Understanding Franz Kafka

Understanding Modern European and Latin American Literature

James Hardin, Series Editor

UNDERSTANDING

Franz Kafka

Allen Thiher

The University of South Carolina Press

Published by the University of South Carolina Press
Columbia, South Carolina 29208

www.sc.edu/uscpress

Manufactured in the United States of America

27 26 25 24 23 22 21 20 19 18
10 9 8 7 6 5 4 3 2 1

Library of Congress Cataloging-in-Publication Data
can be found at http://catalog.loc.gov/.

ISBN 978-1-61117-828-9 (cloth)
ISBN 978-1-61117-829-6 (ebook)

This book was printed on recycled paper with
30 percent postconsumer waste content.

For Irma

Contents

Series Editor's Preface ix
Acknowledgments xi
Chronology xiii

1. Franz Kafka: A Biographical Sketch 1
2. Kafka's First Experiments in Writing Fiction 34
3. *Amerika* or *Der Verschollene* (*The Man Who Disappeared* or *The Missing Person*) 66
4. "The Judgment" and "The Metamorphosis" 98
5. *The Trial* and "In the Penal Colony" 131
6. *A Country Doctor* and Other Stories 163
7. *The Castle* 195
8. *A Hunger Artist* and the Last Stories 227

Epilogue 259
Notes 267
Selected Bibliography 273
Index 281

Series Editor's Preface

Understanding Modern European and Latin American Literature has been planned as a series of guides for undergraduate and graduate students and nonacademic readers. Like the volumes in its companion series, *Understanding Contemporary American Literature,* these books provide introductions to the lives and writings of prominent modern authors and explicate their most important works.

Modern literature makes special demands, and this is particularly true of foreign literature, in which the reader must contend not only with unfamiliar, often arcane artistic conventions and philosophical concepts but also with the handicap of reading the literature in translation. It is a truism that the nuances of one language can be rendered in another only imperfectly (and this problem is especially acute in fiction), but the fact that the works of European and Latin American writers are situated in a historical and cultural setting quite different from our own can be as great a hindrance to the understanding of these works as the linguistic barrier. For this reason the *UMELL* series emphasizes the sociological and historical background of the writers treated. The philosophical and cultural traditions peculiar to a given culture may be particularly important for an understanding of certain authors, and these are taken up in the introductory chapter and also in the discussion of those works to which this information is relevant. Beyond this, the books treat the specifically literary aspects of the author under discussion and attempt to explain the complexities of contemporary literature lucidly. The books are conceived as introductions to the authors covered, not as comprehensive analyses. They do not provide detailed summaries of plot because they are meant to be used in conjunction with the books they treat, not as a substitute for study of the original works. The purpose of the books is to provide information and judicious literary assessment of the major works in the most compact, readable form. It is our hope that the *UMELL* series will help increase knowledge and understanding of European and Latin American cultures and will serve to make the literature of those cultures more accessible.

J. H.

Acknowledgments

Thanks are due to Gordon Weaver, who asked some years ago if I was interested in doing a volume on Kafka's short stories for the Twayne Series in Short Fiction, of which he was editor. Then thanks go to the editor of the present volume, the ever-active James Hardin, for the opportunity to return to Kafka. This volume also owes much to conversations with scholars from various fields through the years, beginning with Germanists like Stanley Corngold and Avital Ronell and extending to colleagues at many places. Through the years students at Middlebury College, the University of Missouri, Universität des Saarlandes, and Sofia University in Bulgaria have also had their word to say about my ideas about Kafka. More recent help came from the staff of the University Library at Cambridge University, who helped me with material in their German collection. Thanks are also due to the staff of Romance Languages at the University of Missouri who have helped with this project and to the Research Council at the University of Missouri, which provided some financial help. And special thanks to my indefatigable critic and companion, Irma Dimitrova.

Chronology

1883 Franz Kafka is born in Prague, capital of the province of Bohemia, in the Austro-Hungarian Empire. His father is Hermann Kafka, wholesale tradesman, and his mother is Julie (née Löwy).

1885 Birth of brother Georg (died in 1887).

1887 Birth of brother Heinrich (died 1888).

1889 Begins elementary school. Birth of sister Gabriele (Elli).

1890 Birth of sister Valerie (Valli).

1892 Birth of sister Ottilie (Ottla).
All three sisters were murdered in the Nazi camps.

1893 Begins secondary school at the German *Gymnasium* in Prague. Friendship with Oskar Pollak.

1899 Friendship with Hugo Berman.

1900 Has begun to read Nietzsche, Spinoza, Darwin. Begins writing.

1901 Begins university studies, briefly chemistry, then law, with some courses on German literature.

1902 Vacation with Uncle Siegfried Löwy, a country doctor. Meets Max Brod, lifelong friend and future editor of Kafka's posthumous works. Friendship with Felix Weltsch and Oskar Baum.

1904 Working on "Description of a Struggle." Reading Grillparzer, Goethe, Eckermann.

1905 Vacation in Zuckmantel, where he has an affair with an unidentified older woman.

1906 Works briefly in a law office, completes his law degree, and, in October, begins a required one-year internship without pay in the law courts.

1907 Working on "Wedding Preparations in the Country." Takes a position with an Italian insurance company.

1908 Takes a position with the semigovernmental Workers' Accident Insurance Institute for the Kingdom of Bohemia. Works here until retirement in 1922. Publishes prose texts in the journal *Hyperion*.

1909 With Max and Otto Brod in Italy at Riva on Lake Garda and Brescia. Publishes "The Airplanes of Brescia" in a newspaper. Publishes two texts taken from "Description of a Struggle."

1910 Begins the diaries. Sees Yiddish theater in Prague. In Paris with Brod in October, goes to Berlin in December.

1911 Friendship with Yiddish actor Yitzak (Isak) Löwy. Reading Hassidic tales. Probably begins writing *Der Verschollene* (translated in various ways, referred to here as *Amerika*, Brod's title).

1912 Gives a talk on the Yiddish language. In summer goes to Weimar with Brod, where they honor Goethe and Kafka flirts with a young girl. Then vacations in a sanatorium. Meets his future fiancée, Felice Bauer, on 13 August and shortly afterward starts to write to her in Berlin. Writes "The Judgment" during the night of 22–23 September. Writes "The Stoker," the first chapter of *Amerika*. Late in year writes "The Metamorphosis." *Meditation* published in December (with 1913 on cover page)

1913 Visits Felice Bauer in Berlin. Publishes "The Stoker" and "The Judgment." In September in Vienna, Venice, and Riva, where he meets a Swiss girl. Meeting with Grete Bloch, Felice Bauer's friend, to discuss his difficulties with his proposed marriage to Felice.

1914 Official engagement to Felice Bauer in June; it is broken off in July. Working on *The Trial*. Outbreak of World War I, in which Kafka does not serve because of an exemption obtained by the insurance institute. Writes "In the Penal Colony" in October and another chapter for *Amerika*.

1915 Meets with Felice Bauer in Bodenbach. Moves for the first time into an apartment on his own. Publication of "The Metamorphosis." Probably begins "The Village Schoolmaster" at end of the year.

1916 Meets with Felice Bauer in Marienbad. Public reading in Munich of "In the Penal Colony." Probably begins to write short stories collected in *A Country Doctor*.

1917 Continuing to write short stories. Second engagement to Felice Bauer. Diagnosis of tuberculosis in September. Takes leave of absence and, hoping for recovery in the country, goes to be with his sister Ottla in Zürau. Writes most of Zürau aphorisms. Engagement broken off in December.

1918 In Zürau through spring. Reading Kierkegaard. Meets next fiancée, Julie Wohryzek, in Schelesen.

1919 Publication of "In the Penal Colony" and *A Country Doctor*. Engagement in spring to Julie Wohryzek. Writes "Letter to His Father."

1920 Begins correspondence with Czech journalist and translator Milena Jesenska. Brief love affair with Milena. End of engagement to Julie at the end of the year. Writes many unpublished texts (found in so-called *Konvolut* of 1920). Begins friendship with medical student and fellow patient Robert Klopstock in a sanatorium in the Tatra Mountains.

1921 Probably begins writing texts collected in *A Hunger Artist*. In a sanatorium until September.

1922 Writes *The Castle*. Writing texts published in *A Hunger Artist*. Goes to live with his sister Ottla in Plana. Writes the posthumously published "Investigations of a Dog."

1923 Vacationing in northern Germany with sister Elli, where he meets Dora Diamant (Dymant) in a vacation colony. In September moves to Berlin to live with her in Berlin-Steglitz. Writing "The Burrow." Leaves hostile landlady to move to Berlin-Zehlendorf.

1924 Returns to Prague very ill, with tuberculosis of the larynx. Writes last work, "Josephine, the Singer." Dora Diamant escorts him to find a clinic, ending finally at Kierling, near Vienna. Dora and Robert Klopstock with him until his death on 3 June. Buried at the New Jewish Cemetery in Prague on 11 June. *A Hunger Artist* published.

1925 Max Brod publishes *The Trial*.

1926 Brod publishes *The Castle*.

1927 Brod publishes *Amerika* (today *Der Verschollene*).

1931 Brod begins editing unpublished short stories with a first volume, *Beim Bau der Chinesischen Mauer* ("The Great Wall of China").

1935 Brod begins publishing first edition of Kafka's *Gesammelte Schriften* in six volumes (new edition of these "collected works" done in 1951).

1937 Brod publishes Kafka's diaries, *Tagebücher,* his edition of the diaries, and *Franz Kafka, eine Biographie*.

1982 Fischer begins publishing its *Kritische Ausgabe,* including the diaries and letters.

Chapter 1

Franz Kafka

A Biographical Sketch

There are many biographies, in many languages, that narrate the life of the German-language Jewish writer Franz Kafka. The large number is undoubtedly a result of the fact that knowledge of Kafka's personal life is important for a proper understanding of his fictions.[1] In fact, much has been written to show that Kafka's personal life offers a key to the meaning of his often enigmatic fiction. However, the attempt to spell out the meaning of his work by relating it to events in his life is often unnecessarily restrictive and usually inaccurate if the biographical reading limits itself to ferreting out putative dramas played out in Kafka's psyche. If it is patent that a full understanding of Kafka's works demands knowledge of the contexts in which Kafka elaborated his fiction, it is also true that these contexts are at once personal and historical. Kafka makes little direct reference to history in his works, yet these works are often a direct reflection of and even a commentary on the historical context in which he found himself, for better or worse, ensnared.

For example, it is of the greatest significance that Kafka was born in Prague, in what was then called the Kingdom of Bohemia, and was therefore a subject of the Hapsburg Empire but died a citizen of the new Republic of Czechoslovakia. In this turbulent historical context Kafka grew up in the world of Judeo-Christian culture, one permeated with Enlightenment ideals but also with a nearly medieval attachment to cultural traditions. Born a member of two minority groups—a Jew among Christians and a German speaker among Czechs—he grew up and had to earn a living in the Catholic world of the Austro-Hungarian Empire, of which the Kingdom of Bohemia was rapidly becoming the most industrialized region. Throughout his adult life Kafka worked in constant direct contact with the growing sphere of industry. Prague, the capital of Bohemia, was also a city in which Judaism and Christianity nestled side by side, sometimes in peace, often in enmity. For Jews had been in Prague since the tenth century, and at times the Jews of Prague made up the second largest Jewish settlement in Europe, after Thessaloniki. But Jews were not the only group to know persecution. For Prague was a city in which German became, in the seventeenth century, the official language only after the Catholic Hapsburgs had eliminated the Protestant rebels who sought independence. Historical monuments to these events are everywhere in Prague, a city replete with memories of pogroms as well as Protestant heads on lamp poles. Memory of Jewish tradition was long there, for, as Kafka knew well, the ghetto area demolished during his youth had—and still has—the oldest synagogue in Europe.

Kafka was also born into the culture of what has come to be called Wittgenstein's Vienna, an urban culture prominent in the development of modernity in the arts, sciences, and philosophy. Kafka cared little for Vienna, was very much a Czech intellectual in preferring Paris, and, like many German-language writers born in the Hapsburg Empire, wanted to live in Berlin. He was nonetheless part of a generation of Austro-Hungarian modernists, a group that included many assimilated Jews. Assimilation meant that their families had stopped speaking a Slavic language or Yiddish, had moved from the villages in which as Jews they had been obliged to live, and had come to cities like Vienna and Prague. Here they practiced religion sporadically if at all and, speaking German, accepted the basic values of the European Enlightenment, at least in its Austro-German form, which sought to accommodate Empire and parliamentary democracy. It is important to remember that Austro-Hungary was an empire in which Jews were only belatedly recognized as full citizens. These Jewish citizens, in both the new German Reich and the old Hapsburg Empire, included some of its most famous subjects—literary men like Arthur Schnitzler, Hermann Broch, and Walter Benjamin or a philosophers like Ludwig Wittgenstein, doctors like Sigmund Freud, and, most famous of all, a Berlin professor with a Swiss passport, Albert Einstein. It is no exaggeration to say that without the contribution of assimilated Jews intellectual life of the German-speaking world would have, to put it mildly, suffered greatly.

The province of Bohemia, roughly today's Czech Republic, had a population made up of an ethnic German minority that coexisted uneasily with an ethnic Czech majority, which constituted approximately two-thirds of the population and which was becoming increasingly restive under what it viewed as German subjugation: ethnic Germans were viewed as something akin to oppressors granted privileges by the Hapsburg authorities. However, in the year in which Kafka was born, the Austrian regime cut in half the amount of taxes a man had to pay in order to be able to vote, and this de facto extension of the right to vote meant that Czechs then became the majority in the regional parliament and could increasingly make life difficult for the ethnic Germans who dominated business and administration (Stach, vol. 1, p. 3). Reliable statistics are difficult to find, but it seems that the German-speaking population in Prague went from a near majority in the mid-nineteenth century to a small minority by the end of the century as the suburbs filled with Czechs coming from the countryside. The old center of Prague remained a bastion of German culture, however. German-speaking Jews like Kafka, living in the city center, inhabited a cultural milieu in which it seems most Jews were German speakers, at least for business and education. The ethnic Germans were of course mainly Catholics. Jews appear to have been a minority in a minority, though statistics vary with regard to proportions at any given date.

Kafka was not excluded from the life of the Slavic majority, however, since he grew up speaking Czech as well as German. His father, a recent migrant to the city, at times called himself a Czech speaker, which stood him in good stead when a Czech mob plundered ethnic German and Jewish businesses in December 1897 (Pawel, p. 42). However, Kafka's father appears to have spoken German at home in his family, and he was educated in primary school in German. Some sources suggest he might have been equally, if not more, at home in Czech. Successful in the wholesale trade of women's accessories and haberdashery, Kafka's father was ambitious and desirous of increasing his status in a world in which German was still the Empire's language of prestige and officialdom—and Czech the language of the street, of a growing working class and of Kafka's employees, but also of a growing middle class, and, above all, of growing nationalism.

Kafka's father, Hermann, came from the village of Wossek (Wosek or Osek in Czech), where a few Jews had been permitted to live in the nineteenth century—for Jews in the Hapsburg Empire were still subject to restrictions on residence and even marriage until 1849. Hermann Kafka was born on 14 September 1852, some three years after his father, Jakob, a kosher butcher, was allowed to marry Franziska, the woman with whom he was living. This marriage was allowed only after the 1849 abrogation of the law forbidding younger sons of Jewish families to marry at all unless an opening occurred in the quota allowed for Jewish families in a given region (Pawel, p. 8). By the time of the law's repeal the couple had already had two of the seven or eight children they would have—for laws against marriage hardly prevented the growth of families. What is of import about the marriage of Kafka's paternal grandparents is not how many children they had, of course, but the very fact that the state had had the power to deprive or to grant to Jews like the Kafkas the right to enjoy such basic human institutions as marriage—this on the basis of ethic identity or religious affiliation.

As a child, Hermann Kafka worked delivering meat from a cart while studying for six years in the *Grundschule,* the elementary school whose language was legally mandated to be German for Jewish pupils. He served in the army for three years, seems to have enjoyed it, and rose to the rank of sergeant. After military service, Hermann was a *Hausierer,* in effect a traveling peddler of haberdashery, who settled at a young age in Prague to make his fortune. In a sense he was typical of the first generation of Bohemian Jews allowed to leave the land and move to the city. There Hermann met Julie Löwy, possibly through the offices of a marriage broker, and, after marrying her on 3 September 1882, he apparently opened a shop for fabrics and fashion accessories (or expanded a shop he had before marrying). Julie had come originally from Podébrady, a town some sixty kilometers from Prague, where her father had been a successful merchant dealing in fabrics and in a sense was already a member of the expanding Jewish middle class. Biographers are in agreement that Julie came from a higher social class than Hermann. In fact, it appears that with her dowry she brought the wherewithal that allowed Hermann to open or at least to better finance his own store. Hermann quickly expanded into the wholesale business of fabrics, accessories, and the vast array of articles that goes with such a trade. He was a very typical successful Jewish urban merchant.

Julie's father had also been a successful businessman and a devoted family man. His first wife died of typhus after bearing three or perhaps four children, including Julie; he remarried and had at least two more sons. The sons were later all active in business of one sort or another, with one country doctor among them, and Kafka had at least epistolary relations with several of his uncles, who also served as models for certain characters in his fiction. Julie's family also counted among its forebears several religious teachers and rabbis, known for their learning and piety, and her father continued this tradition of deep respect for Jewish religious practices. After selling his business and retiring in Prague, he withdrew into private life in order, it seems, to devote himself mainly to reading the Talmud.

Before she married Hermann Kafka, Julie, like most young women of her social class, seems to have had as her main occupation waiting for a husband to come along. Perhaps feeling she was getting old, at age twenty-six she accepted the rather crude and ill-mannered but ambitious provincial businessman and brought to him not only a dowry but a willing partner to work in his business for the rest of their active lives. It has often been noted that young Hermann, living in rather poor conditions, could not help but be attracted to Julie, living in one of the nicest houses in the Altstäder Ring, a prestigious address in the center of Prague.

Kafka was not insensitive to the social differences between his parents, marked notably by their use of language, especially the father's propensity to insults and curses. Religion was a superficial affair for the father, as Kafka noted on several occasions. It is not known how his mother reacted to her husband's lack of piety. The contrast with her father would have been notable. Kafka's first critical biographer, Klaus Wagenbach, stresses that Hermann did not join a synagogue in Prague until 1900 and that he first chose the Czech-language synagogue. He then changed twice to different German-language synagogues, perhaps mainly out of opportunism (Wagenbach, Rowolt, 1964, p. 17). The upwardly mobile couple also frequently changed residences in the first years of their marriage.

Franz Kafka was the couple's first child. He was born on 3 July 1883. The week-old Kafka was circumcised according to Jewish ritual practice—a practice Kafka later described as repugnant after he saw it done according to traditional practice. After this initiatory ritual, however, it would be hard to say that he was brought up according to Jewish tradition. The Kafkas' religious practice was limited to participation in a few of the holidays that assimilated German-speaking Jews usually celebrated, such as Pessach (Passover) and Yom Kippur, the Day of Atonement (Alt, p. 68). In his diary, as well as in his *Brief an den Vater* of 1919 (translated variously, here referred to as "Letter to His Father"), Kafka declared that he found these religious celebrations to be boring and meaningless. Be that as it may, the boy's coming of age was celebrated with a traditional bar mitzvah. What is perhaps most remarkable about the bar mitzvah is that Hermann Kafka sent out invitations saying the invitation was for a "Confirmation."[2] The semantic conflation of Jewish and Catholic rituals seems to point up, minimally, the degree of assimilation that Prague Jews had undergone.

But one should not overestimate this assimilation, however much many in the Prague Jewish community may have desired it. The Jews had finally been granted official emancipation by the Empire, but this was accompanied by growing anti-Semitism among nationalist-minded ethnic Germans as well as among Czechs, who often lumped Germans and Jews together, and this had a very direct effect on Kafka. It was virtually impossible to avoid accepting a Jewish identify when it was forced upon the Jew by an often hostile society—much like the circumcision Kafka did not ask for. Kafka saw that he had no choice but to be Jewish because he existed as such in the eyes of all around him, Jew and non-Jew alike—and it is no surprise that Kafka was later a prototype of the Jew for Jean-Paul Sartre in his book on the Jewish question. Whether or not Kafka or any other Jew wanted it, he was given an identity as Jew by being so in the gaze of the Other (*dans le regard d'autrui*), as Sartre put it in his discussion of how identity is conferred in his *Réflexions sur la question juive* (translated as *Anti-Semite and Jew*). Kafka himself may have often doubted that he had any identity, but he had only to walk in the street to find that one was waiting on him.

After Franz was born, two more sons were born in quick succession, Georg in 1885 and Heinrich in 1887. Both died as infants a year or so after birth, one of measles, the other of meningitis. Infant mortality rates in the late nineteenth century meant that such deaths were not uncommon. Kafka's biographer Ernst Pawel speculates about young Kafka's possible reaction to these deaths and their influence on the development of his character. Pawel thinks that the feelings of guilt that seem to have constantly plagued Kafka were a reaction to his own desire for his siblings' death. Having desired their deaths, deaths that then occurred, he could not escape guilt feelings for the rest of his life. The reasoning is that young Kafka wanted their deaths in order not to have to share their mother's affection. They died, and Kafka felt an irrational responsibility for this "murder" for the rest of his life. This is possible, though I do not think anything in Kafka's work really confirms this idea. It is clear, to be sure, that Kafka was lonely and angst-ridden from early childhood to the end of his life. However, Kafka's ongoing conflict with his father was enough to instill guilt feelings in him from a young age, not to mention the normal guilt that Judeo-Christian belief foists on everybody. Obeying the father is the first rule for all, as Freud among others pointed out. It is also notable that some biographers think that much of young Kafka's unhappiness may have stemmed from the fact that, however much his mother may have loved him, she spent most of her time in the family store, leaving Kafka in the care of domestics. Hence the intense feeling of solitude even in the midst of a more or less normal family life, or what was normal for a Hapsburg Jew who was undoubtedly born with an innate sensibility and intelligence that few others have ever had.

Kafka was not an only child. Three girls were born after the sons' deaths, namely Gabriele (Elli) in 1889, Valerie (Valli) in 1890, and Ottilie (Ottla) in 1892. The conventions of normal family life molded the desires of two of them, Elli and Valli, who followed social norms, accepting what were probably arranged marriages to Jewish husbands. Only Ottla, to whom Kafka was relatively close, broke with this pattern. Influenced apparently by Zionist thought, she acquired something of a proto-kibbutznik mentality, which manifested itself in her decision at one point to go work on the land in a small village, the Zürau, made famous by the aphorisms Kafka wrote there. Independent and unafraid to follow her own desires, Otttla eventually married a Czech Catholic, much to her father's chagrin. It appears that the non-German-speaking son-in-law got along well with everybody in the family, though Hermann Kafka accepted the marriage only after two daughters were born. Ottla was, it seems, an extraordinary person who, to anticipate the dismal development of European history, divorced her husband at a time when marriage to a non-Jew protected her from arrest by the Nazis. She seems to have chosen this separation to affirm her separate Jewish identity and perhaps from a belief that this might save her children from the Nazi camps. In any case, she was then arrested and was last seen alive as a volunteer helping with children on a train to Auschwitz. A comparable fate awaited the other sisters.

Kafka thus grew up with relatively little parental supervision, among various cooks, nannies, and servants. For, by the time Elli was born, the family could afford a servant girl and a nanny for the baby. All domestics were Czech, which meant that as much Czech as German, if not more, was spoken in the Kafka household. This was also the case in the Kafka business. Later Kafka also got some practice in French when a Louise Bailly was hired to be a *gouvernante*. How much French he learned from her and at school is not clear, though he claimed mastery of the language and, in fact, was able to read Flaubert *dans le texte*. More interesting, perhaps, is the fact that the Belgian *gouvernante* seems to have sexually excited the young Kafka, even if she did not actually seduce him—an experience refracted in the adventures of the protagonist of his first novel, *Amerika*. (I will refer to this novel by the title given it by Max Brod, *Amerika,* for there are now at least three translations in English of the title *Der Verschollene,* Kafka's putative title for this novel about "the man who disappeared" or "the missing person.")

Among the memorable hired help who took care of young Kafka was one especially obnoxious cook about whom he wrote that she enjoyed tormenting him while taking him to school each day. She enjoyed threatening to tell his teacher what a naughty boy he was, seemingly causing Kafka to suffer fantasies of impending punishment.[3] This anecdote about the evil cook also points up the minimal presence of Kafka's parents in his life: during the day they were at the store, and at night they played endless card games that were Hermann's main pleasure in life. They were decidedly not Kafka's, and this trivial entertainment became a barrier between Kafka and his family. Though he lived with his family most of his life, Kafka resisted his mother's entreaties to play cards with them, probably as a matter of principle.

"Letter to His Father" was written in 1919. Intended as a settling of accounts with his father, the letter was never given to him. (He did give it to his lover Milena, and Brod was able to publish it posthumously.) In this very long letter Kafka recalls events from childhood and offers what many biographers take to be the description of a major traumatic event in Kafka's life as a child: his punishment by his father by being briefly exiled from the family in the middle of the night. It appears that one night the child Kafka kept asking his father for a drink of water when his tired father wanted to sleep. After the boy repeatedly pestered his father, which Kafka says may have been a bit malicious on his part, the father forced the boy to stand outside in the night on a veranda in the building's courtyard. It is not clear how long he stood there, but it is certain that Kafka never forgot this expulsion. The myth-minded can read in it a symbolic expulsion from the Garden of Eden, and the psychoanalytically minded can see another side of the Oedipal conflict with much the same symbolic value. And the literal-minded can see here a strong affirmation of the patriarch's real power over the boy's life. There can be no doubt that this aspect of the punishment was ever on Kafka's mind.

In 1889 Kafka began elementary school. After four years, he took the secondary school admission examinations and, at a young age, began to attend the humanist high school, the *Altstädter Deutsches Gymnasium,* in the Kinsky Palace in the old town of Prague. He would study at this school for the next eight years. Kafka completed the curriculum, if not brilliantly, with more than satisfactory *Matura* exams in 1901. He was very good in humanities and, it seems, traumatized by mathematics. The choice of a humanistic secondary school was motivated not by Kafka's talents, however, but by the promise of the kind of career to which it might lead: university studies and then a career in law or administration. In effect, this is what happened to Kafka: he became a lawyer and a bureaucrat. Preparation in secondary school for this career included studies that led to Kafka's receiving certificates with the rating of excellent (*Lobenswert*) in geography, history, Greek, and philosophy and the rating of satisfactory in mathematics, German, natural science (*Naturkunde*), and French (Alt, p. 98). Kafka always played down the importance of this secondary education, though he did suggest that it warped him. It is difficult to find Kafka making a single commentary on the content of his studies, though he was not hesitant to criticize what they did to him. In a famous litany from the diaries, Kafka wrote for himself a long list, almost a poem, about how his education stifled him, attributing personal responsibility for this pernicious result to a good many hostile adults.

Whatever Kafka may have thought of this secondary education—and biographers have tended to echo his sentiments that it was worthless—it is clear that the *Gymnasium* was the place where he encountered books, ideas, and friends who pushed him into exploring areas that were crucial for his development. It is true that most of the curriculum taught there, centering on Greek and Latin, does not seem to have made much of an impression on Kafka, though he did have a knowledge of classical literature that allowed him later whimsically to rewrite Homer and Aeschylus. Moreover, it was at school that he began to read the German classics that did count for him: Goethe, Kleist, Grillparzer, Hebel. As mentioned, French was also important. And if Kafka was able to read in the original Flaubert's *L'Education sentimentale*, it is perhaps noteworthy that, as in the case of Kafka's Prague contemporary the poet Rilke, English literature played no important role in Kafka's intellectual life—with the notable exception of Dickens. English had not yet begun its role as the international language; for Prague intellectuals, in revolt against Austrian domination, Paris was the cultural center to which they were most attracted (*dixit* Rilke). In any case, it was during these years of secondary school, under the influence of his friends at school, that Kafka began to read widely, especially Russians such as Tolstoy and Dostoevsky, as well as the incredibly influential German philosopher of the time, Friedrich Nietzsche.

It was through a school friend, Oskar Pollak, that Kafka first encountered Nietzsche as well as other philosophers. Pollak was a brilliant student, a cut above the other students, and an aggressive atheist. He also had some sympathy for the German nationalist movement, especially in arts and letters. He introduced Kafka to a trendy German literary magazine, *Kunstwart,* that opened up an artistic world beyond Prague for him, one in which Kafka encountered the artistic tendencies of the Germanic world (Wagenbach, Rowolt, 1964, p. 40). Kafka thus saw that trends in art as well as literature and philosophy were important for Pollak; in fact, his friend later became an art historian whose work on the baroque was original, though never developed, since he died on the Italian front in World War I. Pollak's importance for Kafka is underscored by the fact that Kafka showed him, as Kafka's letters to him make clear, samples of his first writing, begun apparently when Kafka was a teenager. His letters to Pollak are among the earliest of Kafka's correspondence still extant. In one of them, dated 20 December 1902, a rather bizarre tale about a tall man (*der Lange*) strongly suggests that Kafka was feeling shame or at least unease about being a bit taller than average. This letter about the problems of having a body can count as one of Kafka's earliest examples of writing. As far as one can tell, Kafka showed nobody else his work at the time, especially after an uncle looked at a sample and called it the usual junk.

Another important friend for Kafka's development was Hugo Bergmann, later a professor of philosophy at the Hebrew University in Jerusalem. Young Bergmann was acquainted with the Zionism of Theodor Herzl, a topic Kafka was interested in from a young age. Zionism would be a subject for unending debate among Kafka's friends, especially later with his companion in letters the socialist Zionist Max Brod, a prolific writer who collected Kafka's manuscripts and edited many of them for posthumous publication. Sympathy with socialist ideas was widespread, and arguing for and against both socialism and Zionism, or something like Brod's combination of the two, was a mainstay of Kafka's intellectual development, beginning in school and continuing for the rest of his life.

Another fellow student, Rudolph Illowy, may have introduced Kafka to Darwin. It seems Illowy, later a social democrat, left school for unknown reasons, leaving Kafka the only overt socialist in the class, something he showed by wearing a red carnation. Another friend who developed Kafka's scientific interests was Ewald Pribram, later an American gynecologist who, even before taking a scientific interest in the matter at the University of Vienna, was apparently able to explain to the young Kafka what sex was about. Pribram was also a dandy and a gourmet who showed Kafka that life was more than Zionism and socialism. The same may be said of Kafka's friend Paul Kisch, the future journalist and brother of the more famous writer and journalist Egon Erwin Kisch. Paul introduced Kafka to modern writers such as Ibsen, Strindberg, Hofmannsthal, and Maeterlinck. He may have played a role in Kafka's brief desire to go to Munich to study German literature after he had already begun his university studies.

Kafka read other philosophers at the time, especially Spinoza and Schopenhauer, though it seems fair to say that, under Pollak's influence, Nietzsche was the writer who had the greatest influence on him. Kafka was receptive to the *Weltgeist,* or the intellectual climate in which Darwin's theory of evolution could be combined with Nietzsche's ideas about overcoming nihilism in order to reach a new stage of development for humanity. This was one way of reading the dithyrambs in Nietzsche's *Also Sprach Zarathustra* (*Thus Spake Zarathustra,* as an early translation of the title put it): Kafka was part of an entire generation that was taken with Nietzsche's poetic vision of the "superman" (*Übermensch* or literally "over-person") who would transform values. Moreover, it was Kafka's early commitment to Nietzsche that sparked his friendship with Max Brod. The two met on 24 October 1902 when the young Brod gave a paper on Schopenhauer in which Brod defended Schopenhauer against Nietzsche's critique of him. Kafka defended Nietzsche's viewpoint, and it appears the two of them argued until late. They remained friends until Kafka's death, and it is only just to say that without Brod's devotion to Kafka and his work Kafka would be largely forgotten today.

Kafka had a brief respite from the travails of academic life when, after receiving his secondary diploma, he went on a holiday with one of his uncles, Siegfried Löwy, his mother's brother, who became a country doctor and with whom Kafka apparently got along rather well. Traveling for the first time outside Bohemia to Cuxhaven in Lower Saxony and from there to Helgoland, an archipelago in the North Sea, the eighteen-year-old Kafka made his first real contacts with another world. He returned to Prague to resume his studies, now at the German Charles-Ferdinand University of Prague, since a medical certificate got him an exemption from military duty. Apparently he was diagnosed with *Herzneurose,* or cardiac disturbances of probable psychological origin (a diagnostic manual today says that it can be psychosomatic). Surprisingly, he first enrolled in chemistry in October 1901 but quickly changed over to the law faculty.[4] In the spring of 1902 he fled the law faculty and attended classes in German literature, art history, and philosophy. Literary studies, however, were permeated with chauvinistic German nationalism, which may have contributed to Kafka's decision to drop *Germanistik* and to return to the law, which he took up full time in the winter semester of 1902–1903 (Alt, p. 102).

Kafka went to Munich at the end of November 1903, perhaps thinking about returning to German studies. If so, this was a short-lived project. He returned to Prague to live with his family and to resume legal studies in December 1903. The following July he passed the legal history examination known as the *Romanum,* which marked the midpoint of his legal studies. After this examination Kafka spent the first of a number of periods of rest and recuperation from his putative heart condition in a sanatorium, this one near Dresden. After that he studied mainly civil law, criminal law, and *Staatsrecht*, roughly, administrative law. Kafka's checkered university career came to end at the end of summer of 1905 when he began taking a series of examinations, the *Staatsprüfungen,* that went on until June 1906. He became a doctor of law in June of that year and the next month went again to recover from the stress caused by his studies in a sanatorium in Zuckmantel, a city today in the Czech Republic in the Opawskie Mountains near the Polish border.

This stay has been much commented upon because it appears that while at the sanatorium Kafka had an affair with an older woman. The affair made an lasting impression on Kafka, which Kafka himself suggests in letters, written some years later, both to his fiancée Felice Bauer in 1913 and to his lover Milena in August 1920. This affair would have occurred after Kafka had already been initiated into the mysteries of Eros by a salesgirl in July 1903. Kafka's description of that initiation gives one the impression that the girl was as much a prostitute as a girl seeking pleasure or romance. Whatever love affairs Kafka may have had, it is clear that Kafka frequented prostitutes, as was normal at the time, often with his friend Max Brod—the Brod who tried to eliminate references to these brothel visits when editing Kafka's letters and diaries. Moreover, whatever the precise occasion for Kafka's sexual initiation, it is clear that he was raised in a culture that accepted the traditional double standard for men and women and, as has often been pointed out, that the preservation of the chastity of a large percentage of the female population demanded the prostitution of another large percentage of the same population. To this end Prague had many brothels, as did most other European cities. Kafka may well have had doubts about the moral justification of this double standard. But his own erotic needs led him to purchase pleasure despite his doubts and perhaps anguish about it. By contrast, his father had no scruples about whores, for Kafka brings up the issue in his "Letter to His Father," recalling that his father offered to take him to a brothel so that Kafka would not marry a woman of whom the father did not approve.

Brothel visits were made in the company of a group of friends who became constant companions in Kafka's life. In addition to Max Brod, Kafka made friends with Felix Weltsch, a would-be philosopher, and Oscar Baum, a blind writer and musician. The four frequently met during Kafka's student days and afterward to read their works and offer one another commentary and encouragement. Social life centered on cafés and literary gatherings, such as, beginning in 1906, the philosophical circle that met at the Café Louvre. Here young enthusiasts discussed the work of the Austrian philosopher Franz von Brentano, who, once a priest, now married, had been banished from the university for his refusing to keep his vows of chastity. Kafka also did some work in philosophy as part of the law school curriculum and came into contact with two of Brentano's followers in Prague, Christian von Ehrenfels and Anton Marty. Brentano, whose influence was great in developing an empirical phenomenology, derided attempts to understand psychology in the terms of physical science. His disciple Ehrenfels was important for the development of Gestalt psychology and, also, a more open attitude toward sexuality, for which he won Freud's approval. Anton Marty, a philosopher of language, interpreted Brentano's work to imply a bioracist doctrine. It is hard to say what Kafka took from these thinkers, though it is certain that debates on science and ethics, psychology and language, and, not least of all, sexuality are refracted in myriad ways throughout Kafka's work.

Typical in this regard is the fact Kafka met Max Brod in 1902 at a literary gathering where Brod gave his talk on Schopenhauer before the *Lese- and Redehall,* a literary organization that allowed students to organize interest groups and furthered their interests with a substantial library. Thus, along with his legal education, Kafka pursued a literary and philosophical education in student groups, in cafés, and through contacts with friends who seem to have taken up increasingly more of his time than the study of Roman law and contracts. After he met Baum and Weltsch, he undoubtedly found it more interesting to go with them to, say, the salon of Frau Berta Fanta to discuss Kant, Hegel, Schopenhauer, and Brentano than to prepare for the examinations that utterly depressed him (Alt, p. 117). Moreover, Kafka's attention was drawn to other trends of those prewar years: the cult of physical fitness, vegetarianism, natural living, and the call of the outdoors—the *Wandervogelbewegung,* a movement that stressed the Teutonic side of hiking . He was an avid swimmer. Kafka became a follower of a number of doctrines of which the weirdest was undoubtedly his attempt to eat according to the theory of an American doctor, Horace Fletcher, whose teaching prescribed the number of times each mouthful of food should be masticated (known as "Fletcherism," a term now part of the German language). Thus, Kafka often went swimming, rowed boats, and, to his family's dismay, "fletcherized" at meals. He also spent time keeping up with literary trends as found in journals that were of great importance for literary life, not only *Der Kunstwart* from Vienna but journals such as *Die Neue Rundschau,* founded in 1890, in which Thomas Mann was publishing, or later, after 1908, Franz Blei's *Hyperion,* in which, along with Musil, Rilke, and Hofmannsthal, Kafka himself published texts.

Having passed his law examinations Kafka decided to pursue a career in some field demanding knowledge of the law. It appears he never seriously considered practicing law. He needed a career for practical reasons: an income. In Bohemia, as in Austria, a new lawyer who wanted a career in *Staatsdienst*, or the civil service, had to spend a year without pay working for a court. In April 1906 Kafka began a brief internship in the law office of a Richard Löwy. Then, in October, he began his required year by working for the district court for civil and criminal affairs (*Kreiszivil- und Kreisstrafgericht*) before being assigned in March to the Prague regional court (*Prager Landesgericht*) (Stach, vol. 1, p. 337). With no income, he remained dependent on his family and continued to live with them, which, even after he had income, he did most of his life.

After the initiatory year of work with the court, he went in the summer of 1907 to spend a month with his uncle Siegfried in Triesch, a town in today's Czech Republic with a notable castle. Here he met a young woman, Hedwig Weiler, and continued to correspond with her for some time. She was an intelligent person who was part of the first generation of women to enter the university. Kafka's letters to her are among the most revealing of his youth, for, as Peter-André Alt observes in his biography of Kafka, one sees in this correspondence that Kafka began the *Selbstanklage* or self-accusation that he used later in writing letters to other women in his life, notably to his first fiancée, Felice Bauer, and later to his Czech lover Milena (Alt, p. 169). Kafka wanted to attract the young woman and at the same time explain why it was impossible for them to have a relationship. For some unknown reason—unlike Felice later, Hedwig may have believed him—they broke off contact in 1909, though it is known that she did complete her university studies in Vienna after this.

After completing his internship, Kafka took a position in October 1907 with a private insurance company, the Italian firm *Assicurazioni Generali.* He seems to have been interested in the work and in 1908 took courses in insurance law and bookkeeping at a business school, the *Prager Handelsakademie.* But he could not bear the routine the company imposed and especially the long hours, which seriously interfered with his writing. In June 1908 he took a position with the partly state-owned *Arbeiter-Unfall-Versicherung-Anstalt,* the Workmen's Accident Insurance Institute. To justify his leaving his Italian employers, he showed a health certificate saying, again, that he had "Herzneurose mit regelmässigen *nervösen* Störungen" or a heart neurosis with regular nervous disturbances (Alt, p. 172). This note suggests that, in the medical parlance of the time, Kafka probably continued to have heart palpitations with some irregular beating. But the real motivation for the change of workplace was that the state-run Institute demanded considerably shorter work hours, allowing Kafka to go home at two o'clock.

Whatever the condition of Kafka's heart at the time, it was probably not because of his health that he got the new position with the Institute. Rather, he got it through connections. The father of his friend Ewald Pribram had converted from Judaism to Christianity and was chairman of the Institute's board of directors. He apparently overruled, in Kafka's favor, the Institute's policy of not hiring unconverted Jews. I note this example of influence, which was very much a typical practice at the time, not as something to count against Kafka but rather to point out the more or less institutionalized anti-Semitism that was something of a norm in the Austro-Hungarian Empire despite official attempts at offering full citizenship to Jews.

The young lawyer Kafka thus became a government employee at one of the seven insurance institutes that had been set up in the Empire to meet the needs of a growing workforce. The Prague institute was the largest: 288,094 entrepreneurs were under its purview, which meant that it provided insurance for some three million workers in Bohemia (Alt, pp. 173–174). Taking his work quite seriously Kafka went to a morning course on the preparation of fabrics at the *Technische Hochschule* during the winter semester 1908–1909. This seriousness continued throughout his career, and, by all reports, Kafka became a respected expert in the field of industrial accident prevention. Despite an income that grew through the years, Kafka continued for some time to live with his family in crowded conditions. The travails he experienced that were caused by life in the everyday world would make up a volume in themselves: suffice it to say that, like Virginia Woolf, Kafka often needed a room of his own, or at least one through which members of the family did not pass on their way to other parts of the apartment.

Kafka wrote literary texts throughout his student days, though it is difficult to reconstitute exactly what he wrote in these years. He apparently destroyed most, if not all, of his early texts, such as those he may have sent to Pollak. It is from these years during which Kafka was finishing his studies and looking for suitable employment that we get our first record of what he was writing. Not only did Brod preserve some unpublished manuscripts from the time, but some of what Kafka was writing was eventually published, first in journals and then, in 1913, in his first published book, *Betrachtung* (*Meditation* or *Contemplation*), a collection of his early sketches and prose poems. He may have begun writing these published vignettes as early as 1904. And between 1903 or 1904 and 1910 he also wrote a number of unpublished texts, including what appear to be the beginning of possible novels, *Beschreibung eines Kampfes* ("Description of a Struggle") and *Hochzeitsvorbereitungen auf dem Lande* ("Wedding Preparations in the Country"). In these texts, published and unpublished, we see that Kafka was searching in an uncertain manner for his literary voice. He seems never to have had doubts that he must find it, only doubts about whether he had one to find.

The struggle to find this voice may be one meaning of the title of a very early text, possibly the earliest extant literary text he wrote: "Description of a Struggle." The first version of this narrative was probably begun in summer 1904 and abandoned in 1907. In 1909 Kafka published parts of the text in Blei's *Hyperion*, namely the "Gespräch mit dem Beter"("Conversaton with the Supplicant")and "Gespräch mit dem Betrunkenen"("Conversation with the Drunk"). Kafka began a new version of the text, which resulted in 1912 in "Children on a Country Road" ("Kinder auf der Landstrasse"), subsequently published in *Meditation*. Kafka published other texts in the literary review *Hyperion;* when he selected some eighteen pieces for *Meditation,* half of them had already seen print. *Meditation* was a project much facilitated by Brod, who was instrumental in getting the publisher Ernst Rowolt to ask Kafka for a volume for his Leipzig publishing house. Kafka himself seems at the time not to have considered sending a volume off on his own. The other major unpublished text of this period is, in Brod's title, "Wedding Preparations in the Country," mentioned earlier, which he probably began in 1907. Brod thought that it was the beginning of a novel and got the manuscript from Kafka in July 1909, after Kafka had finally given up on it (Alt, p. 156).

The friendship between Brod and Kafka was such that two years later, in late summer of 1911, they embarked on a joint novel: *Richard und Samuel.* This project did not go far, though part of it was published in the journal *Herderblätter* in 1912 as "Eine kleine Reise durch mitteleuropäische Gegenden," a title whose "little trip" in German becomes for some reason in the 1948 translation "The First Long Train Journey." These texts make up the most important pieces of what one can call the first period of Kafka's writing. It is not perhaps the most impressive list on first glance. Most of these texts have received relatively little critical attention, but we shall take a close look at them later, for they contain some moments of poetic intensity, and some are notable anticipations of Kafka's gift for the comic.

A more or less nonfictional text from this period also deserves mention: "Die Aeroplane in Brescia ("The Aeroplanes in Brescia"). It describes, with Kafka's typical wit, the airshow he witnessed in the Italian city with Max Brod and Brod's brother Otto. It was published in the newspaper *Bohemia* in September 1909. Describing the airplanes and the appearance of the famous aviator Blériot, this bit of journalism may contain the first description of aviation in German literature, or so a number of critics have claimed. In any case, it points up that, with Brod, Kafka also traveled around Europe during these halcyon years before World War I. The trip to Brescia was part of a voyage that included the Italian city Riva on Lake Garda in September 1909. In October 1910 Kafka went to Paris with Brod; and December of that year found Kafka in Berlin for the theater season. In August 1911 Brod and Kafka traveled together again to northern Italy and the region of Lago Maggiore, where they heard of a cholera epidemic in northern Italy, the same to which Thomas Mann gave lasting fame in *Death in Venice*. Unlike Mann's writer, who, entranced with Eros and Thanatos in Venice, stays there, they decided to leave and went to Paris for its art, not to mention its erotic pleasures.

Kafka then went for a week to a sanatorium at Erlenbach bei Zürich. He repeated this sanatorium visit the following year. in July 1912 he and Brod made their last trip together when they went to Weimar, certainly in honor of Goethe's memory, before Kafka went for three weeks to the *Junghorner Naturheilsanatorium* in the Harz mountain—a "nature-cure sanatorium" with vegetarian cooking and "outdoor air" therapy, as one might translate *Freiluft* therapy. Guests lived in little huts, did collective exercises, and went naked in the park. Kafka did gymnastics, sun bathing, and agricultural chores (Alt, p. 210). This was Kafka's first encounter with a Christian milieu, one in which he did not reveal that he was Jewish, at least so long as he kept his clothes on, which he apparently did most of the time.

Kafka's life in Prague included more than work, study, and breathing exercises before an open window. Inspired perhaps by his traveling uncles' tales of America, he began, perhaps in 1911, his first major novel, titled *Amerika* by Brod when he published it posthumously. Modern editors call it *Der Verschollene* after the working title Kafka gave when he published the novel's first chapter in 1913 as "Der Heizer" ("The Stoker") in Kurt Wolff's *Der Jüngste Tag*, a prominent literary journal. As mentioned, the novel now has at least two or three different titles in translation, for which reason it seems convenient to call it simply *Amerika*. Kafka also had time for political and cultural life. It seems he went to a *Klub mladych* ("Youth Club" in Czech), which was dissolved by the authorities, who suspected it of being an anarchist group. Kafka thus had occasion to attend their meetings only a few times; he also went to a workers' association (*Verein*) called Bohemia (Wagenbach, Rowolt, 1964, p. 69). In addition to whatever political contacts he may have made—perhaps it would be more accurate to say, in addition to satisfying his curiosity about contemporary political movements—he also made his first contacts with eastern Judaism in the form of Yiddish theater.

It appears that there were virtually no Yiddish speakers to be found in Prague, though Yiddish was the language of millions of Jews who lived in what is today Poland, Ukraine, and Russia, that is, the unassimilated Jews who practiced Judaism with no overlay of Western reformism. This contact led to Kafka's interest, for example, in the Hasidic groups that practiced a mystical

Judaism that had little in common with reform religion (and little in common with the culture from which Yiddish theater arose). The existence of Eastern forms of Judaism seems to have made an ambivalent impression on Kafka, at once positive in that he here found a living Jewish culture and negative in that he considered many of its practices to be primitive in a repellent way. The rationalist view of a strange culture found expression in at least one of Kafka's fictional works, "In the Penal Colony."

A Yiddish theater company came to Prague in 1910, but it made little impression on Kafka. However, another visit in 1911 by a Yiddish company caught his attention. Kafka went regularly to their performances; he became friends with one of the actors, Jizchak Levi (or Isaak Löwy in German), and maintained relations with him for some time. The dislike that Kafka's father expressed for this actor is a major point of contention in "Letter to His Father," for the father seems to have called him vermin (*Ungeziefer*), not coincidentally the word used for the monster that Gregor Samsa becomes in *The Metamorphosis*. Kafka's enthusiasm for the theatrical company culminated in his organizing a theatrical evening, sponsored by the Zionist student organization Bar Kochba, during which Kafka made a speech to reassure his German audience that they knew more Yiddish than they thought they did. The interest Kafka took in Yiddish culture can also be seen in Kafka's diary entry of 25 December 1911, where he registers his thought about the existence of a *kleine Literatur*, a "minor literature," and its significance in world culture—an idea that has made its way to prominence in the course of the years, even as Yiddish literature, once a living literature in Eastern Europe as well as in the emigration of that culture to New York City, has receded from view.

During this time Kafka was seemingly sympathetic to the Czech nationalist movement as embodied in the Social Democratic Party of Tomaś Masaryk. He regularly read the party's newspaper, *Čas*. He continued to be interested not only in his friends' Zionism but also in the anti-Zionists among Jewish intellectuals, including politicians such as Walther Rathenau and writers such as Karl Kraus, with whom Brod had a quarrel about Kraus's favorable views of assimilation. Brod was now actively committed to Zionism. Moreover, Kafka read the weekly Jewish journal *Selbstwehr*, published in Prague. It called upon Bohemian Jews to return to their religious traditions while demanding the recognition of a Jewish national identity in the Empire—Zionism without emigration. He also heard Martin Buber at this time (20 January 1909) give a lecture titled "The Meaning of Judaism." In brief, Kafka went out of his way to learn about socialism, Jewish culture, and Zionism, though he never really embraced any of these as Brod did. But it is significant that Kafka began to read Jewish texts, such as the Talmud, with some regularity. This interest in Judaism was very personal, and it is only indirectly reflected in Kafka's creative writing, in which, with one exception, there is never a direct reference to Judaism, Zionism, or contemporary politics. I will return to that exception at the end of this study, to ponder why there is an animal in the synagogue.

One of the most problematic aspects of Kafka's life, for his biographers as well as for Kafka himself, was his relationship to his first fiancée, Felice Bauer. What is one to make of the fact that Kafka courted this woman, who lived in Berlin, through more than five hundred letters but rarely saw her? It has been argued that courtship by correspondence was not so unusual for the era, no more so than marriage arranged by a marriage broker, for the relations between potential spouses were often distant and mediated by conventions we can hardly conceive today. (Readers may recall Otto, a character in Fontane's *Frau Jenny Treibel* of 1892, who writes to his fiancée every day but is afraid to see her because of his mother's disapproval.) What is unusual, even for the era, however, is that Kafka spent much of his energy in this correspondence explaining why he could not marry his fiancée, even as he was asking her to marry him.

Kafka met Felice Bauer on 13 August 1912. A distant relative of Max Brod, she was present at Brod's home when Kafka came to see him to discuss the order of the texts that Rowohlt was going to publish in *Meditation*. Kafka was undoubtedly struck by the fact that she was an ambitious young woman of twenty-four who had already achieved remarkable success in the Berlin business world, being the rare example of something like a female executive officer at a major company. Later he and his mother learned that her family background, however, was not one that would appeal to Kafka's family, for investigation undertaken by his mother revealed that Felice's father had left his wife for several years to live with another woman, that a brother was basically an embezzler, and that a sister had an out-of-wedlock child. These facts were for the future, however, and in any case probably made little difference to Kafka himself. The fact that this ambitious and sensible woman was hardly on the same intellectual wavelength as Kafka also seems to have made little difference, nor does the undeniable fact, as shown by a famous photo, not to mention Kafka's own reactions to Felice, that Felice was rather homely. This did not matter, nor did the fact that she was a working woman. Kafka was looking for an ideal mother for an ideal family that he could not father, so perhaps it mattered little who the real Felice Bauer was.

Felice was a modern German Jewish woman, perhaps more German than Jewish, who nonetheless had some Zionist inclinations and went to temple more than occasionally. In fact, on the very evening of their meeting, Kafka proposed to her that they consider a trip to Palestine together. Some seven months would elapse before Kafka would see her again, this after Kafka initiated, on 20 September, the correspondence with her that would last more than five years. It is remarkable that we have Kafka's side of the correspondence, since Felice had to keep it intact for years, carrying it with her even when she emigrated to the United States. Kafka apparently burned the letters she sent him.

What Felice preserved is a record of the strange psychopathology of a writer fighting for his sanity by at once accusing himself and then defending himself—at once prosecuting attorney and defense lawyer staging a trial for which Felice was a privileged witness or perhaps judge. This was clear from the outset when, from the end of October to the end of December Kafka sent her ninety letters, often by express mail and sometimes accompanied by a telegram asking about the letters' arrival. Great claims have been made for the literary value of this correspondence, for its virtuoso display of Kafka's psychodynamics and his gift for perverse argumentation. However, its literary merit is debatable. With regard to Kafka's biography, of course, it is of no small interest that the correspondence reveals a Kafka who yearned to conform to the norms of his culture—to be a married man with children—though he could not stand the thought of being yoked to another being in a relationship that must inevitably limit his freedom, especially his freedom as a writer, by compelling him to honor the norms of the tribe.

Marriage was taking place all around Kafka. His sister Valli married Josef Pollak on 12 January 1913, a marriage that had been postponed because of fear that the Turks might invade the eastern part of the Empire during the first Balkan War. Brod was now engaged to be married. And during that year Elli's marriage had resulted in a second child for her. Kafka could hardly escape the idea of marriage and a family. And it was with the firm intent of pursuing marriage plans that Kafka went to Berlin on 23 March 1913. After he spent much time in a hotel waiting for Felice to show up, they met in an awkward encounter during which they walked around the Grünewald Park. And then Kafka traveled on to Leipzig with friends on 24 March. This second encounter seems to have been a nonevent. In May, however, he went to Berlin again to meet officially the Bauer family, and in July Kafka gave his mother, Julie, a free hand to employ the *Auskunftsbüro*—basically a private detective—to investigate the family background. For her son had already written on 16 June, after a week of composition, the letter in which he officially requested that Felice become his wife. Most notable in the correspondence after this letter is the letter of 28 August 1913, which was accompanied by a list of his faults and which he mailed to Felice with the request that they be given to her father.

Kafka continued a life of his own in all this planning and doubting. In the spring he had started working in a garden in a Prague suburb for the putative health benefits of manual labor. In September he was sent to Vienna to attend a congress for insurance officials who dealt with accident avoidance in the workplace, which was a question on which Kafka was becoming a specialist. He also attended at the same time at least some of the meetings of the *Kongress der Zionistischen Weltorganisation,* the official body of the German-language organization that was promoting the Zionist movement. After Vienna, on 14 September he went to Trieste, then by steamer to Venice for his own purposes, and after three days in Venice he took the train to Verona and from there to Riva, where on 22 September he checked into a luxurious sanatorium. His possible marriage did not stop him from being interested in other women, for in Riva he had some kind of relationship with a young Swiss woman, called G.W. in the diaries. Kafka did not tell Felice immediately about G.W. That confession came later in winter, when their relationship was about to come to a halt.

In the fall of the year, understandably perplexed by Kafka's hesitations, Felice Bauer asked a friend of hers, Grete Bloch, to speak to Kafka about their problems. Grete was rather young to be placed in the role of a marriage broker or at least counselor. She was a twenty-one-year-old *Stenotypistin,* a secretary who could take dictation, and worked for the Zeiss firm in Frankfurt. At the beginning of November she was in Prague and met with Kafka. Apparently she and Kafka got along rather well, too well perhaps, since Brod thought she had a child by Kafka. Biographers today say this was not possible: the dates do not fit. What Grete Bloch accomplished is not clear, though on 8 November 1913 Kafka did make a quick trip to Berlin. It was rather a fiasco. Felice was not at the train station. The next day they walked in the rain in the *Tiergarten,* and then she left for a funeral that afternoon after no real decisive conversation. After this visit the correspondence came to a halt, though Kafka wrote a thirty-five-page letter at the end of the year. Perhaps some letters were sent in December, but, if so, they are lost (Alt, p. 305).

In February 1914 Kafka was again in Berlin on a surprise visit. Kafka saw little, if anything, of Felice, for she had gone to a ball alone. Kafka profited from these unsuccessful visits. During the visit in November, for example, he visited his friend, the novelist Ernst Weiss (who was against the marriage), and in February he visited Martin Buber, the Jewish scholar and philosopher he had heard earlier in Prague. He put Felice's absence to good purpose for a discussion with Buber of an interpretation of the psalms and the "godless judge" of Psalm 82. (Kafka's biographer Alt calls this a discussion of "Gerichtsbarkeit ohne verbindliche Rechtsbasis"—of "judgment without a binding basis in law," a most Kafkaesque theme [p. 377].) He did meet with Felice the next day and even accidentally met again with Ernst Weiss. Berlin exerted a great attraction on Kafka, and one cannot underestimate how cultural life there appealed to him—as it did to Robert Musil, another Hapsburg subject who preferred living there. Berlin was replacing Vienna as the capital of German-language intellectual life.

Despite the not altogether successful winter visit, Kafka went to Berlin again on 12 April 1914 and the next day he and Felice decided on their engagement.

Kafka screwed up his courage to decide that Felice should quit work on 1 August and move to Prague. Moreover, official announcements of Kafka's engagement were published in the newspapers *Berliner Tageblatt* and the *Praguer Tageblatt*. And on 30 May Kafka went with his father to celebrate the engagement in Berlin, his mother and Ottla having gone four days earlier to prepare the festivities. This eventuated in an official ceremony at the Bauer home in the Berlin district of Charlottenburg. But the announcements and the official pomp did not keep Kafka from being immediately overcome by doubts on returning to Prague.

European history was about to directly intervene in their lives, for the respective empires in which they lived would soon be at war against common enemies. On 27 June of that fateful year 1914 the Crown Prince of Austria, Prince Ferdinand, was assassinated in a remote part of the empire, in the Bosnian city of Sarajevo, and Austria soon declared war on Serbia for its responsibility for the murder, as Austrian generals saw it. Few expected that this war declared by an empire against a backward Balkan country would lead to four years of war and millions of victims and to the end of the empire of which Kafka was a paid employee. At the time the event seems not to have made a great impression on Kafka. On the day of the assassination, Kafka went to Dresden, then to Leipzig, and met with various writers—he did this rather than going to Berlin, where he was expected. Grete Bloch had written that she could no longer accept the role of intermediary—she could not understand why he wanted to marry Felice at all—and Kafka decided then to meet with her and Felice in Berlin on the way to a summer vacation he planned to take on the North Sea coast near Lübeck. This encounter was another fiasco (or perhaps a felicitous event, seen from Kafka's own contradictory viewpoints). Felice had read letters Kafka had sent to Grete. Kafka was put on trial, as he wrote in his diary, and in the end it was decided that the engagement was over. He went to tell her parents and then left for the coast with Ernst Weiss and his girlfriend. At least in a photograph from this time, Kafka looks almost happy. And after his return to Prague, the Austrians declared war on Serbia on 28 July.

The astute biographer Klaus Wagenbach was among the first to note that one finds in Kafka's diaries and letters fewer than fifty lines about the war. Perhaps the only clear statement is found in a diary entry from 4 August 1914 in which Kafka speaks of his hatred of all the fighting forces (*Hass gegen die Kämpfenden*) for which he passionately wished everything bad—in short, a pox on all of them. This attitude was undoubtedly motivated more by ethical feelings about the stupidity of the war than by the fact that the war made it very difficult for Kafka to meet again with Felice.

Of course, what interests us most here is what really most mattered to Kafka—the writing that he undertook during these years. In fact, it was during this time that Kafka wrote some of his most important works. Critics often speak of a second period of Kafka's writing career beginning with what he himself knew to be a breakthrough moment when, shortly after meeting Felice, he wrote "The Judgment" in one all-night sitting on 22–23 September. This occurred two nights after he had written his first letter to Felice on 20 September 1912. It is difficult to avoid the feeling that there must be a causal connection between the letter and the writing of Kafka's first major work, which tells of the condemnation of a son by his father because, among other things, he is engaged to what the father sees as a slut. Then, in 1913, he wrote "The Metamorphosis," probably the signature text for Kafka's work for most people, for its portrayal of the hero's transformation into the *Ungeziefer*, the word for vermin that must have been one of the preferred insults of Kafka's father.

With the war under way, from September 1914 until February 1915 Kafka lived and worked with his sister Elli and her husband, in effect for the first time outside his parents' home. He began writing *The Trial* in 1914 and took a two-week vacation to work on it in October of that year. He then broke off writing the novel to work on "In the Penal Colony" and wrote a final chapter for *Amerika*. He continued with variants for a conclusion for the never finished *Amerika* again in 1916. The year 1914 probably saw him working on at least two of the texts that would go into the collection *A Country Doctor,* though the majority of them were written in 1917. In short, despite moments of creative blockage and despite fits and starts imposed probably by depression, from 1912 to 1917 Kafka produced an extraordinary group of literary works in what can be called the second period of his writing life.

Felice did not disappear during the war. Her father died in November 1914, and she apparently wrote Kafka to say that she felt sorry about the "trial" she had inflicted on Kafka in Berlin at the Askanischen Hof, the hotel where she and Grete had confronted him. Felice's mother may have also written to Kafka asking for a conversation. Kafka and Felice arranged to see each other in January 1915 in Bodenbach (Podmocly), an accessible border town. It appears that they had little to say to each other, though Kafka read some of his recent work to her. Nonetheless, their correspondence resumed after that. They met again in May in northwest Bohemia and then again at the end of June in Karlsbad. Kafka went alone to a sanatorium in northern Bohemia at the end of the following month. What his physical condition may have been is not clear. He had been called up for military service in May, and a military doctor had said that he was fit for unlimited service under arms. (Those who recall Grosz's drawing of German military doctors' declaring a skeleton fit for duty may have some doubts about the credibility of their medical judgments.) Whatever may have been the state of Kafka's health in 1915, the doctors' evaluation probably made no difference. The head of the insurance institute had made a request that Kafka be exempted from service on the grounds that his administrative experience made him indispensable to the insurance organization. The Institute was swamped with work because of the war, for Prague was now filled with war wounded needing aid. The request for Kafka's exemption was granted for an indefinite period of time.

With regard to Kafka's health at this time, one may surmise that he may have been a hypochondriac or that he suffered some serious problems caused by a neurological disorder, or that he had bouts of depression, or that he was suffering from a combination of all of these. Any affirmative diagnosis can only be speculative. Clearly, Kafka thought he had some kind of medical problem, and in 1916 he consulted a neurologist about headaches and sleeplessness. The doctor suggested electrotherapy, which Kafka did not want to undergo, and in addition the doctor superfluously recommended Kafka's abstinence from nicotine, alcohol, and meat, apparently not having had much of a conversation with this convinced vegetarian. Kafka's health did not prevent travel, since in November 1916 he went to Munich to read "In the Penal Colony" in a bookstore art gallery. Rilke was in the audience, an audience that apparently was aghast at the cruelty of the story.

Even before this trip, however, Kafka and Felice had decided in May 1916 to spend the forthcoming vacation in July in Marienbad, a resort town made famous by Robbe-Grillet's homage to Kafka in his eerily beautiful film *Last Year at Marienbad*. Taking companion rooms in a hotel there, the couple apparently achieved a successful intimacy, as one said in those days. Felice left after a few days, and Kafka stayed on there for another eleven days. The letters Kafka wrote in the first eight months of 1917 and sent to Felice are lost, but it appears that the experience in Marienbad had convinced them they could live together. Thus, they were planning to get married after the war's end. Kafka's biographer Ernst Pawel construes this to mean that they had reached an agreement in which Kafka demanded a good deal from Felice for this "Marienbad contract": that she would continue to work and forgo motherhood so that he could live as a freelance writer in Berlin. He did not want to continue on in Prague as the secure bureaucrat whom Felice had hoped to marry and who, she undoubtedly hoped, would be the financially capable father of her children (Pawel, p. 347). Kafka yearned to leave Prague and live for his writing, if not write for a living. Perhaps he was even willing to get married if he believed that marriage with a working woman would offer him complete freedom to write. This is largely speculation, of course.

If one desires to speak of periods in Kafka's creative life, it seems appropriate to say that a third period began with his discovery of his tuberculosis. The symptoms of the disease appeared in August 1917, one month after Kafka's second engagement to Felice. Kafka coughed up blood, although, on consulting a general practitioner, he was reassured that his condition was not serious.

Continuing to spit up blood, however, on 4 September he consulted a lung specialist, Professor Gottfried Pick, who diagnosed tuberculosis in both lungs. He recommended that Kafka go to a sanatorium. Kafka had voluntarily spent a fair amount of time in sanatoria and had no desire to subject himself to the kind of routine practiced there on tubercular patients—the kind of treatment, for example, that Thomas Mann made famous in *The Magic Mountain*. On 12 September, having received a three-month medical leave from the insurance institute, Kafka went to Zürau, the village where Ottla had been working on a small agricultural enterprise since April (its owner was their brother-in-law Karl Hermann). This was a small farm of some twenty hectares, roughly fifty acres, with an assortment of farm animals. Here Kafka hoped to find a cure in the clean air by participating minimally in the farm routine.

He wrote no fiction but rather a series of meditations out of which he compiled and numbered 109 texts that have come to be known as the Zürau aphorisms. (These were published in 1931 by Brod and Hans-Joachim Schoeps in the volume *Beim Bau der Chinesischen Mauer*, under the somewhat misleading title *Betrachtungen über Sünde, Hoffnung, Leid und den wahren Weg*, or, literally, "Considerations of Sin, Hope, Suffering, and the True Way"). While at Zürau Kafka also did a great deal of reading, for example, in a twelve-volume edition of Schopenhauer that he had acquired the year before, or, of considerably shorter length, the essay on Palestine that Thomas Mann published in October 1917 in *Die Neue Rundschau*. Kafka apparently liked Mann's apology for aestheticism that Brod had already condemned as narcissistic in his essay *Unsere Literaten und die Gemeinschaft* (roughly "Our Writers and Society"). But despite Brod's arguments, Kafka was much closer to Mann than he was to Brod, who by now was subordinating his work to his commitment to Zionism. In short, during this time, Kafka's reading ranged widely, from Stendhal and Dickens to the Danish philosopher Kierkegaard of *Either/Or, Repetition,* and *Fear and Trembling*.

Kafka decided he should break off the second engagement with Felice because of his health. He went to Prague on 22 December 1917 and three days later met Felice to ask her to accept the end of their engagement. When he took her to the train station on 27 December, he said good-bye in what was to be their last meeting. He also used the time in Prague to get his medical leave prolonged, though a request for early retirement was denied. Thus he stayed in Zürau until the end of April when he returned to Prague and two days later began work again. It appears that during the summer, after his workday, he also worked for an institute for raising fruit, the *Institut für Obstbaumzucht*, in a suburb north of Prague, probably continuing his hopes that contact with nature and the soil might have a healing effect.

In September 1918 his father, now sixty-six, sold his business and retired, having purchased a group of rental flats to provide a future income. He may well have seen that his future business was a risky enterprise in a Prague in which Czech nationalists had already trashed a number of German-Jewish businesses. As the war came to an end, it was obvious that a political and perhaps social revolution was taking place in which the future of the German and Jewish minorities was anything but certain. In the middle of October there was a general strike that called for the creation of a Czech republic. On 17 October the kaiser published a manifesto that offered political self-determination within a federated empire, but the Czech national committee, the *Nationalrat*, rejected this offer and demanded unlimited autonomy, the withdrawal of Czech soldiers from the kaiser's army, and active participation in all future peace negotiations. This occurred as Edvard Beneš, later a president of the Czech Republic, set up a Czech government-in-exile in Paris in October. Interestingly, as German officials at the insurance institute pondered their limited future, Kafka became an even more valuable employee. He was one of the few higher executives who could work competently in Czech.

Kafka's health hardly allowed him to enjoy his privileged position. Suffering weight loss certainly in part because of his bad wartime diet, he, like millions of others suffering near-malnutrition, caught the Spanish influenza in October 1918. He was extremely ill, with a high temperature, and was bedridden for a prolonged period of time, staying in the home of his parents, who took care of him. After a month or more of illness and recovery, he came back to work in a new world: he was a citizen of a republic in which Czech was now the legally mandated official language. Many, perhaps most German employees of the insurance institute where he worked thus lost their job or went into early retirement.

In November 1918 Kafka went to Schelesen, north of Prague, for more recuperation, after which he returned to Prague still weak, and subsequently he requested more time for rest. On 22 January 1919 he went back to Schelesen, where at the Pension Stüdl, the boardinghouse where he was staying, he met Julie Wohryzek, a twenty-eight-year-old Jewish woman. Her father, having been a butcher earlier in life, was now a *Gemeindediener* (the servant called Shammash in Hebrew), that is, the lowest servant in a synagogue. This was not a social position likely to please Kafka's father. Julie had studied in a business school and was working in an office where she had arrived at the position of *Prokuristin,* something like an upper-level clerk. Brod has described her as not at all educated in literature, though she was interested in Zionism and contemporary political issues (at the time she apparently was reading Brod's *Die dritte phase des Zionismus,* or "The Third Phase of Zionism"). Julie left Schelesen in

March with the understanding that she and Kafka would meet again in Prague. Here there quickly developed an erotic attachment that Kafka had held back from earlier. Kafka at first did not inform his family about his relationship with Julie, but, having returned to work again on 1 April, he apparently felt ready to face the world and his family: he became engaged to Julie in September 1919. Kafka's father was predictably against the marriage, preferring, it seems, a brothel to meet his son's needs.

Kafka's relationship to his father was undoubtedly at a new low ebb at this time, for he then wrote "Letter to His Father." The letter is about the only thing he wrote in 1919, though he did see "In the Penal Colony" published at last. If we are to believe "Letter to His Father," when Kafka gave his father a copy of the just published "In the Penal Colony," the father was irritated that his card game had been interrupted and told him to put it on the night table, which may have been the impetus for "Letter to His Father" (Wagenbach, Rowolt, 1964, p. 120). However, despite his father's insults and rebuffs, Kafka persisted in saying that he considered "marriage and children the highest thing one can strive for"—to quote a letter that Kafka sent to Julie's sister on 24 November 1919—to which Kafka typically added that he could not possibly get married.[5]

Kafka could not commit himself to marriage and apparently put Julie off with tales of his incapacities. On 4 November Kafka went to Schelesen without Julie; he met there another young patient, the eighteen-year-old Minze Eisner, to whom he may have been something of a father figure. In any case, no marriage was forthcoming with Julie. At the beginning of 1920, despite his illness, Kafka was promoted to the rank of secretary (a *talemnik*)—a very high clerk with executive status. But in February a specialist said Kafka's tuberculosis had so developed that he must now go to a sanatorium for therapy. With this dire diagnosis Kafka received another medical leave and went to Meran, a spa town in northern Italy, where he checked into a luxury hotel that he could not afford. Moving into a more modest boardinghouse, he found himself in a milieu rank with anti-Semitism.

It was during this stay in Meran that Kafka began in April 1920 what many biographers consider his most interesting correspondence. He began exchanging letters with Milena Pollak, née Jesenská, a twenty-three-year-old Czech journalist who in February had asked for permission to translate "The Stoker" into Czech. Kafka had met her once earlier in a café in Prague a month before he left for Meran. Their relationship developed by correspondence into a love affair. Milena had been born in Prague and was the daughter of an orthopedic surgeon, a notorious anti-Semite who was a professor at the Karls-Universität (which, in 1882, had been divided into Czech- and German-language colleges). Rebelling against her father, Milena became a sexually liberated intellectual, abreast of modern European literature and the political currents of the time.

Outraged by his daughter's behavior, her authoritarian father had once had her incarcerated in a mental institution. Among other things he wanted to keep her from marrying a Jew, namely Ernst Pollak, a sometime banker and ne'er-do-well intellectual who needed financial help from Milena. Moving to Vienna, she did marry Pollak and tolerated his numerous infidelities while starting on her own career. She began to write articles in Czech for newspapers in 1919, publishing essays, for example, in the *Tribuna,* in which writers like Hasek and Kisch also published. By the time of her death, at the hands of the Nazis, in 1944, she had written more than four hundred articles. With regard to Kafka, she published a translation of "The Stoker" in April 1920, followed that year by a series of translations of some of Kafka's shorter pieces. In brief, Milena was aware of what Kafka the writer was about, and when Kafka began writing to her in April he was addressing himself, finally, to a woman who was on equal footing with him.

Their correspondence quickly became a love affair. At the end of June Kafka went to Vienna to meet Milena. They took walks and made love to celebrate Kafka's thirty-seventh birthday. Kafka returned to Prague and felt obliged to tell Julie about Milena, which meant a quick end this time to their engagement. Peter-André Alt thinks Kafka behaved rather badly at his last meeting with Julie on 6 July (Alt, p. 544). The fact that Kafka quickly ended all pretense might give rise to a contrary judgment, if judgments were to the point. Milena also told her husband about her affair, though, in light of the more or less open marriage they had, it does not seem that this had much effect on their relationship. In the end Milena did not want to leave her husband despite Kafka's request. And while Kafka was ending his engagement and Milena was putting her marriage on trial, Kafka's favorite sister, Ottla, was affirming her independence by marrying the Czech Catholic Josef David. The authority of the patriarchal father was duly in question in every quarter.

Meetings between Kafka and Milena were few. They met once again at a half-way point between Vienna and Prague in mid-August 1920, in the border town of Gmünd, where the Prague–Vienna railway made a convenient stop. One wonders what Kafka felt when, upon returning to Prague form Gmünd, he was visited by a friend of Milena, Jarmila Reinerova, whose husband had recently committed suicide after he discovered that Jarmila had been having an affair with Willy Haas, a writer who was an acquaintance of Kafka. Apparently Kafka was intrigued, for he subsequently saw Jarmila a number of times in Prague.

It was about this time that the very sick Kafka began to entertain even stronger fantasies about leaving Prague and perhaps emigrating to Palestine. These desires are of course comprehensible: in the fall of 1920, in November, there were outbreaks of anti-Semitic attacks on the streets of Prague. Czech nationalists attacked German-language institutions, such as the newspaper and the theater, as well as Jewish institutions, which were also German institutions in Czech eyes. It is difficult to separate out anti-Teutonic and anti-Semitic feelings, though it is also clear that, in Prague, Jews were the object of a special rage, for not only were they part of the German-language minority, but many Jews were also among the community's elite of businessmen, doctors, and industrialists—who probably made up some 1 percent of the city's population. *Ressentiment* was papable, as Kafka wrote to Milena, when he broached the subject of getting out of a milieu in which he felt he was a target of hatred. Unfortunately, a medical diagnosis on 14 October 1920 suggested that there was little likelihood that Kafka could travel far: his prognosis, based on x-rays, was that his death in the near future was very likely. (And, as Kafka undoubtedly knew, had he decided to go to Palestine, it was unlikely that the British would have allowed somebody with TB to enter their Mandate.)

The x-rays justified another three-month medical leave. In December 1920 he went to Matliary, in today's Slovakia, located in the Tatras Mountains, a range forming part of the Carpathians, with a number of peaks reaching more than 2,500 meters high. He undoubtedly did not know that he would spend the next eight months here. Some critics speak, making allusion to Thomas Mann's novel, of Matliary as Kafka's own Magic Mountain, for the treatment Kafka underwent greatly resembled the one Mann describes in his fictional sanatorium set in the Swiss Alps: lying each day in a chair on a balcony for sunshine, walks, caloric-rich meals, all in a snowy environment.

Kafka made a new friend here, Robert Klopstock, a Jewish medical student for whom Jesus and Dostoevsky were spiritual mentors. The young Klopstock was the last friend Kafka made. Klopstock was a Budapest Jew who was against Zionism; moreover, he was reading *Fear and Trembling* by Kierkegaard, whose works also accompanied Kafka throughout his life. Klopstock returned to Budapest in June to resume his medical studies, and a correspondence began that shows Kafka was quite taken with the young man. They remained friends until Kafka's death, when Klopstock came to help him on his deathbed.

Kafka remained in Matliary until 25 August 1921, returning to Prague on 26 August. No writing from 1921 is extant, though the notebooks of 1920 are very rich with new texts. Two weeks after his return to Prague, a medical examination showed that his lung infection was now more advanced, and the doctor advised continuation of the stay in a sanatorium. On 8 October he met Milena after a hiatus of fourteen months while she was visiting her father in Prague. A token of his trust in her is that at this time he gave Milena his old diaries, some eleven notebooks, and a dozen separate sheets from a twelfth notebook. This occurred after, in July 1920, he had already given her "Letter to His Father."

Having giving her the diaries, he began to write again in a new diary, with a first entry on 15 October 1921.

Despite his poor health Kafka tried to participate in Prague's cultural life, to go to cafés or to see new films in the cinema. If Brod can be trusted, it was around this time that Kafka, perhaps in late autumn of 1921, wrote a note to Brod that contained his desire that, after his death, everything he had written be burned, by which Kafka would have had in mind all the manuscripts that Brod had collected. Most biographers assume that Kafka did make such a request, and many assume he did so knowing that Brod would not honor it, which was the case. Brod held onto the manuscripts he already had, as well those that were yet to be written. The last years of Kafka's life were witness to some of his greatest writing.

On 22 October 1921, Kafka got an attestation from his specialist, Dr. Kodym, requesting that he be granted early retirement. Instead, he got three more months' leave. Given the state of his finances, he decided to pursue a regimen in Prague that included relaxation exercises (*Entspannungsübungen*), walks, diet, and gymnastics. And on 29 October he showed up for a day of work that was to be the last day he ever worked for the Institute. In November he saw Milena several times, but the old intimacy was apparently gone (Alt, p. 562).

Kafka began to write again in 1922. Pursuing dreams of health, he took up residence in the Hotel *Krone* in Spindelmühle, a small mountain town on the Elbe northeast of Prague. Apparently Kafka was strong enough to undertake skiing and walks in the snow and to begin writing *The Castle*. At the end of February 1922 he returned to Prague and was able at the end of March to read from the novel to Brod. In fact, by the end of June 1922 some sixteen chapters, or more than half of the extant novel, were written. Kafka kept up his creative élan until the end of July 1922, finishing then the twenty-third chapter. However, in the last week of August Kafka stopped working on the novel, apparently not for reasons of health, or not entirely for those reasons, but because he simply was no longer able to keep the proliferating plot in hand. In September Kafka wrote in a letter that he must abandon the *Castle* story for good.

His health kept deteriorating: still losing weight, sleeping badly, he could take walks only with frequent pauses to catch his breath. On 26 April Dr. Kodym certified Kafka's incapacity for work and said that an improvement in his health was not expected in the foreseeable future. Kafka sought again to be granted early retirement. Without waiting to hear the results of his request, on 23 June 1922 Kafka went to Plana in the *Böhmerwald*, the Bohemian forest, where he lodged with Ottla. She and her husband had rented a small apartment in a country house, where she was spending time with her small child. Kafka spent the summer months here, with three short trips to Prague. At the end of

June he was finally granted permanent leave from the insurance institute. Kafka was not the only member of the family to be ill. The reason for one of his visits to Prague was to see his father after he had undergone an intestinal operation. In the middle of July, Kafka gave the manuscript of *The Castle* to Brod, though it seems he tried to continue working on the novel upon returning to Plana in September. Suffering from lack of sleep, Kafka was in a depressive state comparable to that of earlier periods in his life, though this time the medical reasons for it were all too clear. He spent most of November and December in bed.

Perhaps the only thing that may have cheered Kafka at this time was that Jewish-Czech relations improved when the liberal philosopher and politician Tomaś Masaryk came forward with a program for a full social integration of Jewish citizens into the Republic. The government had to face problems with both Czechs and ethnic Germans in this regard. For example, when a Jewish professor was elected rector of the German-language university in Prague, the Czech government threatened to eliminate the university's autonomy if the German nationalists at the university continued their anti-Semitic protests against him. Of course, these positive signs must be read against the rise of political anti-Semitism throughout the Germanic world. Kafka commented little on this ongoing social development, though he kept half-seriously toying with some idea of participating in Zionism. (Brod's eclectic *Sozialismus im Zionismus* was published in 1920—certainly Brod was totally committed.) One can hardly say, however, that Zionism was an exclusive occupation for Kafka, since he continued reading the very Christian Kierkegaard, moving on from *Either/Or* to *The Concept of Anguish* and *Studies on Life's Way*. Kierkegaard's *Sickness unto Death* also remained a reference for him. But it is also true that in late fall of 1922 he resumed studying Hebrew, this time with a young Palestinian woman, Puah Ben-Tovim, who spoke Hebrew as a native language, having learned German as a second language in Jerusalem. She had come to Prague because of its centrality to the European Zionist movement. She was Kafka's teacher until, apparently finding Prague too provincial, she moved to Berlin in 1923. Kafka apparently found great symbolic value in having Palestine come to him in the presence of this young woman who had no conflict at all about being Hebrew. Moreover, Kafka's health took a turn for the better, briefly, with the return of warm weather in 1923. He continued to work on Hebrew and began to review Italian.

In July he went with Elli and her two children to Müritz on the Baltic seacoast, and on the way he stopped in Berlin with the idea of finding a new publisher for a proposed volume of short stories, *A Hunger Artist*. He talked to the directors of the newly founded publishing house *Die Schmiede,* which was the publisher of major writers such as Benn, Döblin, Hasenclever, Kisch, Sternheim, and, of lesser note, Kafka's friend Ernst Weiss. It also published the first volume of Proust in German. Given Kafka's health, it is remarkable that it was during this time that he was writing some of his most impressive short fiction, not only the four texts published in the new volume, such as "A Hunger Artist" and "Josephine the Singer, or the Mouse People," but also a number of major texts that came to be known only posthumously, such as "Investigations of a Dog" and "The Burrow." The year 1922 was a period of marvelous creativity, as 1923 was also to be.

After the negotiations for a forthcoming volume (which were finalized in 1924), Kafka went on to Müritz, where he spent four weeks in the same boardinghouse as Elli and her children. On 13 July he met the twenty-five-year-old Dora Diamant (or "Dymant"), a volunteer working with children at a Jewish vacation camp. Kafka was immediately struck by this comely young woman, a runaway from an ultraconservative orthodox family in Ger, a Hassidic village not far from Warsaw. She had earlier refused an arranged marriage, had been sent to Crakow to become a teacher, and had fled to Berlin. Dora became his devoted partner for the last twelve months of his life. Kafka did not immediately begin life with her, for he left Müritz in early August 1923 without her. But, after spending five weeks in a private room in Schelesen, he returned to Prague on 21 September, and two days later he went to Berlin, where Dora was waiting for him.

Kafka was met by Dora at the train station and moved into a room in Berlin-Steglitz. He had arrived at a terrible moment to be in Berlin, for he soon found himself in the middle of the hyperinflation that quickly impoverished the German middle class. By the end of 1923, for example, it took several trillion marks to buy a dollar, and the cost of living had increased fifteen-fold since the summer of 1922. Kafka found himself living in acute poverty that winter. He depended on delivery of food packages from Prague—even, it seems, sending his clothes to Prague to be cleaned. Moreover, in the fall there were anti-Jewish outbursts in which shops were sacked, windows broken, and Jews beaten on the streets as the National Socialists began their ascension to power.

In January 1924 the couple had to leave their apartment and took a place in Berlin Zehlendorf. Kafka's condition became so bad that he could hardly leave the house. He left Berlin, accompanied by Dora and Brod, and on 17 March 1924 went to Prague before going three weeks later to a sanatorium, *Wiener Wald* in Ortmann, an hour away from Vienna, in order to undergo treatment. Kafka also went to the Vienna University clinic to consult a specialist, Markus Hajk. Dora then decided to take Kafka to a sanatorium in Kierling bei Klosterneuburg, on the Danube north of Vienna, where the doctor could come to treat him. Treatment consisted mainly of drugs for pain since no effective antibiotics were known for Kafka's condition, which by now was a tubercular infection of the throat. This painful condition interfered with his speaking and eating.

Remarkably, he seems to have remained creative to the end and was correcting the proofs of *A Hunger Artist* when he died on 3 June 1924 with Dora at his side. His body was brought back to Prague, where he was buried eight days later in the New Jewish Cemetery. A hundred people or so were at his burial, and there were a few obituaries. Probably none were more prescient than the one Milena wrote in which she observed that Kafka wrote "the most significant works of modern German literature. . . . They reflect the irony and prophetic vision of a man condemned to see the world with such blinding clarity that he found it unbearable" (quoted in Pawel, pp. 448–449).

Milena seems to have intuited that the history of Kafka's literary legacy would intertwine with the catastrophes of twentieth-century history. She could hardly have known in 1924 how accurate she was, for she did not know the posthumous works. *A Hunger Artist* was published shortly after Kafka's death, but none of the novels had been published in 1924, nor had a good many of the major short stories. Brod immediately began editing and publishing Kafka's manuscripts, first *The Trial* in 1925, *The Castle* in 1926, and Kafka's first novel, *Amerika,* in 1927. After the Nazis seized power, nothing by Kafka could be published in Germany, and the publishing of Kafka's manuscripts, including diaries and letters, depended upon Brod's finding outlets in other countries. After the novels, he edited and published various collections of short stories and parables as well as the diaries. These editions are of course landmarks in establishing Kafka's opus, testimony to the fact that Brod worked hard to made Kafka available and marketable. Critics have often condemned Brod for using his editing to transform Kafka into a saint. This is true, but it is equally true that Brod is the man to whom we owe the existence of Kafka's legacy.

Seemingly acting against common sense, Brod remained in the Nazi-controlled Third Reich until 1939, when, at the last moment, he fled with Kafka's manuscripts to Palestine, where he lived and worked until his death, in 1968. He published a six-volume collected works. This edition did not include all the manuscripts he had in his possession. Many manuscripts have subsequently made their way into Western European libraries, notably at Oxford and Marbach, though it appears there are still some things in Jerusalem. The status of these manuscripts has given rise to rather unseemly litigation, since Brod gave the manuscripts to a secretary, perhaps his lover, who was less than reliable. I pass over the details, but as I write these lines, the National Library of Israel seems to have won the legal battle to keep Kafka's remaining manuscripts in Israel and has written to me that it will make them available online. It is unlikely that there will be any great surprises, but some suspense remains.

Brod's editions of Kafka have now been superseded by the *Kritische Ausgabe* or critical edition put out by the Fischer publishing house, edited by a team of scholars who have done an excellent job of collating the available manuscripts, editing them, and bringing some order into our understanding of Kafka's complete works—if there is such a thing. This edition is usually the basis for recent translations, though Anglophone readers are well advised to see what they have in their hands or on their tablet screen when they open a translation: translations based on Brod can differ in important ways from translations now based on the *Kritische Ausgabe*. This is not to say that earlier translations are to be scorned: some of them are very good, though they often not only reflect editing that bent the work to fit Brod's agenda but also change Kafka's syntax and style in ways that are not in conformity with today's desire for more literal translations. Moreover, after the years during which the once émigré press Schocken Books held absolute control over Kafka's work, with the expiration of copyright there has been a proliferation of translations, in print and online, and Kafka's best-known works exist in multiple translations. Any search on the Web, for example, will lead the searcher into a Kafkaesque labyrinth of unending possibilities. Suffice it to say, then, that Kafka is undoubtedly the best-known German-language writer in the Anglo-Saxon world—an extraordinary irony for a writer tortured by doubt all his life about his literary worth. Kafka might well have appreciated his literary fate of proliferating texts and texts about texts, and one can well imagine him writing another parable illustrating that old manuscripts go astray in peculiar ways.

Chapter 2

Kafka's First Experiments in Writing Fiction

Kafka's writing career has been characterized as having three phases. First came his search for voice, theme, and orientation. This search culminated in what he considered his breakthrough story, "The Judgment," which can be considered the beginning of Kafka's career as a major writer—unless one considers *Amerika* to be equally important. The second period includes major stories such as "The Metamorphosis" and "In the Prison Colony" as well as his best-known novel, *The Trial*, and the stories of *A Country Doctor*. Finally, after he realized in 1917 that he had tuberculosis, he began to define anew what writing meant to him, in unpublished ruminations, aphorisms, narratives, and the stories of *A Hunger Artist*. These last years also saw his last attempt at writing a novel, the magnificent failure he titled *The Castle*. I highlight this tripartite overview of the unfolding of Kafka's work, since it will orient us in our discussion of Kafka's works. This chapter begins with considerations of Kafka's first writings, including work he left unpublished as well as the first short texts he published late in 1912 in the volume *Betrachtung* (translated as both *Meditation* and *Contemplation*). In the following chapter I deal with the novel Brod titled *Amerika*, a novel Kafka apparently worked on both before and after writing "The Judgment."In the fourth chapter we consider this breakthrough story of 1912, a story many critics, as well as Kafka, agree was his first important text. "The Judgment" is in many senses the culmination of several years of experimentation. In the same chapter we also consider "The Metamorphosis," the novella that, for many readers, is the most interesting work Kafka ever wrote. Both stories dramatize a son's dilemma and, after *Amerika*, represent Kafka's varied ways of dealing with the figure of the patriarch. And in subsequent chapters we continue in rough chronological order, studying the second and third periods of Kafka's career as it unfolded in his all-too-short life, with chapters on each of the two unfinished novels and separate consideration of short fictions, parables, and aphorisms.

Turning to the first of the two volumes of Kafka's unpublished writings as found in Fischer's critical edition, one finds eleven texts written before "The Judgment." Most of these are of relatively minor interest. However, two are probably Kafka's first sustained attempts to write fiction: *Hochzeitsvorbereitungen auf dem Lande* ("Wedding Preparations in the Country") and *Beschreibung eines Kampfes* ("Description of a Struggle"). (Proper punctuation in English, italics or quotation marks, is uncertain with these texts, since it is not clear if they were to be novels, stories, or what Germans like to call "novellas.") The editors of Fischer's critical edition propose that Kafka began writing "Wedding Preparations in the Country" in 1906 and "Description of a Struggle" in 1907 and that he worked on them both either alternatively or at the same time before giving up on the former in 1908 and the latter perhaps in 1910. Other sources suggest other dates, but this is of no great importance for our purposes, for it is in these two experiments in fiction that one can see what the young Kafka first set out to do as a writer. One may debate the aesthetic merits of the two narratives—John Updike notably trashed them in his forward to the incomplete *The Complete Stories*. The reader with an open mind may find that these clearly experimental texts contain some memorable moments, especially the way they point up the comedy of the act of writing that is fundamental to Kafka's work. In this respect the two texts show that the young Kafka wanted to grasp, among other things, what might be the meaning of writing, for it seems patent that he was not at all clear about what he wanted to achieve concretely in these often disjointed narratives.

For a first perspective on the very young Kafka's thinking about writing, it is worth considering a remarkable text he wrote as a brief dedication dated 4 September 1900. In florid language this dedication shows succinctly that the young Kafka was caught up by current fashions of literary thought; in a few lines he sketches out a lamentation about the incapacity of language to communicate. Sounding as if he had been reading the French symbolist poet Mallarmé on the impossible task of literary language or was anticipating the Austrian poet Hofmannsthal, who in *The Letter of Lord Chandos* declared the failure of language, Kafka asks that one look at all the words that confront one in books, then declares preemptively that words should be able to recall the past but that they fail because they cannot grasp essential things. And in metaphors borrowed from the German Romantic poets, he says that words are bad mountain climbers and bad miners (*Bergsteiger* and *Bergmänner*) since they cannot bring back treasures from the heights or from the depths (*Bergshöhn* and *Bergstiefen*). Literary antecedents notwithstanding, this text is a good example of Kafka's thinking in images to imagine what should be the task of writing and points to a strategy for reading Kafka: he often thinks in concrete images to get around the regrettable fact that abstractions cannot seize what he sees as essential. In this precise text, Kafka makes an ironic turnabout, as if he could suddenly use language in some essential way, and declares that his inscription in these unpretentious pages offers a living thought (*ein lebendiges Gedenken*) that can softly go beyond the meaning of memory. In short, the young Kafka could not set pen to page to dedicate an album to a girl without invoking the aesthetic crisis of his time, though not without good humor that aimed at the act of writing itself. Kafka's view of language's incapacity to access essential revelation, to say the least, dominated Kafka's ruses with language for the rest of his life.

This short dedication shows that from the beginning Kafka wanted to understand his own writing through the writing itself. On one hand, this desire led to his creating marvelous hermeneutic puzzles that turn on their project of explaining themselves; on the other hand, his joisting with language seems to have prevented him from finishing any long narrative projects. He never finished a novel, except *The Trial,* and this work can be called finished only in the sense that it has a probable ending. These repeated failures have been, arguably, influential in part because they are failures. It has become a cliché that the postmodern mind no longer believes in great narrative projects or coherent logical totalities. Kafka's fragments and failures seem in harmony with contemporary beliefs and are among the most cited antecedents demonstrating the successful power of failure. However, I would also stress that, despite or perhaps because of their incompleteness, Kafka's works seem nonetheless to proclaim the necessity of finding an overarching narrative vision of the nature of things. Failure is simply the best one can do, and in his sense failure is successful. Thus, an understanding of Kafka's works entails confronting the frequent paradox of a text's demonstration of a failure to understand coupled with the understanding that recognizing failure is successful understanding. Understanding the lack of understanding is a task that is then imposed on reading and interpretation, for Kafka's work implies that the failure of reading is just a variant perspective on the failure of writing. Let us turn now to "Wedding Preparations in the Country," a narrative Kafka possibly meant to become a novel. He worked on it at least three different times. In its very incompletion, in its literal failure to go anywhere, this narrative about a walk and then a trip that the protagonist takes points up that Kafka was drawn to images of movement, such as in walking and travel, especially to movement that begins and goes nowhere or is broken off. Description of this motion, walking or traveling by train, is the basis for the narrative's unfolding. And thus, logically enough, motion, travel, and walking become metaphors for the text itself since they are, literally, the substance of what the text narrates. In "Wedding Preparations in the Country," for example, after walking to the train station in the rain, Eduard Raban sets off on a trip by train to go see his fiancée in the country. With the hindsight granted by later texts, fictive and autobiographical, not to mention innumerable letters, the reader knows that, for Kafka, as for his characters, marriage is a bond signifying an acceptance of a social pact: the wish to marry shows a desire for integration into society, something like initiation into the sacred mysteries granted by belonging to the tribe. Marriage is ultimately a hope for salvation from the alienation that afflicts the cursed bachelors living outside the saving grace of social conformity. So a trip for wedding preparations is more than a neutral topic. But Raban never even starts preparing his wedding; in fact he barely makes it to the town where, anticipating *The Castle* and its hapless land surveyor, nobody is waiting for him to make an appearance. Moreover, the omnipresent snow of *The Castle* is anticipated here by the constant rain that sets the scene for a trip that goes nowhere or at best to a filthy town, as the omnibus driver says of the desolate town when he finally picks up Raban at the train station in the night.

Of course, Raban, like many of Kafka's travelers, both riders and walkers, has no desire to make a trip. He imagines in advance all the difficulties that make travel unpleasant, painful, and undesirable when not impossible. Like the Kafka later engaged to Felice Bauer, he has no desire to travel to see a fiancée. Unlike Kafka, however, Raban has never traveled. Like one of Beckett's later heroes, all he wants is the pleasant plenitude of staying in bed, of enjoying total, supine immobility. While walking in real rain, he imagines a solution to his problem: he would avoid the trip by finding a way to travel while remaining in bed. He imagines sending his physical body into the country—he watches in his mind as his body goes staggering through his room's door—while his self remains ensconced in bed. He will remain there to dream, though he knows he will need a new material shape for his self. So he pictures himself there in bed as a giant beetle, either a stag beetle or a ladybug; in any case, his self will lie encapsulated in a beetle with its little legs pressed to its protruding stomach. Readers familiar with "The Metamorphosis" will be impressed by these images that foreshadow the tale's giant vermin, though with more precise entomological images. However, the images in "Wedding Preparations in the Country" do not present the bug-man as vermin. Kafka's beetle images for Raban provoke different emotions. The ladybug is, for most Anglo-Saxons as well as Germans, a cute little bug children like to find and play with, whereas the male stag beetle, coming in at several inches long, has pincers that must impress most readers as potentially dangerous and is hardly condemned to immobility. In his imagined immobility, Raban is not unlike Gregor Samsa who, transformed into an insect, then does not succeed in going to work in "The Metamorphosis"; he is also not unlike the Werther of Goethe's celebrated novel who thinks that a beautiful day makes one want to be a ladybug to fly about and gather one's nourishment from the flowers. Raban's stag beetle is minimally an image of hostile alienation, whereas his and Werther's ladybugs are deluded projections of happily belonging to the cosmos. Raban's desire to be transformed into an insect thus embodies comic images of conflicting desires. With such imaginative play, Raban wants to escape the necessity of travel to prepare for a marriage he does not want, even as he prepares for it.

Unlike Gregor Samsa stuck in his room, the daydreaming Raban must travel. Therefore, taking leave of a friend, he boards the train that carries him into the rainy night. He travels on a train filled with small-business people and traveling salesmen. In the train he enters the world of totally practical people; about them he says, with no small irony, that it is wonderful to be like traveling salesmen and travel quickly about, talking just about their wares and nothing else. The absolute banality of their world of practicality is reassuring, for it is the world that, throughout Kafka's work, stands in opposition to the uncertainties of writing and the quest for some elusive meaning. With Kafka's father in mind we can call this realm of practicality, found in a train full of salesmen, the patriarch's business world. Having immersed Raban in this world, with the train ride concluded at its dismal destination, Kafka breaks off preparations for the wedding. Raban goes to a hotel in paranoid anticipation that all will go wrong, and the text ends on this comic fizzle with no conclusion.

It appears that, in this early attempt at narrative, Kafka simply could not image something that might lift the narrative project out of a world of inconclusive decline. One might speak of an entropic fall, though that idea defines a perhaps too precise notion of running down: entropy means quite specifically that that the measure of time is the growth of disorder. We shall encounter images of entropy often enough in Kafka, though with no parameters spelling out how fast or slow his clocks must run (and they do change speed). What we read in the unfinished tale of "Wedding Preparations in the Country" suggests that narration as travel will resemble a kind of asymptotic movement toward failure that will get closer and closer to nothingness, the symbol for infinity in this case being replaced by the image of the fiancée who is never going to appear. (One cannot avoid something of the same impression of infinite dilatoriness in reading Kafka's letters to Felice Bauer regarding his own preparations for a wedding.) Within this pattern of movement in "Wedding Preparations in the Country," there are several remarkable moments; there are a few passages that show that Kafka, perhaps intuitively, was working toward an art form that would endow his movement toward nothingness with the hint of a transcendence that is forever beyond the purview of the text. I offer one example. In describing the omnibus's movement in the dark night, after Raban has reached the town, Kafka writes that the vehicle "drove between houses, and here and there its inner space shared light coming from some room: a staircase—in order to see its first steps Raban would have had to stand up—was built on to a church: before a park gate a lamp burned with a large flame, but the statue of a saint stood out only darkly in the light of a junk store [*Kramladen*]" (*KA* 1, p. 383). Light enters the darkness, flashing like the image of a world beyond the rain, but Raban does not raise himself up to see images of the church, nor does a saint appear other than as a dark presence contrasting with the world of cheap wares that may represent some bedrock reality, that of the world of traveling salesmen and the wares they sell.

Kafka came back to this text twice but could not make it move beyond the rainy night and the world of traveling salesmen. With this example in mind I offer further observations about Kafka's failure to find meaning, here the failure to find closure. Kafka's narrative art seemingly has built into it an incompletion principle. Completion would mean that the text's movement—travel, running, crawling, walking or any other form of *Gehen* (to go or to walk)—has reached some terminal point, some form of closure, but closure can occur only if some successful revelation of meaning occurs at the end of the trajectory. Real closure seals off the world of the text as something other than the space of failure. But, to return to the principle of Kafkaesque paradox, that closure itself would be a failure, since recognition of failure is the sign of a meaningful text. Hence, no movement can ever stop. And no text can really be complete if it respects the incompletion that underlies all motion toward meaning. The very nature of fiction, conceived as a quest for meaning, demands that it recognize, implicitly or explicitly, that it can never be completed.

This incompletion principle leads to a second axiom underlying much of Kafka's fiction. Since the text consists literally in unsuccessful movement toward a goal, depiction of movement is logically the essential characteristic of the text—such as Raban's walking, train trip, and ride to the hotel. Consequently, nearly all of Kafka's texts are, implicitly at least, self-referential in that they are about their own development and movement, toward an encounter with revelation, the law, the Castle, or at least an understanding of why one is seeking to go to wherever it is that one is going, for example, a quest for knowledge if you are an inquisitive dog. Since the text's encounter with whatever might be its goal does not take place, the trip is not completed, and the text often resembles an unfinished allegory, which is to say, a struggle to reach some realm where a meaning might be lodged. Or it may simply be that the narration cannot go beyond the disorder that entropy inflicts on all messages. And even those of Kafka's works that were finished (most were not) and went to publication may portray an incomplete conclusion, one left open or in suspense, such as when the country doctor, unable to return to his home where savage things are going on, seems at the end obliged to wander forever. It comes thus as no surprise that Joseph K. never finds the law or the court presiding over his trial or that K. never makes it to the Castle.

In "Wedding Preparations in the Country" Raban is going to travel to see his bride-to-be. From the point of view of social conventions, this would be a most meaningful trip, leading to Raban's insertion into the web of social ties that haunted Kafka throughout his bachelor life. Raban does not even want to go, but he does go; since in this tale Kafka is still more or less respecting the conventions of realist fiction, he allows Raban only to imagine that he might stay in bed as a beetle, a nonhuman being that is totally but happily excluded from social meaning and insertion into the conventional web of human ties, duty, and intercourse. Realism seems to dictate that Raban get on a train and find himself in the world of commerce and accomplishment and bad weather. But realism's usual demand of closure runs aground here: Raban never gets to his bride because the text is not finished, and the text is not finished because, in a nearly metaphysical sense, he cannot get to his bride—which would entail finishing the message/text. One might say, if one has a taste for theology, that the first sign of the Fall in Kafka is that no travel ever gets anywhere, not on the plains of Oklahoma, or through the chancelleries of the law, or up the mountain to the Castle—to allude to itineraries found in the three major novels. Of course, Karl Rossmann can get on a train for Oklahoma, Joseph K. can visit many places looking for the law, and K. can even look up at the indistinct outline of the Castle. One can also wait for the emperor's message to arrive, just as the Georg of "The Judgment" can send perhaps unread letters to his friend, and the list of failures turning on travel and the movement of messages could be extended greatly. My point here is that "Wedding Preparations in the Country" is a tantalizing introduction to the failures to follow. And the necessity of failure might even explain why, when Kafka did finish a text, he could be dismissive of the closure he imposed on it, as in the case of "The Metamorphosis" and "In the Penal Colony."

In short, once one has grasped that travel and the quest for closure condition each other in self-referential ways that constantly generate paradoxes, one is ready to negotiate Kafka's labyrinthine texts for what they often are: extremely comic self-explorations.

The young Kafka did not return to Raban's travels perhaps because he felt that the quest for failure needed different rhetorical strategies, something other than narrating quasi-realistically a nearly completed trip. And discursive problems aside, Kafka probably dreaded the necessity of inventing a fictional fiancée almost as much as he feared the real marriage that would put an end to the bachelorhood he also dreaded. Be that as it may, in his next major text, *Beschreibung eines Kampfes* ("Description of a Struggle"), Kafka changed his narrative mode. In leaving behind the approximately realist conventions of

"Wedding Preparations in the Country," he decided to experiment with embedded narratives, stories within stories, that often resemble a dream narrative. Embedding narratives within narratives did nothing to bring this tale to an end, and the story's very title seems to be self-descriptive in that the story describes a struggle to go somewhere (and it appears that the title is Kafka's, not Brod's). Certainly Kafka did struggle with the text, for he wrote a first version, then began it again with substantial cuts, and apparently wrote another page or so at a later date before deciding to abandon it in around 1909. This writing did give him, when Kafka excerpted them from the larger manuscript, two short texts that he published in a journal and several that he included in the collection of short narratives and prose poems he published in 1913 under the title *Betrachtung* (referred to here as *Meditation*).

For the reader who is prepared to entertain the idea that Kafka is fundamentally a comic writer, "Description of a Struggle" is a marvelous text because it is one of his wackiest, if not one of his most successful. It begins with a first-person narrator attending what appears to be some kind of social gathering. He leaves this gathering to go on a walk with a new acquaintance; they walk out into a cold winter night to begin a trajectory that will not be completed. Their walk is complicated by various embedded narratives, with variations on the theme of walking (*Gehen*), as Kafka gives free rein to imagistic flights. The acquaintances walk and talk, but this stroll is broken by the first-person narrator's sudden fear that he will be murdered. He tries to flee into the night, only to fall and hurt his knee. The title of the story's second section is translated as "Diversions or Proof That It's Impossible to Live," with "diversions" here for *Belustigungen*, which might well be translated as "entertainments" or "amusements." These entertainments begin in the second section when the narrator begins a new trip by, most improbably, climbing up on the shoulders of the acquaintance. He then rides his new friend like a horse until the friend falls, his knee now injured. The pair hardly know each other, though they are now doubles in bodily affliction. The narrator's ride on his mount is short, leading to the next section, not surprisingly called "Walk" (*Spaziergang*, meaning walk in the sense of promenade or stroll). The narrator walks on, now capable of shaping the landscape to his desire through acts of volition. A true Kafka character, he becomes tired, wants to sleep, and so climbs a tree to sleep dreamlessly, or so the text says. However, the landscape resembles a dreamscape, and the narrator does allow that it seems as if he had wandered into a dream. Climbing down from his leafy bed, he wonders if he has found the region in which to be happy, but once on the ground he discovers that he is in anguish. Moreover, all appears to him to exist only in his imagination.

The next section, called "The Fat Man," begins with the arrival of an obese character who comes onto the scene on a sedan chair carried by four bearers.

He speaks, addressing the landscape, saying that he is especially bothered by a mountain that obstructs his view of what he will never be able to reach: the unfathomable distances of the horizon. The portable fat man is another Kafkaesque traveler. Other aspects are a bit more problematic. The narrator stands before the fat traveler as an observer, watching what appears to be his portly double. The fat man praises the immediate surroundings before going into a river. There are several ways to make sense of this somewhat oriental or perhaps Asiatic-appearing character, besides viewing him as a bearer of the message of the impossibility of travel. He also resembles a prophet or perhaps a Buddha, and with this image in mind it is not too hard to find in him, as several critics have done, a resemblance to Nietzsche's Zarathustra, the "superman" (or "over-man," the Übermensch) who strives to overcome nihilism by seeking wisdom on the mountaintops. For Kafka and an entire generation of young modernists, Nietzsche was the most important thinker of modernity. To them he appeared as something of a prophet, especially for his poetical *Thus Spake Zarathustra*. (Recall that Kafka first met Brod when he had an argument with him about Brod's criticism of Nietzsche.) To be sure, the prophet's appearance as a fat man suggests an element of parody, for the bloated traveler seems to be overly true to the body that Nietzsche praised when Zarathustra put the physical body above the dubious spiritual being that Christianity saw as the embodiment of humanity's aspirations. Kafka may have been in thrall to Nietzsche, but at this point he appears to liberate himself from the philosopher with a fat "over-man" who is not going to make to the mountain on which Zarathustra takes up residence. The *Übermensch* is literally over his bearers, but they sink into the water and drown as the fat philosopher floats away. The water's vengeance, as the river-borne prophet puts it in a Nietzschean turn of phrase, does not stop the fat man from adding to the story's embedded narratives, for he begins to tell another tale, in effect, the story's next section, called "Beginning of a Conversation with the Supplicant."

It seems that the first-person narrator of this next section is the fat man, though some critics have read it differently. It matters perhaps little, since the fat man and the supplicant he describes are largely doubles of each other, and the "I" looking at the supplicant is replaceable by the "I" that narrates the whole narrative. Doubles seems to appear everywhere in the story, which brings up a central issue for the narrative: how do characters exist? In "Beginning of a Conversation with the Supplicant" the fat man is logically the first-person narrator telling about the incomprehensible supplicant who then narrates in his turn. The first narrator begins by saying he went to church to look at a girl but that his attention was caught by the sight of a man who prayed by slamming his head on his hands on the church's stone floor. One is tempted to see here a parody of some of Nietzsche's already nearly parodistic remarks about

Christianity. However, if one recalls that Kafka himself later wrote an enigmatic line saying that writing is a form of prayer, this supplicant may also appear to be enacting a self-directed satire.[1] From this perspective, writing would be a form of bashing one's brains out as one seeks transcendence. Thus, one is not surprised to find in Kafka other images of smashed foreheads, culminating in the head of his animal architect of "The Burrow" at the end of Kafka's life: the blood streaming down the artist-burrower's face lets him know he has been creatively successful in literally using his head for building his maze. Abstractly considered, of course, if prayer and writing are related, they should take the form of address, aiming at a transcendental realm. By contrast, with the image in the church, Kafka offers a supplicant who demonstrates that prayer, perhaps again like writing, means smashing oneself up against inflexible limits.

The supplicant is also, in contemporary terms, the prototype of a performance artist, for, when cornered by the narrator and queried about why he smashes his head, he admits that he prays that way so that people will look at him. He creates spectacle, and it is not hard to imagine the Tate Modern or perhaps the Whitney Museum offering him exposition space. The narrator is dismayed by the supplicant's explanation, exclaiming that it is as if the supplicant were seasick on dry land. In some anxiety himself, the first-person narrator goes on to analyze the supplicant's rather baleful behavior, telling the latter that in his feverishness he has lost the ability to make connections between words and things. This assertion seems at first to be gratuitous, though it justifies the narrator's demonstrating what happens when language loses its moorings in the world. The narrator claims that the supplicant has called the popular tree in the field the tower of Babel and has thought that the tree shaking in the wind is the biblical drunken Noah. These biblical examples are curious cases of using the scriptures for unfounded metaphors, and perhaps they reflect, comically, Kafka's own anguish about metaphor and the abuses of language to which the scriptures used as metaphors lend themselves. Kafka could not abide the deception that, he felt, metaphor introduces into language use, though it can be argued that the metaphor is the rhetorical figure that he most often used in his attempt to convey meanings that escape nonmetaphorical language. Be that as it may, the dialogue here wanders as in a dream, with one incongruous comment calling forth another, so that the identities of the speaker and the supplicant are blurred as they argue about whether the supplicant has understood a word of what the narrator is saying.

If with his head-bashing the supplicant is in some sense a double of the artist—for prayer is also a form of literature—then it is fitting that he, in his disjointed manner, voices some of the concerns of modernist aesthetics. Finding himself in the fallen reality of quotidian existence, he laments the very uncertainty of his being: he is not convinced that he is alive. As the dialogue develops, he shows he is disquieted by a kind of modernist ontological insecurity, a malaise created in the supplicant by the way things seem to be always on the point of sinking and slipping away toward nonexistence. Looking forward to Kafka's Zürau Aphorisms of 1917, in which Kafka yearns for what he calls there the "indestructible," one can say that the supplicant lives in the world of the perennially destructible. Complementary to a yearning for the indestructible is the supplicant's desire to see things as they really are in themselves, in their true being as it were, before they reveal themselves to our perception of them. This idea about perception may clarify the purport of the supplicant's lament, for he seems to voice the concerns of a generation of aesthetic modernists for whom conventional perception reifies things in inauthentic forms. However, it also is doubtful that authentic perception could change the nature of things, since, in truth, the supplicant says, everything rapidly disappears in his vision of the world: houses collapse and people fall dead in the street, whereupon their bodies are quickly stowed in some stranger's house. Kafka's whimsical sense of humor gives rise to the supplicant's hyperbolic list of disasters that are a refraction of Kafka's own anguish about entropic instability. The supplicant's litany of destruction is at the heart of Kafka's text here, as shown by the fact that Kafka repeats it in the second version of "Description of a Struggle," even after, in the rewriting, he gets rid of the fat man and the parody of Nietzsche.

In the first version of "Description of a Struggle," the text continues with still another tale embedded in the already embedded series of narrations. The supplicant begins a tale of his own. Much as in a dream, it is apparent that the supplicant is a double of the other characters, which is reflected in the common knee problem that afflicts all of them. Kafka's work borders here on a type of metaphysical farce that became the hallmark of much writing later in the twentieth century. (Samuel Beckett used, for example, a comparable strategy for creating doubles in *Molloy* and other works in which characters are united, in their dysfunctional bodies, as comic clowns who often can barely stand up.) The body is immediately an issue in the supplicant's tale in which narrator meets a girl who tells him forthwith that it is clear that he cannot deal with truth, because truth is too demanding. Moreover, his incapacity to deal with the truth is not surprising since, as she points out, the narrator exists only as a silk paper cutout that makes a crumpling sound when it walks. The narrator now resembles something like a Balinese puppet. The narration becomes frankly oneiric when the narrator finds himself in the most defective body encountered in Kafka before Gregor Samsa. At this point Kafka pulls out the stops in pushing forward his attempt at dreamlike narration. It is dream rhetoric that provides the model for narrative transformations that are arbitrary, indeed absurd, yet joined by fluid spatial continuity. The narrator is in a space in which he seemingly glides from this encounter with the girl into something resembling a cocktail party at which he insists on playing the piano. In this image he is overtly an artistic performer, though not a very good one, so he is ushered out of the party into the night. As in a dream, the first-person narrator now discovers that he has no name. But, after speaking to a drunk in the street and deciding that the inebriated fellow is a Parisian, he finds an identity in a French name, Jerome Faroche (rhyming with *fantoche* or "puppet" in French). Moreover, he says that he lives on the rue de Cabotin—*cabotin* being French for "bad actor." That association seems justified not only by his performance as a supplicant but also by the entire preceding series of images. One can only speculate about whether Kafka intentionally used bilingual associations here in an imitation of the way dreams mix languages or if this mixing is the result of automatic writing in which associations appear freely as the unfettered mind pursues whatever happens to present itself—a technique that the surrealists of the 1920s hoped would allow the unconscious finally to express itself. It is clear that Kafka, whether through contrived associations or by automatic writing, was experimenting with irrational associations that are comic in their incongruity.

After this narrative sequence, which one might also liken to a riff in an unfolding jazz improvisation, Kafka breaks off the narration based on narrators wandering in contiguous space. The narrative line returns to the fat man and the supplicant. In case of doubt, this section has a title to orient the by now undoubtedly bewildered reader: "Continued Conversation between the Fat Man and the Supplicant." The chubby narrator has indulged in writing, though not without problems. He copied a page from a manuscript and then found that it was not his handwriting. The emotive charge of this oneiric image is great, and it appears to suggest that all writing is problematic: in bewailing the fate of writing, the would-be artist finds that texts are unstable and subject to transformations. Readers may see in this lament a meta-commentary on the text they are reading, though I hesitate to call this image a *mise-en-abyme* or interior duplication in which an image in the text is a representation of the whole text. We see this kind of interior duplication often in later Kafka works. Here the fat man's page of unrecognizable writing seems to be more a fragmentary image of what dreams can produce: nothing is fixed, including the narration itself. Rather incongruously, the fat man concludes his lament with the question about whether one should not be able to live differently. The supplicant's answer is that one cannot. And the biographically minded reader may note that this was the debate Kafka had with himself all his life.

Attention is then again centered on the supplicant when the fat man asks him why he prays. The answer is that, given the fragility of everything, it is a good idea to shout prayers in church in order to be looked at (*angeschaut*) and to acquire a body. This is not the answer the devout might expect, but it sheds some light on what is a body for the Kafkaesque hero: it is something that exists as it is seen. Thus prayer, like writing, is a performance that aims at filling up the vacant hole at the heart of being, where houses and human bodies are sucked in and disappear in nothingness. In the performance the supplicant is seen, and at least momentarily this prevents his disappearance. These disjointed ideas point to a constellation of Kafka's later images in which the precarious body plays a constant role as it is beset by forces wanting to transform it, by disease, starvation, or simply absurd metamorphosis itself.

Dream rhetoric offers a key to understanding why the two narrative voices of this "continued conversation" then meld into a prose poem about destruction and futility, repeating many of the images and themes of the preceding text. The section concludes with a beautiful finale, a short paragraph that offers the paradox that human beings resemble tree stumps in the snow. They are apparently movable, but in appearance only. Kafka liked this paradoxical simile enough to publish this section in *Meditation*. I will discuss it at greater length presently, noting here that it stands in sharp contrast to the other passages in the continuing conversation: it is a unified parable turning on a developed simile. This part of "Description of a Struggle" ends with the declaration that nothing the fat man is going to say can be held against him (or against whomever the narrating voice belongs to) since what he is saying resembles what can be said in sleep. This is not an innocent idea. With it the narrator seems to claim immunity from moral criticism for whatever an oneiric text might cast up and brings up the question about whether one bears responsibility for one's dreams. The intuitive and automatic answer is that one does not, but Kafka is not one to leave an automatic answer unquestioned. Guilt is a pervasive issue in Kafka, and at this point I leave the question open, as does Kafka, though the implication may well be that one is responsible for all that enters one's mind. In any case it all comes to an end as the supplicant himself blows away clouds so that the stars are clearly present.

The title of the fourth section of "Description of a Struggle" has been translated as "The Drowning of the Fat Man." "Drowning" loses, however, the sense of the German title, "The *Untergang* of the Fat Man." *Untergang* or "going under" is a loaded term in German since, among other things, it explicitly recalls Nietzsche and his Zarathustra. Nietzsche's Zarathustra must "go under" in coming down from the mountain to rejoin the frail humanity that, in becoming Christian, has not been faithful to the earth. However one may interpret the sense of Zarathustra's *Untergang* in Nietzsche, and one can say that it resembles Christian asceticism more than Nietzsche would have admitted, it is clear that, in parody, Kafka's fat man goes under in the most literal sense. He is swept away over a waterfall, and down he goes. The potential prophet leaves the narrator in distress, for the latter still has questions to ask the prophet about how to live. The "entertainments" of the opening title now being over, the poor narrator finds that if his lungs breathe too quickly they suffocate from inner poison and that if they breathe too slowly they suffocate from the air that is now not breathable. His lungs cannot find their own rhythm in a world in which it is indeed difficult to have a body.

If the fat man is a Zarathustra figure, the narrator's complaints may reflect the prophet's teachings, notably the idea that those who embrace otherworldly doctrines poison themselves, so that finally the earth becomes weary of them. In fine, for Nietzsche the desire for transcendence is poison. The narrator is having problems not poisoning himself. This complaint seems to be a further development of the parody of Nietzsche, but I stress that parody is not satire: parody affirms even as it takes comic critical distance. Nietzsche remained a reference for Kafka, informing his thought until the end of his life, well after Kafka had taken his distance from him. From this perspective, the narrator's problem with breathing appears as much homage to Nietzsche as parody. For Kafka's Nietzschean generation, moreover, the image of breathing was an image for living. It was a dynamic metaphor, since it implied for this generation the desire to live passionately and perhaps dangerously. Now, for the narrator, this life seems to be an impossibility; with image of stifling impossibility, the narrator seems to be the victim of the kind of moral paradox that modernists often formulated as they sought to break the bond of convention without destroying themselves. Gide, Wilde, and many of other modernists worried about poisoning themselves as they tried to break with a life based on conventional morality that was suffocating—an image Kafka encapsulates with the impossibility of breath. The primary source for these modern "immoralists" was the Nietzsche who proclaimed the necessity of transforming values. Alas, the narrator derives little help from the fat man and the sight of his literal *Untergang*. Drowning is probably not preferable to suffocating.

Kafka finds then another image for despair, one seeming to owe more to Lewis Carroll's Alice than to Nietzsche's Zarathustra. He turns to fairy tales for the story's next images—which is not altogether surprising, since fairy tales often use narration that draws upon the narrative techniques of dreams. As in a fairy tale, the narrator finds that his members are now growing, which puts an end to his walking. In desperate straits he becomes what he calls an avalanche in the mountains. At this point the narrative breaks off, much as in a bad dream, to return to a scene of normal walking, set on Laurenziberg, a real hill, a park area, in the center of Prague, which is one of the rare instances of reference to a real place in Kafka's work. This is the setting for a new section in the narrative that is simply numbered "III," with no title. The new section continues the conversation begun by the narrator and his new acquaintance at the very beginning of "Description of a Struggle." The two men continue to walk in the frozen winter night and begin a discourse on whether the acquaintance's sweetheart is worthy of love if her beauty is only apparent and transitory. The topic is typical of Shakespearean comedy or of neo-Platonist love lyrics, though the inflection given to it here reflects more a fear of women than an attempt to arrive at an idea of what beauty is separate from its carnal embodiment. Much critical discussion has been devoted to Kafka's attitudes toward women, and the walkers' conversation here could accredit the idea that Kafka was as much repulsed by women as attracted to them. Of course, Kafka is not directly speaking here, and it is more accurate to say that the conversation, underlining how ugly the acquaintance's sweetheart can appear, is a self-directed satire of men's expectations, not to mention the impossibility of accurate perception in the first place. Finally, the discussion of the beloved shows that the acquaintance feels trapped by his own desire. No more than Raban or the Kafka of the voluminous correspondence with Felice Bauer does the acquaintance desire to begin his wedding preparations.

Readers may have the impression that they are reading another version of the correspondence, in fact, when the acquaintance says that he can break off the relationship with the girl only by committing a scandalous act or by leaving for a distant land. The narrator retorts that the acquaintance will do no such thing: his only escape is suicide. This is the reasoning of a man who feels trapped by conventional expectations, of a man desperate but unable to break their hold. The narrator offers the acquaintance a consoling lie to show that he, too, knows what it means to be trapped. He falsely declares that he is also engaged. The narrator is seeking solidarity with the acquaintance. They thus become doubles united, in a rather traditional sense, through male bonding, which suggests that their women exist for them mainly as imaginary projections, even if one fiancée supposedly exists.

The bonding of the two males is overtly underscored. Before inventing his consoling lie, the narrator says that the acquaintance bares his chest, in the freezing weather, allowing the narrator to admire the man's beauty—though the acquaintance has apparently unbuttoned to show that the narrator is incapable of being excited by love, just by fear. The homoerotic side of this supposed demonstration is rather comic, and one may wonder if the narrator then says he is engaged in order to cut short the temptation offered by the handsome flesh. Be that as it may, the acquaintance is the more unhappy of the two, the more desirous of escape, since he suddenly sticks a knife in his arm. Though the narrator has suggested suicide as a solution, the acquaintance's blood-letting more resembles a masochistic act than an attempt to end it all. The narrator thinks, for some reason, that the acquaintance has done this gratuitous act for the narrator's sake, and the narrator duly sucks on the wound in the bleeding arm. For some critics this is also a homoerotic act. It could perhaps appear to be a strange ritual in the sadomasochistic drama of the body.

"Description of a Struggle" begins, in the first section, with a description of blissful heterosexual kisses and ends, in the third section, with the image of male bonding in blood. This itinerary suggests that Kafka's aim is to describe the struggles that sexual beings engage in, which would perforce include homoeroticism. However, it is not accurate to speak unqualifiedly of homoerotic attraction between the two men in "Description of a Struggle" because the two are really more like doubles of the same character in a strange dream, walled in at the end on a mountain. If one has trouble ascribing homoeroticism to the scene, it is because the scene is imbued with narcissistic eroticism in which the self takes itself for its own object, as may happen in dream or masturbation. Freudian critics would view this doubling as a projection of the unconscious, be it the fictional narrator's or, through the narrator or through both characters, Kafka's unconscious. (From a Freudian perspective, this projection is, a priori, always true, which greatly weakens the hermeneutic validity of this kind of dream analysis.) In empirical terms, the meaning of a unique gesture, like the knife stuck in the acquaintance's arm, should be read in the context of the development of the narration. This is not always easy. In this precise case, the stabbing resembles a bizarre sacrifice in some primitive ritual as well as a masochistic sexual act springing from narcissistic eroticism. Set in a near dream, it might be taken as a displacement of the narrator's desire or, indeed, a bizarre form of quasi homoeroticism for which we have no precise categories—just this weird image.

The first version of "Description of a Struggle" ends a few lines after the stabbing. It is difficult to speak of a meaningful closure to this narrative, though this blood-letting may be the ending Kafka had in mind. It is difficult to take seriously the narrator's rather comic assurance to the effect that the acquaintance will walk happily one day in the sunshine, and the acquaintance notably does not take solace in the narrator's idea. The bleeding double simply says rather that he must go home since he might have to do something the next day. He might have to answer to the demands of the world of business. The demands of the practical world reign in Kafka's work sometimes like a tragic fate. In contrast to this reference to the practical world, however, the text concludes with the image of a play of light and shadow: a lantern's illumination in the night contrasts the shadows of tree and branches against the snow. The play of light and darkness recalls the images in "Wedding Preparations in the Country" where Raban, in the rain, sees light breaking into the darkness that appears to be the general condition of the world. There the image seems to be almost a mocking promise of revelation for the beleaguered hero. The effect is much the same at the end of "Description of a Struggle."

In the first version of "Description of a Struggle," Kafka uses various narrative modes for a disjointed series of embedded tales: parodistic, satirical, comic, lyrical, oneiric, poetic, with even a more or less realistic moment here and there, though with an expressionist cast. All modes are strung together by motion forward, by the characters walking and almost going somewhere, in contiguous spaces that flow into each other with no logical connections. It is this motion, with absurd transitions, unmotivated juxtapositions, and unexplained events and transformations, that endows the text with the appearance of a dream. Kafka retained these modes for the second version of "Description of a Struggle" (the B version, as it is called in the critical edition). However, in the second version, as I mentioned, he entirely discarded the parody of Nietzsche in favor of the exploration of dream rhetoric. In the B version the fat man disappears and the head-smashing supplicant's tale is joined to the main narration. The second version begins, as does the first, with the encounter between the narrator and the new acquaintance. However, their relation as doubles is stressed earlier than in the first version when, revealingly, the narrator says that whenever the acquaintance's sweetheart kisses him, she also kisses the narrator. He adds that if she steals the acquaintance away, this means that she will steal him from the narrator, though this does not seem possible. He emphatically declares that the acquaintance must forever remain with him—for who other than the narrator could protect such a dumb man—so that the acquaintance will never be free of the narrator. The thought here is muddled, but the narrator's speech to himself reinforce the impression that the "I" and the "he" are much the same and, at the same time, different as in a dream in which the dreamer is at once the observer and the observed or, in other words, oneself and another.

This merging of identities in the second version perhaps makes more sense of the fact that the narrator, as in the first version, suddenly fears for his life—though no motivation for this fear is given in either version. In the second version it might appear that this is as much a fear of suicide as of murder, of a suicide disguised as murder. Suicide hovers on the horizon of Kafka's work and sometimes erupts as a form of self-judgment, as in "The Judgment," in which it takes the form of the father's judgment and condemnation of the son, who then drowns himself. Suicide is thus a judgment by the other, when the other is also one's self—for the son is also the father.

In the second version of "Description of a Struggle" the world sometimes obeys the dictates of the narrator's desires, as when he can shape the landscape according to what he wants. The tale takes a new direction in the story's second part—confusingly labeled with the Roman numeral "I" in the critical edition. Here the narrator again mounts his acquaintance but this times rides into the land of Nobody, where he would like to make an excursion into the mountain with a crowd of Nobodies. This text was excerpted and published in *Meditation,* and I will return to this presently. Suffice it say here that Kafka appears to allude to *The Odyssey* and Homer's depiction of Ulysses's trick when, imprisoned in the Cyclops' cave, the wily traveler tells the Cyclops that his name is Nobody (so that no fellow Cyclops help the giant when he cries out that "nobody" in his cave is endangering him). Kafka's version presents a crowd of Nobodies to accompany the alienated narrator on an outing. However, this short section of the B version ends, as in the first version, with the mounted acquaintance again falling down with a knee problem. The narrator again continues forward, though this time leaving the prostrate acquaintance under the guard of a few vultures. (A vulture appears in a later Kafka parable, "The Vulture," in which the scavenger seems to have replaced the eagle in Kafka's version of the Prometheus myth.) Vultures acting as guards is darkly humorous, another macabre example of the black humor that Kafka used throughout his work in which the ghastly and the horrible are a part of the comic workings of the ever collapsing Kafkaesque body.

The third section (with Latin number "II" in the critical edition) presents another walk, another *Gehen*. For this stroll the narrator prefers a flat surface to the mountain slope that Nietzschean immoralists frequent. Again as in a dream, he wills the path be flatter and lowers it into a valley (which is perhaps Kafka's final parodistic allusion to Nietzschean mountain climbing). The narrator goes into the valley and is soon tired. Fatigue is a near universal condition in Kafka's work, since the ever-frail Kafkaesque body can hardly surmount the obstacles the world unceasingly presents to it—including a lack of beds. Lacking a bed, the narrator climbs a tree and goes to sleep. In the next section (with the Roman numeral "III"), the tired walker now sleeps. In this second version, he dreams, or, as he puts it, he dreams himself into the depths, which allows him to return, as if saved (*gerettet*), to the villages of his homeland. This dreaming leads to a parable of sorts, almost a prose poem, composed of children's voices, which Kafka also published in *Meditation*. The poetic text does not really fit into the development of the dream logic of "Description of a Struggle," though it is very interesting in itself as an expression of the kind of Romanticism that is part of Kafka's panoply of voices. Published alone, as I will presently discuss, the text shows that Kafka was never far removed in his imagistic thinking from the world of fairy tales and folk paradoxes.

It is at this point that the B version turns to the tale of the supplicant who smashes his head in prayer. This time the story is told by the first-person narrator. With somewhat less difficulty than the earlier fat narrator, the first-person narrator of the B version catches the slippery supplicant to find out what he is about. They begin their encounter by conversing about suspicion and guilt, as if the suppliant were guilty of something. Since they readily affirm their shared innocence, the reader may suspect they also share guilt. None of this is all too clear, since neither supplicant nor narrator can clearly define what he wants.

The supplicant asks the narrator if he understands that, if the supplicant proves his innocence, then the narrator must prove his, to which the narrator blandly replies, "Either that or something else" (*KA*, p. 154). Kafka plays with the idea that innocence implies guilt, for guilt somehow precedes innocence. As *The Trial* shows, guilt is the natural assumption about everybody, a conclusion deriving from a belief in original sin. Apparently the narrator and the supplicant believe that they must demonstrate their innocence before they can converse, which leads to a discussion of head smashing as prayer. The supplicant says, as in the first version, that he performs in order to be seen, but in the B version he goes on to discuss reactions to his performance. He contends that the pious find his performance natural and that the others think it is pious. By contrast, however, the narrator does not find head smashing to be an act of piety, or, as he says, "My irritation is disproof thereof" (*KA*, p. 157). To which the supplicant replies that his irritation merely shows he is neither pious nor one of the others. This banter between the doubles suggests a kind of interior monologue of the artist with himself, for the supplicant as performer seems again an image of the artist and by implication of the narrator. In fine, like the artist, actor, and, we suppose, the writer, he performs to be seen and even to be understood—though he is not unhappy that the narrator does not understand him. The supplicant says he want to make the narrator cry—by which one may suppose that he wants to evoke an emotional response, the goal of most artists until a recent date.

However, the most likely emotion elicited here is that of laughter, for Kafka's characters, in their bodily convulsions, engage in pure farce. Their distortions alone would justify the claim that Kafka was influenced by nascent cinema, for the physical comedy of the pair appears to derive from movie farce, with perhaps some traces of the music hall variety act. This is true throughout both versions of "Description of a Struggle." In the first version, for example, the narrator walks bent over double, since he believes it is not polite for him to be taller than his short acquaintance (a bizarre thought apparently Kafka had at times about himself). In both versions the narrator uses the acquaintance as a horse to continue moving forward. And, in section III of the B version, the narrator and the supplicant stand in a stairwell and adopt various absurd poses on the steps, going through some of the most farcical scenes in Kafka's work. The narrator does gymnastics on the steps while the supplicant stretches out, with his face pointed down on the steps, so that the fingers of his left hand touch the wall while his right hand taps on the stair's underpinnings—keeping rhythm perhaps with the gymnastics? It is difficult to interpret farce, any farce, since farce creates a self-enclosed world that rejects the possibility of serious meaning while joyously celebrating the absurdity of the physical world. Kafka's pair of clowns offers the reader the physical image of the marvelously absurd body, undoubtedly springing from Kafka's own distrust of the body.

Kafka gave up on the B version of "Description of a Struggle" around 1910, though the critical edition attributes to it another page, from around 1911, in which one character is kneeing another to keep him awake. This kneeing presents perhaps in miniature another farcical artistic performance for doubles. In any case, by 1911 the struggle with "Description of a Struggle" was over. It is noteworthy that at approximately the same time, in 1910, Kafka began to write his diary. "Diary" or *Tagebuch* is a slightly misleading term for what Brod published under that title. The reader should be aware that Brod turned a series of Kafka's notebooks into diaries by editing and ordering them in chronological order, though the notebooks in question are not, strictly speaking, chronological. The available translation presents the texts chronologically, with many cuts that Brod undertook to shape his image of Kafka (and to avoid references to himself that might be unflattering). Since Kafka himself used the term *Tagebuch* to designate these notebooks, it may seem a quibble to point out they do not entirely resemble a conventional diary. They resemble a diary in that Kafka dated some, but not all, entries. However, much of the material in them is closer to what is found in a sketchbook. They are a very mixed bag. The manuscripts offer, in effect, a collection of personal reflections, meditations, notes on dreams, and comments on daily life, as well as projects for writing and fictional texts, which are now part of Kafka's fictional opus, either because Kafka used them in publications or because Brod put them in his editions of posthumous works. As might be expected from a diary, these manuscripts contribute much to our knowledge of Kafka's life and sometimes offer insights into his ideas about fiction. The range of topics is wide: one learns that Kafka had trouble sleeping, was interested in Yiddish theater as well as theater in general, liked sex and women, feared sex and women, and often had strange dreams.

Kafka began writing his diary about the time he found that he was unable to finish "Description of a Struggle." In a sense, the diary notebooks offered a way of keeping pen to paper while he worked his way toward an understanding of what he wanted to do as writer. In fact, the diary writing appears to be almost the only writing extant for 1911 and the early part of 1912. Kafka failed in an attempt at a collaborative work, *Richard und Samuel,* with Brod in late 1911; one chapter was published with the title "Die erste lange Eisenbahnfahrt (Prag-Zürich), or "The First Long Train Journey." The travel motif with its attendant theme of motion seems to be as inevitable as the fact that the work went nowhere.

The diary entries of these early years offer some interesting examples of the experimentation in writing, fictional or nearly so, Kafka undertook at this time. For example, in the entry dated 10 July 1910 he wrote a series of variations on a theme the litanic repetition of which recalls the texts, say, of Gertrude Stein in which she experimented with repetition in an almost musical sense. In this case,

Kafka used the theme of his unhappy education to create an incantatory mood through repetition of phrases about how harmful his education was. By dint of repetition he could not avoid the conclusion that his education had ruined him, more him than anybody he knew and even more than he realized himself. There is a comic side to this hyperbolic claim, repeated over several pages, as theme and variation, with its expanding litany of complaints, in the deadpan performance of a natural-born *farceur*. With this text Kafka worked out for himself a style of nearly syncopated hyperbole in which each repetition increases the scope of the catastrophe in which a character is involved. This comes from a "diary" entry in which fiction and autobiography merge. In this entry, Kafka wishes for himself in fact a different autobiography, in which, for example, he would have inhabited ruins far from the city in which he had the misfortune to receive his miserable education from all the unintentional miscreants and evil-doers who surround him. With the example of Rousseau's *Confessions* in mind, we can call this an exercise in negative Rousseauism, negative in that Kafka imagines all that has made of him the unmade man, a unique exemplar about which he, unlike Rousseau, is not especially happy.

Fictional texts are also part of the diary, often fictions emerging from autobiography. The story "The Judgment" is anticipated in detail in this regard by the story narrated in the entry of 21 February 1911. In this tale, called "Die stadtische Welt" ("The Urban World"), a fictional Oscar M. feels guilt for wasting his life. Still a desultory student, Oscar has not finished the dissertation, left untouched for some ten years, which would allow him to embark on a career. The autobiographical side becomes clear when one learns that Oscar's disapproving father has virtually disowned him. Oscar promises to show his family a new side. With good intentions, he enters a room in which the father sits, in a kind of inner sanctum, in order to announce that he has a plan to become industrious. This disjointed diary text displays the logical gaps found in "The Judgment," for father and son treat each other in contradictory ways. Oscar finally declares that the man he confronts cannot be his father and leaves to go see his friend Franz, an engineer who has embarked on a career that Oscar's father would have approved. (He is a first version of the friend in Russia who, in "The Judgment," is the son the father would have wanted.) The clear dichotomy of lazy bum and successful man is a projection of the roles projected in Kafka's own relationship with a father who approved of nothing Kafka did. In short, the triad of father, son, and friend sets out the configuration that, radically transposed in 1912, became the basis for Kafka's so-called breakthrough work, "The Judgment." But there is no breakthrough in the diary, and "The Urban World" breaks off without closure. In fact, the next entry is an amusing description of Kafka's visit to the theosopher Rudolph Steiner in which Kafka reports how little interest the impresario of esoteric thought took in Kafka's problems. And so the diary goes on, mixing descriptions of events in Kafka's life, brief fictions, and commentaries on various topics.

Under pressure from Brod, Kafka prepared a book for publication. He agreed to allow publication of some of the texts he had published in literary reviews, to which he added some unpublished pieces. The unpublished texts did not add many pages, but it all added up to a short book he entitled *Betrachtung* (*Meditation* or, more recently, *Contemplation*). It was published at the end of 1912, though it is dated 1913. This anthology of short texts has not fared well with later critics, though it was rather well received by some contemporary reviewers. (The so-called *Complete Stories* does not contain all of them, though other anthologies do, such as the *Collected Stories* edited by Gabriel Josipovici.) *Meditation* offers a collection of minimalist experiments in which Kafka sought, among other things, the art of finding closure for his narrative. To this end, the short texts are often framed as brief revelations, as epiphanies that often ironically reveal that nothing is revealed. This negative quality was perceived upon their publication by the Austrian writer Robert Musil. In his inimitable style, Musil said that the texts offer a "Hinübertönen dieser kleinen Endlosigkeiten ins Leere, eine demütig erwählte Nichtigkeit," or a "distant reverberation of these little infinities in the void, a humbly selected nothingness."[2] In *Meditation*'s selected instances of nothingness, as Musil put it, Kafka traces out textual movements with often delicate irony. He offers paths, as his favored *Wege* is often translated, which, as I now hope to show, lead to more than a few moments of poetic success.

Meditation opens with "Kinder auf der Landstrasse" ("Children on a Country Road"), taken from the B version of "Description of a Struggle." It is narrated by a meandering first-person narrator who, returning to the past, finds himself "saved" as he enters the village of his childhood. The desire to find salvation by returning to childhood is a Romantic leitmotif, taken up by the modernists, frequent from Wordsworth through Proust and Rilke. In "Description of a Struggle" the narrator's return seems to occur in a dream, though this oneiric perspective is lost in *Meditation*. Published alone, the text resembles a foray into the world of fairy tales and folk fables. It describes the play of a child narrator who escapes from his or her home after supper to run riot in the night—the German neutral pronoun allows for either gender, and the tale is as much a girl's narration as a boy's. The child frolics with other children, jumping, rushing about, rolling, and falling headfirst into the night. The child's frolics are not without risks, for her/his headlong leaps might carry the child far beyond a ditch into which she or he falls. Indeed, suddenly the child is headed for the town in the south where fools live, and one knows that fools are never tired—which suggests perhaps that they do not have to go to bed. This received idea that fools (*Narren*) and the mad are never tired is part of universal folk wisdom, though not being tired is something that decidedly does not characterize Kafka's characters. Here childhood—this time of imagined paradise, the once-upon-a-time realm of salvation—is characterized by the temptation to do the impossible: to run away into the limitless distance, which would take the child to the land of fools, beyond reason and limits, and hence beyond fatigue. What else is one to do, the text implies, if one does not want to go home to bed, to that place of protected limits ruled over by conventional parents? One must go beyond limits or else nowhere. "Children on a Country Road" is not the last example of writing in which folklore and Romantic-inspired existentialism overlap in Kafka.

The second text describes a moment in a walk when the narrator faces the "Enlarvung eines Bauernfängers" ("The Unmasking of a Confidence Trickster," though, with Melville in mind, I would prefer "Confidence Man"). In this story the ambulatory narrator also goes on a walk with a superficial acquaintance, realizes that he cannot get rid of the fellow, and, arriving at the place he wants to go, suddenly fears that his obstinate companion is in fact a swindler or confidence man. Why this is so is not clear, no more than in "Description of a Struggle" is it clear about why the narrator fears being murdered by his new acquaintance. In "The Unmasking of a Confidence Trickster," the narrator speaks as if mouthing proverbial wisdom, saying one knows when one is with a *Bauernfänger* because confidence men always place themselves in front of a person who wants to go somewhere and, making themselves as big as possible, try to keep the victim from going there. As the narrator explains it, the trickster thus creates an ersatz goal for us right in our own breast. The trickster works by getting us to stop ourselves, to give up our desire to keep going, to keep walking, to stay in motion. Strongly implied again is the idea that the swindler is none other than the narrator's own self, that the confidence man is the narrator's double. Recognizing this, it seems, the narrator dismisses the trickster and rushes up the stairs to his destination. Going up stairs is a recurrent image in Kafka, comically suggesting ascension and perhaps transcendence. It is at times another comic image of the act of writing itself, which in this case is also the narrator's successful flight from his own self-destructiveness when he becomes aware of the swindler working inside him.

As in the case of the tale of the trickster, Kafka is drawn to images of blockages impeding movement. In *Meditation* he portrays several of these blockages as inner self-deceptions the responsibility for which is often ascribed to exterior objects. This theme is illustrated in the description of movement in *Meditation*'s third text, "Der plötzliche Spaziergang" ("A Sudden Walk"). The definite article in German suggests a generic case of taking a walk, whereas the indefinite article in English is more suggestive of a single occurrence. The different is important insofar as the suggestion of a general description is a deadpan form of comic hyperbole. Moreover, the third-person narrator uses the pronoun *man* ("one") in order to make the generalization from a seemingly objective viewpoint, which naturalizes a daily scene in which contradictory desires are juxtaposed. The narrator says, in effect, that when (*wenn*) one decides to stay home, since one has no reason to go anywhere, for the weather is bad and it is late at night, in short, if one decides on immobility, then if one suddenly decides to go out, with all possible haste, it will be the case that, when one is then totally free in the street, having left behind the family, one can rise up to one's true shape or self (*Gestalt*). My reproduction of Kafka's syntax should point up the contorted reasoning used to describe, ironically, the extraordinary results of such a burst of motion that leads one to rush out into the night. The great results of this motion then are deflated when the generalizing narrator adds that it would be a good idea, to reinforce the effect of this movement toward self-assertion, if one were to go see a friend to see how he is doing. The explosive assertion of freedom functions at best as an excuse to go drop in on somebody. The conclusion is as ironic as is the hyperbole in the idea that liberation consists in kicking off one's slippers and striding into the night—only to find that, once emancipated, one does not have much to do.

The fourth text, "Entschlüsse" ("Resolutions"), follows up on the preceding text's ironic "resolve" to take a walk into the night by offering, in contrast, praise of the narrator's irresoluteness. The narrator observes that if he were to start the motion necessary to remove himself from his miserable condition, if he were to meet people and thus begin making the usual mistakes, he would find that he could move only in circles. Reasoning with hypotheticals and conditionals is recurrent in Kafka, allowing him inevitably to arrive at the worst conclusions. For example, this narrator argues that, if it is the case that he would only go around and around, then it is better for him to remain motionless and watch the world with an animal's stare. "Resolutions" ends in deflationary irony: the narrator observes that, when one finds oneself in a frozen state, the best movement is to run a little finger over one's eyebrow. Whatever the meaning of the gesture—usually absurdly preening oneself—in context the gesture is an ironic marker of incongruity.

Kafka took the fifth text from "Description of a Struggle" and titled it "Ausflug ins Gebirge" ("Excursion in the Mountain"). Here the narrator makes an excursion in the company of a group of nobodies. As said earlier, "nobody" can allude to the scene in which Ulysses said his name was Nobody to the Cyclops Polyphemus. Translation is a problem, since the plural of "nobody" in German does not necessarily suggest, as in English, a group of insignificant people but rather conveys the idea of multiple negations. For his excursion to the mountain, Kafka's narrator uses the plural of the negative pronoun to say he will travel with nobodies, which presents a semantic conundrum, not sociological analysis. In multiplying the negation, he perhaps parodies the idea of traveling with others, or Kafka may have in mind the Nietzschean mountain climber who must travel alone to reach the highest peaks of attainment. Hyperbolic solitude would entail more than one nobody as a companion. And so the narrator comes to the conclusion that to travel with nobodies will be a joyous event, since it would be surprising if nobody did not sing. "Nobody" thus offers a subject going nowhere, but with music, a recurrent image in Kafka for spiritual nourishment, perhaps even transcendence. Music, even if sung by nobody, is an image of plenitude—the negative plenitude Kafka often envisages as the best we can hope for. In "Excursion in the Mountain" the comic play here with negation dramatizes that negation can spill over into life, at least the life of a text.

The sixth text, "Das Unglück des Junggesellen" ("Bachelor's Ill Luck"), is taken from the diary entry of 11 November 1911. Several critics have considered this text's description of the bachelor as a key to Kafka's early work, complementary to his ruminations in the diary, especially in 1910, on what it means to be a bachelor. In brief, it shows that the unmarried man's misfortune is to be excluded from the social world. The image of the bachelor's exclusion resembles in some ways humanity's fall from grace, for, like a solitary Adam banished from the garden, the bachelor is excluded from earthly joys. To illustrate the bachelor's curse, Kafka depicts the unmarried man, never climbing the stairs pressed next to his wife, finding himself thus alone, immobile, sick in bed, or simply at home standing about, while his body and head constitute a useless physical being, one whose forehead at best serves as a place upon which to beat his hand. Like the supplicant in "Description of a Struggle," the bachelor will spend time in head smashing. However, the bachelor's beating his forehead seems more a sign of regret and expiation than of prayer. Prayer and expiation can be, of course, interlinked in the world of the universal fall, and the bachelor's dilemma is to find himself immobile in guilty alienation.

"Der Kaufmann" ("The Businessman" and "The Tradesman") presents a small businessman who has the Kafkaesque gift for using catastrophic conditional sentences to foresee all the possible disasters that could threaten his business. The first-person narrator proceeds by making a list of potential misfortunes—for example, his money is in the hands of strangers who might at the very moment be feasting on it before they run away to America. The narrator adds that, at the end of the business day, he knows a useless desire to be torn away from this world of routine and probable unhappiness. But this is useless wishing. So he goes home, too dirty, torn, and worn to go anywhere else. Alone in the building's elevator, he speaks to himself and, in the imperative mode, tells himself to fly away, to travel, and then entertains the fantasy of rushing through the world, in which he might rob an old man in the street, with impunity, if he so desires, and then ignore the police riding by on horses. This counterfactual is a fantasy, in counterpoise to the opening hypotheses about catastrophes. The fantasy lasts the time of an elevator ride. The elevator comes to a stop—immobility has the last word—and the maid opens the door to the apartment in which the merchant is trapped until the next day. Free movement can be had only when fantasy tramples on the reality principle, to evoke another Freudian notion. In fantasy, the merchant can run freely and sadistically through the streets. This is a darkly humorous text, in which the character's fantasy conjures up the masochist pleasures of loss and the sadistic pleasures of violence. It offers another image of the fallen world of business: it is buffeted by the gusts of imagined motion and fantasy evasion, though, ultimately the practical world asserts its omnipotence, for, come what may, the merchant's shop must be opened the next day.

Subjectivity can also invade seemingly objective observation, as in the eighth text, "Zerstreutes Hinausshaun," literally "distracted looking out." The title in translation, "Absent-Minded Window-Gazing," specifies a location for this looking out. In this text a third-person narrator uses the pronoun *man* to say that when one goes to the window on a spring day and leans one's cheek on the windowpane, one can see a young girl in the setting sun. Then one sees that a man approaches quickly, goes by her, and afterward, the girl's face is radiant. This observation is enigmatic. An immobile observer seems simply to observe motion, drawing no conclusion, though the reader may infer that if the girl had been disquieted by the man's brusque approach, she would have been happy to be safe after he has gone by. The reader may ask whether her radiance is a product of her state of mind or whether it is a projection of the immobile narrator upon what she or he has observed. In either case, there is something threatening about all this, as in a Balthus painting in which a threat seems to hover over an erotically charged scene with a young girl. But it is not clear on which side of the window pane lies the meaning of the observation and the possibility of a threat.

The first-person narrator of the ninth text, "Der Nachhauseweg" ("The Way Home"), is another text that describes movement. The narrator "marches" along, content with himself, finding injustice in the world only in the fact that providence has privileged him above all others. His is not the usual attitude of a Kafka character. The narrator is a forthright megalomaniac who claims responsibility for much of what happens in the world. Perhaps without knowing it, he loses himself in the fantasy that he is responsible for events as various as, for example, the knocking on doors, the presence of lovers in bed in new buildings, or the fact that others finds themselves on the divans of brothels. The narrator's marching produces a delirium that is tempered only when he comes to his room, where, now immobile, he is thoughtful. Moreover, music comes through his window and appears to deflate his imaginary self-aggrandizement. Stationary in his room, the narrator seems most ordinary, while the music acts, by contrast, to point up that his fantastic lunacy is a product of his rushing about. The music imposes on him, with its muted promise of elevation, the recognition that he must live in a quotidian reality in which his fantasies have no place. In this case, the narrator's marching home is much like the merchant's ride in an elevator: it offers the one moment when the ordinary man can, in delusion, reign supreme over the city.

The tenth text, "Die Vorüberlaufenden" ("Passers-by"), offers other variations on the themes of walking, night, and fantasy. It begins with a third-person description of a walk one takes in the night. One can potentially have encounters in which one runs into trouble. In a hypothetical encounter, one (*man*) would not stop a running man who is pursued by another, even if the first man were shabby and feeble. Kafka's characters, animal and human, often spend their time thinking up the permutations of the possible catastrophic results of their acts. The generation of paranoid permutations is recurrent in Kafka, who had the insurance agent's eye for the potential disasters lurking in any situation, an insurance agent with a great comic sense, to be sure. In the night scene of "Passers-by," one might suppose, for example, that the two running men mentioned earlier are entertaining themselves—and that an intervention will be unwelcome—or that they are following a third person, or that the second one will murder the first one—and then the intervener will become involved as an accessory in crime—or that perhaps the first one is armed, and so on. The unpleasant possibilities are endless, and finally one is glad to be tired from having drunk too much, which leaves one the option of remaining still.

The translation of the eleventh text's title, "On the Tram," does not have the resonance of the title in German, "Der Fahrgast." The German title, literally the "travel guest" or the rider on the tram, puts the emphasis on the traveler, whereas the translation suggests that the means of travel is the focus. The traveler in question, a first-person narrator, is on the platform of the tram, allowing himself to be carried along, saying that he has no certainty about his position in the world. The traveling narrator seems to want something certain, and perhaps this is why he is riding on a public conveyance, following a rigidly fixed itinerary, but not even this banal image of the most certain movement gives him a sense of direction. His apparently pointless trip mirrors an incapacity to justify anything. Kafka's tram rider apparently spends his time mainly looking at the world, such as in the tram when he watches a girl preparing to get off at the next stop. He describes her appearance in quick detail, seemingly with the idea in mind that in the clarity of the description, he might grasp something solid. He concludes by wondering why she is not in wonderment about herself: why does she keep her mouth shut and not say the same thing he says, that the whorl of her ear has a shadow at its base? Every detail can be a source of wonder in the fallen world of absurd presence. Yet, there is something derisive about the narrator's absurd final question, derisive and nonetheless expressive of a poetic receptivity to the world and to the fact that people in it simply exist.

The narrator of the twelfth text, "Kleider" ("Clothes"), offers another illustration of Kafka's entropic vision. Clothes offer a pointed example of the fall and decline of everything, especially the most desirable things. The first-person narrator says that he often looks at clothes draped over beautiful female bodies and then reflects on how the garments quickly become worn and wrinkled. This is one of the few texts in which there is no explicit mention of movement and immobility, just an evocation of entropic degradation that afflicts wearing apparel, the movement from one state to another—the entropic movement from order to disorder. The narrator's stare resembles that of the narrator in "Description of a Struggle" in that it fixes itself on the immobility of form that women want to achieve in order to fix their beauty as a permanent state. The narrator projects his vision into a near future to imagine women in front of their mirrors when, at the day's end, they see that all is dirty, bloated, and worn out. Nothing is permanent, and clothes offer only another measure of the fall from grace. It seems Kafka placed this text right after "On the Tram" as a corrective to the male passenger's vision of wonderment, for the text of "Clothes" suggests that when the girl traveling on the tram gets home, her image reflected in the mirror will inevitably show the failure of her attempts at transcending the banal world.

Kafka returns to a more frankly comic mode in *Meditation* with the thirteenth text, "Die Abweisung," translated as "The Refusal," not to be confused with a text Kafka wrote in 1920 and to which Brod gave the same title for its posthumous publication. (The title has also been translated "The Rejection" and "The Dismissal.") The rejection involves a first-person narrator and a pretty girl whom he approaches, only to be dismissed by her. The narrator says that whenever he makes a friendly proposition to a girl he happens to meet, her silent rejection of him is full of meaning. It means that she is telling him that he is not a duke, that he has never, in American Indian fashion, been to the prairies, that he has not been massaged by great flowing rivers, and that he has never traveled on the great lakes. In short, he has not been a hero, cowboy, or Indian, as in a western, novel or film, and has none of the great virtues of those who have been. In his imagination, the man snubs the girl in return by imagining that she, still decked out in last year's fashion, is not going about in a modern automobile, nor is she accompanied by an escort of gentlemen pressed into suits, who follow her in a semicircle while murmuring blessings they shower upon her head. For his image of what the girl is not, Kafka anticipates a future image of paradise yet to be proposed by pop culture, imagining a scene for the girl that would actually be realized in twenty years' time in musical comedy films: the man imagines that the girl, like a star dancing in a film, should but does not trace out a fabulous trajectory leading to a transfigured life in which a ballet corps of Fred Astaires surrounds her as in a Busby Berkeley musical (notable for their remarkable choreography). In a sense, Kafka is inventing Pop Art here, or a negative version thereof, since neither character embodies the Pop hero, and that is what is wrong with them. The girl's rejection of the man presupposes that he should be a heroic traveler, and the man's imagined retort is that she is no sex goddess, since neither is a film star living in those regions where existence is transformed—as later serially depicted by Andy Warhol, Roy Lichtenstein, and other Pop artists. These mutual rejections point up by their comic fantasy that one does not live in a transfigured world, however much such a world makes up our imaginative life—which is the essential vision of Pop Art.

The fourteenth text in *Meditation* is also an exercise in negation. Bearing the humorous title "Zum Nachdenken für Herrenreiter" ("Reflections for Gentlemen-Jockeys" or "For the Consideration of Amateur Jockeys"), the text offers a series of reasons, based on a series of hypotheses, why "we gentlemen" should not want to be first in our horse racing. The reasons derive from a brief series of comic permutations of negative outcomes to explain the undesirability of winning a race—a variant on the theme that one should not desire to finish anything. Using direct address, the narrator tells a gentleman interlocutor that if he is first in the race, he will disappoint his friends who have bet against him, his opponents will be obliged to try to overlook the injustice done to them and will want another race, and women will find his victory ridiculous because he does not know how to deal with congratulations; in any case, it will rain on everybody. Kafka's whimsy here in creating negative results based upon incongruous reasoning sets a precedent for later fables and their marvelously absurd chains of logical reasoning. This quasi parable in *Meditation* is unusual, however, in taking the world of privilege as its source and target, and the pretense of dealing with an imaginary high society makes the irony all the more pointed.

The very short fifteenth text, "Das Gassenfenster" ("The Street Window"), returns to a scene set before a window. In it the third-person narrator observes that whoever lives alone but occasionally desires help in looking at life cannot forgo a window opening onto the street. This prose poem gives a wistful description of what happens when one tries to remain stationary while attempting to look at life. The man who sits by the window will inevitably find that he is torn away by the people and horse-drawn wagons in the street. Despite himself, he will be dragged finally into human harmony (*Eintracht*). The image of street noise and horses and vehicles is an ironic image of human harmony, an image of noise and racket. But it is this noise and racket that engages the observer in the banal, fallen world where people create street traffic as they go about their daily business relations, their *Berufsverhältnisse,* as Kafka, ever the son of a businessman, puts it in the first sentence in this most concise description of the unhappy impossibility of remaining motionless.

Juxtaposed and contrasting with this ironic desire for immobility is "Wunsch, Indianer zu werden" ("The Wish to Be a Red Indian")—meaning today's native American. The wish to be an Indian is the longing to rush away toward the limitless horizon of infinite expansion, realized by Kafka's Indian, who rides his horse not just across the prairie but up into the air. He ascends, losing his spurs, his reins, and finally contact with the earth as the land becomes barely visible and even the horse disappears. In effect the narrator describes an Indian astride a western Pegasus (with Schiller's ballad rather more in mind than Fenimore Cooper's novels). The wish to be an Indian riding beyond all limits, as well as the supposedly Indian-admiring girl in "The Rejection," show that Kafka was captivated by a certain image of the American West found in pop culture. This fascination finds its final expression on the plains of *Amerika* that we will discuss in the next chapter.

In anticipation of *Amerika,* suffice it to say that Kafka was also attentive to trends in then contemporary American history, and one suspects that he was well aware that American historians saw that the frontier had recently been fenced in—as per the historian Frederick Jackson Turner's famous thesis of 1893 that the open range no longer existed since all land in the United States had now been claimed. With his interest in America, Kafka probably knew that by 1887 some sixty-seven tribes had been immobilized on reservations in Oklahoma (only to be victimized once again when Oklahoma became a state in 1907 and these tribes lost their supposed sovereign status). His later "nature theater of Oklahoma" acquires additional ironic resonance when juxtaposed with these facts. And the "desire to become an Indian," in 1912, can be read only as a wish to live somewhere other than there where one is, in a mythic America, despite the fact that American historians had declared that there were no more limitless horizons. So the Indian's horse must fly up into the air to find limitless horizons and infinite expansion, alone, however, bereft of all orientation.

The seventeenth text, "Die Bäume" ("The Trees"), has attracted critical attention because it offers one of the earliest Kafkaesque paradoxes in the form of a parable reminiscent of Greek Stoic reasoning. The parable was written first as a part of a dialogue in "Description of a Struggle." Published alone, the text can be taken as a parable illustrating the type of paradox that the logician Zeno formulated to demonstrate the logical impossibility of movement. Zeno argued that if space is composed of an infinite number of points, an arrow cannot move through space since it would first have to go through any two given points between which lies an infinite number of additional points, which means that in its motion the arrow would have to go through the first two points of an infinitely expanding series, which creates in effect an infinite backward regress. Hence motion is logically impossible. Kafka's version is more intuitive. His narrator writes that we are like tree stumps in the snow. It appears that we should be able to shove the stumps away with a gentle push. But that appearance is belied by the fact that they are fixed to the ground. However, if we look, that, too, is appearance. I take this to mean that appearances lie behind appearances in a kind of metaphorical infinite regress so that movement is impossible—or perhaps the immobility is also belied by appearances. Perhaps all is then impossible. The parable may seem to cut in both directions, thus going beyond Zeno, and to be more reminiscent of the Platonic dialogue *Parmenides,* in which nothing is possible except to affirm the One.

But there are other readings of this mind twister. In one of the few readings that recognizes the self-referentiality that permeates Kafka's work, Eric Baker contends that the text works as an allegory for its own reading, seeing self-reference figured even in text's own black letters on the white page, these figuring the image of black tree stumps set against the snow.[3] The idea acquires some plausibility when one recalls Kafka's fascination with the black figures he drew on white backgrounds, so that the text would be only the appearance of text. Be that as it may, I leave it an open question whether a logician would find a real contradiction in this prose poem, but a poetic reading of the figures here suggests that the conclusion that all is appearance leads to a conundrum not far from Zero's paradox—which still stumps logic—as Kafka's stumps may well do. If all is appearance, then each appearance is only an appearance, and that of another appearance, and so ad infinitum.

Meditation concludes with "Unglücklichsein," translated as "Unhappiness," though the translation leaves out the verb "to be" that is added to "Unhappiness" to create a single word in German. The combined noun and verb convey the idea that the text is about being in this state, unhappiness, a normal state in Kafka. The relatively long text is a narrative of sorts. It begins with the image of a race track, since the first-person narrator is racing around his home as though he were on a track, fleeing the image of the street and screaming when he sees an image of it in the mirror at the end of the room. Apparently the street is reflected back at him from the window. (It is possible that Kafka had in mind Munch's famous painting, first exhibited in Berlin in 1893, or a graphic version thereof with this image.) This screaming calls forth the appearance of a child, who, as the narrator puts it, enters the room like a ghost. The German again allows the child to be a boy or a girl, and translations differ on this point. One may be inclined toward male identity, since the child and the narrator agree that they are related, somewhat as doubles, and the narrator affirms that the child's nature is his. Female gender is also possible, however, as suggested by salacious remarks that a neighbor later makes. After some dialogue with the ghost/child, the narrator appears to be free to leave the room. He goes to the stairs, where he tells a neighbor that he has a ghost in his apartment. The two engage in some banter about belief in ghosts. If one has a ghost at home, it is a matter of indifference whether one believes in them or not, because, the narrator says, the real problem is what caused the ghost to appear. As far as belief goes, it seems that ghosts doubt their own existence even more than we do. Doubt notwithstanding, the male neighbor thinks a female ghost might be useful. The narrator is offended by this idea and declares he will break off all contact with the neighbor if he takes his ghost away from him. Concluding this whimsical exchange—turning on the foundations of our reasons for belief—the narrator can find nothing better to do than go to bed. Thus he concludes his day, immobile, after a day of running around in horror, and all questions of belief seem inconclusive, indeed, of little import.

Ghosts may or may not exist. Their ontological status does not prevent them from visiting us; indeed, they need not exist in order to mirror our inner nature. This image of the ghost may suggest another image of literature for the young Kafka: a visitor whose ontological status is forever questionable but that forces us to look at the reasons why we believe what we believe, including our belief in literature, or lack thereof.

To conclude, I observe that, if one looks only at overt subject matter, it is difficult to generalize about what might unite the texts included in *Meditation*. However, many present a basic Kafkaesque narrative configuration. Most of them describe short voyages, walks, and meanderings that go nowhere except the length of the text for which they are a self-referential metaphor. Most can be described, literally or metaphorically, in terms of a narrator's or character's mobility and immobility. Usually they start to go somewhere and then finish nowhere. In movement or, more likely, frozen in immobility, a narrator or character may try to move toward that realm where some meaning might lie—but with little success. The character may want to avoid the ever encumbered, traffic-filled street, where the business of life goes incessantly on, but it can rarely be avoided. For the world of practical reality is omnipresent in Kafka, as we will now see now in Kafka's first novel, *Amerika*. It is a text that forefronts the banal practical business of life in many ways, as Kafka portrays an involuntary flight to America on which his young protagonist discovers that America is the land of incessant traffic and unending business. Travel remains the central issue, to be sure, motion toward that elusive goal that may or may not be discovered out west in Oklahoma, there where the open frontier no longer exists.

Chapter 3

Amerika or *Der Verschollene* (*The Man Who Disappeared* or *The Missing Person*)

Max Brod published Kafka's first written novel in 1927, after publishing *The Trial* and *The Castle.* He entitled it *Amerika,* a title Edwin Muir and Willa Muir retained for their translation in English. This title has its own history, which older readers may recall, since, with its German spelling, the title served in graffiti for protest movements in the 1960s. *Amerika* was ripe with connotations for a generation in revolt. Today's editors title the novel *Der Verschollene*, a title Kafka used in 1913 when he published the novel's first chapter, "Der Heizer" ("The Stoker"), in Kurt Wolff's literary journal *Der Jüngste Tag.* Recent translators have not been in agreement about what ought to replace *Amerika* in English. In German the title suggested by Kafka is the past participle of a now archaic verb, one nonetheless still used to describe in bureaucratic language a missing person. *Der Verschollene* conjures up a listing in the missing persons' bureau, and it suggests that the person's legal status is in question since it is not known whether the person is alive or dead. This meaning is reflected in Mark Harmon's choice for the title *Amerika: The Missing Person* as well as Michael Hofmann's earlier translation, *Amerika: The Man Who Disappeared.*

It must be said that Brod's *Amerika* is not at all a bad choice for a title, for it points squarely to a central aspect of the novel: America is the hostile backdrop against which the novel's protagonist "disappears" as he makes his way about a land of crowded cities, with their deafening traffic, hostile cops, aggressive women, and opportunistic tramps. It is the America whose description modern Americans have learned from reading progressive novelists and historians: a land of alienating industrialism, frenetic work rhythms, racism, plutocracy, heartless child labor, monopoly capitalism, and lawlessness and, notably by contrast, a land with a people who have a boundless confidence in the country's basic righteousness. Novelists such as, say, the reformer Upton Sinclair of *The*

Jungle and historians such as the progressive Charles Beard of *An Economic History of the U.S. Constitution* would have had no trouble endorsing Kafka's portrait of the United States of the early twentieth century.

Kafka probably read relatively few contemporary American sources for his image of the America he never visited. Among the sources he used, the most important was undoubtedly Arthur Holitscher's *Amerika heute und morgen*, a travel book that progressive American historians could use to document their worst suspicions about the nature of American society in 1910. First serialized in a journal that Kafka read, Holitscher's essays were published as a book in 1912. The book was in Kafka's library (and is available today on the Web). Holitscher, a Berlin journalist, wrote down his critical impressions gathered during his travels in the United States and Canada. On one hand, his book describes a place of boundless opportunity; for example, in Winnipeg, posters advertised land for everybody who would claim a share. On the other hand, in Chicago the traveler could enjoy what Holitscher described as the hell of a stinking city in which traffic was impossible and the poor were everywhere—although a park had been opened to offer cultural and athletic opportunities for one and all. Learning the meaning of "muckraker" while being one, Holitscher was an enlightened, sometimes ironic critic of the New World.

In creating Karl Rossmann, Kafka was undoubtedly sensitive to Holitscher's portrait of child labor, accompanied by an analysis of why the United States was having trouble abolishing the scourge of children in the labor market. And he was certainly attentive to the Berlin journalist's masterful description of migrants in New York, especially their arrival at Ellis Island. Holitscher's description of the horrors of the lives of African Americans must have also made an impression on Kafka. And Kafka's *Amerika* offers direct reflections of Holitscher's critique of a new world that, as Holitscher described it, was increasingly using the systematic organization of industrial labor famously known as Taylorism (after the name of the American engineer Frederic Taylor, who described how to organize every detail of mass production—what Chaplin later showed in *Modern Times*). Holitscher wrote from a broadly socialist point of view, one Kafka shared, to describe an America of robber barons and homeless tramps, of movements to protect the poor and the exploited, and of an oligarchy that was extending its control over politicians as well as factories. All of these elements are found in *Amerika* and its story of a boy wandering in a new world.

Holitscher offers no keys to reading Kafka's novel, just a rather good idea of what a German socialist might have seen in the United States; nor is Holitscher the only source for Kafka's ideas about America. Kafka read widely, including some of the classics of America literature such as works by Benjamin Franklin, and he went to public lectures on the United States. Moreover, he talked to people who had been there, which was undoubtedly the most important source of information for those contemplating emigrating. Kafka's sources for *Amerika* were many, not least of which his views based on his own direct contact with industrial society. In terms of industrial development, Bohemia was the most advanced province of the Austro-Hungarian Empire, and Kafka's work with workers' insurance directly involved him in the realm of work and manufacture. The nature of capitalism was not something unknown to him.

It appears that Kafka never came close to finishing this novel, which sprang directly from his social views and, as a kind of "projective thought experiment," embodied his own desire for escape. A probable history of the novel's writing and partial publication is a story of starting and stopping writing, a record of ongoing successful failure—if we apply to it the principle of incompletion I outlined in the preceding chapter. Kafka may have begun a first version of the novel, of which there is no trace. In all events, America had been on his mind for some time before he began the novel we know today and before he made his "breakthrough" with "The Judgment." A diary entry of 19 January 1911, shows, for example, that he had once considered a story about two brothers: they fight and one goes to America, leaving the other brother behind in a European prison. Escape and breaking away are leitmotifs in Kafka's works, though in *Amerika* the theme of evasion has a specific social and cultural context that it will not have later. It is not clear when Kafka began writing the novel that describes a single protagonist's escape to America. Some critics think Kafka began work in 1912, before he had written "The Judgment." Others say he worked on it mainly between September 1912 and January 1913. In October he read to Brod the previously mentioned first chapter of the novel, "The Stoker," that he later published in a journal. Moreover, in a letter to Felice Bauer in November 1912, Kafka refers to the ongoing project as *Der Verschollene*. And as late as 31 December 1914 he wrote in his diary that he had finished another chapter of the novel during the course of that year.

However, Kafka put the novel aside in November 1912 to write "The Metamorphosis" and, after returning briefly to it, apparently gave up on the novel at the beginning of 1913 for at least a year. He did return to it, and his biographer Reiner Stach, among others, interprets diary comments of 15 August 1914 to mean that Kafka came back to the novel immediately after the declaration of war in August 1914. Kafka also referred to writing fiction, presumably the novel, in diary entries in October 1914 and again in the aforementioned entry of 31 December 1914. At the time he was also working on *The Trial* and had begun a new text, found today in his diary, "Memoirs of the Kalda Railway."

This biographical detail is important: although Kafka wrote additional material for the novel about America after finishing the main body of the novel, Brod used only one part of it for the novel's conclusion, the section called "The Nature Theater of Oklahoma." Declaring this text to be the novel's ending,

Brod created a sense of closure endowing *Der Verschollene* with the optimistic outlook Brod wanted for it. Many critics have noted that Brod's choice of the comically apocalyptic nature theater as a conclusive ending falsifies the novel. Be that as it may, this version of *Amerika* is the novel most people have read—and continue to read since Brod's text in German and the Muirs' translation remain in print and have wide circulation. However, the current critical edition and more recent translations based on this edition offer two additional texts that might just as well qualify as potential endings, one continuing the narration of what has preceded and one pointing to a different direction the novel could have taken. The latter text is called "Ausweise Bruneldas," a grotesquerie portraying "Brunelda's Departure." In this text the protagonist Karl Rossmann rolls the obese woman in a wagon to transport her to what is probably a brothel.

As it stands, the novel has no definitive ending, neither in Oklahoma nor in a whorehouse. Kafka may well have even had some other form of closure in mind. This is suggested by the diary entry of 30 September 1915, in which he compared *Amerika*'s missing person, Karl Rossmann, to Joseph K., the hero of *The Trial*. Joseph K. is executed in what is surely the final chapter of *The Trial*. Comparing Rossmann and Joseph K., Kafka called the former innocent and the latter guilty. Why Rossmann is innocent, I add, is not entirely clear, nor is it obvious why Joseph K. is guilty. I would argue that the opposite could be equally well maintained—everybody around Rossmann thinks he is guilty of something. In fact, both novels show the difficulty of determining what is innocence and what guilt, or they at least illustrate that neither condition is ever clear. Rossmann's constant fate is to be a guilty innocent party, and Joseph K. certainly appears innocent in his presumed guilt.

In this brief diary entry, Kafka went on to say that both Rossmann and Joseph K. are executed, though the innocent party (*Schuldloser*) dies in a gentler way (*mit leichter Hand*), actually, more pushed aside than struck down (*erschlagen*). The English translation of this passage in the diary mistakenly translates "innocent" as "guilty." However, the error in the translation is fruitful in that it leads one to question what exactly Kafka really had in mind: perhaps he, no more than the translator, could keep straight the characters and their guilt. Whatever the degree of guilt that can be imputed to either character, it is noteworthy that Kafka once entertained the idea of Rossmann being cut down at the end of the novel—like Joseph K.—which is not the ending promised by the nature theater Karl sets out to find in Oklahoma. In Kafka's mind, at least in 1915, the boy might have become a genuinely missing person—had Kafka wanted to find a way to continue the plot.

Upon opening *Amerika* in any version, the reader begins the book with a chapter that Kafka himself published as a separate work. This fact may alter the interpretative framework one brings to bear on the first chapter. For it makes a difference if one reads it as an overture to a novel or as a completed narration—or, to offer a third possibility, as one part in a trilogy of tales about "sons," a publication project Kafka had in mind that combined "The Stoker" with "The Judgment" and "The Metamorphosis." (The publisher Kurt Wolff turned it down, though Schocken Books later brought out a version that included all three.) Indeed, the reader may today first encounter the chapter standing alone, say, in an anthology such as Stanley Corngold's recent *Selected Stories* (though "The Stoker" was not included in *The Complete Stories*). Here I will read "The Stoker" as the beginning of Rossmann's adventures in America, though with the suggestion that the reader may also want to read it as part of a trilogy in tandem with "The Judgment" and "The Metamorphosis."

Taken as the beginning of a novel about being down and out in America, "The Stoker" has an ironic closure, for it ends as a possible success story, of the sort for which America—but not *Amerika*—was once famous. At the end of the chapter, Karl, having arrived in America, is found by his rich and successful uncle and hurried off the ship to face the brave new world, in which the uncle has become a rich and powerful man. This fortuitous encounter smacks of the beginning of a Horatio Alger tale of rags to riches. Karl has read such a tale of America, as he tells the stoker, in which a man worked all day in a shop and studied at night until he became a doctor and a mayor. This is notably not the fate of the hard-working student whom Karl later meets, nor, despite the happy beginning, is it Karl's. "The Stoker" is the beginning of the opposite of a Horatio Alger tale. The overture makes a narrative feint by which Kafka sets his character up in order to throw him down, and more than once.

The opening of *Amerika* has some rather clear indices that this is not a Horatio Alger tale. The scene is set in New York harbor, where, to set the plot in motion, the novel's third-person narrator says that the reason that Karl has been sent to America is that the sixteen-year-old boy had been seduced by a serving woman in his parents' home, that she had had a child by him, and that Karl's parents had sent him off to America. This information may or may not be reliable, and doubts are fostered by the narrator's second sentence—one of the most famous in Kafka's work—according to which Karl is looking at the sword that the Statue of Liberty is holding up in the bright sunlight. The sword does not forebode success.

We may suppose that Kafka himself knew well that the statue holds a torch, though some critics have supposed he might have been deceived by a bad photograph of the famous lady in the harbor. That supposition is most unlikely. In fact, Holitscher describes the torch (*Fackel*) with fairly taunt irony at the end of the forty-fourth chapter of *Amerika heute und morgen*. Having described Ellis Island as something halfway between a quarantine station and a prison, the ironic journalist concludes with a mock encomium in which the Statue of Liberty holds up her torch to illuminate the world at night for those coming to Ellis Island—where, as he stressed, they can hope they will not be refused admittance, sent back, or imprisoned.

Whatever Kafka may have thought of Holitscher's irony, the sword seems to be his own invention. In a sense, the image of the sword-bearing "goddess of freedom," as Kafka's German text has it, is an ambiguous rhetorical figure and a superb example of Kafka's thinking in images. The image of a lifted sword turns the narrator into a narrator of symbolic fictions that stand closer to a dream than to newspaper accounts or travelogues. And thus the narrator is as subject to our suspicion as are the thoughts he ascribes to Karl or to anybody else. The narrator is usually privy only to Karl's mind, though the narrator's commentary does not always coincide exactly with Karl's consciousness. While looking at the sword raised menacingly above the harbor, Karl is probably not thinking about the woman and the child he left behind in Prague, though the narrator first informs the reader about them in order to explain Karl's presence in New York. Thus, as the reader sorts out the relations of narrator and character, he or she inevitably asks where the sword came from, which in effect is asking what Kafka, the implied author, is implying with it. The sword minimally implies a parodistic, satiric, or ironic author.

The sword can appear as an emblem of the brutality awaiting those who want to make their way in America. And it also seems to stand as a barrier between the New and the Old Worlds, implying that Karl will never return to the East. In fact, the reader can well imagine that the Statue of Liberty has taken on the appearance of the archangel Michael, who, in familiar Christian iconography, stands to bar the way back into the paradise from which the first innocents were famously banished after sinning. (Or, if one prefers, in Jewish liturgy there are the cherubim whom Jehovah sends to prevent the return to the garden.) With the image of banishment suggested by the sword, Karl's initiation into sex becomes the equivalent of the knowledge that stands at the origin of the Fall—almost, but not quite, for Kafka rarely gives more than a veiled and usually problematic allusion to myth. With the quasi allusion, Kafka hints at a possible allegory, but an allegory that one entertains in order to see that it fails really to encompass the situation. The semantic riches of Kafka's fictions often turn on his offering a meaning through a possible allegory, then suspending it, to suggest that the meaning of the image is finally the hopelessness of making sense of it—though of course one has already made some sense of it, for a giant sword in an angel's hand has only a limited number of archetypical meanings.

Karl arrives in New York and sees Kafka's Statue of Liberty, but he does not think about getting off the boat, even though he is caught up in a crowd that is intent on leaving. The narrative intent again is not realism but something akin to the motivation of the narrative described in "Description of a Struggle": it is narration drawing upon dream rhetoric. In *Amerika* it is an attenuated form of oneiric rhetoric, which is to say that, though the mainstays of realist narration are sometimes not respected, the deviation from realism does not occur in any systematic manner. Causality to explain events is sometimes omitted, probability is often not respected, the incongruous may appear at times to be the norm, and narrative transitions are often simply juxtaposed sequences without explanation—though not always. Oneiric parataxis is often the rule (that is, as in dreams, things simply happen in sequence with no regard to antecedent causes or probability).

Karl has forgotten his umbrella, so he entrusts his "box" of a trunk to a fellow passenger and descends into the bowels of the ship. Though he has presumably been on the ship for a long period of time, he recognizes nothing and begins to wander through a labyrinth of ways and byways that is the hallmark of a Kafkaesque promenade: a *Gehen* going nowhere. As in *The Trial* or *The Castle,* the protagonist can open a door, enter a room, and suddenly find the unexpected, the incongruous, or simply an instant friend, as in *Amerika*. Karl enters the stoker's room, and, in no time at all, the two are intimately connected, as in a dream in which attractions are instantaneous. The stoker complains of mistreatment, and Karl immediately becomes his advocate. They decide to go to the ship captain's room and to defend the stoker against the way his Romanian superior, named Schubal, has treated this German worker. The national identity given here is all the more notable in that ethnic and national identities by and large cease to exist in Kafka after this novel. After meeting the captain, the stoker manages his defense badly, though the trial is interrupted when there suddenly emerges from the bystanders a man who is none other than Karl's uncle. Having been informed of Karl's arrival by the very servant who seduced the lad, the uncle leads the boy away to what appears to be a new life in the so-called New World.

What stands out in this résumé of "The Stoker" is that at least two trials are involved, the first having taken place in Karl's home before he was punished with banishment, the second unfolding on the ship. We know the first sentence: Karl is condemned to exile. The judgment is clear, but it is not certain that we know all the facts about Karl's trial, for the narrator's representation of it is given from Karl's viewpoint. By contrast, we see the second trial, and it appears to go very badly for the inarticulate stoker. But we do not learn the judgment that the captain, who is the stoker's judge, may pass. In other words, we see that, in a fragmented way, trials and judgments make up a major part of characters' experience of the world. Fragmentation of experience is also an aspect of dream representation, and it is characteristic of the world of Kafka's fictions in which the disjointed experience of the law and its uncertain consequences becomes a kind of metaphysical fate.

The novel's first sentence sets out what appears to be a clearly defined state of affairs. Karl has been banished. But the question of his guilt is delayed until the trial involving the stoker has begun. Then the uncle can offer the version he has concocted, apparently on the basis of the letter that the servant has sent him to inform him of the reason that his nephew is on the ship. Concern with certainty about events begins to seem misplaced when the reader must entertain the uncle's version of Karl's fate. The uncle says Karl was seduced by the servant, Johanna Brummer, a viewpoint that suggests Karl's innocence. He is a minor. But then the uncle goes on to say that the boy has been exiled so that the family can avoid paying money to the servant girl and her child. This suggests in addition that his sentence is unjust and that he has been made a scapegoat as his family seeks to avoid both public opprobrium and financial responsibility.

Karl himself then begins to recall the past and to reflect on the event that brought him to his present state. In a description of sexual intercourse, Karl recalls the trivial but troubling trauma of his initiation. In his memory, Karl appears to himself and hence to the reader as a rather passive participant, allowing himself to be led into the woman's room, undressed, and finally led into copulation. Who is guilty? There seems to be a shared guilt in this memory, though the memory also suggests a disparity between the act and the ensuing judgment: none of it seems to be important, and Karl wonders why his uncle is making such a fuss about it. Karl decides that if he ever has a chance, he will try to do something for the servant who has been so good as to inform his uncle of his coming. At the conclusion of this scene, Karl shows that he has a sense of equity—a sentiment that will do him little good in the rest of the novel.

The scene set in the captain's room is clearly a trial of sorts. I have spoken here of a kind of reverse symmetry between the uncertain trial with a certain judgment that has sent Karl to American and the trial that does not result in a clear sentence in the case of the stoker. A reader drawing upon psychoanalysis might say that this curious symmetry corresponds to the kind of dream displacement in which a lack in one part is compensated by a positive event in another part. Be that as it may, these images of guilt and judgment, the omnipresence of trials and sentencing, set forth one of the dominant themes in *Amerika*. Karl will be continually judged and sentenced in the next chapters, and, with retrospective irony, it seems fitting that, for a moment at least, he can play the role of defense attorney for somebody else before becoming the permanent defendant who must defend himself as he sinks in America.

Let us consider Karl as a lawyer. Karl enters the stoker's room and, in a totally unexplainable movement of sympathy, becomes attached to the stoker, accepts what the stoker says as true, and becomes his advocate. The stoker's ranting against his boss, a Romanian, may or may not have some grounds, though the accusation that his nationality has something to do with the fact that the boss unjustly hassles the German stoker sounds much like a parody of the nationalistic venom Kafka himself often encountered. For no good reason, Karl is willing to entertain the truth of the stoker's complaints about injustice and immediately counsels his new friend to go to the captain to defend his rights. Good advice, except, as the stoker knows, he has no right to defend his rights. This is one of the paradoxes of the law—real paradoxes—that permeate Kafka's work: the law may forbid one to have recourse to it in the name of the law.

The stoker knows he should not present his "petition." But with the naiveté of a well-bred adolescent, Karl apparently believes that justice exists at some higher level, which motivates him to accompany the stoker as he seeks justice—though only after the stoker decides he does not care what happens to him. They arrive at the captain's room to find that its entrance is incongruously decorated with a pediment supported by caryatides. It is a parodistic image redolent of the entrance to a temple or of a modern courthouse in an eclectic style—in short, of a high temple to the law. They enter the room and hear salvos from warships in the harbor, resembling offscreen sound effects that suggest some unmentioned dimension to the text. These decorative touches also suggest the incongruities of a dream world in which the quest for justice is questionable, if not laughable. This impression is underscored when they are immediately rebuffed by an attendant; he is aware of the fact that the stoker has no right to seek his rights, tells him to get lost, and also tries to chase Karl away, the narrator says, as if the boy were vermin—an *Ungeziefer*. This is a term that Kafka uses as image of those who are outside the law and even humanity, most famously in the case of Gregor Samsa of "The Metamorphosis."

The trial begins despite the fact that the stoker has no right to a trial. Karl then addresses himself to the captain as if the boy had known the stoker for years and knows that only slander can account for the stoker's fate. ("Slander" here is the translation for the term *Verleumdung*, a notion Joseph K. invokes when he first supposes that only his being slandered could account for his being arrested at the beginning of *The Trial*.) Only slander, Karl reasons, could account for the stoker's failure to receive his deserved recognition. Karl shows himself to be a good lawyer since he discourses with conviction about something he knows nothing about. The head purser (or paymaster) is ready to rebut Karl's arguments with what is apparently evidence, and the captain, seemingly like an impartial judge, intervenes to hear the stoker's testimony. But the latter makes a shambles of his own case by his incoherent presentation, and Karl ends up quarreling with him.

Nonetheless, Karl apparently believes in his case, and at this point he thinks of a higher forum in front of which justice might be had. The question thus arises as to whether the novel and its implied author share the belief that some kind of forum of higher law might be found for the stoker's case or any other case, perhaps a forum embodying natural law that transcends local interests. Since in most of Kafka's subsequent work the law is notable by its absence, one may wonder if the belief in such a forum is a sign of either Karl's immaturity or his delusional nature—or perhaps even of his having been educated to believe that the law exists as an objective fact. In any case, Karl loses himself in a kind of lawyer's delirium, as he imagines, as if he were confronting a jury, that he knows the strengths and weaknesses of the men standing around the room and that they have some role to play in the trial's eventual outcome. Karl is clearly not a good judge of his situation.

Much as in a dream, this fantasy is broken off, only to be replaced by another, when Senator Jacob steps forward to identity himself as Karl's uncle. He makes a quick defense of Karl's own questionable past, for to mention his guilt to pardon it, says the uncle. The rich uncle's presence seems to portend that Karl's sentence will be considerably lightened. The uncle takes Karl away from the trial, though not without seemingly adjudicating it, at least for Karl. The uncle observes that, on one hand, the stoker will get what he deserves and that, on the other, there are questions more important that justice, namely discipline. And with regard to discipline only the captain can rule. Implicit is this distinction is something that Karl does not want to admit: that his thirst for justice may well have less importance than the defense of order. Reflected in this distinction is something like the proverbial declaration Goethe made in which he said he preferred injustice to disorder. For this distinction will be in the background of much of what happens to Karl subsequently, as when, for example, he is sentenced to banishment by his uncle for his disobedience or when he is chased in disgrace from the hotel he works in for failing to obey a rule. In both of these cases, discipline in capitalist America seemingly trumps justice. And it is not an indifferent matter that, seen through Karl's eyes, discipline is often imposed by an order as arbitrary as the disorder it claims to want to overcome.

The stoker's trial continues even as Karl is being led away. Schubal shows up with his group of "witnesses." Karl's emotional involvement with the stoker results in behavior that borders on the pathological: he kisses the stoker's hand and breaks out crying. The uncle is insightful when he says that the stoker has thrown a spell over Karl. Indeed, the stoker's trial might be likened to a kind of enchantment worked by some evil principle using magic to mold events. The impression of an ongoing bewitchment is enforced when Schubal's witnesses line up, as in a dream, to wave at Karl, from three windows no less, as the boat carrying the boy and his uncle from the ship is rowed away toward the docks. The scene offers the kind of visual disassociation found in oneiric narratives when the viewer himself is viewed, here in a mockingly friendly way, as if Karl's own vision were turned against him. But, as if seeking to reassure himself, when Karl looks at his uncle, he sees him looking away, perhaps as if in contemplation of the discipline he will impose on Karl. Thus concludes the opening chapter. In the next chapter I discuss further the idea that Kafka thinks in images. In this context let me note that there are few moments in Kafka's work in which the images are powerful images of vision itself, undermining itself, much as in an expressionist painting: Karl sees his solitude even in the world abounding with images of others, both looking and then not looking at him.

Whether or not the first chapter works as a short story is a debatable point, but it is certainly a powerful beginning to the novel. "The Stoker" sets in motion an unbroken narrative movement that continues for the next six chapters, ending with Karl a captive of Brunelda and her tramps. It is well known that Kafka usually wrote in unbroken spurts, without revisions, a way of working that allowed him usually to finish only short narratives. However, the seven chapters of *Amerika* seem to have followed one after another with more continuity that one can find in virtually anything else in Kafka, including the two other novels, both of which can be considered as in some ways more successful works than *Amerika* for the way they develop Kafka's images with singular perseverance. But *Amerika* is unique in that Kafka's narrative action pursues a continuous logic leading from the ship to Karl's final imprisonment in Brunelda's apartment, from which, reduced to slavery, Karl could be freed seemingly only by a deus ex machina.

Kafka found the impetus for continuity in the ongoing process in which Karl is the object of trial and judgment. This process results in Karl's ongoing decline in America, literally from a high position, lodged in the rich uncle's tall building, to his fall out of society to end up in Brunelda's apartment, where he is lodged again, ironically, in an upper story from which he can look down on society, literally into the street in front of the apartment where local judges are elected in violently chaotic elections. Karl is a young protagonist who should learn through this process, which some critics have likened to that of an aborted bildungsroman, or novel of initiation and education for which Kafka's beloved Goethe established the model in his *Wilhelm Meister's Apprenticeship* (1795–1796). There is little doubt that Goethe, along with the Flaubert of *L'Education sentimentale* and the Dickens of *David Copperfield*, was constantly on Kafka's mind as he wrote the novel, though the novel's relation to Goethe, or to Flaubert or Dickens for that matter, may be more one of parody than of imitation. In the course of his education, however, young Karl seems to learn little from his repeated failures: he is a benighted initiate until the end, a sprightly perpetual victim, an innocent who does not wise up very much.

Through Karl the reader is offered views of a semifantastic America in which the reader finds the all-pervasive presence of trial and judgment. Whether these views can be taken as a portrait of America and of capitalist society in general or whether Kafka is more concerned with the metaphysical nature of reality, these are issues that intertwine in the novel's development. What is certain is that Karl's misadventures spring from a series of judgments. In this regard the novel is something like a trial performance for *The Trial*. True, Karl is not subject to accusation by unknown authorities. He knows all too well who accuses him, though that hardly mitigates his fate: the power to condemn and punish is always in the hands of others, which is to say that other parties have a power that appears nearly omniscient at times.

The first judge is this series is, after Karl's father, the uncle, who seems at first to be well disposed toward his nephew. He takes him in and provides him with all that a young man might need to make his way in America. The uncle is, however, judgmental from the beginning. He admonishes Karl about the dangers of standing on the balcony and looking down to gawk at what goes on in the ever busy street. According to the uncle, looking down into the street is a sure source of perdition—which is perhaps borne out in irony when Brunelda later tries to force Karl to use binoculars to view the street. The uncle's admonishment comes after the uncle has warned Karl about judgments formed by newly arrived immigrants who are bewildered precisely because of the seductiveness of first impressions. Judgments, the uncle implies, are to be made only by people of experience—such as the uncle himself. Moreover, as the chapter progresses, it becomes clear that Karl is to take the uncle's word as law. The uncle lavishly gives Karl many things—a weird mechanical desk, a piano, English and riding lessons—but always under conditions that the uncle rigidly sets out for him. The uncle is in effect a surrogate patriarch whose word is the law, in the most literal sense, which means that Karl, who has been judged in Europe by the law of the father and banished to America, finds himself once again subject to a patriarch's power.

Inevitably, Karl infringes the law, though he does so with no criminal intent. No rebel, he has no desire to put the uncle's precepts in question and does not mean to be disobedient. But disobedience occurs. A friend of the uncle, with much insistence, invites Karl to come spend an evening and a day with him and his daughter in the country. The uncle finds that this will involve too many infringements on the order he has established for Karl. And, without openly forbidding Karl to accept the invitation, he shows great displeasure at the fact that Karl intends to go with the friend despite the uncle's display of disapproval. Karl merely sees a contradiction in his uncle when the uncle says that it is out of the question for Karl to miss his English lesson, which in effect means that the uncle is forbidding the visit. And so Karl departs for the country, unaware that he has brought about his own condemnation and banishment from an American form of Eden—a New York high-rise equipped with all the latest machines.

The third chapter's title, "Ein Landhaus bei New York" ("A Country House near New York"), sets the scene for the judgment that one of the uncle's friends, Mr. Green, delivers in the form of a letter. Mr. Green is an intruder at the house where Karl is a visitor, and from the outset Karl is perturbed, without knowing why, by Green's presence. Green is unaware of what is in the letter he will deliver at midnight, though he is astonished that Karl might have received his uncle's permission to make the visit. Obviously, Green is more aware of what the uncle's word means than is Karl. So the evening unfolds as a rather unhappy event. Karl has no appetite, for Green's presence casts a pall over the dinner. Clara, the host's daughter, leads Karl into the interior of the house, which reveals itself to be another Kafkaesque labyrinth. Here Clara may have sexual designs on Karl. She masters him with judo and, in a remarkably comic moment, carries him around as if about to deliver him up to a rape. Karl escapes, wants to go back to the dining room, and gets lost in the halls and stairs. His walking in darkness toward a difficult goal is a Kafkaesque prelude to the failure to make some discovery that might bring about hope of salvation. For, while seeking what he hopes will be a friendly reception in the dining room, all Karl finds are endless corridors, a chapel, empty rooms, and darkness, to paraphrase his perception of his wanderings in the maze set in an American country house. He is finally saved by a servant and then returns to Clara's room to play piano. The most oneiric moment occurs when, out of the blue, it turns out that Mack, an acquaintance who is also Karl's riding friend, is now sleeping in Clara's bed and has listened to Karl's performance. Mack judges it to be pleasant if not free from error—a minor judgment in this case.

Mack's almost favorable judgment is something of a foil to the judgment to come. Like an avenging angel sent on a mission, Mr. Green obeys the order given to him by the uncle, which is not to deliver the uncle's letter to Karl before midnight. There is a catch-22 in this situation. Karl has decided to return to the uncle's home early enough to be in time to obey him. But the necessity of remaining until midnight to receive the letter makes Karl's project unfeasible, and the delivery of the letter finally renders Karl's intentions nugatory. Ever a lawyer, Karl does try to quibble about this point with Mr. Green after the latter has read the letter informing Karl that, because of his disobedience, he is never to return to the uncle, nor is he to attempt to communicate with him. No more than Adam could appeal God's judgment about the sin in the garden can Karl hope to have recourse against this judgment that refuses in advance all appellate procedures. The uncle's principles have been violated. The sentence is irremediable. With "The Judgment" in mind, the reader may compare the uncle's sentencing of Karl to the judgment uttered by the father against his son Georg: death versus exile. Death by drowning is more severe perhaps than exile, but eternal exile, as the Judeo-Christian tradition has it, has become the fate of humanity. An allegory about Everyman or *Jedermann* is thus lurking in the background of the narrative movement, eventuating in the judgment of a Ross-mann. It is lurking, albeit evasively, so that one can only be tentative about seeing a universal allegory in Rossmann's fate of perpetual banishment. (The hyphen placed in Rossmann points out there is a *Ross* or "horse" in the name, perhaps suggesting a dunderhead if not the eternal traveler that is another image suggested by *Jedermann*.)

Given a push by Green, who fulfills his annunciating function to the end, Karl goes through a mysterious little door and, as in a dream, finds himself immediately on a road. Equipped again with his trunk and umbrella, he begins that most Kafkaesque of activities, walking toward an unknown destination. A bit of guidance is given to the reader, however, by the next chapter heading, "Der Marsch nach Ramses," which should be given a Kafkaesque reading as the walk or march toward Ramses. (Mark Harmon got it right; the Muirs did not.) If Americans read too quickly, their American eye may read "Ramsey" in place of "Ramses," since the former is a real city near New York City toward which, in a realist novel, Karl might well be headed. However, for whatever reason, with his spelling Kafka has interjected a name used by pharaohs, one of whom supposedly had dealings with Moses—which, arguably, subtly recalls the movements of the Jewish people in their trials and banishments. Be that as it may, Karl is now on the road, a wanderer with all that implies about his trip and banishment.

He stops at an "inn," not unlike a protagonist in eighteenth-century fiction, and shares a room with two tramps who appear to have been sent by providence to be instrumental in Karl's further trials and judgments. In realist terms, they are representative of the armies of poor who have walked America's roads looking for work. They claim to be mechanics on the way to Butterford, a fictional town, with a nicely Anglo-Irish ring to it, where there is work to be found. After a night in the shared room, the threesome set out on a walk along a roadway along which drive endless streams of trucks headed for New York—traffic reminiscent of the bustle of the street in *Meditation*'s "The Street Window," as well as the unending flow of vehicles at the end of "The Judgment."

The tramps' names are suggestive of their role in Karl's itinerary. One is the Frenchman Delamarche, whose name, redolent of a march, can be literally translated as "On Walking" or "About Walking." The other vagrant is supposedly an Irishman named Robinson, though this is later called into question, since the text says that Irishmen are not named Robinson. Of course, a very well-known Robinson is Defoe's unfortunate sailor, and it seems likely that Kafka is playing with ironic associations to foreshadow where Karl's walking may end: with a metaphoric shipwreck on the equivalent of a desert island. With little difficulty the two tramps convince the naive Karl of their good intentions, even as they use his money. At the end of the day, they send him to get food in a hotel along the route, the Hotel Occidental. Compliantly, Karl goes and returns from his task to discover that his new friends have opened his trunk and pilfered things, perhaps even stealing the only photo he had of his family.

When a hotel employer comes to find Karl and take back the basket Karl used to carry the food, Karl leaves his friends and returns to the hotel, where the head cook (the "manageress" in the Muirs' translation) has offered him accommodation. His friends seem more like petty criminals than mechanics, but Karl promises to press no legal charges against them if they return the photo. Karl's sentimental desire for compromise has no visible results, though his rejection of his ne'er-do-well associates underscores his determination to lead an upright life. At this point in the novel, Dickens's influence seems manifest, for echoes of a right-minded Oliver Twist or a victimized David Copperfield reverberate in this portrait of the good and virtuous boy—caught in a world full of Fagins.

Banished twice now, Karl remains perpetually innocent as he enters employment at the hotel. The head cook, a woman from Vienna who once worked in Prague, takes a fancy to Karl and gets him a job as an elevator operator (or liftboy) running one of the hotel's thirty elevators. The work requires the boy to work twelve-hour shifts on an alternating day-night schedule. Karl, now saying he is fifteen years old, adapts to his difficult new life style, and the makings of an Horatio Alger story seem to be in the offing. He works hard, is reliable, and, when he has time, studies business correspondence with a virtuous young woman who has become the head cook's secretary. As elsewhere in Kafka, the promise of success is shown with new clothes, though the gold buttons and braid on his liftboy's uniform do not hide the fact that the jacket is too stiff and wet with the sweat of the many boys who have worn it before him. Karl complains about nothing, neither the exhausting work schedule nor the terrible conditions in which he must try to sleep in the elevator boys' dormitory, where smoking pipes and boxing seem to occupy the boys far more than sleep or study.

It is against this backdrop of virtue and resignation that Karl is once again judged and condemned or rather condemned and then judged, since the sentencing precedes the trial in this case. For, at the outset of the sixth chapter, "Der Fall Robinson" ("The Robinson Case"), Robinson shows up drunk one night, wanting money from Karl, and vomits in the hotel. The chapter's title shows that a legal case is now unfolding, namely the Robinson case, though it is the unfortunate Karl who is adjudicated. Despite his best intentions, Karl knows that weighty precepts have been violated and that he is guilty as least by association. In the case of infringements of the rules that regulate business practices, one hesitates to speak of the law, yet it seems the case that these rules have the force of law for business. And there is no doubt that through his wretched behavior Robinson may have driven away guests and certainly has besmirched the hotel—with a suggestion in German of defilement. Karl's association with Robinson suggests Karl's guilt. The inevitable conclusion is that Karl himself is a drunkard or that he has pilfered the hotel larder to provide his impecunious friend with booze or perhaps has even stolen money from the guests for this purpose.

After this quick survey of possible and plausible charges, Karl knows he must try to get rid of the condemning evidence: he hustles the intoxicated Robinson off to the dormitory so that the tramp can sleep off his drunkenness. But Karl's unavoidable act of self-defense entails more guilt, this time not by association but by commission: to get rid of Robinson Karl must momentarily leave the elevator. And in so doing he violates one of the sacred rules governing his employment. No sooner done, no sooner convicted, for, upon returning to his elevator after a few minutes' absence, he finds that another boy is running it. The judgment, through the agency of the head waiter, has been rendered immediately.

Dream logic may appear to organize the sudden operation of the law here, though the stringency with which it is applied reflects social reality. If not a direct reflection of what Kafka saw in the legal workings of Austro-Hungarian bureaucracy, this stringency certainly reflects widespread stories about the harshness of the American industrial system and its repression of workers. Moreover, Karl's banishment from the hotel has already been decided when Karl goes to the head waiter's office to be interrogated; the questioning is a pro forma bit of procedure. The head waiter is accompanied by a head porter decked out in a splendid uniform, the trappings of power that he intends to use in order to exploit Karl sexually. Karl believes that his good intent should protect him from severe punishment, though he is quickly disabused when the head waiter screams his sentence at him: dismissal. The head porter then seeks to compound the crime by accusing Karl of not saluting him every time the boy sees the mustachioed sadist. Karl realizes that the verdict is irrevocable, for it is the product of the judge's immediate anger. Or, as the narrator puts it in a concise but contorted phrase, in both Europe and America the defendant learns the judgment as it springs from immediate anger or rage of the judge's shouting mouth (*Der Verschollene*, *KA*, p. 228: "es wird so entschieden, wie einem in der ersten Wut das Urteil aus dem Munde fährt"). The ultimate ground for the law is patriarchal rage but also, as becomes clear in this scene, sexual lust.

This scene of judgment is one of the most powerful moments in all of Kafka's work. Part of the scene's power derives from the pointless development of a hopeless reopening of the question of the grounds for sentencing, showing the impossibility of Karl's justification. The head cook and Theresa come down to see what is happening to their favored liftboy. Their presence allows the accusers to bring up additional charges, groundless as the reader knows but not without some probability of merit, as Karl recognizes to himself. The prosecutor argues that Karl has been profligate, spending his nights in town, and is guilty of low associations. The head waiter wants to convince the head cook (who is probably his lover) that Karl has been a thief. He comes up with two charges of theft, one involving a theft from the hotel storeroom and the other a theft from some other source of money—thievery that in turn explains the presence of the drunk Robinson. Karl must own up to his responsibility for Robinson's presence in the dormitory, which he cannot deny, and thus he is obliged to speak the fatal words that he is guilty (*KA*, p. 243: "Schuld also bin ich"). Critics who want to find premonitions of Stalinist purge trials in Kafka can start here, even before *The Trial*. *Amerika* forcefully and convincingly demonstrates that the near-innocent can always be forced to admit their guilt, since everybody is always almost guilty of something. In Karl's case, he cannot deny two facts: his momentary absence from the lift and Robinson's drunken presence. From these admissions the accusers can easily deduce Karl's guilt. In Kafka's world innocence can never be proven since guilt, at least some form of guilt, can always be shown. This was the lesson Camus took from Kafka for Meursault's trial in *The Stranger:* the prosecutor can always show that one has done something wrong.

Karl's trial is a depiction of the arbitrary workings of power. In the head waiter's case, it seems that he uses his power to gratify a fairly base desire to show vaingloriously that he has some power because of his position in the hotel hierarchy. In the case of the head porter, his will to power deviates into a sadistic desire for sexual gratification. Signs revealing the porter's desires are clear. He holds tightly to Karl, squeezing him during the trial as if he had some special design on him. When Karl tries then to leave the hotel, the porter seizes him and pushes him into his lodge. Saying he intends to continue the investigation, he proclaims that, as head porter, he is above everybody and thus entitled to search Karl. This means that, while defending the interests of the hotel management, he wants to "take pleasure" from Karl: "will ich dich geniessen," as he forthrightly puts it (*KA*, p. 262). Karl escapes from the porter's clutches and forces his way out of the lodge only at the last moment, with his clothes largely torn from his back.

Banished from the hotel and barely dressed, Karl finds a bloody Robinson on a stretcher on the street in front of the hotel, where the liftboys have deposited him after boxing his ears. Karl then takes Robinson by taxi to where Robinson now lives with Delamarche and Brunelda, a woman whom Delamarche has robbed but to whom he is now servant and lover. Brod gave the next chapter the curious title "A Refuge" ("Asyl"), which can be explained only by Brod's desire to impose a happy ending on the novel (unless one supposes an ironic intent on Brod's part). Brunelda's apartment can be called a refuge only if a prison is a refuge, for Karl enters into permanent internment here. The three exercise power over Karl by threatening him with trial and judgment. Their entrapment unfolds in a rather diabolical way, again showing that Karl's near-innocence is no defense against the wiles of those who have power over him.

Karl and Robinson arrive in a taxi in an obviously poor neighborhood, one that contrasts notably with what the reader has seen up to this point—townhouses, mansions in the country, and a hotel for the rich with high-speed elevators. In this new neighborhood a used-clothes peddler hawks his wares in the street where the taxi stops, while a man with a nose rotten and half eaten away watches them. The unscrupulous taxi driver finds a way to increase his fare, while a suspicious policeman draws near to observe what is going on. In a poor neighborhood, the law stands on guard, ready to impose its sanctions for any real or apparent violation of the law.

The policeman is a visible sign of the law's presence, and his attitude suggests that the law's first presupposition is that anyone unfortunate enough to be in this miserable place is probably guilty of something. Of course the presence of the police in poor neighborhoods is a sign that authorities want to maintain order there, be it Prague or Chicago. But the symbolic threat they represent for the innocent was perhaps even greater in Prague than in Chicago, since European investigating officers did not necessarily assume innocence. As Karl's case demonstrates, the very fact that he is being investigated assumes that he may be guilty; hence, he may be arrested before charges are brought forward or even named. In Karl's case it suffices for the policeman to look at him for the thought of possible incarceration to spring up in Karl's mind; to coin an expression that neither Sartre nor Foucault invented, *le regard du flic*—the cop's gaze—presupposes guilt. Ghetto dwellers may retort that it was, and is, no different in Chicago.

Karl knows he wants to escape from Robinson and Delamarche, and he also knows that anything he does is likely to be taken as a sign that he is guilty of something. While in the street Karl first tries simply to leave, but the neighborhood children rush to tell Delamarche, as if Delamarche had some authority here. And the policeman is already ready to stop Karl, since he assumes that the only reason Karl would want to leave is that he has a reason to flee. The policeman demands to see Karl's papers, which the Anglo-Saxon reader should understand as a normal police prerogative. For in European lands one does not venture forth on the streets without the obligatory proof of one's identity—meaning a proper document. Karl has no papers. He barely has any clothes. And he must also explain that he has no job. Delamarche cleverly intervenes to manipulate the situation so that Karl's only recourse can be to turn to Delamarche if he does not want to be taken in custody for further questioning by the police. The Frenchman increases his power over Karl by supplying information to the policeman that Karl does not want to give about his recent employment. With corrosive innuendo, Delamarche suggests that Karl warrants investigation for his dubious past. With neither proper clothes nor papers, and facing imprisonment for the lies that the head porter will tell if Karl is taken back to the hotel, Karl then breaks away and flees. He has no way to prove his innocence.

Kafka masterfully sets up a situation in which every "fact" becomes proof of the opposite of what the reader knows or assumes it actually means. Karl has no jacket because, as the reader knows, he was nearly raped. For the policemen this is proof that Karl is a ne'er-do-well, if not a hardened criminal. Karl has no employment. Ergo, he must be a thief. Such is the way of the world in which the innocence of poor people is never to be assumed.

Karl flees, and in so doing he enters another labyrinthine space in which ways and byways open up and go nowhere. First, he flees the policemen until, as if in a dream, Delamarche appears from nowhere and pulls Karl into a doorway and saves him from the pursuing officer. Now, having Karl firmly in his power—for Delamarche can have him arrested whenever he desires—Delamarche leads Karl up the meandering stairs and through the halls leading to the apartment he occupies with Brunelda, a fat diva whose lover he has become after having spent all her money. Space frequently dilates in Kafka, and so does time. For it now appears that Karl and the criminal tramps have been separated for months, and not simply the two months Karl worked at the hotel. Kafka expands time, as in a dream, prolonging it when needed, in this case long enough for the tramps to have encountered Brunelda, to have pilfered her money, and to have moved into a dismal flat in a poor neighborhood. Months in this drama of the fall from innocence have no more significance than days.

With regard to space, there is the suggestion that, in this building of wandering stairs and halls, they are lodged in a brothel, though this occurs only once, when Delamarche comments on the women Karl sees in the stairs. Delamarche says that they are a disgusting bunch whom he could have gotten rid of if he denounced them to the police. Later, in the fragment narrating Brunelda's breakfast, it appears that they are living in some kind of rooming house, since an old woman there cooks for some thirty renters. Whatever the exact nature of the prison in which Karl is now enslaved—and Kafka himself may not have decided what kind of bordello-boardinghouse he wanted for Karl—it is clear that it is a chaotic, filthy place that Kafka describes in some of his most comic descriptions. Karl's downward trajectory, from the hyperordered world in which his uncle lives down to the ramshackle area where Delamarche and Robinson serve Brunelda, is a classic illustration of the kind of fall that characterizes entropy: the passage of time is a function of growing disorder. Hence the ease with which time often expands, for growing disorder is a constant in Kafka's world, and time seems to exist as a variable in function of growing chaos.

With Karl having come to the bottom of the downward trajectory, so to speak, it is difficult to see where Kafka could have gone with the novel. Sending Karl to prison might have been one option, but, as the seventh chapter shows, he is already imprisoned in Brunelda's apartment. He puts up a fight but is overcome, for he is no match in strength for the older Delamarche. He is also imprisoned by the nature of the situation in which he finds himself: escape means the police will pursue him. There is no road leading out of the chaos. This dead end is pointedly illustrated when, at night, Karl converses with a student who happens to be studying on the balcony next to Karl's balcony. As mentioned earlier, the student certainly offers one more proof that the Horatio Alger myth is indeed a myth. The young man works long hours at a store, in the employment of a scoundrel, and receives a miserable pittance for a salary. At night he studies, going without sleep he desperately needs. Black coffee keeps him awake. He continues to study even though he knows he has little prospect of escaping the poverty he lives in. He has little hope, since, as he asks with a rhetorical flourish, what chance would he have as a doctor, were he to finish his studies, in a country already full of quacks?

The student is the vehicle for the expression of Kafka's final irony about the law. Dismissing the possibility of getting ahead, the nocturnal student quips that it is easier to be elected a district judge that to get a job as a doorkeeper (*Türöffner*) at the store where he works. The irony of the student's comment stands out against a demonstration of what it means to become a judge in America. For, during the earlier hours of the evening Karl, looking down from his balcony, has witnessed an electoral rally for a local judge. As he watches, Brunelda tries to force him to look at it through binoculars, but Karl thinks he sees this spectacle quite plainly without them. What he sees is indeed clear. A candidate orates, a waiter serves drinks, and from the surrounding balconies other orators perorate so that nobody understands anybody. The street fills up with spectators, music roars, and headlamps of cars illuminate the whole affair until, at one coordinated moment, all the headlights are smashed, leaving the candidate lit only by the uncertain light of street lamps. He is, it appears, lost in the dark, which Karl can see with no need for modified vision.

The juxtaposition of the prospective judge's electoral campaign with Karl's need for justice is striking. The counterpoint is another reductive rhetorical flourish, for it underscores that Karl has little hope for justice in a land in which justice will be decided by the candidate who can offer the most alcohol. There is an historical side to this portrait, and Kafka was perhaps familiar with representations of American elections in which the drunk and vomiting voters are led to vote for the appropriate candidate. (A good example is provided by George Caleb Bingham's painting *The County Election,* a nineteenth-century work showing the falling-down drunk voting on election day.) Kafka was undoubtedly bemused by the very idea that judges should be elected, since even the monarchy of the Austro-Hungarian Empire had accepted, with the liberal Constitution of 1867, the guarantee of the independence of judges. Be that as it may, the farcical electoral campaign, with its violence, points up that Karl must depend on his own resources if he is to find justice in America. Those resources are at this point most meager indeed.

Karl's enslavement in the land of liberty may seem a logical end point in the novel. It certainly was the end of the inspiration that guided Kafka for seven consecutive chapters. After the series of judgments, Karl is in an impasse, and he can go nowhere. Brod wanted to get Karl out of this impasse by using the fragments Kafka wrote about the nature theater of Oklahoma as if they were a conclusion. These fragments also start the novel's movement: in them Karl is headed west, to that frontier that Kafka alluded to *Meditation,* there where one might ride free like a wild Indian. However, it is hard to see that Oklahoma and its theater have much to do with the novel as developed in the first seven consecutive chapters. In the first of the theater fragments Karl is free, but there is no explanation of how this came about. He is simply again in the street, where he sees the poster for the nature theater and its offer of work and happiness.

However, if one turns to the earlier mentioned critical edition of Kafka's work published by Fischer or to translations based on it, one finds two additional fragments that confirm that Kafka was stuck, perhaps caught up by the incompletion axiom that I have suggested underlies much of his work. Each fragment is remarkable in its own way. The first fragment begins with Robinson's waking Karl for his day of labor as a slave to Brunelda. Karl looks up and sees, as frequently happens in Kafka, a space he has not seen before: here Brunelda is being bathed by Delamarche. This scene is close to pure farce as Brunelda screams out orders, demanding a series of things without which she cannot possibly be bathed, and Karl and Robinson scurry around the messy apartment in which they are supposed to find the missing objects. They also observe the show provided by Delamarche and Brunelda as the Frenchman tries to comply with her orders, is screamed at, and, according to Robinson, spends time kissing his fat lover. Karl has now decided that he will remain here—if he were to leave he'd find no better job and he might end up in jail. So he observes and tries conscientiously to follow orders by sorting out piles of junk as he and Robinson seek in vain, for example, to find Brunelda's indispensable perfume. After helping with her ritual bath, the two then go to get breakfast for her, at four o'clock in the afternoon. They again run into filthy disorder in which an old woman, the cook, tries, more or less, to put something together after having served her numerous roomers much earlier. In one of the funniest scenes to be found in Kafka's work, they concoct a breakfast out of disgusting leftovers. This fragment ends with Brunelda's laying down precepts to Karl, namely that he should not imitate the lazy Robinson. Karl is rewarded for his diligence with a handful of leftover cake. This fragment succeeds in carrying the comedy of entropy and ensuing chaos a bit further downward.

The fragment shows that Kafka is a great comic writer, but the mechanical repetition of events and gestures—what the philosopher Bergson saw as the essence of the comic—does not advance the narration beyond the continuing downward spiral. By contrast, the second fragment, "Brunelda's Departure," opens up the narrative space. Karl is in the street outside the apartment, where, with help from the student, he has carried the immobile Brunelda down the steps in something like a wheelchair (in a *Krankenwagen,* a term today for ambulance but in context clearly meaning a rolling chair or perhaps a child's wagon—Mark Harmon's "invalid cart" seems right). It is early in the day, and Brunelda is covered with a cloth so as not to arouse excitement or attention as Karl pushes her through the streets. This seems to be a permanent departure, since the student apologizes for past behavior as they all say good-bye to one another. Karl then begins to push, only to be interrupted by a policeman who wants to know what is under the cloth. But by now, the text says, Karl knows how to deal with policemen, and he tells Brunelda to show the agent a document she has received. It is not clear what this document is, but from the policeman's reaction it appears it may be some kind of permission or medical approval to practice prostitution (which was and still is legal in some European countries, often under medical control). The policemen notes with a smile that she is "that" kind of girl (*KA,* p. 381: "so ein Fräulein ist das Fräulein?"). And so on they go, Karl wheeling his charge to Enterprise No. 25, where, arriving late, he is greeted by the unfriendly manager with the observation that in that house there are no excuses for tardiness. Karl observes the incomprehensible filth that covers everything and, while he meditates on the task of cleaning, Brunelda reveals herself to the satisfaction of the manager whom, apparently, she will know how to handle. So it ends.

This enticing fragment suggests that Kafka considered taking Karl's fall a step further downward or perhaps opening a way by which the now experienced young man might make a career in something; exactly what is not clear, but less than honorable work is not excluded (one can imagine something like

David Copperfield becoming a pimp). The last paragraph affirms that now Karl no longer heeds caustic remarks but uses his strength and does not hesitate to curse at lower beings. In other words, with this wacky image of Brunelda in a cart, Kafka seems to be trying out the image of a new Karl, stripped of his Dickensesque naiveté and innocence, entering the jungle, and ready to engage it. This was a thought experiment of brief duration, though one that teasingly points to a possible new plot line.

A rather different thought experiment lies behind the two fragments that Brod used for his ending for *Amerika* when he melded them together in one chapter under the title "The Nature Theater of Oklahoma." Most critics have seen in these fragments an attempt to dramatize a kind of secular salvation, though some have also seen in them a parody or a satire of the very idea of salvation. The multiple incongruous juxtapositions and events certainly suggest parody with a satirical edge. With regard to satire, as frequently is the case with Kafka, one cannot pinpoint any distortion in the text's images that would allow an obvious juxtaposition of that distortion with an external image in the world that is the object of the satire—unless a general satirical evaluation of religion and doctrines of salvation underlies the entire episode. This is not to be excluded.

There is no obvious connection between this episode's events and Karl's preceding life. He appears as a protagonist who reads a placard advertising jobs for everybody with the Theater of Oklahoma. It says that all who go to the Clayton race track will be hired. Two things immediately stand out about this beginning. First, this poster represents a version of the type of American advertising that traffics in hyperbole and half-truth. It offers the unlimited promise of some product or opportunity, often with utopia on the horizon. That is the nature of much advertising. Second, however, Oklahoma seems a most unlikely place for a theater, today or yesterday, in which to find happiness.

With regard to the second point, when Kafka was writing this wacky text, Oklahoma had only recently been admitted to the union, in 1907, though "Sooners" had crossed the boundary lines much earlier than was legal, in order to be the "soonest" to grab land. With statehood, Oklahoma ceased in a sense to be a last frontier. Moreover, it was a state largely populated by southerners who brought their racist mores with them. It is nearly certain that Kafka encountered an image of the racism found in Oklahoma in Arthur Holitscher's *Amerika heute und morgen*. In it Holitscher included a chapter, "Der Neger," in which he wrote a severe critique of the way America treated its black population.

Moreover, Holitscher reproduced in the book a photographic image of two lynched African Americans, one hanging prominently in the foreground, one less visible in the background, with the caption "Idyll aus Oklahoma" (with Oklahoma apparently misspelled in the original edition as Kafka then misspelled it himself). The picture is uncanny, for the black victims, hanging there dead, are accompanied by a group of young white men posing proudly. Three of them are wearing bowler hats much like the one favored by young Kafka, as one sees in a well-known photo of him. If we accept the idea that Kafka was influenced by Holitscher, and especially by the photo portraying an "idyll in Oklahoma," it is then certain that Kafka was engaging in savage irony by situating his theater there. However, there is nothing in Kafka's text to make this irony apparent to a then contemporary German reader—unless we suppose that Germans in 1912 were well aware of the racism present in America, which is after all quite probable. Moreover, the fact that Karl later says his name is "Negro" depends for its irony on some awareness of America's racism. In fine, Karl's taking on the name of "Negro" as he is going to an Oklahoma known for lynching presupposes that the reader will have some recognition of racism there if his name is to have any significance. It had significance for Kafka, to be sure.

The hiring for the theater is taking place in Clayton. Some critics have pointed out that "clay" is contained in his town, perhaps a "ton" of it? Clayton is also a suburb outside St. Louis, today a financial center, situated west of St. Louis at the end of Forest Park (a twin to Central Park in New York). Kafka may well have heard about Clayton and its proximity to St. Louis from the advertising blitz that had been undertaken throughout Europe for the World's Fair held in Forest Park in 1904. Posters were seen throughout Europe advertising the fair as a stupendous achievement that any European could see after a mere week of travel. It was, as one poster immodestly put it, "Man's Greatest Achievement." Austria had a pavilion at the fair, as did "The German Empire," and the exposition catalogue was available in German translation. (Henry Adams went, but, despising St. Louis, he could not wait to get back to London.) Kafka's Clayton requires that Karl take the underground to get there, which seemingly conflates it with a New York suburb that is too far distant for one to walk there easily from the city itself. There was no metro in St. Louis.

The posters that advertised the World's Fair give a good idea of the hyperbolic claims of the advertising of Americans used to peddle medicine, soaps, miraculous household products, wagons, and tools. There were also posters promising utopia to those who would settle land in the West, in Canada as late as 1912. This kind of image is central to Kafka's presentation of the paradise promised by the poster for the nature theater. This is largely an American phenomenon, since advertising was first received with some hostility in German-speaking countries. America seems to have been the land of choice for the development of ecstatic visions to be delivered by the consumption of selected products. The promise of attaining some kind of bliss or transcendence was, and perhaps still is, a model for advertising, and it appears that Kafka was attracted to it by the fact that advertising looked like a secular version of discourses that fascinated him from childhood on: religious discourses promising the revelation of transcendence and access to utopian salvation.

Karl has initially some doubts about the poster's claim, since it notably neglects to mention the pay for working in this theater. With self-directed irony, Kafka has his character reflect that nobody wanted to be an artist but everybody wanted to be paid. Yet, Karl cannot resist the blandishments of advertising that, like a secular evangelic message, says all will be received, all will be taken in, and that it is sufficient for job seekers merely to present themselves. Ernst Pawel notes in his biography that Kafka's stay among Protestants probably gave him some impetus for this vision of evangelical universalism: specifically, the attempts at conversion inflicted on Kafka at the naturopathic sanatorium at Jungborn in July 1912 acquainted him with the promise Protestantism holds out to those who will simply "come forward" to receive the Word. Or, as the biographer put it, "the Jungborn experience—both its physical setup and its chiliastic pretentions—contributed in some measure to his conception of the paradisiac 'Oklahoma Open Air Theater'" (Pawel, p. 261). Kafka was undoubtedly fascinated by the ease with which, by a single act of volition, those thirsting for salvation could convert and be saved—a far cry from the necessity of blood and birth by which one becomes a Jew (which meant that one could not stop being a Jew in Europe). Kafka was willing to draw upon all manner of religious and metaphysical discourses to find the stuff of his fictions, and, not surprisingly, Protestantism was not insignificant for a tale of America by a writer who came, after all, from the city of the Hussites, those proto-Protestants whose descendants were repressed in the seventeenth century by the Hapsburgs with their own versions of lynching.

Advertising works, and Karl spends the money necessary for a trip to Clayton. Upon arrival, he is greeted by the sound of trumpets or, perhaps more accurately, by a cacophony produced by innumerable trumpets, each blowing without concern for the others (perhaps an image of Protestant individualism). The trumpets are played by women dressed as angels, standing on pedestals of varying height. The number and size of the pedestals are set off by the fact that virtually nobody is listening. The angels announce salvation to general indifference, which contrasts notably with the busy scenes of traditional Christian iconography in which angles blow horns while the elect are sorted out from the damned. This astonishing image of angels and trumpets is also extremely funny, for it is incongruous beyond measure, yet seems to translate directly a certain type of religious experience, at least as viewed from the outside. One thinks immediately of Swift's satirical perspective in his descriptions of extravagance among dissenters, Cartesians, and other nonconformist believers whom he savagely ridiculed.

All of Kafka's extravagance takes place, moreover, on a race track. Heinz Politzer pointed out in his study of Kafka that the improbable race course used for recruiting is probably inspired by a well-known seventeenth-century poem, "Abend" ("Evening") by the protestant Andreas Gryphius.[1] "Abend" ("Evening") is a baroque work in which the turbulence of the world is compared to that of a race track, the image of which is already found in Kafka's "Unhappiness" with its race track in a living room. The comparison with the baroque poem is fruitful. It points up the parodistic quality of Kafka's image, especially the absurdity of a representation using a baroque image of angels blowing trumpets while would-be actors and mechanics seek placement at one of the interview offices lodged in betting booths. In his poem Gryphius turns to his God to ask that he be snatched from this "valley of darkness" and taken away. Indeed, the poet's plea that a hidden deity snatch him up to heaven seems echoed in Karl's dire need of such help: *ergo* Oklahoma.

At the race course, Karl walks through the row of trumpeting angels, talks to a white-clad female acquaintance on the way, and then goes to find the recruiting officer for this strange enterprise. We might call it Kafka's version of the *theatrum mundi* since it appears Karl is going to step forward into the world as a stage, working for a theater that is an image of all that is found in the world. This image of the world as a stage is another baroque image with roots in the seventeenth century, notably in dramatists like Calderon and Shakespeare.

The homeless Karl intends to embark on a new adventure, though, like the Karl thrown out of the hotel, he has no papers to show when he reaches his first interview. However, it is less important to have documents for this all-embracing theater than to have a profession, since the theater needs and takes everybody. The interviewers are hiring far more than actors. Karl decides to say that he is an engineer, since that it what he once hoped to be. Salvation is not gained only by hoping, however; it requires deeds. Karl admits that he is a once-upon-a-time student from a European intermediate school. With these qualifications Karl is rated at what appears to be about the lowest rank in the enterprise. In effect, he is deemed suited for low-level technical work, which, once the interviewer has felt Karl's arm muscle, appears to mean manual labor. In a short time, Karl has descended from his hopes to be on the top of the hierarchy to the bottom, a movement that reprises the movement of the chapters preceding this finale, if finale it is, much like a musical reprise of theme and variations. The fact that Karl has given his name as "Negro" adds to the impression that he is at the bottom of the hierarchy, about to become again something close to a slave. In any case, he is hired, his name is added to the list of those new recruits on the theater's announcement board, and he can attend a bizarre banquet for those who are departing for Oklahoma.

The festive banquet the narrator describes is redolent of a religious celebration of some sort, whether a Jewish ritual such as the Passover feast or the Christian Last Supper. It also resembles a parody of the visions of plenty found in medieval and Renaissance representations of the Land of Cockaigne or, in Germany, *Schlaraffenland,* where good food and drink are available in unlimited supply (lasting until the imbibers pass out drunk, as in Breugel's well-known painting "Land of Cockaigne," which depicts peasants stretched out unconscious on the ground). In Kafka's version of the land of plenty, huge birds are passed around, and wine pours into the festive celebrants' glasses without their making any effort. The contrast here with the novel's unrelenting story of descent into penury, of judgment and trial, is total. Kafka's vision of salvation is, at least in this banquet, a materialistic heaven that represents the most stereotypically American aspect of the novel's vision of the New World: the legend of total happiness brought about by the total satisfaction of all material needs. In a sense this was and perhaps still is a predominant image of America that circulates in those parts of the world where the poor dream of a land of Cockaigne in which one does not have to worry about hunger.

The fragment narrating Karl's encounter with the theater breaks off when the newly hired recruits board a train. With some justification, Brod melded a probable last fragment Kafka wrote to this scene of boarding the train. It should be noted, however, that the description of Karl's travel found in Brod's amalgamated version is a separate fragment, one that logically follows Karl's boarding the train after the preceding portrayal of his recruitment. However, the fragment depicting the boy's travel can stand alone. As a detached fragment it recalls some of the texts published in *Meditation*, for it offers a description that evokes the possibility of endless travel through open spaces. The fragment opens up the very Kafkaesque prospect of travel without end, of going perpetually toward the unknown, and hence of finding no respite in the quest to give meaning to the quest. Indeed, the fragment shares motifs with a text like "The Refusal," in which an accosted woman rejects a prospective male suitor, presumably noting that he is no wide-shouldered American with an Indian's stature, with honest, steady eyes and skin massaged by the air rushing over the expanses of grass and their rivers. Karl seems on his way to a place where he can become such a Westerner with a windswept complexion. And with Oklahoma in mind, one also thinks of *Meditation*'s "The Wish to Be an Indian" in which the speaker imagines flight forward, as if one were an Indian, on a running horse that ascends into the air, losing contact with the earth and then dissolving into the air, now without a bridle and finally without a horse's neck or horse's head. These texts recall that the wide-open expanses are favored images in Kafka, spaces to be traversed and to get lost in.

To illustrate this point I quote the last lines in the Muirs' sometimes lovely translation of the scene describing the images of an unlimited space filled with imaginary mountains:

> The first day they travelled through a high range of mountains. Masses of blue-black rock rose in sheer wedges to the railway line; even craning one's neck out of the window, one could not see their summits; narrow, gloomy, jagged valleys opened out and one tried to follow with a pointing finger the direction in which they lost themselves; broad mountain streams appeared, rolling in great waves down on to the foot-hills and drawing with them a thousand foaming wavelets, plunging underneath the bridges over which the trains rushed; and they were so near that the breath of coldness rising from them chilled the skin of one's face. (*America,* trans. Willa Muir and Edwin Muir, p. 268)

This description bears the same relation to the reality of a train trip from the eastern part of America to Oklahoma that Caspar David Friedrich's mountain landscapes bear to the Baltic sea coast where this famous Romantic painter was born. In both cases we confront a kind of soulscape or psychic projection in which the artist represents images produced by his inner vision. In Kafka's case these images also represent a desire to escape and an implicit recognition of the impossibility of escape, for Karl's vision cannot encompass this landscape of mountains in which vision can only go astray. Friedrich's imaginary mountains, by contrast, often suggest a vision at home in the sublimity of the natural world. Kafka's mountains are sublime, but in a way that threatens the viewer with loss.

To finish this discussion of this unfinished novel, I want to approach Oklahoma from a different angle, first from a personal perspective, in order then to make a few general observations about the nature of this strange and unique novel. While reading the novel's conclusion, I have more than once instinctively recalled an experience from my childhood time spent in Oklahoma, the memory of which was transformed by an adult experience. That experience was to see, as an adult, a serial cowboy film that I had also seen as a child in Oklahoma. The serial, called "The Phantom Empire," features the "singing cowboy" Gene Autry, who called himself an Oklahoman, though my association of the film with Kafka is mainly a result of the fact that as a child I saw the serial when my family lived in Oklahoma. In this serial the redoubtable Gene Autry takes on a highly technologically advanced alien civilization living under the earth and planning to assault at least Oklahoma, if not the entire planet. As an adult, years later, viewing the serial on television, I saw that it was a Republic Pictures product from the 1930s, reprised in the 1940s for Saturday matinees, which accounted for the fact that the underground empire was a 1930s art deco fantasy, both in its images of buildings modeled on the Empire State Building and in its underground décor in which the futuristic scientific instruments of the hidden civilization were all examples of the design of that era (or roughly what one can see in a Flash Gordon film of the time). Most interesting, this film combines the innocence romance of the western with the cutting-edge evil of science fiction, with an overlay of the cowboy musical. It mixes genres and styles, combining the kitsch of the Boy Scout activism with H. G. Wells and a soupçon of futurism.

The relevance of this serial's campy play with genres for a reading of *Amerika* is that, when the two are compared, it points up that Kafka has done something comparable. Kafka's work has more metaphysical intent than a portrayal of a civilization gone bad with science, but the influence of the genres of pop culture is strongly present in the novel. In fact, the pop representation of modern civilization in Kafka is not unlike what one sees in early Hollywood science fiction as well as in expressionist painting or even futurist painting. Almost systematically, in fact, Kafka sketches out in each chapter a kind of pop vision of space that sets the scene for the often comic mixing of genres—bildungsroman, Dickensian pathos, sci-fi, and futurism—in which operate the mechanisms for judgment that await the young hero who crosses from one side of the Atlantic to the other. Let us consider some specifics.

First, the New York harbor and the ship. The harbor is the scene of the menacing archangel, the futurist Statue of Liberty with a sword, though this display of menacing power lasts only a moment. Karl is quickly lost inside the ship, where the unknown byways lead him on a descent into the unknown, if not into Hades, then to a baroque court where the hero undergoes initiation. He is quickly lost in these spaces, though above him shuffle thousands of feet while engines throb in the distance. This is more redolent of Fritz Lang's *Metropolis* with its lines of marching zombie workers than of an adventure tale. The harbor comes back into view after Karl has entered the captain's quarters and takes on the remarkable appearance of some mythological beast from an expressionist setting: the skyscrapers stare at Karl with 100,000 eyes while great ships crisscross the scene and the guns of warships thunder in salute.

In the second chapter, "Uncle Jacob" in the Muirs' translation, the image of the city is that of a scene of perpetual motion, seen from Karl's balcony, where in foreshortened perspective people and vehicles rush about, providing an expressionist vision of the ongoing destruction of vision, for it is as if a glass roof over the scene were being constantly smashed. Experiments in Cubism at this time were achieving comparable effects with the fragmentation and distortion of vision. A sense of incipient violence is present when Karl, not realizing that he has already been condemned, travels out of the city with Mr. Pollunder.

Traffic moves ceaselessly about them, giving the impression of a whirlwind as it changes direction every minute. Kafka adds explicit social commentary to this futuristic vision when he depicts strikers who threaten the flow of traffic, for they are depicted as a mass of humanity forcing its way forward, singing, while mounted police protect travelers and keep the way open for the constant movement of vehicular traffic.

In the inner labyrinth of the country house Karl encounters Clara, the judo specialist who may be about to deflower our hero for a second time. His naiveté is patent, and his getting lost in the house points up his need for help. This bildungsroman, if *Amerika* is in part a representative of the genre, unfolds here in a space that underscores, in darkness, the hopeless of Karl's prospects for education. Learning to negotiate labyrinths without help from the gods is often impossible. The labyrinth is a constant image in Kafka for the hermeneutic quest, and here it serves as an image of Karl's failure to understand his lack of understanding. In the country house it thus shows how far Karl is from even remotely grasping the meaning of his fall.

Expelled from the country house, Karl then finds himself again "on the road," as Kerouac later put it in the novel of that name. The image of traffic Karl encounters is again futuristic in its portrayal of the unceasing movement of machines that dominates everything. To be sure, Kafka does not share the enthusiasm that Marinetti and the futurists had for a future in which machines would be the model for humanity. *Amerika* shows that he did not endorse Marinetti's 1909 Futurist Manifesto, in which the Italian proclaimed that a roaring automobile is more beautiful than the Winged Victory of Samothrace. But Kafka certainly put roaring cars into this novel in a way that the futurist would have recognized to be prophetic of the future. And in a vision that is, alas, prophetic of American cities today, while on his way toward his next judgment, Karl does not see a single car stop, nor does a single passenger get out of one. Cars roar along like autonomous beings in this America.

The Hotel Occidental, with all the irony implicit in its name redolent of the open expanses of the West, is also a place where the machine reigns. It has a vast number of elevators, speeding up and down twenty-four hours a day: Kafka could have had in mind that New York's Woolworth Building, being completed as he wrote the novel, would not only be the world's tallest building but would also have the fastest elevators. Karl's work is to be an extension of the elevator, working the lever that takes him and his passengers from floor to floor. The fifth chapter, "The Hotel Occidental," ends, in fact, on the strange image of the elevator shafts, surrounded by glass, behind which one can see masses of hanging bananas. Kafka's thinking in images is again illustrated in this incongruous example in which the machine and a fruit from the tropics are juxtaposed to suggest some kind of futurist scene. New technology meant that large fruit companies were making tropical fruits readily available in the most distant places, even in futurist elevators.

When he is trapped by the vicious and lascivious head porter, Karl views the work of the subordinate porters: they resemble machines for the dissemination of information, an arduous task they can handle for only an hour at a time, after which, with the ringing of a bell, they are automatically replaced. Then, after this hour-long shift, their heads, like overheated machines, must be cooled with water, so intense is the work dealing with the pressing demands of the crowds of seekers of information perpetually amassed before the subordinate porters' windows. And when Karl looks to see if he can hope for help and rescue from the head porter's clutches, all he sees are the six underporters, three of whom talk without stopping on their modern telephones while the other three make notes to be handed to the speakers and three boy assistants seek telephone numbers in huge telephone books. In this preview of the information society, telephone communication apparently excludes any hope of any other communication, so that Karl must rely entirely upon his own wits to escape the porter's grasp. He escapes, only to run into another unbroken line of automobiles that block him, leaving him to wonder if he ought to climb through one of them, before he is called to take care of Robinson lying on his stretcher.

Perhaps Brod thought "Refuge" a good title for the seventh chapter because here the dominance of automobiles, elevators, and other machines ends. The futurist vision, or perhaps nightmare, is over. True, Karl runs into a labyrinth in his attempt to escape the policeman, and he must negotiate endless stairs to go up to Brunelda's apartment. These shabby images tie in with Kafka's images of recurrent themes of wandering and quest, of loss and deception. In any case, Karl's nightmare takes a new shape as it becomes a comic descent into chaos. Significantly, machines do reappear at the electoral rally unfolding in the street at night. Automobile headlights illuminate the candidate, at least until they are smashed by the opposition. The machine is a source of light, but one easily challenged by violence in the generalized quest for power that Kafka often saw at work.

My final point is that Kafka created a quite heterogeneous work in presenting the boy who is missing. Perhaps the central paradox is that the boy who is missing is not missing from the novel named for the missing person. It is never really made clear who precisely might be missing him, if indeed he is missed, though it may be that the missing person is the missing hero of a typical bildungsroman. But let us not overburden the interpretation of *Amerika* with paradox. Rather, I prefer to underscore what I see as the central issue in these interrelated fragments—the way Kafka has integrated recurrent mechanisms of judgment into the narrative development while bringing out both its dark and its comic sides. Of course, there are other interesting approaches one can take in reading this novel. It can be read as a straight autobiographical fantasy, a projection of Kafka's desire for escape and his recognition in advance that escape is impossible: in this case the missing person cannot, ironically, go missing. From another perspective, *Amerika* can be read not only as a parody of the idea of bildungsroman but, more generally, as a satire of edifying literature. It can be read as a kind of sociological inquiry, a portrayal of the workings of modern industrial society.

This latter reading has occurred frequently. Indeed, in the first major attempt at interpreting the entirety of Kafka's work, Wilhelm Emrich's *Franz Kafka*, the renowned critic made a judgment to the effect that, in *Amerika*, Kafka created a novel that belongs to the most perspicacious novelistic revelations of the nature of modern industrial society that one can find in world literature, since in it "the hidden economical and psychological workings of this society and its demonic consequences are mercilessly laid bare."[2] This view of the novel as a form of social critique and, indeed, an indictment of modern society is not without justification. However, one can argue that, starting with Balzac and Dickens, there have been many writers who have been perspicacious about the nature of capitalism and industrial society. But socially oriented writers have usually not set out to write, for better or worse, novels like *Amerika* in which the novel makes not only an indictment that incriminates society but also seems to transcend the historical specificity of industrial capitalism to dramatize flaws in the nature of existence itself. Industrial capitalism was and is the modern form of what Kafka saw as the current manifestation of the inevitable failure of our desire not to fail. It is the constant backdrop for the drama of the decline and fall that were increasingly the subject of Kafka's work after Karl's disappearance in America. The capitalist bureaucratic state and the world of business do not disappear in later Kafka, but they are rarely named with historical specificity as in *Amerika*. Let us now turn to one major exception to that generalization and consider the son's fall in "The Judgment," a son who has a friend who fails in business in St. Petersburg.

Chapter 4

"The Judgment" and "The Metamorphosis"

Before *Meditation* could appear in print and after he had begun work on *Amerika,* Kafka experienced what he saw as a breakthrough in his quest to become a writer. It occurred in a night of intense writing on 22–23 September 1912, during which he wrote the story "Das Urteil" ("The Judgment"). Critics often approach this unsettling tale of a son's suicide by drowning using Kafka's own commentary in the diaries. They may also quote "Letter to His Father," the long letter Kafka wrote but did not deliver to his father in 1919. In the letter Kafka explains to his father why he feels persecuted by him, whereas the diary entry, written after Kafka had finished "The Judgment," shows Kafka trying to figure out what he had accomplished in this overflowing of inspiration. However, the diary entry is really of nugatory interest, for it consists mainly of Kafka's discovering that he had Felice Bauer in the back of his mind when he wrote the story, which is hardly surprising.

More interestingly, "Letter to His Father" does have parallels to the conflict of father and son presented in "The Judgment." Of course, there is a circularity involved in projecting the story onto the letter and then using the letter to read the details of the story. Both Kafka and his fictional character Georg certainly had problems with their fathers. That Kafka, unlike Georg, did not commit suicide suggests significant differences between Kafka and his fictional character, a businessman about to get married. What is of interest is that the letter highlights how Kafka experienced the power relationship embodied in his father's dominance: Kafka experienced it as a demand that he negate his own existence. Thus, he experienced his relation to his father as misery and fear. Much of Kafka's work turns on the consequences of questioning or refusing the demands of power that relentlessly commands obedience simply in the name of an obscure or unfounded law. This is the sort of law that fathers embody. Their demands are unfounded, perhaps absurd, but overwhelming. This is spelled out in the letter of 1919, in which Kafka explains to his father that he has constantly feared him because the father has constantly appeared gigantic to him in every regard. The power that this fear engendered is, as Kafka put it, the power of the tyrant whose word cannot be contested. The tyrant has his undisputed right simply because the tyrant is a tyrant: that is the nature of his being. In other words, as the letter puts it, the tyrant has his power because of who he is, not because of any thought or idea that might ground this right. In short, power is arbitrary and emanates simply from the patriarchal presence. It is an irrational power, uncontestable as it is arbitrary, uncontestable because it is arbitrary.

It is primarily for this insight into the nature of patriarchal tyranny that the Nobel laureate Elias Canetti said that Kafka is, among all writers, the greatest expert on power.[1] We have seen this expertise at work in the first episodes of *Amerika,* in which Karl is the victim of repeated judgments. With regard to "The Judgment," it seems that what Kafka experienced as a breakthrough came when he directly confronted the image of patriarchal power through a literary work. He confronted it by portraying the psychodynamics involved when patriarchal dominance expresses itself in the arbitrary but absolute use of its ungrounded power of judgment—or power *tout court.* The history of twentieth-century tyrants suggests why Canetti thought Kafka's portrait of the patriarchal tyrant all too accurate for both the private and the public spheres. For the history of the demise of the Enlightenment in the twentieth century in Europe is a history related to the rise of the patriarchal dictator.

What is essential for understanding "The Judgment" is that pronouncement of the father condemning the son is grounded in his arbitrary power. It may be arbitrary—for what grounds the feeble old man's power except his patriarchal presence?—but his power is absolute, as absolute as the death to which the son consents in self-execution. The son's suicidal obedience is a ghastly demonstration, though with much black humor, of the fundamentally irrational workings of the power fathers have over sons and, by implication, patriarchal social institutions and laws have over all. The recognition of the arbitrary nature of power, Kafka seems to imply, does not diminish power. "The Judgment" is an example of a completed work with a neat, definite close, perhaps the only one with which Kafka was really satisfied. Perhaps this is because it unflinchingly demonstrates the consequences of accepting the father's power. Kafka's characters are often dismayed by power, and rarely do they openly contest it, but Georg seems unique in his unquestioning embrace of the paternal judgment. He embraces self-destruction.

Kafka is hardly alone in believing that the patriarchal model of dominance has been the basis for much human misery. In this regard Kafka was at one with many thinkers of the Enlightenment. It is worth considering briefly in this regard the example of the German philosopher Immanuel Kant, who set out as axiomatic the necessity of throwing off the power of patriarchy as embodied in family, church, and state if one is to be a free moral subject. In his essay of 1784, *Was ist Aufklärung?* (*What Is Enlightenment?*), Kant succinctly described the necessity of growing up to be an autonomous subject as the essential program of Enlightenment. This is something with which Kafka, the "eternal son," as his biographer Peter-André Alt titled his biography of Kafka, undoubtedly agreed even if the son struggled all his life to stop being a child. Enlightenment comes from freeing oneself from what Kant called tutelage, for to have real freedom the moral subject must lead a life dictated by his or her reason and not by exterior authority of any kind. In "The Judgment" Kafka took on the task of showing the difficulty, perhaps the impossibility, of complete human emancipation. It is not surprising that the left-wing defenders of Enlightenment in Germany—Adorno and Benjamin, for example—found in Kafka a fellow traveler on the path toward emancipation.

Let us now consider "The Judgment" in detail. It is narrated by a third-person narrator whose point of view is largely congruent with that of the young businessman portrayed in the story, Georg Bendemann. Other characters are mentioned in the narration, though Georg's father is the only other character who is directly seen through Georg's eyes. Thus, the reader knows the father's viewpoint through his dialogue with Georg. A friend of Georg is also mentioned, though he is never seen, since he is far away in Russia. This narrative configuration means that the reader must decide whether or not Georg's viewpoint, as reflected through the narrator's commentary, is reliable. This is a contested issue. Some critics think Georg is hypocritically untrustworthy or unreliable, especially Freudians, who view Georg as the expression of some unconscious locus or force that cannot be named in the text. From our perspective, however, Georg can be taken to be reliable. There are no obvious indications that he is malevolent or hypocritical, which does not mean that Georg may not be wrong. He is not aware of guilt, conscious or unconscious, in the way he views the world and himself in the world. From this perspective, he appears at the end to be a victim of arbitrary power despite his partial grasp of the facts. At the story's outset he has not yet understood the nature of the power that his father can exert over him. Georg has perhaps been deluded even if he appears to believe he is being honest with himself and with others.

The story begins with Georg at home, immobile in his room, sealing a letter he plans to send to the friend in St. Petersburg in distant Russia. The friend functions as a negative image of what Georg is, that is, as an image of what Georg is not. Since the friend is not planning to get married, some critics see him as an idealized image of the Kafka who knew that only in bachelorhood could he become a writer. This is dubious, however, since the friend is a businessman who has little to do with writing. He has traveled far away and, in the midst of revolutionary turmoil and violence, he has not prospered, so that he cannot plan to get married, as the more prosperous Georg now plans to do. Having found a fiancée, Georg is finally, after much hesitation, going to write a letter to tell his friend of his forthcoming marriage, a sign of his success, in contrast to his friend's failure.

If we step back from the immediate detail, we can see here a variation on Kafka's theme of the impossibility of going anywhere: this theme is reflected in the friend's having traveled far away and most especially to Russia, setting between him and the friend the immense space that messages can hardly traverse. For Kafka, as for his fellow Austro-Hungarian writers Robert Musil and Joseph Roth, Russia signified the end of the earth, a place beyond civilization that Kafka characterized, in the diary entry of 5 January 1912, as the place for the most extreme experience of solitude. (Comparable notions about Russia are found at the beginning of Musil's *Young Törless* and in the narration of military experience in Roth's *Radetsky March*.)

In the context of the early twentieth century, Russia suggests more than solitude and loss; it is also a place of revolution and pogroms. In fact, Kafka names the Russian revolution of 1905. This occurs when, confronting his father later in "The Judgment," Georg thinks of his friend's having told him that, on a business trip to Kiev during the revolution, he saw a priest who incised a bloody cross in his hand, apparently to incite a crowd to action. Then, after he father asserts himself, Georg reflects on the violence that has wrecked the friend's shop and destroyed his business. He imagines the shop's shelves in ruin, its gaslights falling down, and the destruction of the shop's wares. Georg's friend is thus the occasion for what is one of the few allusions to historical events in Kafka's work: the October pogrom in Kiev and the subsequent doings of the proto-fascistic "Black Hundreds" who joined up with the police to chase and kill liberals and Jews in St. Petersburg and elsewhere in the aftermath of the 1905 revolution.

The question of extratextual reference is a constant question in Kafka criticism, and Georg's thoughts on the Russian revolution underscore the range of this reference. Many critics maintain that nothing "real" seems to appear in Kafka's work except the references to Prague in "Description of a Struggle." Of course, critics are willing to recognize that "real" historical entities like God, the Bible, Western law, icons and parables taken from Jewish and Christian tradition, the torture practiced in the Middle Ages, and similar external entities are alluded to by Kafka, often in indirect and contorted ways. This means that extratextual reference of some sort or the other is a constant issue in interpreting Kafka, quite simply because it is constantly, if obliquely and distortedly, present. But it is also the case that Kafka rarely, if ever, wrote an allegory with clear and direct univocal reference to the historical world. (I take it for given that allegories usually refer to other texts that deal with the world and not to some noncodified or extratextual part of the real world.) So, if direct historical references are very infrequent, indeed nearly nonexistent in Kafka's work after "The Judgment," it is also true that reference to the history of Western culture are omnipresent, though nothing is directly cited that would create a consistent, limited univocal allegory. In simplest terms, Kafka is not paraphrasing the Bible. What the reader regularly confronts are self-consciously defective allegories that in an obscure fashion refer to the history of Western culture; they represent in a sense the shards of that culture as it remains half-consciously embedded in our modern conscious. And these quasi allegories are self-conscious in the indirect way they designate their own failure to make any precise contact—thus, they are most successful when they demonstrate their failure.

The historical references to Kiev and St. Petersburg in "The Judgment" are exceptions in that they directly refer to a very unfavorable moment for Jews and liberals in the Russian empire. But even this seemingly precise reference is subject to interpretation. Is the priest whom Georg's friend saw inciting the crowd to violence, perhaps against Jewish merchants? Or is he offering his bloody hand in imitation of the stigmata that marked Christ's body? Is this a sign that the friend has gone astray in a land of fanatics? Or in a land of believers who might contest the power of the state? The friend's stay in Russia seems to Georg to have resulted in a disaster for the friend, but all that is happening at such a distance that Georg can only picture it in dismal images centering on the shop he imagines to be destroyed, highly probable images but only imagined images nonetheless.

Georg thinks of his friend not only as a fellow businessman but also as an "old child." This expression is another sign that the friend is some kind of double for Georg, for the story's narrative development then shows that Georg himself is an aging child unable to free himself from the tutelage of parental authority. It should be a sign of his maturing that he has decided to become engaged, and what was said earlier about the meaning of marriage applies a fortiori to the bachelor Georg's case. It is naturally to be assumed that he has matured because he accepts the duties that social conventions and religious law lay upon him. Now he is going to marry Frieda Brandenfeld—whose initials are the same as those of Felice Bauer, as Kafka noted with apparent astonishment in his diary. Georg's Frieda, unlike Kafka's Felice, comes from a very good family, or so he thinks. All seems quite proper, and so when Georg goes to tell his father that he is going to write to his friend about the engagement, Georg has no idea that his father might harbor hostile feelings about his fiancée and the forthcoming marriage.

Georg is not reckoning with the father's desire to exercise his power. The revelation of the father's desire unfolds in a dramatic conflict, much like the agon in tragedy, between father and son. Readers with a sense of theater may in fact see something like a second act beginning in Georg's tragi-comedy when he enters the father's room, a dark space in which the father is lodged like some kind of foreboding oracle. There the patriarch reads newspapers, as does Gregor Samsa's father in "The Metamorphosis." The newspaper offers another image of writing, perhaps a degraded image, or a counterbalance to the writing Georg wants to send to his distant friend. Images of writing in Kafka are rarely innocent, and the newspaper may seem to be a sign that the narrative is in the father's hands.

Georg's mother having died some two years before, the son now lives alone with the old man, who, though apparently feeble, is nonetheless still active in the family business. Georg's subordination to the father is immediately evident, for the first thing he thinks upon entering the paternal space is that his father is still a giant (*Riese*). This is the same paternal image found in "Letter to His Father" where Kafka tells his father that, for Kafka the son, the father was always giant-like in every respect, and so appears at one point the threatening father looming up in "The Metamorphosis" over his insect-son, the son to be chastised and chased back into his room.

This impression of a giant may or may not be literally true, but the father is a giant for the child, and this impression creates the lasting paternal imago that Freud describes as the image every child has interiorized of the father: it is the image that is the basis for the genesis of the superego that exercises power over the child *cum* adult. In this respect it is quite accurate to speak of a parallel between Kafka's drama and Freud's allegory of the father's dominance through the agency of the superego. Kafka himself apparently saw some parallel with Freud when he commented on "The Judgment" in the diary with the enigmatic phrase "Freud naturally." (In this entry of 23 September 1912, Kafka reflected on his story's relation to several other writers as well as Freud.) Thus, the aging but psychologically powerful father begins manipulating Georg by feigning at first not to know that Georg has a friend in St. Petersburg. Georg, perhaps taken in, good-naturedly assumes that his father has forgotten and tries to remind him, as if humoring the old man. Considering the apparent enfeeblement of the father, Georg begins to feel guilty for not having given him better care and to think of ways of improving the sickly old man's living conditions. At this point the father appears very old to Georg, with a toothless mouth and unruly white hair, though this appearance is belied by the look he gives his son: the pupils in the father's eyes stare intensely at him as if magnified to a larger than normal size. Power is inscribed in the gaze.

When the father affirms that Georg has no friend in Russia, the ambiguity seems intentional, for the father may be denying that the distant person is a friend of Georg—or denying that such a person is in Russia. The latter denial seems to be the first implication. The father appears to be laying a trap to catch Georg so as to be able to affirm his paternal power. The narrator then describes a strange image that falsely implies the father's lack of power when Georg picks up his father and carries him to bed so that the old man will be more comfortable. The son answers positively when the father then asks, with pointed ambiguity, if he is "covered up" properly, for the German verb Georg uses implies both stifled and buried as well as tucked in. The father is certainly not stifled, for he then leaps up and, standing on the bed, towers over the son to proclaim that the friend in Russia is the son the father would have wished for himself. It is at this point that Georg imagines the friend and the violence inflicted on him in Russia. The distant catastrophe—at once historically real and a product of fantasy—conjures up an image of the violence now to be worked on Georg. To intimidate the son, the father mocks him and, imitating a wanton woman or a whore by pulling his robe up, accuses Georg of defiling his mother's image by lusting after another woman. This is a decidedly different view of what marriage usually means. In describing the father's treatment of Georg at this point, some critics have spoken of the father's creating a double bind, a notion used by Gregory Bateson and other thinkers in the 1950s to describe how families create mental illness. The double bind does describe Georg's situation: the parent issues self-contradictory commands so that whatever the child does, the child is wrong. To Georg, the commands would be, implicitly, that the son should get married and, explicitly, that son should not grow up and leave home—and defile the mother. Having opted for marriage, Georg has disobeyed the second order, though not to marry, as Kafka well knew, was to infringe the law commanding the most sacred duty.

The father maliciously asserts that Georg's sexuality entails a violation of the child's sacred duty to the parent. With this sadistic flourish the father illustrates a permutation on the classic Oedipal schema according to which the son desires to possess the mother and kill the father. Here the father wishes to kill the son because the young man does not want to remain true to the mother. It seems all permutations are possible in an irrational world dominated by arbitrary power. For example, the mother's power over the child could be transferred to the father, or so Georg's father proclaims in triumph. And to clinch his victory, to increase Georg's disarray and humiliation, the father suddenly claims that he writes regularly to the distant friend, sending letters that the friend reads while he crumples up Georg's epistles without bothering to look at them.

Images of writing almost always have a self-referential aspect in Kafka's work. In "The Judgment," writing and sending letters suggest a form of motion and travel, for messages must traverse the immense distance that separate Georg and the friend. If a message were to get to its goal, it would represent a momentary triumph over the constant fall into disorder. A received and read letter might convey some essential information, perhaps offering a glimpse of revelation. Sending messages is an important theme in Kafka, especially in a novel such as *The Castle* and in short stories such as "The Village Schoolmaster" and "A Message from the Emperor." It is a theme that usually illustrates failure. Often messages are a possible double of the narrative text that describes their failure. Messages and letters often go astray, or, if they arrive, they cannot be understood; if one thinks one has understood, one may be guilty of an erroneous interpretation. Any text can be wrongly interpreted, including the text in which this message is sent, which is again a self-referential message. For the fictive text describing the message that fails is also a message.

Whatever the case with the friend and the letters he reads or does not read, the father's claim of successful communication is part of the manipulation by which the father assures his power. Georg now wonders if he has ever successfully communicated, and in doubt he is shamed by the father's proclamation of his son's multiple inadequacies, especially when Georg is compared with the father. The father is a successful master of contradictions, for example when he shouts that Georg has been wrong, in this as in everything, to believe that the father spends his time reading newspapers; then he throws down an old newspaper Georg has never seen before to prove that he does not spend his time with newspapers. This is a splendid image of contradictory manipulation: the father proves he doesn't read newspapers by hurling one down.

The father accuses Georg of hesitating to grow up, which is true in that Georg submits to the father and false in that he wants to get married (and perhaps leave home). Drawing on such self-contradictory propositions, critics can argue pretty much anything they want about Georg, though it is only against the assumption of Georg's basic good faith that the father's abuse of power stands out. The paternal will to power becomes clear when the father makes another contradictory indictment, bringing up what are the strangest charges against Georg. The father claims that for Georg to grow up, the mother had to die and his friend had to perish, the latter now having become so yellow that he is good only to be thrown away—like an old piece of paper, perhaps a newspaper. Georg's only defense is to accuse the father of being a comedian, a charge the father gleefully accepts. At this point some critics think that Georg is in some sense guilty, though the idea is difficult to justify in any ethical or legal sense, and it is difficult to see why one would agree with the father when he charges Georg with being egotistical and even devilish. Georg's ineffectual answer to his father's accusation suggests Georg is simply not adroit. Saying that his father has been lying in wait for him, Georg clearly shows he has no defense against the father's power over him. If they both agree that the father is an actor, perhaps it is because they both know that the old man has been concocting a scenario by which the son is to be condemned. With his scenario based on double-bind sadism, the father affirms his arbitrary power and takes over the son's imagination: the son imagines that he is guilty as charged and thus submits to the sentence of death. This acceptance is the ultimate, brilliant demonstration of the father's power.

It is plausible that, with this sentence, Kafka may have had in mind that traditional Judaism allows the father to enact the symbolic death of a son who has not respected the law. Undoubtedly, Kafka often had Jewish tradition in mind, but he was also aware that the empire he lived in and worked for was also founded upon patriarchal power. The Hapsburg emperor, portrayed everywhere as father figure, was a powerful image. Moreover, Jews looked to the emperor as the powerful if distant beneficent father to protect them from their Christian neighbors (not to mention against the anti-Semitic czar in Russia, against whom the emperor soon waged a war that most Jews heartily endorsed). Family, religion, and state formed, for Kafka, an overlapping series of structures in which power was grounded, circularly, in the patriarchal imposition of the law that grounded the patriarchal structure and hence affirmed the father's power to ground the law. Ultimately, the law was an extension of the father's will. The father's word suffices, and the son is sentenced to death by drowning. This sentence also harks back to older traditions coexistent with the beginnings of the purest patriarchy, to a moment when immersion in water could purify the family or the tribe of impure elements. It is not for mere rhetorical flourish that the father has castigated Georg as a kind of devil. In eliminating this devil, the finale of "The Judgment" enacts a parodistic exorcism by water.

The story's final paragraph is replete with Kafka's favored, often comic images. The servant whom Georg encounters on the stairs shows revulsion and covers her eyes to avoid seeing this impure being upon whom, in pointed anticipation of Gregor Samsa, nobody can look. On the bridge over the river, Georg hangs onto the balustrade as a hungry man clings to food, an early image of the longing for nourishment that, after Gregor Samsa's hunger, culminates in a hunger artist's starvation. Georg swings over the railing like the gymnast he once was, to his parents' approbation, though his body is now in the service of the fall to which he has been condemned. Finally, as the obedient son falls into the water, he affirms to his parents that he has always loved them. This is one of the most savagely ironic lines in the entire work of the ever-ironic Kafka, for in it he neatly affirms that love is part of the grounds for the power with which the parents can destroy the child. Of course, the father's power is literally affirmed here by his power to kill, arguably the ultimate foundation of all power. In fine, the good son affirms that he is the good son by killing himself in due execution of the paternal command.

The final sentence of "The Judgment" has elicited much commentary. Set off as a paragraph, the sentence says in effect that, at the moment Georg drowns himself, an unending flow of traffic was going/went over the bridge. The word for "traffic" is *Verkehr,* and it can also mean "intercourse," with the same two meanings that the word has in English. However, Freudians notwithstanding, there is nothing in the text that supports the idea that *Verkehr* suggests here that somebody might be having sex, least of all Georg.

If one reads the sentence carefully, it is clear that the narrative point of view is now that of a necessarily omniscient narrator who stresses that, at the time of Georg's death, the unending motion of the fallen world continued or was continuing, undoubtedly indifferent to the public execution that was taking place there in the street. The difficulty with translating this sentence is not the ambivalence of the word *Verkehr,* which is adequately translated by "traffic." ("The world's unending intercourse" does not work.) The real problem with translating the sentence is offered by the verb *gehen* ("to go"). In the sentence, it is used in the German simple past. The Muirs' translation puts the verb in the past progressive tense ("was going"), a tense construction that does not exist in German but which is an understandable choice. However, the verb could also be translated as a single act ("went"). In other words, the translator into English (or into a Romance or Slavic language, with their imperfect tense) must decide whether this traffic surged forth to accompany the execution at one time, as a single event, or whether the forward motion of the traffic was the ongoing backdrop of the world's busy movement, continuing indifferently as it always does, and hence contrasting ironically with Georg's fall, which is indeed a unique event.

This latter reading seems preferable, for the implication of the practical world's ongoing indifference to Georg has a powerful emotional tonality. Moreover, the roar of unending traffic is a recurrent image in Kafka, as in the world, especially in *Meditation* and *Amerika*. To offer a comparison, the contrast between Georg's fall and the world's ongoing bustle is not unlike, say, the scene in the painting, usually attributed to Bruegel, called *Landscape with the Fall of Icarus*. In the painting, the world plods on indifferently, with its daily business of plowing and sailing, while the famous son's legs stick up from the ocean's surface just before he sinks and drowns after he has challenged divine order. Quite the opposite effect is achieved if one translates with simple past "went," which might suggest that the traffic surged forth one time, almost in reaction to this self-inflicted murder on the bridge. That effect would be rather like the sudden gathering of a heavenly host to mourn the death of the savior.

After the exhilaration of writing "The Judgment," Kafka in late 1912 wrote another story about an unhappy son. This story is probably the work most associated with Kafka, for the giant insect portrayed by the tale has become a not infrequent image for book covers and *New Yorker* cartoons. This image comes of course from *Die Verwandlung* ("The Metamorphosis"), the story of a salesman who wakes up one morning as a giant insect. It is undoubtedly also one of the reasons that "Kafkaesque" has become a common adjective, meaning the uncanny, to describe an unusual or weird occurrence for which there is no explanation. To be sure, *The Trial* and *The Castle* enlarge greatly upon what "Kafkaesque" has come to mean, but these novels propose no single image to rival that of a giant insect, offering a résumé of their portrayal of what it means to be crushed by unknown bureaucratic forces in a hostile, absurd world.

The fame of "The Metamorphosis" is justifiably due to the way it forces the reader to confront the inexplicable from the very first sentence, undoubtedly one of the best-known first sentences in world literature. It says that one morning Gregor Samsa woke up from restless dreams to find himself changed into a giant vermin—"zu einem ungeheuren Ungeziefer verwandelt." The sentence is provocatively enigmatic, for the third-person narrator, who enunciates it with no apparent irony, observes with deadpan neutrality a simple matter of fact. After reflection, of course, the reader may decide that the assertion resembles a proposition found in mythological discourse, maybe in Ovid's *Metamorphoses,* or perhaps in a religious fable, or in fairy-tale and folktale variants on metamorphosis, or in fantastic stories for which the classical Latin tale of metamorphosis, Apuleius's *Metamorphosis or The Golden Ass* could be a model. However, nothing in the rest of Kafka's story suggests that the first sentence is an introduction to some mythological discourse, since nothing else in the story appears to deviate from the norms and conventions for narrating what we usually take to be reality. Reality just happens to have, suddenly, a giant vermin inhabiting it, and the rest of the story tells how the characters deal with this fact, including, of course, the protagonist, Gregor Samsa.

Upon further reflection, the reader might wonder whether the opening sentence is the statement of an insane person, for psychiatric literature has made us familiar with those who believe they are Napoleon, or are on the moon, or are made of glass. But, again, nothing in the rest of the story suggests that we are in any sense reading the representation of an insane person's discourse, neither, directly, the narrator's discourse nor, indirectly, Gregor's. The sanity of the author Franz Kafka is a different matter, but in fact we have little reason to question it. *Au contraire,* there are reasons to believe Kafka was hyperlucid, however much anguish he may have known and whatever may have been the images that haunted him.

Finally, we may be tempted to interpret the first sentence as the introduction to the narration of a dream, which would allow us to hang onto our conventional expectations about the representation of reality and bracket off the story as a psychic phenomenon, the solipsistic product of a mind lost in the nightly delirium of dream. For if the sentence is not an introduction to a myth or to fantasy derivations thereof or to a bout of insanity, then it might seem that only in dream can a son, a normal businessman, wake up to find himself converted into some kind of loathsome beasty resembling a big beetle or, indeed, a cockroach. The dream alternative suggests itself to the reader who has seen the use Kafka made of the rhetoric of dream discourse in "Description of a Struggle." But, as if in anticipation of this reading, after mentioning Gregor's restless dreams of the night before, the narrator begins the second paragraph by explicitly denying that this is a dream. His intent seems to be to say that dream hermeneutics are excluded. However, there is a slight ambiguity to this assertion. It is not directly attributed to Gregor's consciousness, though in context it reads as an answer to Gregor's mental question that opens the paragraph with a direct quotation. Gregor asks himself what has happened to him. Answer: it was no dream. This statement is rhetorically from the third-person narrator's viewpoint, though it can read as if it were a continuation of the direct quotation of Gregor's thought without the narrator's intervention. Gregor is awake, though the uncertainty as to who exactly thinks it is no dream opens the door to the possibility that it is a dream—if the assertion is Gregor's thought. In other words, if the reliable narrator asserts from his viewpoint that it is no dream, then it is no dream, for the rest of the text turns on the reader's acceptance of the narrator's reliability. However, if the assertion that it is no dream is Gregor's thought, then who knows? For the denial of dream in a dream is not uncommon. Gregor's consciousness is a problem for both him and the reader. Nonetheless, in the following I assume it is not a dream. Gregor will not wake up from it.

The reader with a bent for rhetorical questions can then ask whether the assertion that Gregor is an *Ungeziefer* should be taken as a metaphor. This question has taken up a great deal of critical discussion. The reader's mind may boggle at the thought that the assertion "Gregor is vermin" is in some sense metaphorical, since the assertion is semantically to be taken as quite literal. However, there is much semantic slippage in the term "vermin" (*Ungeziefer*), for it applies to a very large, indeterminate category of insects and even small mammals, generally associated with the filthy conditions in which they live. The word *Ungeziefer* has a wide range of connotations, suggesting the need for Jewish purification rituals, the German fear of defilement through dirt, childish associations with bugs, and general fears of degradation arising from disorder. Of course, it can be a pure metaphor: apparently Kafka's father called the Yiddish actor who was Kafka's friend vermin—a clear example of an extremely insulting metaphor.

However, the opening sentence says that Gregor Samsa is, literally, vermin. He is not said to be like one, nor is he simply compared to one; he is not the object of a simile or an analogy. There is no ambiguity in the statement that he is one, as he himself can plainly see when he looks down upon his now chitin-plated belly and squirming legs. Apparently he had a normal belly the night before, but now he sees that literally he is some kind of vermin. One may then ask whether he has literalized in his body a metaphor that might have been used against him. If so, then one can say that in becoming literal, the metaphor itself has undergone metamorphosis; and it is no longer a metaphor, no more than Gregor is still a Gregor, which he is and he isn't.

It is well known that Kafka considered metaphor to be a sign of language's weakness, of its incapacity to reach essential things directly. As he wrote several years later in a diary entry dated 6 December 1921, it is metaphor that makes him despair of writing. The very recourse to tropes implies recognition of language's failure. Yet it has been argued that Kafka is a creator of metaphors, or perhaps antimetaphors, like few others in the history of literature. Kafka's very example in numerous texts sometimes seems to suggest that one has no choice but to use metaphor to get around the incapacity of language to name things directly. It is an incapacity that the use of metaphor itself demonstrates. It is hard to deny that metaphors are to be found lurking at least as possibilities in much of what Kafka writes: trials that are life, castles that are transcendence, mice and dogs that are people. Perhaps to his chagrin, Kafka found himself wedded to a religious viewpoint that he did not want to honor, a view that presupposed that, after the world was named by divine logos, humanity's fall set up the conditions in which metaphor is necessary. But Kafka also knew that this tale of the fall of logos itself could be considered a metaphor, all of which suggests that it is necessary, given the alienation that the Fall inflicted on humanity, to literalize metaphor for whatever communication one might hope to make—in order to get around this metaphor of the Fall.

Kafka thus involves the reader in questions about the nature of language from the very beginning of the story, which means that he involves the reader in more general questions about the nature of literature. With the opening statement's deadpan realism, Kafka short-circuits the reader's immediate desire to see a wiggling metaphor or a six-legged symbol in Gregor's clumsy body. This is not to say that the image of the vermin may not be read at some level as the symbolic expression of a psychological state, perhaps Gregor's, perhaps Kafka's, but the image has to be read first as a concrete presence that disrupts the order of the conventional world that the modern reader more or less expects to be the basis for realist fictional narration. The same reader will make an exception in the case of narration that, following the rules of a so-called nonrealist genre, deviates from the normal order, as in fantasy and fairy tales, dream narration, or imitations of insanity. The reader may recall in this regard fantastic works by Gogol, E.T.A. Hoffmann, and the Dostoevsky of *The Double*, all of whom have, among others, been nominated as Kafka's precursors related to his creation of the big bug. The question is then what genre Kafka is following, or alluding to, or possibly satirizing.

The concrete image of vermin in distress as he/it tries to manipulate his/its new body disrupts the conventional order of realism that, however, the rest of the narration relentlessly maintains. The polarity maintained between the fantastic and the real means that Kafka is not exactly writing, strictly speaking, a realist text. For, in maintaining the incongruity between the initial disruption and the ensuing respect of realist conventions, Kafka keeps up an extraordinary equilibrium that makes of "The Metamorphosis" one of the great works of comic literature. This comedy is generated precisely by the fact that there is no deviation from the conventions of realism in the rest of the story; what happens is what in all probability would happen if Gregor really were to wake up a type of vermin with multiple legs, or so the story implies. In the narration itself, the narrator remains deadpan: no magic is invoked to explain this transformation, no psychic distortions. It is simply the case that the plausible order of the real does not hold sway one night, and for some unknown reason—if there is a reason—Gregor Samsa wakes up to find his body is now that of a large insect.

Thus one is not certain whether one can understand "The Metamorphosis" in terms of the literary genre Kafka has almost used since it is not clear what genre he has actually used. I stress here that the genre of a work of fiction often dictates what can happen in it. A fairy tale, a detective story, or a romance each presupposes and then narrates certain types of action. Surveying the possible genres involved, one might conclude that "The Metamorphosis" belongs to the genre of the fantastic tale. Entertaining that hypothesis, one can turn to the literary theorist Tzvetan Todorov and his seminal *Introduction à la littérature fantastique* (1970; *The Fantastic: A Structural Approach to a Literary Genre,* 1973). Todorov defines fantastic literature as a work that introduces what appears to be an initial suspension of the laws of reality: something happens that defies the conventions of realism. After this suspension, the fantastic usually takes one of two forms, the uncanny or the supernatural. In the case of the uncanny, a natural explanation of the fantastic happening may be found; with the supernatural fantastic, the laws of nature have been suspended because of some superior or supernatural reality. But in "TheMetamorphosis," it is notable that, after seemingly beginning a fantastic tale with its suspension of the laws of reality, Kafka follows neither path described by Todorov: there is no explanation found within the realm of nature for the metamorphosis, and there is no recourse to any possible explanation lying beyond the realm of natural law. (Todorov did not think Kafka's work is an example of the fantastic.) Gregor's transformation just happens, and that is all the text ever says about it. So, in terms of genre, Kafka seems to ask the reader to entertain the fantastic as a genre and then to deny that what has happened is the fantastic. This is another way of describing the ground rule for the creation of the comedy that ensues in "The Metamorphosis," for the characters themselves behave in conventional—exaggeratedly conventional—ways in response to the unjustified monstrosity: the son become insect.

These comments on genre should point up that Kafka's comedy depends not only on his maintaining a perspective that sets in relief the incongruous but also on the fact that Gregor's presence is comic only insofar as it is viewed inappropriately—which to say, as if his metamorphosis were somehow something to be dealt with in everyday terms. In and of itself he is simply monstrous, which perhaps explains why Kafka did not want to have a visual representation of a cockroach on the cover of the book edition of "The Metamorphosis." He did not want readers to think that it is a horror story. The reader, like the parents or Gregor himself, must not simply view the insect body, they must consider it and, being normal readers and parents and salesmen, consider it always inappropriately from some perspective or the other, usually from Gregor's perspective on himself, though also as a viewer watching how the other characters in the story react to Gregor and to one another. They all react with realistic responses that are farcical in their lack of appropriateness. Probably, there is no appropriate response to Gregor, which is another aspect of the fact that the tale is not a typical illustration of the fantastic. The fantastic genre presupposes there can be found an appropriate response because of an appropriate explanation. Gregor's case is indeed sui generis.

The constant intersection between the monstrous and the conventional recurs throughout the story. Let us now follow some of the ramifications of the initial event, especially the demands it makes on perspective and vision. For example, what does the newly fledged cockroach look at after surveying his numerous skinny legs? In Gregor's case he contemplates a picture on the wall that portrays a woman with her arm stuffed into a heavy fur muff. This is hardly the first thing one would expect but seems motivated by the simple fact that it is part of a realistic décor. The ambiguous image endows the scene with a peculiar erotic charge, for there is a bit too much fur in the image. With this image, irony has now entered the textual play, and critics rightly see here an ironic allusion to the founding book of masochism, Sacher-Masoch's *Venus in Furs* (*Venus im Pelz,* published in 1870). Moreover, Kafka undoubtedly knew, if Gregor perhaps does not, that the Austrian writer Sacher-Masoch used the name "Gregor" when he enjoyed being tortured by his fur-clad mistress.[2] Does the icon on the wall suggest there is something masochistically incongruous in waking up an insect and looking at a picture calculated to bring about erotic titillations? Does the incongruity between hard chitin and soft fur suggest some further ironic dimension? This is neither the first nor the last incongruous image of eros in Kafka's work, though perhaps nowhere else does one appear quite so ironically inappropriate.

The contrast between vile vermin and fur-decked beauty is less comically unsettling than the fact that multilegged Gregor's main concern seems not to be wondering about his new state; rather, he starts to worry about how he will make it to work on time. Realism is affirmed as the (ironic) genre for textual development. The practical world rules over the salesman's life in every situation, and, though Gregor is no longer Gregor, he still is Gregor the workaholic. He has a train to catch, and, faithful to the work ethic of his practical life, vermin or not, in his identity as Gregor he believes that he must be on way in order to make sales. The only apparent problem for the moment is that he does not understand how to maneuver his new limbs so that he can get out of bed—a most plausible concern for anyone who wakes up with more legs than normal. And so Gregor begins a not altogether misplaced meditation on what a miserable life traveling salesmen are obliged to lead. His meditation would be entirely justified in a realist framework, set up to indict capitalism and current society, though it may also appear that Gregor has greater problems at the moment than to bewail social injustice. Incongruity rules comically supreme.

He cannot even report in sick, which, indeed, his metamorphosis, conceivably a deviation from good health, might justify; he dares not be ill and ruin his track record for days without a sick report. A metaphor is hovering above the text here, since illness could offer an explanatory trope for Gregor's condition. As Kafka the insurance lawyer knew well, disease and sickness are among the most frequent metaphors to which we moderns have recourse when something goes wrong, and Gregor is tempted for a moment by this solution: he is ill. Pathology might then characterize Gregor's case, though it is not possible to say exactly how. The pathological obeys some law of etiology, or at least we so hypothesize, but nothing of that sort is used to explain Gregor's anomaly.

The medical metaphor continues comically at work when Gregor does not open the door to his room. His family's first assumption is that he must be ill, for nothing else could realistically explain his behavior, and so Gregor's sister, Grete, is sent to fetch a doctor. Interestingly, nobody thinks of sending for a priest, rabbi, or exorcist, since sin is no longer an explanatory principle in the modern world. The comedy then veers toward a version of bedroom farce that could be visualized on a stage with a different character at each of the three doors of the bedroom. Each character yells to remind Gregor that he is late—father, mother, and sister. What is logically entailed by metamorphosis is now carried out with comic pseudo-precision, for Gregor, 100 percent nonhuman in his physical parts, can answer only with a chirping or squeaking sound (*Piepsen*), this despite Gregor's apparently human consciousness that the narrator, with limited omniscience, describes and quotes, without comment. The narrator informs us that Gregor plays down to himself the importance of his altered voice by reflecting that it is in all probability caused by a cold, a typical ailment of traveling salesmen, a profession he continues to curse as he tries in vain to get ready for the day's work. Like his parents, Gregor realistically uses medical reasoning, for his new condition is indeed not redolent of human good health.

The philosopher Bergson might have described Gregor's reactions to his new body as a form of the comic in which mechanical actions are grafted onto the human, for in his repeated attempts to get ready for work Gregor acts like a machine destined to work according to the rules of the market he serves—even when facing inconvenient impediments such as the failure to master his numerous new legs. Or one might reverse the terms and see the human grafted here on the mechanical, for the insect body does resemble a kind of grotesque machine that Gregor, like a Cartesian pilot-soul lodged in a body-machine, must learn to manoeuver from within. In any case Kafka's sense of the mechanical nature of the body's motions, a source for the farce in "Description of a Struggle," underlies the deadpan farce that ensues when Gregor masters the technique necessary for a giant insect to get out of its human bed. The struggling salesman gives himself a time limit—by a quarter to eight he must be up and going—in order to motivate himself to accomplish this feat. Gregor had undoubtedly been reading self-help books.

Social rituals and business decorum are also called upon in "The Metamorphosis" for comic effect. A company "manager," the *Prokurist* who seems to stand second in command in Gregor's company, comes personally to see why Gregor missed his early train and has not begun his workday. With the visit of this representative of the exterior, practical world, the reader learns more about Gregor's standing in that world or, more precisely, in the world of work that has been Gregor's only world outside his family circle. In this scene Kafka brings the two worlds together so that the reader sees that Gregor has been extraordinarily limited by constant work, work interrupted only by moments of repose at home. The description of the manager's visit would be a scene of banal realism if Gregor were not hidden behind the bedroom door responding with squeaks while the mother is apologizing for the son with the obvious plea that he must be ill, the sister is sobbing, and the father is speaking to the closed door. The company representative becomes indignant that Gregor will not open and consequently threatens him. Kafka creates here a farcical version of the genre painting that an eighteenth-or nineteenth-century painter might have made to show the pathos of distress in the family—though the incongruity of it all transforms the scene's pathos into farce. To be sure, the manager's threats show that Gregor and his family have been entertaining illusions about

Gregor and their situation. In fact, as the story then shows, everyone seem to be deluded about the reality of the others' situation.

The description of Gregor's opening a door by figuring out how to hold a key in his insect mouth is the comic prelude to Gregor's first appearance to the world. The scene is viewed from Gregor's perspective. First, he looks at the window through which he sees the opposing building, a hospital, undoubtedly the appropriate building to be found next to Gregor's apartment, and ironists can delight in one more inappropriate allusion to illness. The ensuing scene is a domestic one that represents items symbolizing everyday life, replete with Kafkaesque newspapers and, on the wall, a portrait-photo of Gregor, from his army days, looking down in uniform at the vermin that begins to chirp an absurdly long speech to defend himself as a worthy employee. Like Joseph K. arrested one morning in *The Trial,* Gregor believes he may be the victim of slander. Gregor's self-defense here is, needless to say, incongruous as well as pointless, since, after all, it is highly unlikely that a visitor would stand still to listen to a speech given by a giant cockroach. Realistically, then, and to Gregor's chagrin, the *Prokurist* flees. In keeping with his relentlessly inappropriate view of things, Gregor thinks his failure to explain himself may endanger his job since the boss will think he does not want to work as hard as he should. The discrepancy between reality and response is again, to say the least, remarkable. Gregor represents to himself his situation as one in which he must convince the manager of his desire to work—or else the family will starve. There is a touch of Dickens in this conventional realism.

How does one usually react to the presence of large vermin in the house? The father reacts most naturally by arming himself with stick and newspaper to chase Gregor back into his room, as one might do with a rat that has ventured into one's home. The farce of body mastery continues when, facing the father, Gregor must figure out how to put his body into reverse. The father's hissing is an added note of realism, though the confrontation itself seems to many critics to be laden with symbolic meaning: it portrays the father–son confrontation that is the kernel of the Freudian Oedipal clash. There is here of course a father–son clash, though this is hardly an unconscious feature of the text. Kafka's comedy of representation is self-consciously in conformity with the dictates of the allegorical realism found in a Freudian perspective on family relations. The father's attack, pushing the bug back through a too-narrow door, is a marvelous parody of a Freudian reading of family dramas in which the father represses the son's desire. Gregor's father does what every Freudian father supposedly wants to do to his son: emasculate him in defense of his paternal power. Indeed, his paternal desire for power shows itself to be even more satirically Freudian in the second part of "The Metamorphosis."

The second part of this three-part drama describes the new rituals of family life as the family becomes accustomed to living with the vermin they continue to call Gregor. It also narrates, in good realist fashion, flashbacks that throw new light on the present scene of dereliction. The second part begins by bringing up the question of food, realistically considered in terms of Gregor's new needs. In Kafka's work, food and nourishment often play an important role in creating a quasi allegory. To be sure, the food motif reaches its ultimate expression in the hunger artist's turning starvation into an art form. Kafka's distrust of metaphor notwithstanding, nourishment is a near trope for an indefinite spiritual substance and even redemption. In "The Metamorphosis" Gregor begins to grow hungry, though, unlike the hunger artist, he discovers a nourishment he likes. Though at first dismayed that he longer delights in the fresh and pure milk that Kafka himself drank for his health, Gregor discovers that he likes garbage. Indeed, with only a few experiments, the devoted sister discovers that kitchen refuse is what the vermin prefers. There is self-directed irony in the fact that, as vermin, Gregor feeds on what Kafka's narratives regularly produce: the litter, filth, and trash toward which Kafka's world naturally tends in its entropic development. Gregor would be at home in Brunelda's apartment in *Amerika*. There is, to be sure, an ironic use of realism again, for what else would a cockroach desire to eat? With his remaining human vision of things, Gregor senses, in distress, that his preference for detritus is a measure of his fall. Of course, his preference for refuse also foreshadows his own demise as garbage, the end product of textual entropy.

Locked into his room and fed on table scraps, Gregor has as his main activity to listen to the family and learn what metamorphoses are taking place among them. He discovers that they are not so helpless as he had been led to believe, for the father has money Gregor did not know about; his plans for paying off his father's debts were founded on false ideas about the father's precarious situation. Unbeknownst to him, the family has not been spending all the money Gregor has given them each month. In short, Gregor, like his predecessor Georg, has been deluded.

Gregor also learns that his sister cannot abide looking at him, no matter how much time passes. The passage of time is realistically noted by the narrator's observation, such as, "Once, when already a month had passed since Gregor's metamorphosis" (*KA*, p. 157). There is something comic about this realist measuring of the unfolding chronology, as if each singular event in the routine of being a monster could be mapped out by the calendar. Marking time also allows Gregor to reason, using pseudo-probability, that the familiarity brought about by the passage of time should habituate his sister to his appearance. However, she refuses to enter the room when he is not hidden under a couch. Gregor's expectation that she might one day get used to him is another part of the comedy generated by his incongruous delusions. That probability can be measured by time is another such delusion. Set in contrast to expectations about the passage of time, however, is the fact that Gregor becomes accustomed to being vermin rather quickly, that is, almost as soon as he can use his legs!

With flourishes of pop rhetoric, Kafka ironically uses conventional kitsch to motivate much of the second part's narrative. After the routine of living with the giant bug has set in, Gregor's mother decides that she must see her son. She cries out her need in comic pathos: she is the good mother after all. This development is again a parody of what one might find in, say, eighteenth-century realist genre painting in which distraught parents and children engage in emotional posturing (though no giant insects figure in Nicolas Maes's or Jean-Baptiste Greuze's pictorial dramatizations of unhappy mothers or filial piety). In his own eyes, too, Gregor remains an ideal son. From his filial perspective he sees a concerned mother who naturally wants to come in to see him. She wants to see if he is eating properly, how he is behaving, and, in the most comic use of the medical metaphor, if he has perhaps gotten a bit better—"ob vielleicht eine kleine Besserung zu bemerken war" (*KA*, p. 158).

Despite the sister's revulsion, in keeping with realist conventions about family duty, she wants to help Gregor. With sisterly concern she notes that he has begun to crawl about, going up the walls, and hanging from the ceiling. With the precision of banal realism, the narrator describes her motivation to make things easier for Gregor by removing the furniture from his bedroom. His mother joins her daughter in the task at hand, though, using a mother's reasoning, she then decides that this is not a good thing to do, since it might make Gregor think that they have given up hope for an improvement in his condition—her realistic thinking will not relinquish the medical metaphor.

Upon seeing his sister at work, Gregor is panic stricken at the idea that, without the furniture, all the vestiges of his human past will disappear. Coming out of hiding, he runs about and finally fixes himself upon the picture of the woman in furs, covering it with his stomach and feeling comfort there by pressing it against her. This display of eroticism foreshadows, in comic grotesquerie, the forthcoming parody of explicitly Freudian encounters. Indeed, in this scene Gregor thinks of attacking Grete if she touches the picture—which the reader who does not see in this threat Gregor's final defense of his humanity can view as a variant on the incest motif found in the story.

The mother sees Gregor and, realistically enough, passes out. Grete goes to get medicine for her, Gregor follows to help, and the father arrives. The confrontation at the heart of the Freudian family drama is now prepared. And it is at this moment that Gregor, looking up from the floor, has a new perspective on the father, who, no longer the tottering old man of earlier days, appears in the uniform of a bank employee, well groomed and with powerful boots whose giant soles threaten to crush the astonished son. Many critics speak of the father's metamorphosis, though his is not a permanent change, and his appearance depends more on the son's perspective on the father and his power, not unlike the variation of the father's appearance in "The Judgment." Endowed with the accouterments of power, the Freudian father can punish Gregor for having broken out—as Grete says when speaking of her brother's bid for a brief liberation.

The only available weapons the father finds are apples, and accordingly he begins to "bombard" his son with fruit. Apples are often, as innumerable paintings have shown, associated with original sin in the Western, biblical iconic tradition. Kafka uses the association with a comic reversal. Rather than granting knowledge of sin, as weapons, the forbidden fruit is a weapon to be used against sin. Their round shape may also suggest another Kafkaesque reversal of perspective: rather than tearing out Gregor's testicles, the father implants globular objects in Gregor's back. And the parody of a son's Freudian fears of castration is completed when the mother comes out, her clothing falling from her, as she goes to embrace the father and, united with him, to plead for Gregor's life. Gregor's vision fails him at precisely this moment. Thus he cannot witness the "primal scene" that Freud saw as everybody's initiation into sex and paternal power—when, as a child, one sees the father possess the mother. Freudian theory holds that the viewer of the scene usually represses memory of the image. In Kafka's version thereof, Gregor's vision indeed fails at the crucial moment. In both versions, then, the result is more or less the same: the rebellious son attempts to erase or block the image of the father's power. And so the second section ends.

The third part of "The Metamorphosis" can be likened to the third act of a tragi-comedy. The curtain goes up on a Gregor who, again closed up in his room, is wounded, as is the symbolic fate of every son who has threatened to replace the father. The family leaves the door ajar as a gesture of sympathy for the absent son, which allows him to see that the father now appears the victim of the usual entropic downfall found in Kafka's work. Unable to stay awake in the evening, he falls asleep in his uniform, on which dirt has begun to accumulate. Gregor's perspective is that of a privileged witness to the drama taking place outside his room. In the evening, while the father dozes, Grete and the mother work unceasingly at various tasks. Gregor spends insomniac days and nights remembering a few friends and a couple of women and, caught up in ongoing delusion, thinking that he may soon take up his old life. New developments also take place in this microcosm of the fallen world. For example, an old widow is hired to help with cleaning. She is not afraid of Gregor, though she does not clean his room, contenting herself with occasionally disturbing him and taunting him by calling him old dung beetle (*Mistkäfer*). Whatever her entomological gifts, her apostrophes foreshadow Gregor's fate, especially when the new cleaning woman threatens to bash him with a chair if he does not stay in his place. Gregor the dung beetle is now condemned to live in growing disorder and filth.

The family takes in three boarders who resemble one another as three peas in a pod: three men with full beards, and all three equally without manners. The three resemble cartoon figures or characters in stage farce in which several characters act in unison. Their function is to humiliate the family with their imperious demands, while, unknowingly, showing Gregor how remote he is from the practical world in which men eat meat and potatoes with unrestrained fervor. In his room Gregor hears the boarders chewing, and he ponders again the food that he needs while the three mechanically gnash their teeth. These practical meat eaters have little in common with Gregor, or with Kafka, for that matter, though they bear a distinct resemblance to the father whom Kafka portrays, in "Letter to His Father," as capable of crushing bones with his teeth. By contrast, Gregor again foreshadows Kafka's hunger artist, for he knows a new hunger born of unsatisfied desire.

The desire presses itself upon Gregor when, by chance, one evening Grete plays the violin for the three boarders. Drawn by the music, the filth-covered Gregor sticks his head into the room where the family and renters are assembled. The latter are clearly unimpressed by Grete's playing and blow their cigar smoke out of their noses and mouths in a sign of impatient nervousness (with cigars that are like parodistic Freudian symbols of their power). Gregor listens and wonders what nourishment he needs. In his reverie he wonders whether music shows him what he needs, despite the fact that the narrator earlier has said that Gregor was not interested in music, that he wanted simply to help his sister in her study of music.

Music is an ambiguous topic in Kafka. It does not appear that he personally was greatly drawn to music, even if in Europe and especially Germany music was often considered the apex of artistic achievement. Kafka did not go to concerts as frequently as he went to the theater or cinema. However, at times, as in "The Metamorphosis," music is portrayed with the suggestion that it is the supreme art form or at least an art that offers spiritual nourishment. Music offers the deceptive image of a, if not the, transcendence that can be found nowhere else—or so argued the philosopher Schopenhauer, whom Kafka, like everybody else in his generation, read with intense interest. Perhaps Kafka attributes to Gregor his own attitude toward music: realizing that it is something that he, as a fallen being, cannot properly understand while at the same time recognizing that music can offer a nourishment beyond language, not to mention garbage. Music can even overcome language's entropic fall. Having said this, I stress that Kafka's attitude toward music seems at times to have varied, as we shall see in his very last story, in which he depicts a singing mouse, whose squeaking performances may well cast some doubt upon the supreme place often attributed to music. As shown by Nietzsche's early praise of and then rejection of Wagner, music was the subject of many a claim and counterclaim in the German cultural sphere. Nietzsche himself finally accused Wagner, as well as Schopenhauer, of being against life. Kafka knew Nietzsche's work very well.

So we can ponder the role of music in Kafka from several perspectives. From Gregor's perspective, music appears to perhaps transcend his fall, and he asks himself whether he is really an animal since music so engrosses him (*KA*, p. 185). This is the desperate thought of a human being who sees himself now in a fallen world of dirt in which he, the filthy insect, kicks up dust whenever it moves. (A metaphor is perhaps lurking there. . . .) However, Kafka cuts off any effusiveness about metaphysics and music by returning suddenly to incest and a parody of romantic fiction. Gregor fantasizes that he might beckon to his sister, bring her into his room, and not let her out again. He would explain his plans for her career, she would cry from happy emotion, and he would kiss her on the neck, now free of any collar. The suggested image of passionate insect kisses is not the least noteworthy example of Kafka's black humor, especially as it depicts family harmony.

In the scene with the three boarders, Kafka returns to the farce produced by respecting realist conventions. As verisimilitude demands, the guests are decidedly not happy to see Gregor crawling out of his room, and they are quick to announce their immediate departure (though not without wanting breakfast the following morning). The farce centering on the three gentlemen is contrasted with and offset by the question of Gregor's identity, which Grete broaches. She tells her parents that they get must try to get rid of the beast (*Untier*) they have been harboring in their midst, since it cannot be Gregor. It cannot be Gregor, since if it were, then it would realize that it cannot be there. Grete is a logician of a Kafkaesque sort, for she spins out a near-logical paradox. How can one be what one cannot be? If the beast were Gregor, then it/he would not be here, since it would have seen long ago that it/he is impossible for the others (*KA*, p. 143). Theological and metaphysical issues about identity, implicit in the story from the beginning, surface here in Grete's remarks. Suffice it to say for our purposes that if identity coexists with the body and its material being, then identity becomes most problematic, for the body is the locus of the fall; alternatively, the body reflects entropy, which finally denies identity to any body that has no constancy, except deteriorating change. Variations on this theme of the instability of the material body underlie the perceived threat of metamorphosis, which, from the Greeks and Romans through the current epidemic of vampires, is one of the constant themes of our culture.

Kafka was apparently not happy with the conclusion he came up with for "The Metamorphosis," and some critics have echoed Kafka's harsh negative judgment about the ending of his novella. However, it seems to me the published conclusion carries out with complete consistency the logical result of the fall of the body in time, that is, of the entropic development that subtends the entire novella. Gregor's dwindling away is complete when the forbidden fruit, stuck in his back, rots away and dust collects on the infected area. The narrative point of view ceases of course to coincide with Gregor's consciousness after he gives out his last breath, but few readers are probably greatly bothered by the change brought about by the fact that it is a newly omniscient narrator who tells of the family's fate after the hearty cleaning lady, having found Gregor's dead remains, informs the family that she has swept it out with the usual dirt. What readers undoubtedly do notice is a new perspective on the family: the three family members are ready to begin anew after Gregor's disappearance. Ignoring the demands of the three boarders—Herr Samsa resolutely tells them to get out—the three family members decide to go out of town to enjoy an outing. And, in hope of a new future, they join together in what is perhaps the unique case of a happy ending in Kafka's work, which probably made Kafka think he had truly failed by not failing.

Recalling the proposition, sketched out in the second chapter here, about the axiom of failure that underlies Kafka's work, one can speculate that Kafka was unhappy with the happy ending because, with this success, he had committed a logical failure. The family basks in its freedom after Gregor is gone, which means that the norms of conventional literary representation have won out over Kafka's deep conviction that successful representation can result only in failure. So one can read the diary entry of 19 January 1914, in which Kafka complains to himself that the ending of the work is unreadable and regrets that a business trip did not prevent him from finishing it. Perhaps only a writer like Maurice Blanchot, committed to the belief that literature is always a record of its own failure, could sympathize with Kafka on this point. For, through his essays written after the Second World War and published in book form in 1981 in *De Kafka à Kafka,* Blanchot has been an influential interpreter of Kafka, and it is interesting to see that, with incredible empathy, he could read the final lines of "The Metamorphosis" with a kind of horror. He is especially drawn to the image of Grete. Now that the parents think it is time for her marriage, she stretches out her young body, as if in anticipation of the joys of eros. For Blanchot this moment of awakening to life and its sensuality, this renewal of hope, this sign of the girl's desire to live, is the most horrible moment in the story: it is the most terrifying (*éffrayant*), since the girl wants to live, which, says Blanchot enigmatically, is a desire to escape the inevitable.[3] The inevitable is failure.

Up to this point I have largely interpreted "The Metamorphosis" using its narrative rhetoric and themes. Of course, almost every theme may seem to justify a theological, psychological, or philosophical inquiry. It is an understatement to say that for this reason a work like "The Metamorphosis" is particularly good at providing grist for every type of critical mill.

Blanchot, with his view of the essential self-referentiality of Kafka's work, can illustrate one aspect of the way the story opens up onto metaphysical speculation. The French writer thinks that the central theme of "The Metamorphosis" is an illustration of the torment of literature that, having for its object its essential lack (*manque*), drags the reader into a spiral where "hope and despair respond to each other without respite" (pp. 72–73). Life is exile from meaning, says Blanchot, and thus literature, in reflecting life, can be about only its own failure to mean anything. I think Blanchot is right to the extent that he shows that Kafka's texts are thus essentially self-referential in their designation of their failure to mean, from which pattern, apparently, the successful ending of "The Metamorphosis" represents a deviation.

One can reasonably ask why the meaning of metamorphosis should be construed as reference to literature. The answer is that this self-referentiality is unavoidably there precisely because Gregor's metamorphosis into an insect, with no explanation, turns him into a sign that denies meaning even as it challenges the reader to find a meaning—which is an essential function of a literary text. Critics from the earlier mentioned Wilhelm Emrich in the 1950s to the present have made this kind of argument. Gregor is a sign that one must interpret even as one knows that nothing can justify the belief that one has found a final meaning, for to find a final meaning would entail a denial of the literary text's functioning. Starting with his book *The Commentators' Despair* (1973), Stanley Corngold has been the major American critic to interpret the fall of logos in Kafka in these terms, especially with regard to "The Metamorphosis." In essays and books Corngold has advanced the view that Gregor is something like an opaque sign, a representative of language's despair about itself and the possibility of communicating anything. Corngold makes a powerful argument, making of Gregor an inexplicable demonstration of the inexplicable.

Nonetheless, readers do fix on various meanings that Gregor's chitinous body seems to suggest, often relying on elements of Kafka's biography or other of Kafka's works to buttress their argument. For the theological mind, Gregor's metamorphosis may well be suggestive of the universal Fall that humanity undergoes by being born into the Judeo-Christian world of original sin. Sin seems to attach to the body itself. Kafka certainly meditated on the doctrine of original sin and was not insensitive to the idea that the human body is itself the locus of the Fall. However, with regard to "The Metamorphosis" it may be asked why everyone in Gregor's world is not a cockroach since the fall into sin, as well as bodily existence itself, is perforce a universal fate. Moreover, the sister seems, to Blanchot's chagrin, to escape that fate rather handily. To the psychoanalytical reader, say, one who has read Walter Sokel's *Franz Kafka: Tragik und Ironie* (1964), Gregor may appear to be the victim of his Oedipal complex, another universal fate, though it is clear that Kafka parodies that possibility explicitly in the text (which is another side of self-referentiality in that the story anticipates interpretations of itself in the very unfolding of its plot).

Scoffing at theology and psychoanalysis, the Marxist or sociologically minded reader, with theorists like Adorno or Lukas in mind, may retort that Gregor's metamorphosis shows that he is a victim of the capitalist system, especially as expressed in his vociferous chirping against the harsh fate of traveling salesmen—being an insect version perhaps of Arthur Miller's Willy Loman in *Death of a Salesman*. It is true that Gregor may be a badly treated salesman, and, if he is not entirely delusional, he is right that he must put up with a dreary workload, though one hardly comparable to the slave-like treatment imposed on Karl Rossmann in *Amerika*.

However, to read "The Metamorphosis"as a Marxist allegory is usually dismally reductive, for Kafka's allegory offers no reason for this ordinary salesman to be singled out for metamorphosis. To which the critic determined to find Kafka's biography in everything he wrote will reply that Kafka is literalizing in Gregor what Kafka encountered in his daily family life. For example, the term "vermin" was used by Kafka's father to reprove what he did not approve—such as probably Kafka himself. But however suggestive may be this quasi fact, the real father's use of the term *Ungeziefer* as a derogatory metaphor really does not explain why this character, Gregor, in this story, "The Metamorphosis," undergoes such an absurd fate.

Let me now enlarge upon the meaning we might make of Gregor's metamorphosis, as well as Georg's suicide, with a few critical remarks, going beyond the commentary I have made up to this point, remarks that I hope are also applicable to the entirety of Kafka's work. In this regard earlier I discussed the problem in Kafka brought up by the question of whether elements in his texts make reference to historical or extratextual objects and events. The image of a man transformed into a large insect does not seem to have an extratextual referent, though both men and vermin exist in great numbers outside the textual world found in the story. In itself, that thought may not seem very helpful at first, though it does point up that Kafka's images come from the world. And, as Wittgenstein said in his Tractatus at about the time Kafka was writing "The Metamorphosis," the world is all that is the case, including all possible combinations of images or *Sachverhalte* that make up the facts of world. Fiction demonstrates, moreover, the remarkable fact that, once named, even fictional facts become part of the images of the world. Fictional images are images of the world we know once these images are represented. They become, as it were, thoughts about the world as well as in the world, so that countless times we have all, I assume, thought about a world containing Gregor Samsas. Through literature, the most improbable images become part of thought processes dealing with the world.

In his thoughts about the world, Kafka was rarely a discursive thinker, but he intuitively knew that his images were about the world as much as they were in the world. Thinking in images, he knew his images were taken from the world—for there is no other place to find images. This means that ultimately image-thoughts can be about only the world and relations in it. By saying Kafka was not a discursive thinker, I mean quite literally that he thought in images and hence could represent these images to convey thoughts. To this end he represented these images in writing. In contrast to thinking in images, discursive thought functions by extracting, as it were, abstract relationships from the images the world offers, finding laws and mathematical formulas as well as discursive generalities and relationships to simplify the messiness of the infinitely many images the world offers. In contrast to discursive thinking, thinking in images involves taking images from the world and placing them directly in relationship with one another, often in relationships never seen before, which may be then be interpreted in abstract terms. This is one function of literary criticism. Another function of criticism is to determine the context in which these images are to be placed for their relationships to be read. The challenge offered by "The Metamorphosis" is that the image of Gregor Samsa cannot, it seems, be converted into discursive thought—without making it part of an allegory, a symbol in a discursive system of thought. Or, conversely, Kafka has offered a new image to the world through which we can begin to think in new, discursive ways. It is a bit as if we saw the birth of the first, unique unicorn before there came to be a world of unicorns.

Let us look at this question of the image in historical terms, for it is noteworthy that Kafka began writing in an era that produced a great deal of experimentation, in art and literature, with the direct presentation of images having meaning without an immediate context. This came from a belief that the image in itself could communicate without being embedded in, say, an allegorical context provided by a preexisting story or myth. In the wake of Goethe's preference for symbol over allegory, symbolists and realists alike sought the exact image to signify directly a world. Mallarmé and Flaubert are associated with the most successful attempts at, respectively, using the unique image for symbolism and for realism. And one can also look outside the sphere of literature for the role images play in thought. In the late nineteenth and early twentieth centuries, thinking in images was hardly an exclusively literary matter. Thinking in images is to be found in science and philosophy. I pursue briefly this point here, since it offers meaningful analogies for understanding the entirety of Kafka's work.

In the world of science, Kafka's contemporary Albert Einstein described how he thought in images, not with mathematics, in formulating the first limited theory of relativity in 1905. He pictured to himself the consequences when, given that light travels at a constant speed, a light beam is perceived by two observers at different positions, say, one in a moving train, the other exterior to the train. One can visualize that time is perceived differently at the two positions, relative to the inertial system of the observer.[4] After developing the special theory with its images of moving trains and light beams, Einstein introduced acceleration into his picture of relativity by imagining elevators and objects falling within them, which led to the general theory of 1916. Without wanting to make of Kafka a scientist, I propose that one can see that comparable thought experiments, working out the consequences of relations pictured in the imagination, are found throughout Kafka's work.

Here I have already suggested that in "The Metamorphosis" Kafka asks what would happen if one woke up one morning and found that one was now an insect (or, later, what would happen if one found one morning that one had been arrested or was always hungry, or deathly ill, or a bridge, and so on). Kafka appears to violate the laws of reality, which Einstein also did. One thinks of Einstein violations of the then received views of temporality and space. In the end, with his theory of clocks that slow down, he redefined our received views. One might say Kafka offers an unending fantastic event, whereas Einstein ends by making the once fantastic a part of the real. In any case, with the image of vermin, Kafka is undertaking a thought experiment that, once the first image is posited, his fiction carries out by exploring the realistic probabilities of what might happen once the order of the real is contravened—contravened just one time. In "The Metamorphosis" the fiction turns on the use of an image to allow Kafka to experiment by asking "what if" and then following the probable results. What if the insulting metaphor Kafka's father used were suddenly not a metaphor? Which brings us back to the question, what if one day a dutiful son and practical businessman were to awaken in the so-called real world and find that he had been transformed into an *Ungeziefer*? The thought experiment is then to imagine what might be the consequences of this break in the order of banal reality, as imagined in the workaday world of Prague of 1912.

Science is hardly the only domain in which thought about, and with, images was taking place. Philosophers also tried to understand the iconic nature of language. Indeed, some critics believe that Kafka was receptive to Fritz Mauthner's critique of language in which Mauthner derided language as an instrument of true knowledge. He found in it an instrument for communication based on likeness but deformed by metaphor. In Mauthner's view, language is an imperfect product of evolution that can only imperfectly serve any human purpose, such as the defective representation of *Ähnlichkeiten*—similarities. Thinking in images might be conceived as a way of directly confronting the predicament posed by, or imposed by, language's approximations of images. If language offers only defective images, then it might appear that one strategy to get around it would be to think as directly as possible in images, such as in Kafka's work.

I would argue, in addition to Mauthner, that a useful analogy with Kafka's work is found, in philosophy, in the thinking about images undertaken by the Austrian thinker whom I cited earlier, the Ludwig Wittgenstein who tried to describe language as a servant of images and almost succeeded. In the *Tractatus* Logico-Philosophicus, published in German in 1921, Wittgenstein postulates that all language can do, when it does not lose itself in the abstractions of metaphysics, is to picture the relations of those images that are found in the world. Language is essentially iconic, and thinking in images is the only meaningful thinking one can do. In some ways Kafka resembles a comic Wittgenstein who takes pleasure in showing the disjointed images the world contains, and hence he shows the world that is indeed the case, a very wacky case.

In considering thinkers who theorized about images, one must also mention the Austrian doctor-philosopher Freud, whose work Kafka knew and used for his own purposes. Freud was in thrall to the power of images, which he envisaged as something like the ultimate reality at the disposal of the psyche in representing itself to itself. Thus he tried to elicit chains of images in his psychoanalytic practice. Turning to dreams, he analyzed them in the belief that the real life of the psyche comes forward in those enigmatic images that emerge at night when the superego is (almost) put to sleep. It is not hard to see some parallels between Kafka's creation of oneiric images and the Freudian search for those dream processes that portray the dramas of the psyche, dramas whose images psychoanalysis, like a form of literary criticism, transforms into discursive thought by interpreting them in light of Freudian theory. Kafka does no theorizing, though I have suggested that he turns theory into images, often in parodies that may well underscore the inadequacies of theories purporting to explain the working of the human mind—an abstraction in itself.

These references about various way of thinking about and in images point to Vienna as a center for the development of a modernist understanding of images and thought. (Einstein was not part of Viennese culture, though he had a brief stay in Prague, where it appears he may have met Kafka.) By focusing on modernity's belief in the power of images, one enlarges one's understanding of the rhetoric of modernity. This modernist context, as suggested earlier, offers an approach to Kafka's experimentation in narratives like "Description of a Struggle," which appear to borrow their techniques from the rhetoric of dream with the labile interconnections of changing images. But the use of the representation found in dreams is hardly the only kind of thinking in images in Kafka. Indeed, he seems always to have been looking for different techniques that would allow him to undertake imagistic thinking in narrative, including realist narration, folk and fairy tales, and fables. Quite simply, Kafka thought in images from his earliest days until the end of his life.

To clinch this argument, let us turn to the beginning of Kafka's life and an early example of this thinking in images, found in an often quoted letter, dated 27 January 1904, that Kafka wrote to his friend and near mentor Oscar Pollak. In describing the goal of writing, he wrote that one should read books that bite and stab the reader. He asked, If a book we are reading does not wake us with a blow of the fist on our skull, to what end are we reading the book? Rejecting happiness as the goal of reading—since one can be happy without reading—he concluded these thoughts in the letter by saying that, like a suicide, a book must be an ax striking the sea frozen within us.

One is tempted to translate these violent images into the discursive thought of psychology or philosophy. One can say, probably correctly, that, with the image of the ax, the young Kafka envisaged literature as a way of breaking down the reification of perception that blocks our receptivity to the world. Many modernists, as different as Proust and the Russian formalists, had in mind something comparable to this goal. Or one might interpret the image of the ax to mean that Kafka wanted to force the reader to recognize the limits of what can be said about things of transcendental interest. What can be said discursively is not much, an idea with which Wittgenstein agreed, as he implies in the concluding seventh aphorism of the *Tractatus* to the effect that whereof one cannot speak, thereof one must be silent. A book qua ax would show those limits of language and smash through them like an ax blow cracks ice . . . perhaps. So we might say that with the image of the ax Kafka is showing us what can be done, pointing to a way toward the mystical that Wittgenstein held to be beyond language's capacity to articulate. With the ax Kafka is pointing to that breakthrough he always wanted to achieve, one that might be likened to a suicide, an experience about which there is perforce little discursive thought. It is uncanny that several years after writing this letter, he did think he had achieved his literary breakthrough with a suicide, namely Georg's.

Let us clarify a point about Kafka's thinking in images, perforce couched in language, as he experimented to see whether they offered access to whatever might lie beyond language. What lies beyond language is perhaps impossible to know. However, it is clear that Kafka did not think that beyond language lies a realm of ineffable feelings, as the Romantics often held. Rejecting this idea, he wrote a letter, dated 18–19 February 1913, to Felice Bauer to tell her that it is a fallacious belief to think that the limitations of language stand out when one compares language to the infinity of feelings to be expressed. Rather, for Kafka the critical issue is language's inability to get directly to essential things, and they are not inchoate feelings.

What does the idea of thinking in images bring to an understanding, if understanding is to the point, of Gregor Samsa? As an image, a comically detailed image in language, the insect seems to break down the way in which neat conceptualization limit the world. Hence one might speak of its ax function. The image of the man-vermin does so with a strong emotional component, for disgust, repulsion, or fear can coexist with the comic incongruity of the image. Saying this, I use discursive language to say that the polyvalent image points us toward all the conflicting directions that Kafka felt in living, at once rejection and the intoxication of creation and the impossibility of overcoming the body that chained him to existence, as well as the hilarity of having such a weird thing as a body in the first place.

I am not alone among critics to have suggested analogies between Kafka and Wittgenstein, though most have not insisted on the analogous role of thinking in images found in the young Wittgenstein and Kafka. I want to conclude here, however, with considerations of the later Wittgenstein's thought and analogies with Kafka. Wittgenstein rethought the iconic nature he attributed to language in the *Tractatus,* but, in reducing the role images play in what he called language games, he continued nonetheless to be concerned about the way images function in language use. For example, he asked how one talks about the ambiguous image that can look either like a duck or a rabbit. Depending on the aspect that one perceives, the same figure changes from one animal to the other without the figure changing shape. (This ambivalent duck-rabbit image, first noted by the American psychologist Joseph Jastrow, is available in many versions on the Web.) This is aspect perception. It plays a key role in Wittgenstein's later philosophy, in which he thought that seeing things as something is essential to understanding how we mean things with images. The simple example of the image of the duck-rabbit and the not-so-simple interpretive games it may involve can illustrate a central problem in dealing with Kafka's images. The varying ways language has meaning dependent upon aspect viewing finds an analogy in Kafka's images. Depending on our perspective on the images—which is within limits a matter of choice—we can view images as different things with no change in the image's shape. For example, many of Kafka's images can be seen either as subjective projections or as objective dramatizations of the world—ducks or rabbits, as it were. It depends on the aspect that one perceives. Moreover, this means that, after viewing a duck or a rabbit in the figure, one can switch over to the other aspect. This interpretive freedom is a normal part of dealing with the world and its images, at least some of its images, especially the labile images of the world that a writer selects for iconic representation.

Kafka was aware that his texts present images that change their aspect depending on the perspective of the viewer. Sounding like late Wittgenstein in a letter of 10 June 1913 to Felice Bauer, he spoke precisely of the perspectival viewing found within "The Judgment," telling Felice that the story cannot be explained, for the friend in the story is hardly a real person. Rather, since the story is perhaps the tour or *Rundgang* around the father and son, the changing image (*wechselnde Gestalt*) of the friend is the result of a perspectival change (perspectivische Wechsel) regarding the relationship between father and son. Kafka's own formulation makes it clear that he was well aware that his texts oblige perspectival viewing, taking the reader around the image and allowing the reader to perceive different aspects.

Perhaps no image in Kafka lends itself more to aspect viewing than Gregor Samsa. From one perspective, Gregor the vermin is an image of alienation from language and hence community. He is a thing. But, from another perspective, he/it is the image of an alienation in which the helpless sufferer is locked within a repulsive body. He is human. From one perspective, he is "it"; from another, it is "he"—all referring to the same image. Grete wants to limit the aspect viewing to one image so she can get rid of it, but it is also he, the brother. Aspect viewing thus brings up the question of personal identity. What is identity when the image is the same but the iconic aspect can be radically different according to the perspective? Only the cleaning lady seems immune to the problem, for she knows a beetle when she sees one.

The critical reader wants to translate Kafka's often weird and distorted images into discursive thought, using the language of psychology or philosophy or the rhetoric of literary criticism. One uses such language when one says, for example, that with the image of an ax Kafka envisages the function of literature to be the breaking down of the reification of perception that prevents our receptivity to the world. Or, to consider again "Description of a Struggle," with its image of a supplicant who smashes his head in prayer, one can say in discursive terms that Kafka wants literary communication to force the reader to recognize the limits of what can be communicated. And the image of a suicide, if considered an act of violent expiation, might appear, to use discursive terms, to communicate the recognition that ungrounded guilt pervades our cultural space and condemns us one and all. All of this discursive thought may be true, but of course it lacks the specificity of Kafka's images: the book conceived as an ax suggests many other possibilities or aspects that wincing readers can pursue as they change their perspective on the image. The critic can point out that the image of Georg's suicide in "The Judgment," his plunging down into the water, seems to have something in common with the young Kafka's ax hitting the frozen sea within. And we can conclude that, with the image of Georg's self-execution, with his going under, Kafka found his ax, for with it he broke through the ice and found the writing that indeed acts like a suicide.

Chapter 5

The Trial and "In the Penal Colony"

Kafka had made much progress in 1914 in writing *Der Process* (Kafka's spelling of *Der Prozess* or *The Trial*) when he interrupted work on the novel in order to write a story, *In der Strafkolonie* ("In the Penal Colony"). He returned to the novel but did not put it into finished form (which has made it a virtual requirement for future editors to argue about how to order the text). Written in tandem, the novel and the story share a kind of reverse symmetry: the novel portrays a trial and execution from the perspective of a condemned man, whereas the story shows a judicial condemnation viewed by a presumably objective viewer. In *The Trial* the law and the courts that apply the law are shadowy, neither named nor seen. By contrast, in the story, the procedure for adjudication and the application of the law are explained in detail to the observer, a traveler visiting the penal colony. Indeed, the application is supposed to be demonstrated to him when the law is written out on the defendant's body—or such would have been the case if the execution had gone as planned.

If we entertain the idea of aspect viewing, introduced in the previous chapter, it may appear that Kafka intends, in *The Trial* and "In the Penal Colony," to elaborate, on a large scale, contrasting perspectives on one image that contains two aspects, that of the trial and the judgment. I have suggested that, depending on the perspective adopted, Kafka's images can appear to be either projections of a subjective world or dramatizations of the objective world. Both perspectives are equally plausible with regard to "The Judgment" and "The Metamorphosis." In *The Trial* and "In the Penal Colony" Kafka has in a sense made a first choice for the reader by choosing two aspects of perspectival viewing with regard to the image of law and justice. Since Kafka did not complete *The Trial*, one may assume that he felt he had not worked out the question of perspective to his own satisfaction. But, with the publication of *The Trial*, the completed work "In the Penal Colony" takes on new dimensions. The representation of the image of the law, throughout *The Trial* and "In the Penal Colony," works to change the reader's perspective on the law, as it appears and disappears.

The Trial centers on an ordinary man, the bank employee Joseph K., who is arrested one morning and is then tried without knowing what the charge is or even where the court is. He is not told what law he has violated. He is simply told that he is under arrest, but he is not incarcerated. As the novel develops, Joseph K. increasingly resembles a man stumbling forward in the dark, looking for clues to his own fate. He becomes convinced that he is on trial, a *Process,* even if it is handled by judges he is not allowed to see. He then hires a lawyer, tries to make useful connections, and attempts to figure out what is an appropriate response to his unseen accusers. He remains uncertain about what to do until finally two executioners call upon him and kill him after he rejects their suggestion to commit suicide. Joseph K. offers at once the image of a unique man and, from another perspective, in an almost medieval sense, an image analogous to the Everyman of the fifteenth-century morality play (or *Jedermann,* updated in a modern version in 1911 by Kafka's Austrian contemporary Hugo von Hofmannsthal). Joseph K. is an Everyman who, in being executed in a remote quarter of his city, by clown-like executioners, is also an absolutely unique case. The reader is challenged to decide whether the novel offers an image of universal fate, namely that we are all "condemned" to die, as the banal judicial metaphor contained in ordinary language puts it. Or, alternately, one could view Joseph K. as an individual in a specific culture in which one lone man must cope with the bureaucratic machinery of a developed industrial society.

A conspectus of the novel's reception by a few major critics shows the perspectival viewing of critical response to the novel. On one hand, critics have often seen the novel's plot as an allegory about the arbitrary but absolute power of bureaucratic structures; on the other hand, they have seen it as a dramatization of a guilt-ridden self, acting in an allegorical representation, often as a projection of the image of that self on the world. From this latter perspective critics see in the condemned man an expression of an individual self, perhaps Kafka's, perhaps the Jewish self in Kafka, or perhaps a projection of the psyche of the character Joseph K. Or, equally often, they see the novel's central image as an allegory of humanity's universal absurd fate or, less metaphysically, as an image of the fate of a man condemned to live in a bureaucratic state in which alienation is a universal condition. The latter reading may culminate in viewing the novel as an anticipation of the workings of the Nazi or Communist totalitarian state.

A passage in Kafka's diary, dated 23 July 1914, is often cited by critics to show that Kafka was dramatizing his own psyche in *The Trial.* In this entry, written after Kafka had broken off his engagement to Felice Bauer, Kafka discusses his meeting with her in Berlin in a hotel room, which, he says, resembled a "courtroom." Kafka felt he was on trial for not wanting to be married, and of this he was certainly guilty. The Freudian critic Walter Sokel even suggests that, upon dissolving the engagement at that time, Kafka felt guilty not just toward Felice but also toward his own family and in general toward the "course of life" (*Lebensstrom*).[1] Kafka felt guilty that he had not had the strength to continue with plans for marriage, to found a family, and, in short, to be normal—meaning the normal son who accepts the tribe's law. Sokel sees these three moments of guilt as inherent to the structure of the novel. From the Freudian viewpoint, guilt is finally the expression of the son's feeling about having been found lacking when judged by the father interiorized in the psyche of every son. Joseph K. is thus guilty, since it suffices to have a father to be guilty. Variants of this subjective perspective are repeated dozens of times in studies of Kafka, perhaps the most interesting expression of which is to be found in Canetti's reflections on what he calls Kafka's "other trial"—his project to marry Felice.[2]

Contrasting with the thinking of scholars like Sokel, who uses Freud with much finesse, is another type of subjective reading of *The Trial,* represented first by Wilhelm Emrich. Emrich sees "the court (*Gericht*) as the mirror image of K.'s soul (*seelisches Spiegelbild K.s*)."[3] The trial is an expression of Joseph K.'s inner condition, which Joseph K. himself obscurely realizes for a second—that he himself bears responsibility for his being arrested. Emrich's perspective sees an allegory of subjectivity turning on the idea that Joseph K. is guilty precisely because he subsequently denies his guilt. Since it is a psychic allegory, Emrich argues that *The Trial* contains no religious dimension, which means the court has no relation to the divine. I personally find Emrich's reading unconvincing, finally, because one cannot eliminate contradictions in the novel and nonetheless view it as the image of a psyche rent by contradictions. Nor does the subjective locus of guilt require that an angry deity, to paraphrase Pascal, not be lurking somewhere in the novel.

Another type of subjective perspective views the trial, born of K.'s anguish and doubts, as an image set in a dream. A variant of a Freudian perspective, the representation of images such as those found in dreams are considered to be a mimetic projection of unconscious inner states. It must be said that Kafka himself unintentionally invited the reader to adopt the oneiric perspective when he wrote a short story narrating "Ein Traum" ("A Dream"), in which the dreamer is Joseph K. Kafka published this short story in *A Country Doctor*—when he apparently had no intention of publishing the novel to which the story seems to belong.

Minimally, "A Dream" shows that at one point Kafka had the idea to associate a dream with a Joseph K. (and one can argue he used the same name for two different characters). In the story, Joseph K. approaches a festive graveyard, sees two men plant a tombstone, and watches as an artist begins to put gold lettering on it, after which he falls into the grave that has been prepared for him: he looks up from the hole and sees his name on the tombstone. Thereupon, as the last line says, in enchantment he awakes. Comparing *The Trial* to this story, the reader may note that the two men holding the gravestone correspond to the two assassins who kill Joseph K. and that the story's artist somewhat recalls the painter in the novel, Titorelli. These are teasingly imprecise analogies. If, as most scholars think, "A Dream" was written some time after Kafka abandoned *The Trial,* then it appears that Kafka may have returned to his unfinished novel in a desire to find or create a vantage point from which to view it himself. He perhaps wanted to experiment with the idea that his image of the trial could be viewed as an oneiric image produced by Joseph K.'s mind lost in a nightmare.

The image of Joseph K. as a figure of a universal allegory offers a plausible objective perspective on the novel, especially, if one reads it unmotivated by the desire to seek out the image of Kafka or his putative guilt. A number of influential writers have espoused this view of Joseph K. Notably, the young Albert Camus saw a universal allegory in the novel's religious inspiration, a work almost illustrative of what Camus saw as the essential and universal absurdity of human existence. In *The Myth of Sisyphus,* Camus writes that in *The Trial* we see "the moving face of man fleeing humanity, finding in his contradictions reasons for believing, raisons for hope in fertile despair, and calling life a terrifying apprenticeship of death."[4] To my mind it is not clear what this hope in despair might be. Perhaps Camus wanted to differentiate Kafka's putative allegory from his own allegorical novel, *The Stranger,* which can be read as a commentary on or even a correction of *The Trial* in its portrayal of Meursault, an "absurd man" condemned to death by a court that judges him unworthy of life.

Camus's contemporary and one-time friend, the writer and philosopher Jean-Paul Sartre, also saw *The Trial* as a text illustrating the objective world, though in more specific terms than Camus, since Sartre suggests, in his earlier mentioned essay on Jewish identity, *Anti-Semite and Jew* (1946), that perhaps one can see the hero of *The Trial* as the European Jew who constantly finds himself engaged in a long trial in which he does not know his judges and hardly knows his advocates or what he is accused of. The Jew knows only that he is considered guilty, with a judgment perpetually put off, so that each precaution the Jew takes only reinforces the belief in his guilt until, sometimes, as in the novel, he is dragged off and killed on a vacant lot.[5] Sartre thus viewed *The Trial* as an allegory of the trial inflicted on European Jews by the omnipresence of anti-Semitism, which eventuated in the death camps. One may conclude that atheist French philosophers saw a more objective image in Joseph K. than German professors, who, perhaps because they shared Kafka's cultural context, viewed Kafka's work as the projection of his psyche. This appears to be a normal state of affairs, once we accept that Kafka's images permit or even demand aspect viewing as a part of their interpretation, which is, to say with Wittgenstein, a normal part of much language use.

These perspectives on *The Trial* can orient us in our viewing *The Trial* from within, as it were, as well as from without. The notion of aspect viewing suggests that at any given moment in the novel the reader may see a universal allegory or a nearly demented projection of anguish in a disjointed narrative that changes the perspective in each chapter. Moreover, whatever the perspective one adopts in reading *The Trial,* one should not lose sight of the importance of the Judeo-Christian cultural context. It is in this context that it makes sense to consider that the supreme function of language is to gain access to the law and the originating logos and to reveal what one must do to undertake the impossible task of regaining the lost paradise of humanity's origins. The quest for the law is thus incumbent upon all. In addition, it is of singular importance that in Jewish tradition priests and judges have an overlapping function in revealing the law and judging in God's name. *The Trial* is replete with absent judges and perhaps an absent deity, but it does offer a priest, supposedly with connections to the judges, who interprets the law for Joseph K. The novel also has a talkative artist who is something of a priest-judge, an artist undoubtedly emblematic of the fact that, in the wake of Romanticism, modernity has made of the artist a surrogate priest and scribe who should be able to offer essential revelations. Kafka's artist, like his priest, is associated with the judges. Both are faint but distorted reflections of those who were once responsible for finding God's will as revealed in the Torah and who were then responsible for the adjudication of legal matters—much as Hebrew scribes once did.

Thus *The Trial* draws on Christian and Jewish tradition for its chiaroscuro images of guilt and innocence. Not only is a Catholic priest an interpreter of the law for Joseph K., but the vision of original sin that hovers over the novel owes as much to the Church's prosecution of sinners as it does to the Jewish myth of the fall and expulsion from the Garden of Eden. Indeed, it is pointless to argue which tradition offers a more pointed version of the original sin and guilt for which death and, especially, knowledge of death's inevitability are the punishment.

Both Jew and Christian may, for different reasons, be sensitive to the way Kafka's invisible courts and judges are also redolent of the Church's judicial structure and the way the ecclesiastical courts were organized in a system parallel to the official courts of Christian monarchies, often acting as a shadowy system working behind the façade of the official juridical system. For the Church traditionally claimed for itself the role as the unique interpreter of the scriptures and thus the final arbitrator of the meaning of the law. With regard to procedure, analogies to *The Trial* are found in the way the Church tribunals, unlike the common law courts, did not (and do not) follow the adversarial system in applying the law. Based on the Roman civil law, the procedure of a canonical court was akin to the inquisitorial system, with judges leading the investigation (which is still true of many European judicial systems). Joseph K. might think that the defendant usually has the favorable presumption of law, but he would be well advised to know that in the canonical court there are also situations in which the burden shifts to the defendant: the assumption is that he is guilty.[6] Or, as the very Christian Kierkegaard's priest notes at the end of *Either/Or,* one is always wrong against God.

Many readers will read Kafka from the perspective of European history as it murderously unfolded after Kafka, which means, as suggested earlier, that they see in *The Trial* a foreshadowing of Hitler's totalitarian state or Stalin's regime, built on the assumption of universal guilt. There is much to be said for this perspective, for it is certain that the lawyer in Kafka was clearly sensitive to the possibilities of the abuses of bureaucratic power, even before the Nazis and the Communists established their police states. But one should be aware that the Austro-Hungarian bureaucracy for which Kafka worked was not part of a totalitarian state, whatever might have been its deficiencies. In fact, Kafka's own work in the state insurance firm allowed him on occasion to play an adversarial role in favor of workers' rights. But, if we use a double historical perspective on *The Trial*—looking forward and backward at the same time—we can see that, if Kafka anticipates in the novel the creation of, say, the nightmare bureaucracy of some modern states, then it is in large part because he meditated on the possibilities inherent in that bureaucracy in the more or less liberal empire in which he worked.

Kafka's view of a totalitarian bureaucracy in *The Trial* was doubtless influenced by the Russian novelist Dostoevsky. Kafka was especially sensitive to the allegorical chapter in *The Brothers Karamazov* called "The Grand Inquisitor," probably the most important European political allegory written before *The Trial*. In Dostoevsky's novel the rationalist brother Ivan tells his Christian brother Alyosha about a "poem" he has written describing Christ's return to the world after fifteen centuries' absence. Christ walks in the streets of Seville, bringing joy to the populace, but then is confronted by the Grand Inquisitor, who promptly arrests Him. Promising to burn Him at the stake the next day, the Inquisitor explains to Christ that it has taken all this time for the Church to rid the world of Christ's pernicious influence; as the priest-judge explains in chastising Him, Christ promised freedom to humanity, which is the last thing that humanity really wants or even needs. The Church has corrected Christ's error, and the Inquisition has been established to maintain the order that the Church has finally established. Christ, the paradigm of innocence, is condemned as guilty by the priest Inquisitor—policeman, judge, and executor in one office. In fine, the Church bureaucracy uses its courts to maintain a reign of universal guilt to ensure its power over the innocent, not unlike the way the Soviet bureaucracy under Stalin inculcated a belief in universal guilt in order to ensure its hold on power. Moreover, as a student of Jewish history, Kafka could hardly have been unaware of the use of the Church's legal power specifically against Jews. The Spanish and Portuguese inquisitions sought to police belief and condemn those who even secretly might harbor unacceptable ideas. With this compelling example in mind, I would argue that *The Trial* thus finds its origins as much in the history of Christianity as in Jewish tradition or in the oppressive possibilities Kafka saw in modern bureaucracy.

After these general considerations of perspectival viewing and context and before making a more detailed examination of *The Trial,* I offer a practical caveat: there are two versions of the novel now on the market, with translations based on both (and there are probably other versions available on the Web). The first version of the novel, until fairly recently the only one, was compiled by Brod, published in 1925, and translated by the Muirs in 1937. A second version has been proposed by the Fischer critical edition of 1990, edited by Malcolm Pasley. This later edition follows the manuscripts more closely than Brod's version. To be sure, Brod's arrangement of the chapters is largely followed in the critical edition, and in the case of the novel's first chapter Brod's editing may actually be preferred. The critical edition separates the section called "The Arrest" from those sections entitled "Conversation with Frau Grubach" and "Then Fräulein Bürstner." Brod combined the three sections into one chapter. There is something logical about Brod's editing: in his version the chapter begins and ends with the novel's protagonist, Joseph K., in the same position, namely in bed.

The novel begins when Joseph K. awakens, in bed, and waits for his breakfast, but to no avail. At the end of the chapter, in Brod's version, after being arrested and spending a day in the office, he goes to bed, though not without having kissed his neighbor Miss Bürstner with voluptuous relish. Beds are important images in Kafka. From *Amerika* to *The Castle,* his exhausted heroes are always looking for one, or, finding themselves in one, they then talk, have new experiences, and occasionally get much-desired sleep. Gregor Samsa undergoes his metamorphosis in bed; Georg's father undergoes his transformation in bed when he rises up like a giant. Beds are for Kafka a recurrent locus of fatigue, dream, and revelation. Moreover, since the chapters of *The Trial,* like those in the two other novels, are often disjointedly independent units of narration, Brod's framing the first chapter with a bed as its central locus gives the chapter a significant unity. It suggests that Joseph K.'s awakening is a passage into a new world, one born of sleep, and one that is encapsulated by the waking and sleeping moments. It reinforces the oneiric perspective, though of course that does not eliminate other perspectives.

In short, the Anglophone reader may well consider picking up the Muirs' classic translation, still in print, and then comparing it with any of several recent translations to get a sense of the importance of editing. Whichever edition readers open, however, they find that the first sentence sets out the novel's central image in concise form: "Jemand musste Josef K. verleumdet haben, denn ohne dass er etwas Böses getan hätte, wurde er eines Morgens verhaftet" (*Der Process, KA,* p. 7). We can gloss and translate this often-commented-upon three-part sentence by reading that somebody in the exterior world must have slandered K. or was spreading lies about him, since, without his having done anything wrong—apparently he thinks he is innocent—one morning he was arrested. The German is not so straightforward as my gloss suggests, since, as critics have often noticed, the subjunctive mood "hätte" in German indicates that this is Joseph K.'s opinion of himself: he thinks he is innocent. But the subjective coloring leaves open the possibility that he may not be.

It is notable that, as we noted earlier, in his diary Kafka considered K. to be guilty, which leads many critics to read the novel as if K. were guilty of manifest bad faith by not recognizing his guilt. I find this idea difficult to accept. One does not have to think that Kafka was wrong about Joseph K., though this is possible, to think that in his diary entry Kafka was considering the final result of Joseph K.'s trial: the execution of Joseph K., like a dog, does indeed show that the court found him guilty. But almost any reader who is innocent of or ignores Kafka's diary will probably find K. innocent on the basis of ordinary jurisprudence. By ordinary standards he has committed no crime. (Joseph K.'s behavior with women has provoked hostile reaction among some critics, but it is usually not a criminal offense to be an arrogant cad.) However, the laws by which the hidden court judges are also hidden, so we must read with a double perspective: K. offers an image of innocence from one perspective and an image of guilt from another, which is a difficult perspective to adapt, to be sure, since we do not know where to position ourselves to have that perspective. Perhaps this is no more difficult, however, than trying to figure out why all of humanity is always guilty.

From a strict Judeo-Christian perspective, Joseph K. is guilty as the result of original sin, the original infringement of God's word, or the patriarch's law. As the Zürau aphorisms make plain, Kafka was fascinated by the myth of original sin, which he, in a rather original way, attributed to impatience. A modern reader of *The Trial* like Camus revolted against the idea that one could be guilty a priori, and so Camus proclaimed, in *The Myth of Sisyphus,* that once we recognize the world's absurdity, then we feel our innocence through and through. Camus believed he saw the remains of religious doctrine in Kafka and for that reason did not confer total "universal" status on Kafka's work, which he otherwise saw as exemplary in its confrontation with the universe's absurdity. However, Kafka was also revolted by the idea of a priori guilt, and we shall see that Camus's revolt against the idea of original sin is outlined in Joseph K.'s conversation with the priest in the penultimate chapter of *The Trial* when he wonders how an ordinary human being can be assumed to be guilty when he is not even granted access to the law. Joseph K. thinks throughout the novel that he is innocent.

Guilty or innocent, he surely does face the absurd. The confrontation with events that are absurd by all standards begins in the first chapter; and it is an understatement to say that the irrational invades Joseph K.'s bedroom. He is arrested by two agents or guards, who have no means of affirming their identity. They do not know why Joseph K. is arrested or what may happen to him, nor are any laws cited that he may have violated. Joseph K. is simply arrested and ordered to dress in absurdly appropriate black attire in order to meet the supervisor in the next room, which is also the chamber of Miss Bürstner. Nothing much happens there, however, for Joseph K. learns that, although he is arrested, he is free to go to work. He learns that his insistence on his own innocence is not helping his case. From one perspective, it appears that K. could be having a bad dream, for these incongruous events are linked in a way that recalls the absurd concatenation of events in dream. But, from another perspective, it appears that things are unfolding as they really might if the irrational were to invade the conventionally real world. It is as if, for example, some arbitrary power were abusing its capacity to determine reality—somewhat as if agents of the Inquisition had come for a visit. This is not unlike what we have seen in "The Metamorphosis," in that Kafka asks what would happen if the order of conventional reality were one morning disturbed. Demanding an explanation for this disorder, the reader's mind flits about trying to think of the hidden laws that could justify K.'s arrest and thus render it explainable. The thirst for rational realism is, as Kafka knew well, unquenchable, but no more explanation for the arrest is offered than for Gregor Samsa's metamorphosis.

Joseph K. is now, or will be, or perhaps even has been on trial. The philologist can point out that the German word for "trial" is *Prozess*, earlier spelled *Process,* the spelling Kafka used. The earlier spelling shows that the word comes from the Latin *processus,* which gives English the word "process." *Process* in German retains the meaning of a series of causally related events, such as a chemical "process," as well as the meaning of "trial." The word can designate both legal proceedings (a *Verfahren*) and a phenomenon embodying natural laws (typically, a *chemischer Prozess*). Kafka was quite aware of both meanings, one designating legal proceedings and the other, the unfolding of natural phenomenon. Kafka was a lawyer by training, though his first choice of university field had been chemistry, a *Fach* that he admittedly did not study very long. But the double meaning of the title allows another double perspective.

From an objective perspective on the work, the reader may see that the law in the name of which K. is condemned to death is as much a part of nature as of culture. It may be part of the necessary working of natural law, law conceived as a description of natural necessity. Alternatively, of course, the law may also be part of the arbitrary working of prescriptive justice or the law that uses cops and judges. The aspect viewing here is subtle, reflecting the fact that the relation between prescriptive law and descriptive law is complex, for its history begins with the history of the idea of law. The ancients were able to conflate the two. To moderns, like Kafka and Camus, the natural law that condemns all to death can appear to be a form of injustice, and they may appear accordingly to judge natural law by human law. Aspect viewing comes into play, for the same *Process* can be viewed as natural or unnatural as the viewer changes perspective, though whatever the perspective one adapts, Joseph K., guilty or innocent, is condemned. The basic figure remains.

In the first chapter Joseph K. is arrested for a crime that is not revealed to him, nor is it known by the third-person narrator, whose point of view is largely congruent with that of Joseph K. That law, prescriptive or descriptive, is presumably known in the upper hierarchies of a bureaucratic structure whose existence is only dimly seen. The protagonist must largely infer its existence after it has singled him out for arrest. This mysterious administration is not the one that openly tries ordinary criminals with ordinary judges and prosecutors. Joseph K. is a personal friend of the state prosecutor, but the supervisor of the case tells Joseph K. that his friendship has no meaning, since ordinary members of the regular judicial system are not involved in his case. At this point, if readers are not satisfied to see in his arrest something like the working of the courts of the Inquisition or those of the modern secret police, then, frustrated by the elusive possibilities, readers will probably adopt the subjective perspective on the image of the arrested Joseph K. and decide that his case is a paranoid fantasy. (But, as American writers as various as Philip Roth and Thomas Pynchon have shown in their Kafkaesque fictions, paranoia is also real.) With his opening chapter, then, Kafka obliges the reader, like Joseph K., to question and, in questioning, to wonder what the law is. One reasons, blindly, that the law exists; it must exist, since we desire to know it—a plausible non sequitur. One wants to know the law, for how can one be sure one is innocent if one does not know the law that one may have violated without knowing it?

The quest for the law is (narrated by) the text narrating the quest for the revelation of the law. The text is perforce narrating its own existence, for the novel itself is the quest, the motion forward, the *Gehen* toward something. The quest exists only insofar as it is narrated. Writing is also a "process" forward, literally and metaphorically, undertaken to garner some form of scriptural revelation, such as what constitutes the law. The novel is at once a tale about Joseph K. and the self-referential tale of its own existence as writing. It is a self-reflexive narration of the process by which the protagonist wants to go toward the law. This is not unlike the movement we saw in Kafka's earliest narrative experimentation, "Description of a Struggle." Walking, going, moving—these are all so many analogues for the text's own progress/process toward the ever-elusive goal of the movement—the revelation of what is the goal of that movement. The goal is not really spelled out in "Description of a Struggle." In *The Trial* the literary text itself is a process, and another meaning of the novel's title comes fully into play from this perspective, the movement toward the revelation of the unknown law.

In the first chapter the quest is initiated. The chapter shows the location for the quest, the ordinary world of Joseph K. He lives in a properly constituted, well-ordered state where the laws are enforced, he says, and where hard work is apparently rewarded, since K. is doing well at his bank. His life obeys routines, with much work and a weekly visit to a prostitute—the normal erotic outlet for unmarried men, as in the Prague of Kafka's youth. Sex is not a neutral theme here, however, and as the novel develops, it offers at times a vision of a kind of pan-eroticism that engulfs the characters. This does not mean that Joseph K.'s life is to be taken as exceptional in any respect, including his eroticism, though eroticism is omnipresent. The only break with conventional reality occurs on this strange morning when Joseph K. finds himself under arrest.

The second chapter brings another interruption into Joseph K.'s well-ordered life, though it is what one might expect if one were arrested but not in jail. He receives a telephone call telling him that there will be an inquiry or hearing in his case (*Untersuchung*) on the next Sunday morning. Or, more precisely, the text reads that he had received a call before the day on which he went to the inquiry. Kafka effects a kind of narrative distortion in his tense sequences. The first sentence of the second chapter announces this telephone call using the past perfective passive of a verb that literally says that he had been informed ("K. war telephonisch verständigt worden . . ." [*KA*, p. 49]). He had been informed before when? one asks; the answer is that it had occurred before he went to the inquiry. This distortion opens up a temporal hiatus between the first chapter and the second; there is no real linking of the two. Only the sense of the narrative shows that one chapter has to come after the other in some way or other, though there is no clear indication of time's passing. This is true of the subsequent chapters, and it is little wonder that some critics quarrel about the proper order of the chapters leading up to the last one. Kafka thought disjunctively, and there is often no sequence in which the flow of temporality is spelled out to link up one event to another, much less one chapter to another. This is another way of saying that Kafka was not a traditional novelist in any strict sense, and one does well to approach each chapter as a narrative unit, or perhaps poetic totality, with only the first chapter and the last having an undisputed temporal sequence: K. is arrested, and, at some indefinite later time, he is executed.

The second chapter, "First Investigation," is even more absurd than the first in terms of flouting and parodying the realist conventions of fiction. It begins with the implausible idea that the appointment for the examination is scheduled on Sunday morning for Joseph K.'s convenience. He goes to his appointment with only sketchy ideas about where it is to take place. The investigating commission holds its sessions in a poor part of town, in a huge tenement house in which Joseph K. wanders around about while peering into working-class apartments to see whether he can find the investigating commission at work. He happens upon the right door, enters a room jammed with people, and is immediately recognized, for now, in a scene reminiscent of Alice at the court in Wonderland, he is told that he should have been there an hour and five minutes earlier. K. speaks, and the right half of the room applauds. The examining magistrate appears to know him, though he thinks Joseph K. is a house painter.

It is not surprising in this absurd scene that a distorted image of writing shows up as part of the décor, one mocking our belief that the law might be written down somewhere. Here writing is to be found presumably in the notebook that the magistrate fumbles with. It is a tattered notebook that Joseph K. thinks might contain something relevant to his case. He tells the magistrate so, and then he picks up the tome and "hold[s] it up fastidiously between his fingertips by one of the middle pages, so that the closely written, stained, yellowing pages hung down on either side," as John Williams has recently translated it (*The Essential Kafka,* p. 35). Something appears to be scribbled on the dirty pages, though Joseph K. will never know what it is because, as he says, he can only pick it up but never read it. A possible image of the law in this scene is thus that of unreadable text found in a dirty notebook that is about to fall apart (not unlike the instructions for the execution machine that the traveler cannot read in "In the Penal Colony"). The humorous self-referentiality here points up where the novel is going: toward the demonstration of its own inconclusive and hence unreadable character. Having held the unreadable text and finding nothing he can use, K. then expounds his own version of his case, telling the crowd in somewhat contradictory fashion that his is an individual case but one typical of many people. In a sense the novel is the process of demonstrating that Joseph K.'s contradiction is correct. He is killed alone and as an individual, but the end of the case is typical of that for many, arguably of all people.

The incongruities in the rest of the scene reveal aspects of the universally unique: from one perspective, the arbitrary workings of power, and, from another perspective, the specific comic nightmare in which Joseph K. the bank employee finds himself trapped. Comic incongruity is underscored from every perspective. Joseph K.'s speech is greeted by somebody shouting "bravo" while men in the front row tug at their beards. Less comic, however, is the moment when his oratory is interrupted by screams in the back of the room as somebody tries to rape a woman. As in an erotically charged dream, sex manifests itself everywhere in the novel, though its violent irruption here serves to underscore the lawlessness of the law. And the final comic nightmare quality is created when Joseph K. sees that everyone in the crowd is wearing a badge that seemingly identifies them as all belonging to the same organization, regardless of the side for which they applaud. Some hidden power seems to unite all in a derisive system that Joseph K. wants to flee at the end while shouting imprecations.

In most, if not all, editions of *The Trial,* the next important narrative unit is that bearing the heading "Im leeren Sitzungssaal/Der Student/Die Kanzleien" ("In the Empty Meeting Room/The Student/The Offices"). (This is the third chapter in the Muirs' translation; in the unnumbered chapters of the critical edition, it is the fourth chapter.) In this chapter Joseph K. goes without being summoned to the tenement again on a Sunday, only to find that the commission is not meeting on that Sunday. He is met by the wife of the court attendant (the *Diener* or servant), who tells him he is not allowed to look at the books the examining magistrate left in the room, which is now converted into an apartment in which the attendant and his wife live when the commission does not meet. (The same type of multifunctional dream-space is found in the school house of *The Castle.*) In these books Joseph K. is again confronted with images of writing or what he believes should be writing, since he first thinks they are law books. As the scene unfolds and the sexual attraction between the Joseph K. and the woman develops, he looks at the books, only to find that the first is full of pornographic images and the second is a sadistic porn piece about a wife's suffering at her husband's hands.

The pan-eroticism of the whole novel, as in an erotically charged dream, is reflected satirically in this image of the putative texts of the law by which one sees that these magistrates are more interested in sexual titillation than in legal arguments. Their books are conveyors of porn, and the only discernible law is the law of desire, which is a point Joseph K. makes about the court later in the novel when he defends his own interest in women against the priest's criticism of him on this point. The rest of the chapter continues the comedy of the intertwining of eros and power, for a randy student appears who carries off the woman to deliver her to an ever-randy magistrate, leaving the now-randy K. to suffocate in the recurrent stifling atmosphere that makes it difficult to breath.

Most editions have as the next and usually fourth chapter "Fräulein Bürstner's Friend," though this chapter is relegated to an appendix in Fischer's critical edition. One will probably approve the latter's editorial decision if one finds that the short chapter contributes little to the novel, other than to suggest briefly that Miss Bürstner may have some relation to the trial. Indeed, the chapter has little to do with the trial, though it does show Joseph K. pursuing his erotic interests. The reader learns that Miss Bürstner has invited a young woman to be her roommate—perhaps out of self-defense against Joseph K.? In the absence of Miss Bürstner, the young woman informs him that Miss Bürstner does not desire to talk to him. Joseph K.'s reaction is to tell himself dismissively that Miss Bürstner is just a little secretary whom he would have no trouble seducing. If Joseph K. were on trial for his thoughts, his unspoken arrogance would undoubtedly weigh against his moral character. Thus the chapter is something of a footnote, an interesting one, to the erotic comedy in the rest of novel.

A perverse variant on the erotic comedy is illustrated by the oneiric sadism of the next chapter. By all lights it is one of the most extraordinary in the novel. Titled "Der Prügler" ("The Flogger" or "The Beater"), it is the fourth chapter in the critical edition, though it has no precise temporal connection to the chapters before and after it. It begins on "one of the next evenings" in an indefinite sequence of events when Joseph K. happens to be in the bank and hears a sound behind the closed door of some storeroom that he had never looked into before. Doors are key transition points in Kafka's narratives, often opening up on the incongruous and the surprising. In this scene, upon opening this door, Joseph K. discovers that the two men who had arrested him—Franz and Willem—are there with a third man, who, with a rod (*Rute*) in his hand, is about to begin beating them. They are going to be punished, they say, because Joseph K. had complained of their thievery to the examining magistrate. Joseph K. is naturally flabbergasted: ritual sadism is, unbeknownst to him, taking place in his very workplace. With dream-like incongruity there follows an argument about whether justice would be served if the two men were to strip naked to be properly flogged. The flogger is convinced their punishment is just, for with his rod he will inscribe justice on the nude hide of the two miscreants. This sadism foreshadows the execution machine that writes the law on the skin of the always guilty defendants of "In the Penal Colony." Comparing the rod with the penal colony's writing machine, we may well see a near metaphor in the flogger's rod: it is a pen that writes out the law in the only way it can be understood, that is, in pain inscribed in the flesh. The chapter's final twist of black humor is Joseph K.'s discovery the next day that the scene is being repeated. The Freudian might say that Kafka has enacted a savage staging of the triumph of the superego's sadism, though whose superego is perhaps not clear—though obviously that of a paternal imago with a whip. In any case, the sadistic scene is openly hidden in the bank itself. The scene suggests that the operations of power permeate a society in which the violence grounding power is alternately hidden and seen. One need only open the door.

The next three chapters of *The Trial*, as usually arranged, have an overarching unity in that they deal with Joseph K. and the lawyer his uncle finds for him. It may seem logical that he should seek a lawyer, for the very idea of a trial implies the need for the arrested party to have a lawyer to represent him. Joseph K. first thinks he can deal with the miserable business all by himself. But, in the sixth chapter, titled "The Uncle—Leni," his uncle comes from the country to explain to him that family interests are involved in the affair. Joseph K. owes it to them to have adequate representation, as we are wont to say in English about finding a clever shyster. Kafka's own troubled relations with family and father are undoubtedly reflected in the image of the imperious uncle, though one needs no biographical information to see that Kafka presents an image of the way personal and family ties mediate relations of power. The uncle functions as a quasi patriarch vis-à-vis Joseph K. and, as such, demands that he subordinate himself to the interests the uncle claims to represent. The uncle seems to be part of a nearly feudal or clan society in which all interests are tied up with and subordinate to the family. The notion of a dominating family contrasts notably with the earlier presentation of Joseph K.'s solitude.

The uncle blusters his way into the lawyer's house at an undue hour, finds that his old friend, lawyer Huld, is sick in bed—another Kafka bed—and is received by Huld despite the time and his condition. (I pass over the dark ironies found in the meaning of Huld, an archaic term for "grace.") With satiric intent, Kafka shows that unusual ways of conducting business can be taken to be normal. In fact, a magistrate is also visiting lawyer Huld at this hour, though this magistrate, an apparently influential "head of the chambers," remains in the dark, hidden, for the first part of Joseph K.'s visit. Lawyer Huld has already heard of Joseph K.'s case, for, paradoxically, in the world of hidden courts there are few secrets.

Kafka's erotic comedy continues here, for Leni, the lawyer's female servant and perhaps lover, draws Joseph K. out of the room. In a discussion of his case, she recommends that he merely confess, telling him that then all will go better. Leni is not only a surrogate priest recommending confession; she is also another erotic maniac, sprung free of a dream narrative, for in short order she has Joseph K. in her power. They are soon down on the floor together, much like Kafka's easy lovers in *The Castle*. Kafka's comically hyperbolic image of the force of desire seems complementary to the desire for power. In *The Trial* they are arguably very much the same desire in complementary manifestations, as in the court, where rape is apparently an everyday activity, or in the lawyer's home, in which a potential client quickly finds himself rolling on the floor.

Clocks speed up when hyperbolic desire engulfs the characters: Joseph K. emerges from his encounter with Leni to find that his uncle has been standing for hours in the rain waiting on him. Needless to say, Joseph K. has not made a good first impression, as his outraged uncle tells him, a fact confirmed in the next chapter, when, in the course of the legal blather, the lawyer tells Joseph K.

that his conduct toward the visiting magistrate, now named the "head of the chambers," has hurt his case.

The seventh chapter's title sets out the cast of characters that occupy Joseph K. in the chapter: the lawyer, a manufacturer, and a painter ("Advokat/ Fabrikant/Maler"). The chapter begins on an indeterminate winter morning at some indefinite time after the first encounter with the lawyer. Joseph K. has seen him again a number of times, and now a month has passed since their last encounter. Sufficient time has passed to allow the trial to so grow in importance that it has now become Joseph K.'s only preoccupation. He is having trouble keeping his mind on his work at the bank, and his rival, the "deputy manager," has been able to take a manufacturer's business away from him. Despite this adversity, Joseph K. decides he must write up a defense statement, what he calls a *Verteidigungsschrift,* for he believes his lawyer has not yet even submitted a petition (*Eingabe*) to represent his case to the court. He now has little confidence in his lawyer, who talks much but apparently does little. In short, Joseph K. has reached the point where all he can do is think obsessively about the trial: "Often he had considered whether it might not be good to write out a defense statement and to give it to the court. In it he would present a short life history and on the occasion of each important event in it he would explain what were his motives for acting and whether, in his present judgment, this conduct could be approved or rejected, and also what grounds he could adduce for this or that decision he made" (*Der Process, KA,* p. 149).

Though such personal writing is not officially permitted to the defense, it is tolerated by the court; even though Joseph K. has been told by his lawyer that written petitions are of little use and that only his lawyer's personal relations have any importance for the case's outcome and, moreover, even though he thinks a petition probably will not be read, Joseph K. seems now to believe that a written plea on his behalf is a key to his salvation.

Writing is no easy task, since he knows neither the law nor how he violated it, so the written justification he outlines for himself must logically foresee all conceivable possibilities of some fault on his part. This means, as the text quoted shows, that a biography as a form of defense is a potentially infinite task. It demands an accounting of every detail of Joseph K.'s life, along with a justification of that justification, ad infinitum, as the grounds for the grounds for the grounds proliferate. Any writing that would justify itself—and the petition itself would be one more act, so he would have to give the grounds for writing it—is potentially without end, since every justification requires a justification. This passage about writing at the beginning of the chapter is one of those key moments in Kafka's work when the necessity of finding grounds for finding grounds reflects back upon the futile comedy of writing itself. Joseph K.'s potentially infinite task of writing a defense plea is one of the most poignant of Kafka's many images of writing in his work. For Joseph K.'s projected defense statement is another image, tinged with black humor, of the impossible and hopeless task of representing the text that might offer grounds for why it exists.

The comedy of representation is also found in Joseph K.'s visit to the artist Titorelli. Recommended to Joseph K. by a manufacturer who happens to know about his trial, this painter is a friend of the court and therefore perhaps has influence. He also brings to the novel, by way of the incongruous images found in his painting, another version of the way representation functions—iconic signs in this case. This artist works in the service of power and is something of a parody of the image of the artist as ideologue serving the reigning elite. And, as an artist, Titorelli is also a distorted double of the writer himself. Iconic images are often present as comic foils in Kafka's work to suggest doubles for the writing. In *The Trial* an earlier example is the portrait of a judge found in the room in which Leni seduces Joseph K. Looking at the portrait, he asks her what rank the judge has, for the judge is sitting on a throne (*Tronsessel*). Since he is merely a judge in charge of inquiries, his position hardly justifies a throne, but Leni adds that it is all invention, since in reality the magistrate sits on a kitchen chair on which an old horse blanket is tossed. The split between pretense and reality seems evident. However, on reflection, one realizes that the judges may well act as if they were sitting on thrones, for their power is part of the total power of the seemingly omnipotent court system. A false appearance corresponds to a reality that Joseph K. cannot fathom.

After receiving counsel from the manufacturer, Joseph K. visits the artist in hope that the latter may help him with the trial. Though familiar with the halls of power, the artist lives like a caricature of the bohemian artist. He inhabits a tiny garret that hardly has enough room for his easel and bed. The gap between the artist's pretentions to influence and his shabby daily reality is enormous, and one wonders how this artist could be affiliated with the court as *Vertrauensmann*—a term that could be translated as "intermediary" or "representative," with connotations of familiarity or trust. The artist's function here is shown in his work. Notably, Joseph K. sees another portrait of a judge in which the judge is portrayed royally as sitting on a throne, not in the traditional position of repose but at a moment when he is threatening to rise up. An image of angry power animates the menacing figure, having little of the equipoise associated with deliberative justice.

Titorelli also shows Joseph K. a pastel representing justice. The representation is another distorted image, not unlike the image of liberty in *Amerika*, whose Statue of Liberty holds up a sword, not a torch, to greet the newly arrived immigrant. In Titorelli's pastel the goddess of justice is, as traditionally represented, blind and holds scales, but there are also wings on her feet redolent of the goddess of victory, and Joseph K. notices she also resembles the goddess of the hunt. Titorelli's conflation of goddesses seems to offer a résumé of the aspects of the kind of justice that has power over K. Notably, blind victory in the service of the hunt suggests a succinct, if incongruous, résumé iconic of the novel itself: justice automatically and blindly pursues K. until, like a successful hunter, it kills him. From this perspective, Titorelli's hodgepodge representation of justice is another form of inner duplication, a *mise-en-abyme,* by which the novel comically represents itself within itself.

It is not surprising that Titorelli, with his knowledge of the court system, sounds more like a lawyer than an artist when, considering Joseph K.'s case, he advises Joseph K. on the strategies he might adopt to keep from being condemned. The most striking aspect of the artist's consideration is the fact that he knows of no case of a final acquittal granted on the basis of innocence. That, he says, is only the stuff of legend. And so it goes with the history of Western culture's attempt at revealing justice and the law.

The three chapters narrating Joseph K.'s dealings with the lawyer come to a conclusion with the scene presenting the lawyer's demonstration of his will to power in the eighth chapter, "Kaufmann Block—Kündigung des Advokaten" ("Merchant Block—Dismissal of the Lawyer"). Believing, probably correctly, that his lawyer is accomplishing nothing, Joseph K. goes to him with the intention of dismissing him. He finds that another client is already there, and he, too, is enjoying Leni's general fondness for the accused, it seems, merely because they are accused. This client, a merchant named Block, is talkative and tells Joseph K. that he had retained the lawyer some years earlier and is now spending nearly all his money and time on his case, in part because he has secretly hired additional lawyers. Block is fearful of missing any chance he might have of influencing the court. Block is, at least from the lawyers' viewpoint, the ideally submissive accused. Block's submissive position stands out when the lawyer then uses Block to demonstrate his power to Joseph K. in order to dissuade his client from dismissing him.

Before this scene, Joseph K. gets rid of Leni and enters the lawyer's bedchamber to announce his decision. The lawyer does not take it seriously and accuses him of being impatient. Impatience is not an indifferent matter in Kafka. One recalls that the Zürau aphorisms state that impatience, with negligence, is the main sin from which all others derive. And, in what reads like a commentary on *The Trial,* Kafka goes on to say in the third aphorism that it was because of impatience that people were driven out of paradise and because of impatience they do not return (*Nachgelassene Schriften und Fragmente* II, *KA,* 113). Whatever its theological implications, the aphorism shows the centrality of the "sin" of impatience in Kafka. In a certain sense, impatience motivates the refusal to accept the order that rules over things. This, according to the aphorisms, lies at the origin of the fall, the *Hauptsünde*—the major sins of impatience and negligence. And Joseph K. has become impatient with the way things are. He does not wish to conform to the order that the lawyer represents, and herein lies the origin of the revolt exemplified later by Camus's "absurd man" and exemplified immediately in the novel by Joseph K. with his refusal to acquiesce to the patent absurdity of things. Kafka continued to develop this theme of refusing to be ignored in *The Castle*.

The order of things is demonstrated to Joseph K. in one of the most remarkable scenes in Kafka's work. The merchant Block is called before the lawyer. Remarking that it is often better to be in chains than to be free, the lawyer proceeds to show the recalcitrant Joseph K. how accused parties can be treated. To this end, the Dostoevskian lawyer begins to humiliate Block. Bound in psychological chains, as it were, Block is patient. Tolerating every humiliation, he shows he obviously has no desire to escape the court's jurisdiction or to question the lawyer's role in representing him before it. The lawyer's humiliation of Block offers Joseph K. a sadistic illustration of power, for the lawyer forces the merchant to fall on his knees and to kiss his hand in order to avoid losing the lawyer's service. This is a gesture not unlike that of believers who genuflect before a high ecclesiastical figure whom they believe they need to represent them to a deity. The narrator, directly filtering Joseph K.'s vision, concludes by remarking that Block was no longer the lawyer's client, he was his dog—a comment doubtlessly foreshadowing the moment when, at the novel's end, the narrator says that K. has been murdered like a dog. His revolt does not change his fate.

It is notable that the condemned prisoner in "In the Penal Colony" acts like a canine before being placed on the machine that he does not understand. In both novel and short story, the dog offers the image of the submissive animal, marked out to obey the master's orders, obliged to accept what it does not understand until the end. Of course, the lawyer is just one part of the concerted plan to humiliate client-dogs: it is the hidden trial itself, the "process," that is the great instrument of humiliation. The lawyer rubs this fact sadistically in when he asks what Block might think if he were to learn that after all these years his trial has not even begun yet, that the opening bell has not yet even been rung to start the proceeding—indeed, it may not even be the case that a bell is ever rung to start a trial—and even this idea about how trials unfold is subject to interpretations. Which is of little importance, the lawyer mockingly says, since Block would not be able to understand them. The interpreting of interpretations will be left for a later moment in the cathedral when Joseph K. meets the priest.

Joseph K. leaves the lawyer, and it seems he has finished with the arrogant shyster. Joseph K. is obedient only to a certain point, and revolt is clearly simmering beneath the surface. However, Leni telephones him in the following chapter, "Im Dom" ("In the Cathedral"), to sympathize with him, or so it seems, and the call itself suggests that the lawyer might make a return in K.'s life. The telephone call also shows that this ninth chapter comes logically after the three preceding chapters dealing with the lawyer, though little else does. Be that as it may, this chapter contains, as an embedded narration, "Vor dem Gesetz" ("Before the Law"), a parable Kafka published separately in *A Country Doctor*. The parable brings up again the question of hermeneutics, which in Kafka means the art of finding grounds for the grounds for an interpretation—something the lawyer sneeringly tells Block that he is not capable of. However, Joseph K. will have his chance at interpretation in this chapter, beginning on an indeterminate miserable rainy day when he is scheduled to escort around town an Italian client who speaks a dialect Joseph K. cannot understand. The Italian fails to show up for a meeting at the cathedral, so Joseph K., a connoisseur of his city's artistic treasures, begins to wander about the unlighted church trying to see in the dark what he might have pointed out to the missing visitor.

In the darkness, he is suddenly addressed by name by a young priest, standing illuminated above him, in a small pulpit. The priest says that he is the prison chaplain (*Gefängniskaplan*). He has been sent to discuss Joseph K.'s case with him. The oneiric nature of the priest's implausible apparition is striking, though one might also compare it to a baroque painting, something on the order of a Caravaggio-like moment of illumination. The chaplain, like Joseph K. himself, thinks the case may well end up going badly, since, the chaplain says, it is believed that Joseph K.'s guilt has been proved. Joseph K. makes the point that he is innocent, though this time he enlarges upon this defense to wonder how human beings in general can be guilty. To which the priest replies that his is precisely the attitude of all guilty men—therefore the conclusion of guilt is implied in advance if the accused claims to be innocent. The priest's logic is impeccable, if absurd. Their exchange shows that, much as at the first hearing, Joseph K. is again arguing his case for humanity in general, whereas the priest speaks for those who argue for universal guilt, a Judeo-Christian viewpoint that is easily demonstrated by assuming that only the guilty say they are innocent. Their exchange occupies the rest of the chapter, the most poignant moment occurring when the priest shouts down at Joseph K., standing in utter darkness, asking him whether he cannot see what stands before his very eyes. Indeed, he cannot, though the priest seems to want to make him feel guilty for not being able to see in the dark.

The priest comes down from his pulpit, and Joseph K., considering him a benevolent interlocutor, is grateful for the chance to continue the discussion of his case. The priest tells him not to be deluded (or deceived or in error, as one variously can translate the *Täuschung* that Joseph K. should avoid). Joseph K. wonders quite properly how he could be deluded or under any misapprehension about his own guilt. The question of guilt and error segues into the narration of "Before the Law," the tale of a man who comes from the country to find access to the law. The priest says he will tell this parable to help Joseph K. understand the law, since this parable is supposedly an example of what is found in the "preamble" to the law, though the parable is not the law itself. According to the priest, the parable is an annex to the law. It is an interpretive text or commentary on the law illustrative of a precedent, somewhat like judicial commentaries on the common law or an interpretive parable as found, say, in commentaries on religious laws, of which the Jewish Midrash and its exegesis of the Torah is an example. In the context of the novel and its rhetorical strategies, the parable is another example of inner duplication in which a narrative is a reproduction in miniature of the novel as a whole. The man's desire to have access to the law is a clear inner duplication within the novel of the action of *The Trial* itself. The parable thus offers an image of the novel's project; it is an image representing Joseph K.'s quest for the law, *The Trial* itself, and it is thus a self-referential text in that it refers to itself as a parable about reading the parable. In this maze of self-referentiality the logician may venture to point out that any self-referential statement, taken as a basis for deductive reasoning, can generate contradictions, so that one should be prepared for the fact that the priest and Joseph K. arrive at no understanding of what the parable is about.

The parable is simple. A man from the country comes to a gate that gives entrance to the law. The gatekeeper tells the man he cannot enter now. So the man waits and waits, spending his life at the gate, interrogating the gatekeeper, uselessly bribing him, looking at the fleas on the gatekeeper's coat, and wasting away. After many years, the man is dying and, never having gained entrance, finally asks why, since everybody wants access to the law, nobody else has ever showed up to seek entrance. It is because, the gatekeeper says, this gate was meant only for the man from the country. And he closes it as the man dies.

Joseph K. is outraged by the parable, feeling the man has been cheated. His reaction shows that the interpretive parable must itself then be interpreted, for it is not at all obvious what the tale of the man from the country might have to do with justice and the law. The priest counters Joseph K.'s charge by saying that the man has been deceived only if there is a contradiction between the fact that he cannot enter the gate and the fact that the gate was meant only for him. I point up the priest's viewpoint because it does not change, despite a possible infinite spin-off of interpretations—these being a sign of the interpreters' despair, as the priest puts it. The reader is in Joseph K.'s position vis-à-vis the priest, and thus the parable offers a mirror image that shows readers their task when making sense of "the process"—of the trial and of the process of making sense. Of course, no amount of interpretation can change the fact that the man was not let in through the gate that was meant only for him.

Facing the hermeneutic tempest of competing interpretations, Joseph K. nonetheless shows his sense of justice. He realizes that if the gate is open only to one person, then it does not provide access to the law at all: the very idea of law as a unique way is a contradiction in terms from the rationalist viewpoint that undergirds one side of Kafka's work. For the Enlightenment rationalist, the law is universal and hence accessible to everybody. Here it is clear that Joseph K., like the traveler of "In the Penal Colony," is endowed with an Enlightenment mind that affirms that the law must be for all. When the law is arbitrary, when it allows of unique applications, then it is not the law; it is a tool for arbitrary power. This is indeed the sense of the chapter's end when the priest tells K. that it is not necessary that we find all in the parable to be true; rather, we need only accept it as necessary. But when arbitrary necessity takes precedence over the truth, then the law is merely a tool for the application of power, an idea Joseph K. underscores by observing that in effect the priest's view makes untruth or lying into the basis for the world's order: "Die Lüge wird zur Weltordnung gemacht" (*KA*, p. 303).

The priest's final comment is, enigmatically, that the court wants nothing from Joseph K., that it receives him when he comes and releases him when he goes. The reader may with justification think that this comment is not true: Joseph K. will not be freed from the trial. But other responses to the priest's comment are possible, for example, that of the ever enigmatic Walter Benjamin —to quote probably the most quoted commentary on Kafka. Benjamin comments on the priest's puzzling statement with his usual suggestive opacity, saying, "With these words . . . is really said that the court does not distinguish itself from any given situation. That is true of every situation, however with the presupposition that one understands them not as being developed by K. but rather as exterior to him and, as it were, waiting on him." Benjamin seems to suggest that the court is intrinsic to all existence since it is an undifferentiated part of every situation. Benjamin's commentary on commentary evokes the comment from Kafka's biographer Reiner Stach that nobody has gotten closer than Benjamin to the iron kernel of *The Trial*—all are free, yet whatever one decides to do, one remains a "case" for which there are already rules, measure, and institutions, so that "one's most spontaneous, felicitous movement remains within the closed horizon of a thoroughly administered and planned world."[7] It is noteworthy that Stach, biographer and social historian par excellence, interpreting the semimystical, semi-Marxist Benjamin, opts for the most objective image possible of the significance of Joseph K.'s paranoid passage through the dark cathedral: the world of the trial as the world of administration. However, it seems that Benjamin's remark could just as well apply to the psychological or metaphysical nature of existence. Such is the aspect viewing Kafka's work allows and, indeed, demands.

In the final chapter, prosaically called "Ende," the unknown and unseen administration sends two assassins to render judgment. They kill Joseph K., gruesomely, with a knife. *The Trial* is one more of Kafka's major works of his early career that ends in death. Gregor perhaps starves to death, perhaps pines away because of his lack of desire to live, whereas both Georg and the self-sacrificing officer of "In the Penal Colony" commit suicide. Only Joseph K. is murdered, after he refuses to accept the option of suicide. Joseph K.'s refusal of suicide, after his attempt to refuse the jurisdiction of the court, can well be described as the revolt of the lucid person who, in the face of the absurd, refuses to collaborate with the absurd—as Albert Camus undoubtedly understood when he described "absurd man" as one for whom suicide is the only serious philosophical problem. To be sure, Joseph K. barely resists his two assassins, but he remains lucid to the end, recognizing the utterly absurd physicality of a death that is no different from a dog's death.

Behind *The Trial*'s single-minded portrayal of Joseph K.'s demise lies a medley of metaphysical ideas and religious doctrines, with literary devices drawing on parody and comedy, often self-referentially. Images drawn from mythology, philosophy, science, and religion are mixed in Kafka's savagely dark comic view of the trial and its inevitable judgment. But the great strength of Kafka's collage in discourses is precisely that, in avoiding any systematic allegory based on one doctrine, he creates a web of fragmented possibilities for allusion and interpretation, which in turn create the possibility for perspectival viewing discussed here. Kafka is our postmodern contemporary in this regard, in his relentless and ironic portrayal of the debris of our myths and traditional beliefs, as well as the half-assimilated philosophical and scientific views that continue to populate our intellectual landscapes. Much the same can be said about Kafka's other trial (besides the one Canetti attributed to Felice Bauer), the trial that, at least in writing it, Kafka juxtaposed with the trial Joseph K. undergoes. For the trial of the dog-like prisoner, which becomes the immolation of the trial's own judge, calls upon the same sources of Judeo-Christian tradition and European legal doctrines, but set out in the bright sunlight of an unnamed island. Here the quest for the law takes the form of sudden revelation for the unsuspecting.

The connections between the story "In the Penal Colony" and the novel *The Trial* are multiple, and one need not know that the story was also written in 1914 to see that the mixture of discourses in the short story resembles greatly the intertextual collage found in the novel, which is hardly surprising insofar as both portray the punishment of the condemned in the name of the law. The great difference is of course that the law in *The Trial* is never accessible to the condemned, whereas the law in "In the Penal Colony" is made painfully known to the condemned by being inscribed by needles on his skin. But the two works resemble each other in that, in both, once a person is accused, guilt is never doubted. Being accused is enough to confirm guilt, a clear statement of principle that the judge-officer of "In the Penal Colony" makes to the traveler. Then, as the Bible puts it in a different context, revelation is made flesh: the law is made manifest by being written onto the condemned man's hide. Christian flagellants might hold that the context is not so different.

Contrasting with biblical or ecclesiastical notions about the law and punishment is the Enlightenment viewpoint represented by the traveler. He largely shares the understanding of justice that characterizes Joseph K. (as well as the implied reader). Like *The Trial,* "In the Penal Colony" is narrated in the third person from a narrative point of view that coincides with that of the traveler, who tells of the sense of malaise he feels on viewing the punishment machine in operation. That the story is thus largely narrated from the traveler's Enlightenment viewpoint means that the traditional practice of this unnamed island is set off in all its barbaric otherness. Eschewing dream narration, moreover, Kafka allows his narrator to view the world with the crisp accuracy of hyperrealist science fiction, setting out, with the detail found in a technical manual, a description of how to use a punishment machine. (Not for nothing was Dr. Kafka a specialist in industrial accidents.) The result is a type of comedy different from that found in *The Trial.* It is a comedy that turns on the logical application of the absurd in a world illuminated by both the sun and reason. It is a comedy based on the incongruity between modern humanistic doctrines and a traditional, historical practice kept alive by belief.

The penal colony's historical practice of writing the law on and in the condemned prisoner's flesh reflects the traditional belief that the law and logos are two sides of the same coin. Both Greek metaphysics and Moses contribute to this belief that writing—the Word—exists as a means of gaining access to the law and, in a religious context, of finding justification, redemption, and salvation. The identification of writing with the revelation of law is literally incorporated into the workings of the punishing machine, for it is a machine that reveals the law and thus the crime in the condemned prisoner's flesh. Hence, there is no need for a trial as in *The Trial* with its drawn-out "process." In the prison colony, the condemned learns immediately what he is accused of when the machine writes out the law on his body. By granting access to the law through this inscription, by making the Word flesh, the machine should bring about some redemption that, alas for the true believer, the traveler does not see inscribed on the dead officer's face; he does not see what the narrator calls the promised salvation or *Erlösung*.

The fact that the story is set in a distant penal colony may also seem like an idea from science fiction. However, the colony is not a pure fiction. Such colonies existed, established by various European countries, the most famous of which was undoubtedly Devil's Island, on which the French Jewish officer Dreyfus was imprisoned after being framed by the French army for selling military secrets. Kafka was quite aware of the Dreyfus affair and the anti-Semitism that it fueled, as indeed were all European liberals, who saw that this injustice was a serious threat to republican and democratic institutions. However, something like Devil's Island is only an analogue for the story's island, not a reference. One can say much the same about the Christian vision of the incarnation or the Jewish belief in the divine origins of the written law. Kafka's collage of discourses alludes to major doctrines and institutions in the history of Judeo-Christian civilization, especially the institution of law, in all its forms, including Roman law, in which Kafka, unwillingly perhaps, had expertise. The historical development of the law, or lack thereof, is a recurrent referent in much of Kafka's fiction, and his later dog-narrator in "Investigations of a Dog" may well feel that that development has been such that one has lost sight of the Word. Needless to say, Kafka's dog does hold a Hegelian vision of the necessary progress of reason in history.

"In the Penal Colony" narrates events that take place in a prison colony visited by a traveler, *ein Reisender*. The translation "explorer" for traveler suggests that he is a scientific voyager, though this is not explicit, nor is it clear that he is charged with any special mission. It is as an outside, objective viewer that the traveler is asked to witness an execution scheduled for the colony's punishment machine, which he agrees to do. The process, a twelve-hour ordeal, is a practice that is probably about to be abolished by the colony's new and more enlightened commanding officer. The machine's keeper, an officer who is among the last to believe in the machine, tells the traveler that the executions were once celebrated by multitudes who came to view them as if they were a public festival. (Historical echoes reverberate here with images of public executions and the crowds that came to enjoy them, as when the guillotine was working regularly to offer beheadings as spectacle.) The present execution, however, is to be witnessed only by the officer, the traveler, and a soldier who holds the prisoner in chains, like a dog on a leash.

After preparing the machine, the officer suddenly entreats the traveler to help him in his scheme to defy the new commandant and to preserve the machine and the old order. When the traveler politely refuses, the officer, in an unexpected move, releases the prisoner and gets on the machine himself. He programs it to write on himself "Be Just." But before the old machine can begin to inscribe this rather vacuous imperative, it breaks down and begins to spew forth its innards in a comic display of malfunction bordering on farce. In the end, the dysfunctional machine does not write on the officer. Rather, it impales him with a spike through the forehead. The officer will not have learned to "Be Just," an imperative that can be taken as the basis for law; though the reader may suspect that the grotesque image of the spike through the forehead points to another and perhaps universal basis for the law: the murderous application of power.

In a brief and bizarre epilogue, the traveler returns to town, where, in a teahouse, he comes across the old commandant's gravestone under a table. Kafka is never loath to engage in expressionist parody: the traveler learns that according to prophecy the old commandant will rise up again, apparently from under the table, and lead his adherents to recover the colony. The absurd allusion to resurrection surely embodies critical irony vis-à-vis the pretentions of religion, in this case, the possibility of recovering a mythical lost plenitude. The self-immolation the officer has inflicted upon himself and the tomb beneath the table round out Kafka's portrait of belief and believers. After this, the traveler is in a hurry to leave the absurd prison colony. Pointedly, as he leaves, he refuses to aid the soldier and prisoner who, after the judge-officer's suicide, now want to accompany him. He repels them and leaves alone. He is not one to be helping refugees.

The story's central focus is on the *Reisender*, the traveler or explorer (the German term can also designate a traveling salesman, such as Gregor Samsa). Recalling Kafka's earlier writing, we can call the traveler a person in movement, one of Kafka's voyagers, on the way from one point to another, much like the text itself, with no precise itinerary except that inscribed by writing-motion itself in its uncertain quest for meaning. The penal colony is a point on a line tracing out a trajectory, though in this case the trajectory is as much in time as in space, for, to quote again Walter Benjamin, Kafka himself is an explorer of the oblivion in which "what has been forgotten of the prehistoric world, forms countless, uncertain, changing compounds, yielding a constant flow of new, strange products."[8] Benjamin's central insight that Kafka's historical sense is often oriented toward a nearly prehistoric past certainly applies to "In the Penal Colony." The traveler's trip to the island is as much a trip back in time, to a primitive past, as it is a trip in space to the margins of civilization where the latest form of the application of the law takes place—incarceration in the prison colony. And the island's execution machine, modern in that it is a perfected mechanical device, is prehistoric in that it embodies primitive notions about the law and punishment, and these notions about the law have hardly disappeared. True, it appears the machine is on the point of being abolished in the immediate future—though that future is not present yet. Ironies about European past and present abound.

At first the traveler appears to serve as a foil. His viewpoint is the vehicle for a description of the barbarous machine. Endowed with a modern liberal sense of civilized practices, he first resembles a Western observer come to observe a primitive ritual existing outside the pale of Western civilization. He is analogous to a missionary come to observe cannibals, to offer a stereotype from the colonialist era. However, the prison colony itself is a product of colonialist modernity. Assuming this is the case, one comprehends that the traveler is a liberal who views the foundations of his own civilization: the trip to the colony is also a trip showing up the history of Europe's own cultural practices, especially with regard to application of the law and punishment. And since, wherever the law gets hold of the condemned person's body, that past continues to exist, the traveler's perspective illuminates his own world. It is a world in which humanity continues to want access to the law and salvation in the same primitive terms as its forebears. From this perspective it is little wonder that the traveler is in a hurry to leave the horrid place. He must feel something akin to a desire to flee from himself and his own past.

The reader only infrequently has direct access to the traveler's consciousness, however, and Kafka uses the narrative point of view very selectively to maintain a distanced perspective. The narrator's viewpoint and the traveler's coincide, for example, when the narrator reflects that the traveler is not afraid to refuse to help the officer or when the traveler understands that the machine's guardian should want, out of the strength of his belief, to immolate himself on the machine. Much of the time, however, the narrator's viewpoint offers a distanced objective perspective that allows for simultaneous detachment and horror and, finally, a sense of comic incongruity. The narrator's detachment allows the reader to see that the traveler is fascinated by the fact that he finds something like a primitive culture preserved on the margins of civilization and that at the same time this past is also the present moment of his own civilization.

Kafka was fascinated by true believers. It is well known, for example, that he was equally drawn to and repelled by the practices of Hasidic Jews from Eastern Europe. With the image of the punishment machine Kafka offers a wacky but literal image of the way the true believer once perceived that the law and the Word were connected, with a kind of material self-evidence that we hardly understand today. This image conveys one meaning of the belief that the Messiah makes the Word into flesh. Kafka also saw this as another way of literalizing one meaning of the crucifixion, a ghastly image in literal terms of the flesh revealing the Word. Kafka's image of law and punishment draws upon a medieval sense of material literalness such as one can find in Dante's *Inferno*. In Dante the truth of judgment, the truth of the justice of the law, is also inscribed in and on the bodies of the damned in the form of a punishment that takes the physical shape of their sins, all of this in conformity with the rational decrees of divine logos. By the early twentieth century, however, the visionary truth of Dante's cosmology had been largely reduced to the claims of marginal beliefs and fanaticisms. Yet, Kafka's work reveals ironically that belief in the Word is still influential in our lives even after the advent of a modernity that has only ambiguous ideas about the grounds of the law. The traveler has entered a time warp created by the double perspective the story offers, where one sees the law as it once was and, in tatters, as it perhaps really is: an imperative backed up by the threat of a spike through the head.

There are other, overlapping textual sources that find resonances in the writing machine that kills. On one hand, a banal German proverb holds that he who does not obey must feel—which is certainly demonstrated by the fate of the disobedient soldier about to be strapped onto the machine. On the other hand, great monuments of our cultural history reverberate here, with multiple biblical overtones. For example, the machine is set in a sandy valley surrounded by naked crags. A number of biblical valleys suggest themselves as analogues, such as the valley of tears; Gehenna, the Jewish prototype for hell; the valley of Joel 4, the valley of the Last Judgment; or the valley that was the scene of Christ's passion. All of these allusions work, disjointedly, to point to the past world in which it supposedly made sense to speak of the union of flesh and the Word or the revelation of the law in material writing; the allusions are utterly dysfunctional in that they take place in a modern world for which the discourse of revelation has ceased to have meaning.

The machine itself is dysfunctional, for no spare parts are available to keep it running as it once did. The machine is described with a technological precision that comically contrasts with the way it flies apart once the officer finally sets it in motion after having strapped himself onto it. Kafka creates one of his finest black farces in the unfolding of this scene. For example, the officer, because the penal colony is short on parts, has not been able to replace the felt bit that, in recent usage, at least a hundred condemned men have had placed in their mouth. The bit is so filthy that this time, when the stinking felt is placed in condemned man's mouth, it causes him to vomit all over the machine. A defender of tradition, the officer places the blame for this accident on the modern philanthropy of the island's women who, in misdirected charity, gave the victim sweets before his execution. The interaction of body and machine sets out a farce based on pure bodily dysfunction and gesture and, finally, on mechanical incongruity. Moreover, the disjuncture between pretense and reality is total when the machine breaks down. Rather than inscribe the law, it spews parts out in a farcical display of its capacity to throw out an indefinite number of cogs and wheels, much as in those silent film comedies in which machines demonstrate their humanoid capacity to go berserk.

Contrasting with this farce is the guardian officer's explanation that he has a near-sacerdotal function to care for the machine. He is a fanatical true believer who with enthusiasm, like a convinced priest speaking to a novitiate, gives the traveler an account of the machine's history and its function. Like a living anachronism, the officer has dedicated himself to the preservation of tradition in the era of modernity. With his writing machine, he has openly dedicated himself to the preservation of the written law. The officer is aware of his special status, for he proudly tells the traveler that it was despite his youth that he was appointed a judge in the penal colony and thus became the former commandant's assistant. Like a high priest, he knows more about the machine than anybody else and, with proselytizing pride, he willingly explains it. In this regard, he is the very opposite of those unseen judges in *The Trial* who have access to the unknown law. But if the officer is an example of a judge who knows the law and the sacred principles it embodies, then, as this farce shows, the law has come upon hard times.

The officer's work as judge has been facilitated by a guiding principle: guilt is never to be doubted. In this regard, I suggested earlier that he seems to share that axiom with the invisible judges in *The Trial*. By endorsing this basic principle that underwrites the Judeo-Christian tradition, he knows that all are guilty. By always applying this principle, the officer can work with a speed that is rarely found either in *The Trial* or in any other European judicial system. The officer sees no problem in the fact that the soldier, supposedly disobedient during the night, is to be executed a mere few hours later. The principle of assumed guilt means that no trial is needed, since the condemned, always guilty, will discover what they are guilty of at the moment of the revelation. The officer's belief in his principle obviates all discussions, all interpretations, and all the problems presented in *The Trial*. The hermeneutic puzzles of "Before the Law" do not exist for the officer-judge of "In the Penal Colony."

Belief is the essence of certainty, belief without foundation to be sure, though the officer thinks that he can justify his belief by calling upon memory. To this end, he claims to remember when the justice served up by the machine was a public event. Then, he says, the law was made manifest to the crowds that gathered in the valley to see the judgment. Children were held up so that they could clearly see the edifying spectacle. The officer himself always had a child in each arm so that all could be absorbed by the look of transfiguration (*Verklärung*) that would appear on the face of the guilty sufferer. Justice, in all its radiance, was thus self-evident, and, at least momentarily, all gathered in the valley could see it. Such is the power of the claim of memory to anchor belief.

Suffice it to say that nothing in Kafka's work ever vouchsafes any credibility to memory. Memory is one more groundless discourse, though frequently recalled in ironic nostalgia.

Like most believers, however, the officer has more than memory as evidence for his claims. He has writings, texts, in which are preserved the arcana of the machine's functioning; specifically, he has writings about the machine in the form of the first commandant's plans for it. These plans are a possible guide, one supposes, for interpreting the machine, in other words, a potential guide for hermeneutics. The guardian insists that the traveler look at these plans so that he can appreciate the commandant's design and intent. A polite observer, the traveler looks at the plans with much interest, but he sees only a "labyrinth-like series of repeatedly crossing lines that covered the paper so densely that only with great effort could he make out the white interstices" ("labyrinthartige, einander vielfach kreuzende Linien, die so dicht das Papier bedeckten, dass man nur mit Muhe die weissen Zwischenräume erkannte") (*Drucke zu Lebzeiten*, *KA*, 217). From Borges to Robbe-Grillet and Umberto Eco and beyond, the labyrinth has been taken by postmodern writers as a, if not the, key metaphor for writing. As this passage shows, Kafka is a major source for the image of the maze that is a double for writing and, in Kafka, for the law itself. The officer urges the traveler to read this labyrinth, but all the observer can recognize is its artistic quality. "Es ist sehr kunstvoll," he says (*KA*, p. 217)—"It is very artful"—but he can decipher nothing.

The traveler is an explorer in the sense that he must negotiate cultural practices—beliefs and customs—that an outsider cannot understand so long as he stands outside them, that is, does not believe them. He is like an anthropologist trying to enter a cultural maze from which he is excluded by his Enlightenment skepticism. Thus, the traveler cannot accede to the officer's beliefs, and, when the latter understands this, he releases the prisoner and decides to replace him himself. He becomes a martyr to his faith, a witness who then demands that the traveler read the papers that describe how the machine operates. The officer must of course spell out for him the brief text that he is going to have inscribed on his own body, "Be Just," since the traveler still cannot decipher what is written there. All he can do is politely assure the officer that he believes the text is there, written out as the officer claims.

Every reader will ask why the true believer decides to kill himself on his own machine: what transfiguration can he seek in writing a vacuous imperative on his own body? If we take the judge-officer's first principle at its word, then he is guilty like everybody else and deserves to be put on the machine. Such is undoubtedly the power of the true belief to which the martyr is witness. But why "Be Just"? This commandment is perhaps the most general of all legal principles, something like the precondition for obedience to the law, and it has a biblical ring of being the foundation of ethics. It has all the force of "Be Good" for ethical thinking. There is something darkly satirical in this command, for in its generality the imperative is the most necessary and perhaps emptiest of all commandments, though one that all sinners have undoubtedly violated.

Wanting to inscribe the foundation of the law on his own body, the officer is deprived of the satisfaction of being a sacrificial victim to this commandment. With the machine's breakdown, the law manifests itself not as revelation but as a mangling in one last bloody murder. An empty law, a broken-down machine for murderous epiphanies—this is apparently what the past has bequeathed to our legal thinking. To conclude our comparison with *The Trial,* it appears that the spike and the knife embody Kafka's vision of the tribe's primitive way of enforcing justice, found at the end of the novel as in the short story.

After leaving the officer with a spike protruding from his forehead, the epilogue-like narration adds that the traveler returns to the colony's settlement, where he finds other vestiges of the past, especially in the teahouse that exerts on him, as the narrator says, "the power of earlier times" (*KA,* p. 246). Legends continue to exert their power. Curiously, the soldier accompanying the traveler tells him that the judge-officer probably did not mention that it is here in the teahouse that the old commandant has been buried, since the officer was ashamed of this humble and indeed rather absurd burial place for his leader. The legend's promise of resurrection immediately points to an overlap with Christianity, though one can enlarge the legend's referent to include any messianic movement that makes an appeal by the very humbleness of its origins. The commandant's grave is marked by a slab that says that the followers of the commandant will, according to prophecy, take power when he arises after a certain number of years, though for the moment his followers may bear no name. With this legend Kafka offers a condensed version of the doctrine of messianic belief in Western culture, probably beginning with the Jews of Jeremiah 20 who burn with the Lord's name sealed secretly in their hearts. It continues, of course, with the various Christian beliefs in resurrection, finding its most recent version in the Marxist utopians who believe in the coming of an eschatological revolutionary final judgment, at the end of history, when the prophet's followers will take power.

In conclusion, the vexing question of Kafka's conclusion prompts one to ask, Is Kafka's ending a successful closure to this powerful text, surely one of the most impressive in all of Kafka's work? If we refer back to the principle of incompletion that I adumbrated in the second chapter, then we may judge that the story's completion is the sign of a certain lack of success, an idea reinforced by the way the traveler flees. The fact that at the end he threatens the soldier and the prisoner with a rope so that they desist from trying to go with him has strange implications, and critics have not been happy with what they take to be the traveler's less than generous disposition. Perhaps Kafka's own ill humor is expressed in the menacing gesture at the end, since he was obliged to find some kind of closure so that he could publish the story. Or perhaps, as I suggested earlier, the traveler's disgust with the prison colony itself is enough to account for his desire to banish every trace of it from his presence and escape the recognition that he carries traces of a prison colony within himself. That disgust is enough to explain the hostile haste with which he departs, leaving the prisoner and the soldier to fend for themselves in whatever regime the new commandant may impose. At the end, with ironic bad humor, Kafka seems to show that the only ending he could envisage was flight, a continuation of perpetual movement, and hence no closure at all, just motion forward and away from another scene of writing's failure.

Chapter 6

A Country Doctor and Other Stories

World War I was under way and the Austrian-Hungarian Empire was becoming aware of what a disaster it had set off, like a chain reaction, by declaring war on Serbia when Kafka wrote a diary entry in which he listed for himself what he had done in 1914. By 31 December 1914 he had finished "In the Penal Colony" and a chapter of *Amerika,* but he had completed neither *The Trial* nor any of several other texts he had begun. At the end he wondered why he was drawing up such a list, since it was not like him to do such things. His question to himself suggests some dismay that he was beginning new projects without finishing old ones. Two of the new projects are, to be sure, among Kafka's most interesting stories, namely "Der Dorfschullehrer" ("The Village Schoolmaster," also known as "The Giant Mole") and "Blumfeld, ein älterer Junggeselle" ("Blumfeld, an Elderly Bachelor"), the latter abandoned probably in early 1915.[1] After beginning these texts Kafka wrote little for a number of months until he began making sketches for an unfinished play and then, in 1917, began writing stories that became part of *A Country Doctor.* The short stories from these three wartime years, as well as the meditations of 1917 known as the Zürau aphorisms, concern us in this chapter.

The two abandoned texts of 1914–1915 were among the first of Kafka's works that Brod published posthumously. "The Village Schoolmaster" and "Blumfeld, an Elderly Bachelor" are quite different from the immediately preceding works in which Kafka dealt with trials and judgments, and they are also quite different from each other in content and technique. The first deals with investigations into the putative existence of a giant mole, and the second describes the banal life of a bachelor who happens one day to find two animated balls bouncing about his apartment. The stories share a commonality: as in "The Metamorphosis," in both stories the world of daily reality is or has been interrupted by an apparition that contravenes our sense of what can realistically happen in the world. Giant moles and animated bouncing balls are usually not part of our daily reality. They inhabit the world of the fantastic; one again recalls the fantastic as described by Tzvetan Todorov in his *The Fantastic: A Structural Approach to a Literary* Genre. As I pointed out in the third chapter, Todorov describes the fantastic work of fiction as one in which the laws of reality are violated and the perturbed viewer of this violation then seeks a cause for the apparition that is upsetting the normal order of things. Often the mystery is explained rationally, as in science fiction, and reality is reaffirmed, but it may not be resolved, as in Romantic fictions about ghosts, and the supernatural is affirmed. In the latter case the *étrange* hovers over the world (Todorov's *étrange* has been translated into English by the rather Freudian term "uncanny," though "bizarre" or "weird" are also appropriate). As we saw in the case of "The Metamorphosis," Kafka may begin a fantastic work, but that does not mean he follows up on his fantastic beginning.

Unlike the unflappable narrator and the pedestrian characters in "The Metamorphosis," however, both the first-person narrator of "The Village Schoolmaster" and the character Blumfeld are disquieted by the violation of the laws of reality. Perturbed, they both try, more or less, to figure out how to accommodate their desire for rational order to the apparition of the irrational. It is a secondary issue whether these unfinished tales respect the putative rules for the genre called the fantastic, but it is important to see that, insofar as they are fantastic, they involve a transgression of the laws of reality in a very strong sense. As in the case of "The Metamorphosis," in neither story does Kafka give an explanation for this transgression. He gives us the uncanny without causation. The events are often comically transgressive but transgressive nonetheless, and in defying the conventions that define the real they call into question the possibility of rationally understanding the world. This questioning is explicitly the case in the epistemological meanderings of the narrator's mind in "The Village Schoolmaster," implicitly so in the farcical comedy narrated in "Blumfeld, an Elderly Bachelor."

"The Village Schoolmaster" is narrated by a first-person narrator who wants to investigate a rural schoolmaster's investigations into a giant mole that the schoolmaster has discovered in his remote village. "The Village Schoolmaster" tells us little about the existence of the giant mole—a marvelous beast perhaps two meters long—and relatively little about the perturbation caused by the mole's problematic existence. The story focuses on research into the mole, for, as narrator tells it, the mole's existence has set off a series of investigations. In illustrating the process by which new phenomena are integrated into that body of codified propositions we call science, "The Village Schoolmaster" is the first of Kafka's several satirical epistemological fables and points to later works such as "Investigations of a Dog." In them the question of knowing how we know comes to the forefront, usually to no end. Wanting to know how we know is, moreover, a variant of the quest for knowledge of the law, of the prescriptive law that condemns as well as the natural law that should prohibit the unheard of. In this regard they are not so far from the concerns of *The Trial*.

"The Village Schoolmaster" is narrated by an openly biased investigator who begins his report by expressing his disgust with moles. Since the whole business with the giant mole has fallen into oblivion, he says his real intent is to investigate not the phenomenon itself—the schoolmaster did that—but why such an extraordinary phenomenon has been forgotten. The beast is of no real interest, once it has been naturalized by the very fact that it was a topic of investigation, this despite the fact that the schoolmaster was not a competent investigator. The fact that the investigation was assigned to the incompetent schoolmaster is as extraordinary as the existence of the beast itself. So the narrator, a businessman from the city, has taken it upon himself to find out why the schoolmaster's treatise and a supplement he wrote some years later have not aroused curiosity. To avoid being prejudiced by the schoolmaster's writings, the businessman does not read them at first. On reading them later, he finds that his writing and that of the schoolmaster do not agree on some essential points. Nonetheless, they both think they have proved the existence of the mole.

In this satire of scientific investigation, Kafka's narrator embarks on considerations of writings about writings, hypotheses about hypotheses, and the procedures for knowing that we know. As readers of Kafka's "The Burrow" are aware, moles have interesting metaphorical potential because they create mazes and connections that generate labyrinths of hypotheses. One might say that in "The Village Schoolmaster" it is the investigator himself who burrows from one treatise to another in an attempt to find writing that brings to light the existence of the usually problematic animal.

But the businessman's defense of the schoolmaster results in misunderstanding, suspicion, and, finally, in not much at all. The well-intentioned narrator does reach an understanding with the old teacher, who perhaps does not appreciate, as does Kafka's reader, that, in trying to communicate about the old man's communication, the businessman is attempting meta-communication—messages about messages, as information theory puts it. But most messages go astray, and meta-communication fares no better than the first instance of communication. The narrator can send a report back to the city, but naturally it gets lost. He sends a second report, but journalists assume that his second communication is only a repetition of the first and dismiss it as a ridiculous redundancy. And, as the narrator explains, if he were to send another report, it would make no difference, for official science would take the report and make it disappear into the sum total of knowledge that naturalizes the world by describing it as a whole made up of rules without origin.

The narrator becomes discouraged and tries to remove from circulation a pamphlet he has written, one that in any case few have read. On the basis of personal experience, he can then explain to the schoolmaster the hopelessness of the latter's efforts. Just suppose, the narrator says, some professor had given one of his students the task of following up on the schoolteacher's discovery, and suppose the student had successfully developed it; the schoolmaster's name would have been honored and perhaps he would have been brought to the city and given a grant and recognition, but the schoolmaster would have immediately been considered too old to begin a scientific career and would probably have been left in his village. The schoolmaster's discovery would have been further developed, but he would not have understood it any longer, since, like all discoveries, it would have been integrated in the totality of knowledge and so would have stopped being a discovery. Once a discovery is integrated into the totality, according to the narrator, it disappears, so that only a schooled eye can recognize it. Science entails the disappearance of the individual fact—say, a giant mole—by connecting the discovery to more general axioms (*Leitsätze*) whose existence we have never heard of and that, in academic strife, are drawn up into the clouds. Hence the absurd, the irrational, and the fantastic can always be accommodated by science, or so the texts implies in describing the *process* of science. At this point it appears that Kafka has Aristophanes rather than Newton in mind, for the Greek comedian's image of Socrates floating in the clouds seems more pertinent here than the image of the rational scientist explaining the laws of nature.

In fine, the narrator tells the schoolmaster that knowledge is always about something other than what we think, which means that, in Kafka, the random appearance of a singular object can always be covered over by the construction of harmonious wholes. Thus, the fantastic is simply swallowed up by being assimilated to laws. And the whole of science can be viewed then as a region of meta-commentary that hopes to stop self-reflexivity and questions about how one knows that one knows. Hence, science is of little solace to the individual who is confronting a giant mole and who wants to know concretely what the law is—here on Zarathustra's earth perhaps—when the law seems to hide up there, in the clouds, beyond our daily world, where it may lie in *The Trial* or *The Castle*. With the bravura demonstration of the hopelessness of understanding giant moles, the tale comes to closure. The schoolmaster continues to smoke his irritating pipe, and the narrator wants to make a quick and final good-bye—like the quickly departing traveler at the end of "In the Penal Colony."

The giant mole is never seen in the tale, at least not by the narrator, and the reader may doubt that the schoolmaster ever saw the fantastic beast, though the mole's existence is finally of little matter. By contrast, the reader is obliged to believe the third-person narrator of "Blumfeld, an Elderly Bachelor." There are no indications that he is not reliable. So the reader is as surprised as Blumfeld when, one evening, on returning from work, Blumfeld finds two animated balls in his apartment that noisily bounce up and down as they follow him about. If one disregards the narrator's reliability and reads this scene as a projection, then one may use a perspective informed by psychology and think that the bachelor's loneliness has called into existence, through hallucination, strange companions to distract him from his despair. Aspect viewing also allows critics to read this tale as a biographical-projection of Kafka's own fear of bachelorhood, written between Kafka's two engagements to Felice Bauer. It is then relevant that the story repeats images of a bachelor's fears, of his loneliness, that resemble those found in "Bachelor's Ill Luck" in *Meditation*, where the lonely bachelor goes up the stairs to his empty apartment. The good humor suggests, however, other perspectives on Blumfeld. For example, he is a bachelor who has thought of getting a dog to accompany him in his lonely hours, but his fear of the dirt and disorder the dog would bring dissuades him. The bachelor has comically contradictory desires, for he wants to maintain his habitual order while regretting that he, unlike an old maid, cannot find some clean little beast, fish or bird, to satisfy his needs for companionship.

In short, psychological and biographical readings of the text do not quite account for the comic strangeness of what Blumfeld encounters: two white, blue-striped celluloid balls that bounce up and down and seem animated by intentions. In dealing with this fantastic apparition, Blumfeld uses scientific reasoning and entertains a first hypothesis: there must be strings attached to them. Empirical observation shows that they move all by themselves. Blumfeld's reaction is surprise, then dismay, then irritation, and, finally, a very unpleasant feeling, for the balls follow him around. He seizes one, and the other begins to show signs of distress for its companion. Blumfeld ponders catching both of them but, comically, decides it would be demeaning to take advantage of his size and lock them up. He decides to pursue his evening routine, since, as the narrator says, up to this point in his life, in all exceptional moments when his strength did not allow him to master the situation, Blumfeld has had recourse to the temporary expedient of acting as if he did not notice anything. Kafka implies with humor that this strategy for mastering the uncanny is not unusual.

With the pretense of not noticing anything, Blumfeld, viewer of the fantastic, hopes it will change itself into something routine. This strategy is also portrayed with humor in the twentieth of Kafka's Zürau aphorisms. It says that leopards break into the temple and drink the contents of the sacrificial vessels; this transgression repeats itself again and again so that finally the leopards' coming is reckoned into the ritual and becomes part of the ceremony itself. And so the fantastic becomes part of the banal and the routine, which is not unlike what happens to the fantastic when science takes hold of it. Alas, Blumfeld is not as successful as the keepers of the vessels, for the balls do not conform to his desire, which is that the unusual should also have limits. Notably, when he goes to bed, they go under his bed and bounce there, too, though by placing of rugs under the bed the resourceful Blumfeld can dampen their noise. The next day he seeks to get rid of them by giving them to a child.

Whether Blumfeld's gift is a successful strategy for overcoming the uncanny is not made clear, since in the second part of the story the narrator describes Blumfeld at work. Here the normal order of things holds sway. Blumfeld is not appreciated by his superior, is overworked, believes he is the only bulwark between order and chaos, and, in general, has a miserable time of it. However, his workaday world mirrors in a comic way what happened in his apartment, for he has two assistants who behave mechanically like incompetent puppets. They do nothing but get in the way of work—not unlike the pair of assistants K. has in *The Castle*. Blumfeld's two assistants curiously mirror the fantastic disorder created by the two balls in Blumfeld's apartment, though the relation between the fantastic and the workaday world is not developed in the unfinished text.

What is suggested is that the movements of the assistants recall the jumping of the balls, all this comically intensified by the fact that, physically, Blumfeld and his assistants are crowded together in one small office in which the assistants have no place to sit. They cannot move about in a reasonable way, so they bend, fall over, and bang themselves against things while hassling the women who do the real work of making linen. The story becomes a physical farce. One assistant, liking only certain jobs, wants to sweep up and struggles with an old servant to whom is entrusted a broom that the assistant tries to wrest from him. Thus ends the tale of the bachelor's foreordained loneliness, with no real closure but not without sprightly scenes in which the fantastic and the quotidian mirror each other. It is tempting to see in this story another reflection of the conflict between the world of art and the dismal practical world often found in Kafka's work. Then the fantastic bouncing balls would find a place in Blumfeld's apartment as an ironic reflection of the poetical world that, when it invades the real world, can be singularly disquieting.

After these two experiments with the fantastic, Kafka wrote little until undertaking another curious experiment, his one attempt at writing a play, the unfinished "Der Gruftwächter" ("The Warden of the Tomb"), written sometime in 1916 or 1917. Biographers agree that this dramatic piece reflects Kafka's reaction to the ongoing war and the possible demise of the Hapsburg Empire. The aging Hapsburg emperor Franz Josef died in 1916, but, as Bernd Neumann observes in his sustained reading of Kafka's work in terms of his reaction to the war, the Austrians were already seeking a way out of the war, which, as Kafka could see, would probably mean the end of the empire.[2] In its unfinished state, the play is of little interest, though noteworthy for the fact that the prince in the play wants to place a guard at his family tomb. This resembles another version of the gatekeeper motif in Kafka: guardians at the gate are employed to keep out those who are seeking something, such as access to the law, in "Before the Law," and perhaps access to the dead emperor and what he once stood for. We shall find other dead emperors in later stories.

Kafka had another creative period in 1917, which culminated in the fourteen stories of *Ein Landarzt* (*A Country Doctor*), published by Kurt Wolff in 1919. Some of these stories use the fantastic as an investigative technique, though the stories are not in general examples of the fantastic. Some are partial fantasies, which is to say that the story at times uses nonrealistic narration with a quasi-allegorical dimension. Some of them use the rhetoric of dream narration, and then "fantastic" is a synonym for "oneiric." The fantastic can also invade the narration with the rhetorical purpose of signifying the way a text narrates its quest for its own meaning, often ironically, through fantastic allegory, dream rhetoric, or near-hallucinogenic meditations couched as fantasy. In fine, most of these stories involve some form of self-referential allegory about the difficulty, if not the impossibility, of moving toward meaning and represent a development of what we saw in "Description of a Struggle." Kafka's self-referential allegories are richer in these later texts, for they also point to moments in history, to a past in which narratives might once have made sense but that, with the passage of time, can now deliver only mute messages. History has become a more problematic issue for Kafka, for he saw historical time as a movement toward dissolution. The war going on about him in 1916–1917 was not likely to give him the lie in this regard.

Let us now consider these stories individually, for they are nearly all of great interest. The first story, "Der neue Advocat" ("The New Lawyer"), combines fantasy, fragments of allegory, and a reflection on history in an exemplary fashion. The third-person narrator says that there is a new lawyer in town, a Dr. Bucephalus, about whose person little reminds readers that he shares his name with the famous horse of Alexander of Macedon, the world conqueror. This opening gambit opens up a narrative space between fantasy and fairy tale, and a humorous one at that. Given the identity of the lawyer, the narrator can draw certain conclusions, for the famous horse's presence now measures how distant the present moment is from that glorious moment in the past when one could travel as conqueror to India, when traveling somewhere was possible; today, the narrator says, no one knows the way to those royal gates in the East that the royal sword once pointed to. We have no sense of direction.

Thus today Alexander's great horse is reduced to the dismal state of being a lawyer whose only solace for going nowhere is to immerse himself in law books, that is, in dusty old tomes read by lamplight. Little remains of the past, then, just collections of the law reduced to writing. Nothing remains of great deeds, for the very meaning of history now seems to be simply the accumulation of dust. The text's multiple forms of ironic self-reference are clear once readers see that they, the readers, are in the same position as the horse-lawyer: looking at a text that should confer some access to the past by pointing the way to that glorious moment when one could move toward victorious self-fulfillment. However, the text one reads falls far short of that goal. Today, as the narrator muses, one could commit murder, but what is the meaning of that? Implicitly compared with the grand massacres of the past, even murder today is shorn of interest, just another banal event. All one can do in the present is to look at dusty old pages left over from the movement of history.

The implicit comparison of past wars with present murders suggests a perspective on the rather enigmatic twelfth story, "Ein Brudermord" ("A Fratricide"). It describes in quick detail a nocturnal murder that occurs, presumably today, on a city street. The assassin, Schmar, stabs Wese. Wese dies, his blood seeping into the ground as his life ebbs away. Although the deadpan and sadistic description of the murder resembles the opening of an expressionist film noir, the image of blood as well as the text's title recall the first fratricide, in Genesis 4:11, when Cain slays Abel and he is cursed by the ground that swallows up his brother's blood. The ironic difference between the mythical past and the bloody present is sharp, for today, as in "The New Lawyer," we have murders, but they are bereft of meaning. By contrast, Cain's crime inflected history: it is that archetypal crime that lies at the origins of unceasing warfare and crime. No murder today could have such meaning, for history offers no meaning, an idea of which the murderer Schmar seems aware when he asks the dead body, lying on the ground, what sense is there in the mute question that the dead body poses by simply lying there. With regard to Cain, his story in the Bible is a shadow text, a semi-allusion the reader uses since it seems indispensable for meaning. As throughout Kafka, the Bible is rarely mentioned but always a possible allusive referent, if for no other reason than that it is the exemplary form of writing that once granted access to supreme meaning, the laws, revelation, in short, the Word.

After the implied allusion to the Bible and after Bucephalus's law books, a third image of an ancient text is found in the fourth story, "Ein altes Blatt" ("An Old Manuscript" or, more recently, "A Page from an Old Document"). The title has an abruptness in its literal meaning, "an old sheet of paper," with the implication that it comes from an ancient tome, perhaps one shredded by the very barbarians it describes. The decaying page might be one left over from, say, the southern Sung Dynasty of the twelfth century, when the barbarians swept—or sweep—down from the north threatening to destroy Chinese civilization. The verb tense is tricky here: does the old text exist today, or was it once lying about in the past, telling of an even more remote past? Are the barbarians here now or then? None of this is clearly spelled out. And the Sung dynasty is just one of many possible contexts, one plausible historical allusion in the intertextual game suggested by an undated old page in which a shoemaker describes the horrors of life after the nomads from the north have arrived and roam at will throughout the city. The emperor remains in hiding in his palace, whose gates are closed, while the nomads freely destroy things, jabbering with their incomprehensible sounds and savagely eating meat. They tear raw flesh from living animals, and even their horses eat the meat. Like the vegetarian Kafka's father, they gnaw bones with their teeth.

The self-referential irony here is more than biographical, for it turns on seeing that the very text Kafka has written and that the reader is reading can also be compared to an old page; it is a page that has come down to the present, reminding us that the barbarism we face has long been here, ravaging then as now our homes and businesses. Moreover, the gate to the Imperial Palace was closed then, as now, and no messages come from the emperor now, any more than then, telling us—average craftsmen and businessmen—how to survive. The emperor has indeed ceased to be, in the twelfth century or in 1916.

The distant Chinese emperor is a favored image in Kafka; he lives in that always distant place where the law was kept and from which messages might have come (but do not) delivering to us essential truths. Kafka's liking for this image of the distant emperor—god, father figure, source of wisdom, or the kaiser himself—shows itself in his detaching for publication in *A Country Doctor* an excerpt from the unpublished "Beim Bau der Chinesischen Mauer" ("The Great Wall of China"), a text to which we will return presently. For inclusion in *A Country Doctor* he titled the excerpt "Eine kaiserliche Botschaft" ("A Message from the Emperor"). The message is ultimately that no message can ever traverse the great spaces that separate the now-dead emperor from you, his subject who dreams of receiving a message from the center of authority. But, since space is infinitely divisible, the messenger may go up and over steps and walls for a millennium, but there is no hope of leaving the palace. Infinitely divisible space cannot be traversed even by the kaiser's emissaries, any more than an arrow can fly from point A to point B when an infinite number of points lies between any point A and point B. The logician can point out that Zeno's paradox thus explains why messages cannot leave the sender. Kafka's text adds that nonetheless a receiver is wistfully dreaming of them.

The very short fifth story, "Das Nächste Dorf" ("The Next Village"), also asserts the impossibility of going somewhere. In it the narrator recalls that his grandfather used to say that he could not conceive how a young man might decide to ride to the next village without using up his life span, since the time for a habitual, happily unfolding life would not be enough time for such a ride. The critic Walter Benjamin gave this parable to his friend the playwright Bertolt Brecht to interpret. Brecht held the rationalist view that the paradox was underpinned by the same Zeno's paradox referred to earlier: the infinite number of points between any two points on a line precludes motion. But Benjamin rejected this interpretation, saying that the grandfather does not submit distance in space to logical analysis. For Benjamin, memory is the issue: the older we get, the more memory looms, the more quickly time goes by, until finally the grandfather can scarcely imagine a sufficient amount of time for the shortest journey.[3] Accelerating time devours itself. Whichever perspective one takes on the trip, the result is that reaching any goal, traveling to a distant or the nearest point or sending a message there—in short, all belief that motion can reach a goal—is only a wistful dream.

The impossibility of reaching an elusive goal is also depicted in the parable "Vor dem Gesetz" ("Before the Law"). Narrated in *The Trial* by the priest in the cathedral, the parable takes on other interpretative possibilities when read without the novelistic context. In the novel, the parable should illuminate Joseph K.'s trial, since the parable supposedly refers to a case like his. In *The Country Doctor* the parable appears to be an even more directly self-allegorizing text, suggesting that the reader may wait forever for the tale to deliver up its meaning. Moreover, if one accepts the Kafka scholar Hartmut Binder's idea that the gatekeeper speaks contradictorily, then it appears that any interpretation of his actions is more or less valid.[4] From this perspective, the gatekeeper says in effect to the seeker of the law that he can come in and that he cannot come in. From such a contradiction, anything can be deduced. However, it is not clear that there is a contradiction involved in a proposition that joins the idea that this gate may be open some day to the seeker but not now and the idea that the gate is meant only for the seeker. It is of course possible that the rules for entrance are so abstruse that on one level they may prohibit what, on another level, they are supposed to allow. This would also be a contradictory situation, but it is not spelled out. Moreover, one cannot be sure that the gatekeeper speaks the truth. Perhaps the seeker of the law has been deceived, though that is not clear. The only certainty is that the seeker came from the country very desirous of finding the law and that he died while waiting to be allowed to have access. And that may be a rather literal and noncontradictory description of the way Kafka viewed the human condition.

Kafka often faced his hermeneutic impuissance with humor, for hermeneutic possibilities are rarely without a comic dimension when allowed to proliferate. Consider in this light the eleventh story, "Die Sorge des Hausvaters" ("The Cares of a Family Man" or, more recently, "The Worry of the Father of the Family"). The tale itself begins with philological considerations of an object or, more precisely, the word that names the object, the "Odradek." Critics lacking

Kafka's sense of humor have tried to embroider these considerations, with disquisitions on the Slavic and German roots of the word. These critics have not seen that the very presence of the Odradek is a parody of the possibility of interpretation.

The text itself asks whether the word come from a Slavic or a German source—which is a self-referential question about Kafka's own cultural origins and hence the text's. In any case, "Odradek" is a unique word that fulfills a unique function. It is not quite a proper name, even though it refers to but one object in the world, and the ambiguity created in German by its capitalization makes it unclear whether or not it is a proper name. (All nouns are capitalized in German.) In the German text, in fact, Odradek is first referred to as a word (*Wort*), not a name. To be sure, it is not a simple inanimate object; it is a fantastic living creature that is said to inhabit the narrator's house, though it also resembles a weird object, described as something like a flat, star-shaped spool of thread with a crossbar sticking out from the middle of the star and another strut that allows the object to support itself and move about. It is impossible to catch. It is in the house for months at a time, disappears, reappears, and says it has no permanent residence. The first-person narrator, a family man, is perturbed by the little creature, for he thinks it might outlive him and stay around to see his grandchildren. Somehow his duty as a father seems challenged.

Kafka's tale depicting the Odradek resembles in part a fantastic tale and in part a scientific puzzle with philological overtones. First, the presence of the word is as mysterious as the presence of the fantastic creature itself, though presumably there would not be a word without the object. In the background lurks the Greco-biblical doctrine of logos, according to which in the beginning was the Word from which creation sprang. Can a word call into being a new creature? The narrator suggests this possibility by puzzling over the origins of the word before turning to the thing itself—a unique thing corresponding to a unique word. This is a paradoxical state of affairs to be sure, for our Greek doctrine of logos calls for every word to embody a concept or an idea (*eidos*) representing many things, unless it is a proper name. Is it a proper name? That does not seem to be the case since the narrator wants to define the word, which *sensu stricto* one cannot do in the case of a proper name. Thus the "Odradek" (or perhaps better in English "odradek") obliges us to look at the way we negotiate the relationship between language and the world, which is to say, badly when dealing with something unique. The unique inevitably perturbs one's relationship to the world.

"The Cares of a Family Man" offers a new word to bring some semblance of reality to the transgression of the natural laws that describe, if not prescribe, what might live in our houses. The father of the family must keep some order in his home after all, even when the fantastic threatens it. So language is called upon to naturalize the fantastic. This is an interesting proposition. Generalized, it suggests that an essential function of language is to keep us from being worried, if not terrified, by the apparitions that reality throws at us. Language's essential function is thus to tame the world. "Odradek" is not an entirely successful word in this regard, for the father remains worried. After all, the mere word has given him little purchase on the elusive thing that slips in and out of his life. And, he wonders, for how long will this be the case? It seems that the possible longevity of such a derisive little creature might make a mockery of the father's desire for perpetuity, especially in the eyes of his descendants.

For a complementary view of words and things, the reader can consider a tale from 1917 that Kafka did not publish, "Eine Kreuzung" ("A Crossbreed"). The story's first-person narrator seems to have great affection for the fantastic animal, half-kitten, half-lamb, he has inherited. He has no name for it, neither proper nor generic. He cannot bring himself to do what he calls the reasonable thing: kill it. The family's tradition seemingly lives on in the unhappy beast. One wonders, then, if, by analogy, the children of the father who fears the Odradek will not love their inherited fantastic being, simply because that is the nature of family affairs. One loves what comes from the past simply because it comes from the family tradition, that is, the past. Such is the irrational power of time that even a fantastic crossbreed continues to live with us, kept because it is simply part of us, with or without a name.

To return to *A Country Doctor* and a quite different problem of interpretation, the reader may well ask why there are two stories in the collection that describe eleven males—the ten engineers and a servant in "Ein Besuch in Bergwerk" ("A Visit to a Mine") and the eleven sons described by a father in "Elf Söhne" ("Eleven Sons"). The latter has been elucidated by the fact that Max Brod said that Kafka once remarked these "sons" designated eleven of his own stories. The Kafka scholar Malcolm Pasley later proposed a key for reading them in an essay on Kafka's "mystifications." Pasley also says of "A Visit to a Mine" that the ten engineers minus the servant are ten writers mentioned in an almanac owned by Kafka.[5] Given Kafka's penchant for self-allegories, or allegories that turn the text toward representing itself, there is perhaps something to the idea that in these two texts Kafka is whimsically referring obliquely to writing and writers, including himself. In describing his sons and, perhaps, Kafka's own writings, the father-narrator is critical of all them. It is true that Kafka was an exceedingly harsh critic of his own work. However, the key Pasley proposed for relating each son and an extratextual text is not very convincing, and one may just as well find that the father's criticism simply illustrates the way fathers in Kafka's work—and life—are never satisfied with anything.

Are we to see contemporary writers behind the parade of engineers in "A Visit to a Mine"? If they are writers, then they are also burrowers, so many writer-moles, going down into the earth, where they appear to the narrator, a worker in the mine, as superior beings. In his description of the engineers, the worker-narrator lists their capacities and the knowledge they possess, the techniques that make of them higher beings who inhabit a realm that the workers in the bowels of the earth will never know. Or, as the narrator puts it, the workers think they know their mine and its rock formations, but what the engineer finds in his soundings lies beyond their comprehension. The engineers are not unlike those savants who purport to know the law of giant moles and who perhaps have access to some transcendental reality, which writers, not to mention judges, should also have. In this tale, these beings with superior knowledge go down to visit the realm where ordinary mortals live, work, burrow, and seek to understand the infinite forking ways of the labyrinthine world. In his narration, the narrator seems to speak for all of us living underground when he recognizes that we shall never understand what the engineers find. "A Visit to a Mine" seems thus to be a deflationary comic performance in the game of artistic self-referentiality in which the narrator occupies a position analogous to that of the reader as he observes a sunken world forever beyond comprehension despite the presence of those from above who seem to understand it.

The artist's plight is made explicit in two other texts in *The Country Doctor,* the short third text, "Auf der Galerie" ("Up in the Gallery"), and the longer concluding story, "Ein Bericht für eine Akademie" ("A Report to an Academy"). "Up in the Gallery" is one of the most powerful of Kafka's short prose poems. Set in a circus, the text first asks the reader to consider what might happen if it were the case that a circus performer, a tubercular trick horsewoman, were to ride unendingly around on a staggering horse while her boss drove her on for months on end with his whip to the roar of the orchestra and the steamhammer-like applause of the audience. We are then asked to suppose that a young spectator ran down from the gallery and, throwing himself into the show, yelled, "Stop" in the midst of the ongoing fanfare from the orchestra. This first paragraph asks a question in which the artist is seen as a sick, driven being, going forward indefinitely, round and round, while the audience seemingly delights in this torture, which goes nowhere. The artist's *Gehen* is here without end. However, at the beginning of the second paragraph we read that the preceding state of affairs is in fact not the case. So apparently no young hero will rush forward to save the rider; no heroics are forthcoming.

Instead, one learns the circus rider's art is well prepared and that she is a beautiful, well-dressed lady whom the director helps as if she were his granddaughter and that he even hesitates to use the whip to give the signal to begin her act. Watching her with great attention and with marks of obvious concern and finding her talented beyond belief, he seems relieved to lift her finally from the horse and to mark a clear end of her riding around the circus ring. She is happy and seems ready to share her good fortune. And, with this happy spectacle in view, the spectator in the gallery lays his head on the railing, sinks into the final march as if he were in a dream, and unknowingly sheds tears—and so it ends. Does the spectator cry because he cannot heroically intervene? Or because the art he has witnessed is just a well-arranged show in which there really is no danger, barely the appearance of it; there is just the shallow pretense that the artist moves around with gestures that might have significance, for example, making a *salto mortale* in which her leap has only the appearance of risk? From two perspectives, the text contrasts two types of artistic endeavor. One is driven by the whip to continue an unceasing circular movement toward no goal in particular, with no end in sight. This is art without closure. The second image is the artist as pampered star, as a perfumed being who respects limits and is integrated into the careful production of a harmless spectacle. Closure is certain and known in advance and is a sorrowful spectacle, at least for the viewer, who perhaps would have been happier to run down to stop the spectacle if it had been of the first sort, a sadistic performance without end. With the image of art that integrates the spectator into it, Kafka proposes a self-reflexive image of art as a quasi-fraudulent enterprise, no matter what its nature.

The artist as circus performer is also at the center of "Ein Bericht für eine Akademie" ("A Report to an Academy"), though this central theme may be obscured somewhat by the more impressive fact that the performer is an ape that has become human. The text entertains obvious allusive relations, ironic and indeed satirical, with various Darwinist doctrines from the beginning of the twentieth century as well as with the then contemporary anti-Darwinist attitudes that parodied Darwin and his German disciple Haeckel for believing, as anti-Darwinists put it, that humans used to be monkeys. Moreover, the traditional Western aesthetic doctrine declaring art to be imitation is just as salient a text as that of Darwinism for reading the story. If the goal of art is imitation—or "mimesis," as Aristotle called it in saying that it was an instinctive activity—then the artist is a mimic, which means he apes things.

Ordinary language use reflects mimetic theory as well as popular ethnology (including *Homo sapiens*). We were once wont to say that in imitating things one apes things, using the verb "to ape" or, in German, äffen, "to fool," but also "to ape" or imitate such as an *Affe* or ape supposedly does, as well as to *nachaffen* (pejorative for "to imitate").[6] So Kafka's conceit recalls that the central aesthetic doctrine of Western culture proposes that the artist and the ape share common traits.

Add a dose of Darwinist parody and what could seem more natural than that an ape should, having become human, become an artist, when artists are in general apes? From this perspective there is of course a large dose of autoparody in Kaka's portrayal of the artist-performer as an ape-become-human. This strategy is not original with Kafka. He found the image of the artist as ape in the work of one of his favored writers, the pre-Darwinian Romantic writer E.T.A. Hoffmann, who portrayed an ape as artist in "Nachricht von einem gebildeten jungen Mann" ("Report from a Cultured Young Man"). In this story, Milos, a well-educated ape turned performer, writes to a friend to report how he has learned to ape all the mannerisms of Europeans of good education and become something of a consummate artistic charlatan. Kafka's tale of an ape makes ironic allusion to Hoffmann and the Romantic tradition of the fallen artist, not to mention doctrines about the state of humanity since its fall from its mythical origins into a Darwinist world of evolving beasts.

Kafka's ape has apparently read Darwin and, appropriately enough, is willing to narrate his tale to a scientific body interested in evolution. He relates that he was captured by businessmen who saw in nature a source of profit, which offers a rather exact representation of what entrepreneurs were doing in the European colonization of Africa. Shot and then placed in a cage, the ape was mimicked by the sailors who transported him. Like the sailors in Baudelaire's poem "The Albatross" who humiliate the bird that is no longer able to soar above them, Kafka's crew members tormented their captive with imitative mockery. Observing their childish sadism, naturally enough the ape conceived the Aristotelian idea that imitation is the first human activity. In fact, in their sadistic play they gave the ape the idea that by imitating them he could also find a way out, to find the *Ausweg* that becomes the goal of his life.

In the description that the ape, now named Peter, gives of his intolerable imprisonment, one encounters another metaphorical description of the grounds for art. Art is a desperate attempt to get beyond the bars of the cage that confine the artist in a realm he cannot abide. It is noteworthy that the ape was not seeking freedom; he wanted simply a way out. He describes this desire in telling how he learned to imitate, which was not difficult, even if he felt some repulsion toward the cheap booze, the *Schnaps*, that sailors imbibe. Then, he says, when faced with the alternative of a zoo or the stage, he did not hesitate: he would use imitation to find his way out. As he aped humans, his ape-nature began to disappear, and with little difficulty he was soon at the level of the average European. Thus Peter can perform on the stage like any other would-be artist and so gives a performance nearly every night. Like every artist, he has his wounds and, like every romantic, is quite willing to show them, though this may upset some who find such exhibitionist behavior, involving one's intimate self, to be in less than good taste. But, as Kafka implies with sharp irony, it is thanks to such wounds that we have our ape-performers.

In "A Report to the Academy," Peter directly addresses the academy and does not emphasize his role as performer, though it is clear that it is as an artist that he avoids cages. In a manuscript Kafka began another version of the tale with a first-person narrator who is not Peter. The narrator comes to interview Peter, and the ape's role as artist is emphasized. (This text is available in *The Complete Short Stories*.) The narrator first talks to Peter's impresario, then gains admittance to talk to the ape himself. The satire of Darwin or misrepresentations thereof is evident when the narrator congratulates Peter on having set a record for having gone from ape to human in five years. But one also sees here Peter's aversion to humanity. In the published text the theme is not developed, though it is touched upon. Peter recognized that he needed a way out, but he has only contempt for much touted human freedom, such as he sees when two trapeze artists perform. One artist hangs by his hair from the teeth of the other. This freedom, Peter declares, is a mockery of nature. To which he adds that the idea of sublime freedom is a trap for humanity, leading to sublime disillusionment. Here Peter sounds a bit like a character in Dostoevsky, or at least one who has meditated on the Grand Inquisitor's disquisition on the evils of freedom. In the text found in *A Country Doctor* Peter in fact remains true to his animal nature in one respect—his love life. His lover is a half-trained chimpanzee in whose eyes he sees the confusion (*Irrsinn*) of an animal torn from nature, thrust among humans. It is a look he cannot abide. One feels that Peter reads in that look a reproach for his own desertion of nature for humanity, for the artist's existence as an ape aping others.

Some critics see in "A Report to an Academy" an allegory about the Jewish writer encountering the difficulties of assimilation into non-Jewish culture. Kafka was quite aware of the problem, though it is not obvious that he was dealing with Jewish assimilation in the portrait of the ape qua artist. From this perspective, one of Kafka's goals was to show the distance the assimilated Jew had come since leaving his origins in the orthodox Jewish community—which is thus likened to an ape's state of nature? If one perspective on the tale suggests the problem of assimilation, a change of perspective shows the ape-artist nonetheless seeking a way out, a release from the bonds laid upon by the society before which he performs. Assimilation, for the ape as artist, means performing so that he finds a way out. Perhaps Kafka felt that Jews do the same thing, but that is not obvious. However, those who find in Kafka a reflection of the problems of Jews in Christian society can point to another text in *A Country Doctor* about which one cannot avoid concluding that Kafka was engaging in savage irony about Jews and the problems of assimilation. Kafka was obviously creating a comedy in "Schakale und Araber" ("Jackals and Arabs"), the basis of which is the situation of the Jews in Europe in 1917.

In this tale the narrator is a traveler who has come to the desert from the north, a traveler not unlike the European of "In the Penal Colony." The traveler is camping in the desert when he is accosted by a jackal, which tells him how glad he is to see the traveler, since the jackals have been waiting for one like him for many years. The wacky allusion to a messiah cannot be dismissed. The jackals live among Arabs, for whom they have contempt. As the old jackal says, no jackal has ever feared an Arab, a cursed group that eats meat and despises carrion. Yet, despite their supposed lack of fear, the jackals await a savior to deliver them. The narrator tells the jackal that he has no competence in the matter and supposes that jackals and Arabs have a quarrel that has gone on for a very long time and will end only with the extinction of their blood. The old jackal says this idea agrees exactly with the jackals' traditional belief; then, while the narrator is held tight, pinned down by two young jackals, the older one explains to the narrator what he wants him to do. The jackal proposes to give him a pair of rusty scissors with which he will slit the Arabs' throats, exactly as the Arabs do to innocent lambs, according to the morally outraged jackal.

The narrator's Arab guide shows up and, laughingly cracking a whip that drives off the jackals, explains that this is the jackals' old routine. Every European who comes to the desert is treated to the same spectacle (*Schauspiel*). The scissors have always been a part of the relations between jackals and Arabs and will be until the end of time. For the jackals are in effect the Arabs' dogs, he says, even better than European dogs. The Arab has a dead camel brought to the camp and set out in the desert. The jackals cannot resist. The steaming corpse draws them and, even when the Arab cracks his whip at them, they run away only to turn around and quickly come back to sink their teeth into the dead flesh. The Arab laughs, calls them wonderful animals, and seems even to take pleasure in the fact that the jackals hate the Arabs. With that the European traveler moves on.

My résumé should point up that, if one identifies the jackals with Jews of any sort, then it may well seem that Kafka is hardly philo-Semitic in this story. *Au contraire*. However, we know that he first published "Jackals and Arabs" in a Jewish journal, the Zionist *Jude,* published by Martin Buber. In publishing Kafka's work, in 1917, Buber wanted to call both this story and "A Report to an Academy" parables. Kafka refused to allow Buber to use the term "parables" (*Gleichnisse*) for the stories and said they were two animal stories (*Tiergeschichten*).[7] What is of interest in this is not so much Kafka's waggish sense of humor but the fact that Kafka first offered "Jackals and Arabs" to a Jewish readership, one largely composed of Zionists.

Kafka was very interested in Zionism at this time, though he was not a Zionist (nor does he seem to have become one). Another perspective on the tale suggests that Kafka was asking assimilated Jews what could it mean for an enlightened European to envisage a political state built on an outmoded religious tradition. From this viewpoint, the tale appears humorously critical of the idea of a state founded on a dubious tradition of millennial resurrection. Moreover, Kafka's critique may seem savage with its satirical image of the Jewish tradition as one propagated by scavengers, in effect, a parodistic image of the anti-Semitic image of Jews as parasites who live off others. The image is perilously close to the images of the Jew used by European anti-Semites during and after the Dreyfus affair (such as one can see in the graphic work, done after he moved to Paris, of Frank Kupka, a Czech artist and a contemporary of Kafka). One can enlarge the context for interpreting the story by recalling that the Dreyfus affair had unleashed a wave of anti-Semitism that used graphic imagery to portray the Jew as some kind of animal, a scavenger when not a predator (or a fat parasite eating the people in Kupka's case). With the ironic aplomb of which he was master, then, Kafka has taken the stupidity of anti-Semitism and turned it into a satirical allegory about the impossibility of finding paradise.

In his late work on Kafka, Walter Sokel argued that Kafka used the obvious Messiah figure in "Jackals and Arabs" to make a critique of religion analogous to Nietzsche's evaluation in *On the Genealogy of Morals,* in which Nietzsche portrays asceticism as an expression of the will to power on the part of hypocritical religious parasites.[8] In this light the jackals are an ascetic group dominated by hatred, whereas the laughing Arab, with his Nietzschean contempt for them, is free of such self-denigrating feelings. He enjoys his power. The jackals represent those ruled by what Nietzsche called *ressentiment* and slave morality, responsible for an inversion of aristocratic values. Lying systematically, the jackals condemn those who eat the meat they kill with their own hands, for the jackals can feed only on what somebody else has killed. The jackals thus dream of a savior because they are crippled by their own weaknesses and hypocritical pieties. From this Nietzschean perspective, the story's satirical viewpoint is eminently rationalist, and Zionists readers in 1917, contemplating life in Palestine, might well have reacted by wondering about their project. Or, with less critical distance, they might have wondered about an apparently anti-Semitic tale published in a Jewish journal.

With no reference to contemporary history, the collection's title story, "Ein Landarzt" ("A Country Doctor"), is remarkable for the way Kafka perfected in it his use of the dream-like flow of narration to narrate the tale of the traveling doctor who will never find his way back home. Kafka's biographer Reiner Stach thinks that Kafka also drew upon Hassidic folktales, such as a tale in which a proverbial rabbi has a horse that can fly great distances in no time at all. Kafka was apparently reading *Sagen Polnischer Juden* ("Tales of Polish Jews") in 1916. But whatever Kafka may have taken from these traditional tales, the concept is transformed in the way it is incorporated into a story that is closer to a nightmare than to a magical folktale.[9] It is worth considering briefly that if Kafka drew upon fairy tales, it was undoubtedly because traditional tales often resemble nightmares that have been tamed by various distancing conventions, such as a happy ending. Yet, between the bracketing effected by the fairy tale's usual opening of "Once upon a time" and the sometime happy ending, such tales often narrate irrational series of events that defy the reader to explain them. For example, how does one explain the fact in the Grimm Brothers' "Six Swans" that, while the six brothers transformed into swans bide their time, speech is forbidden to their sister, who knits shirts from nettles that will transform them back into humans? Or the fate that decrees that dancing to death with red-hot irons on her feet is meet punishment for Snow White's stepmother in Grimms' original version of this fairy tale? Terrifying dream transformations and savage punishment resembling paranoid delusions are the stuff of many a fairy tale.

The fairy tale as a genre, with its arbitrary but implacable laws and its constant metamorphoses, is undoubtedly behind much of Kafka's work, not least of all for its comic potential as a generator of incongruities. This is well illustrated by what appears to be a version of a fairy tale, namely Kafka's "Der Kübelreiter" ("The Bucket Rider"), a story that was to appear in *A Country Doctor* but that, after Kafka removed it, was published later in a Prague journal. During the freezing winter of 1917, plagued with war shortages, especially of heating coal, Kafka wrote this whimsical but serious tale of a man who has no coal for heat and decides to ride his bucket to the coal merchant to beg him for just a small amount so that he will not freeze. Like the unfortunate victims of fate found in Andersen's fairy tales, the bucket rider is denied his desire for coal by the merchant's malicious wife; with no coal, the man must ride his bucket off into the land called *Nimmerwiedersehen*—the land of never seeing each other again. In this tale the distance established by the tale's fantastic title sets up a buffer against the reader's immediately empathizing with the suffering that the war was inflicting on real victims freezing without coal. Kafka's humor often achieves this effect.

Dream rhetoric and fairy-tale techniques are melded in the first-person narration of "A Country Doctor." The doctor relates that he must set out on a trip that, it turns out, he will never be able to complete—offering one more instance of the infinite distances that are ready to defy the successful completion of any enterprise. But the doctor is neither a metaphysical searcher nor a seeker of revelation. He has a practical mission: to go on a snowy night to the aid of a patient. This seems at first impossible, since his horse is dead and nobody will loan him another. Yet, when he opens the door of a long disused pigsty, behind the Kafkaesque door appears a groom with two powerful horses to hitch to his wagon. Jerked forward by the powerful beasts he cannot control, the doctor surges into the night, and, as he leaves, he hears the groom breaking into his house so that he can ravish the doctor's serving girl. Freudians make much of this scene, for it certainly seems that somebody's id is unleashed once the magic door is opened.

As in a dream or perhaps a Hasidic fairy tale, the doctor makes the ten-mile trip to the patient in a second. Upon arrival, he is lifted from his wagon and carried to the patient, a boy in bed who tells the doctor he wants to die. Still thinking about the fate of his servant girl, the doctor examines the boy while, rather like the two unruly assistants in *The Castle,* the horses stick their heads into the room through the open window. At first the doctor believes the boy to be healthy, but then, while the horses whinny, he discovers a wound, like a blossom the size of the palm of his hand, in which worms are wriggling. The boy is decidedly not healthy, though what this wound might be is not altogether clear. Perhaps the boy has received what all must receive: a blossom from which he will die—a Kafkaesque oxymoron for life itself. The harried doctor cannot decide, and so he laments his difficulties as a mere country doctor, badly paid, unable to protect his servant, called out by a bell into the endless snow—and, despite all this, the people expect him to replace the priest with his supposed omnipotence as a doctor.

Now the boy expects the doctor to save him, and people come to observe, like unexpected visitors in a dream who show up to peer at the scene. Having taken off the doctor's clothes, they put him in bed with the boy while the village schoolmaster leads a choir in singing a ditty encouraging the murder of doctors. Moreover, since his patient now wants to scratch out the doctor's eyes, it is obviously time for the doctor to make his escape, as he says, and so he leaps through the window to get on a horse. But, lo, the oneiric steeds can now make no headway against the night, and the snowy wastes lie like an infinite expanse that the horses' slow plodding will never cover. The text's final lines are among the most powerful in Kafka's work for their depiction of going astray, of the impossibility of crossing any expanse, of reaching any meaningful closure:

> I shall never arrive home this way; my flourishing practice is lost; a successor is stealing from me, but to no avail, because he cannot replace me; in my house the disgusting groom is raging; Rosa is his victim; I do not want to think about it anymore. Naked, exposed to the frost of this unhappiest of ages, with an earthly carriage, unearthly horses, I, an old man, wander aimlessly around. My fur coat is hanging at the back of the carriage, but I cannot reach it, and not one of this agile rabble of patients lifts a finger. Betrayed! Betrayed! A false ringing of the night bell once answered—it can never be made good again.[10]

The doctor's lament reaches a crescendo, comic in its hyperbole but nonetheless an expression of the anguish felt by the traveler who cannot return and who, if he could, would find only ruin.

Kafka punctuates this fantastic story with proverbs, as in the final line quoted earlier, that stand out as near comic platitudes. Kafka uses clichés, proverbs, and limericks that seem to have the function of making the dream resemble a folk-tale. For example, when the doctor kicks open the pigsty and finds the groom down on his hands and knees, the servant girl notes, with notable comic under-statement, that one never knows what one is going to find in one's own house. Then, when the doctor complains that the villagers refuse to loan him a horse, he concludes with humorous banality that it is easy to write prescriptions but hard to come to an understanding with people. Later, dealing with the boy and his wound, made perhaps by an ax, the doctor comes up with an expressionist proverb according to which many a person offers his flank but hardly hears the ax in the forest, much less that it is coming nearer. These formulations, like bits of fixed folk wisdom, act as nodal points in the text, rather like crystallizing moments that organize the absurd narrative. Or, from a Freudian perspective, these fixed phrases of sententious rationalization resemble ironic condensa-tions, such as Freud was wont to find in dream rhetoric. Undoubtedly there is a satiric intent in these would-be proverbs, serving to point up a sharply ironical vision. For the proverbs and clichés in the text are ironic condensations of woe-fully inadequate interpretations of the unexplainable flow of fantastic events in which the doctor finds himself trapped. All that is certain is that once one has answered the bell in the night, the die is cast. We shall return to this question of the call in the final chapter, but it is clear that the call to serve and to help is a vexing question for Kafka, increasingly an ethicist in his later work.

Kafka wrote a number of texts in 1917 and early 1918 that he did not publish. Some are not finished or are mere fragments, but several are major achievements, and most are available in translation. Embodying Kafka's domi-nant themes, they also show Kafka's ongoing experimentation with technique. For example, one of his most expressionist and comic texts is "Die Brücke" ("The Bridge"). Continuing his experiments with perspectival viewing, the text offers a first-person narrator who declares that he is stiff and cold since he is a bridge, lying over an abyss. If the speaker is a human being, then the claim to be a bridge is a metaphor, the figure Kafka distrusted greatly. But if the speaker is literally a bridge, then we are perhaps confronting an allegory or a parable. It appears we may view the talking bridge as either a human or an allegori-cal object according to the perspective we adopt. The text offers a rather pure example of perspectival viewing, for Kafka has set up a situation in which the speaker can change form before our eyes, so to speak. If human, he seems to be a speaker representing one of the tortured views of the artist that Kafka holds; if an object, it seems to be a part of a parable about the impossibility of going anywhere. Indeed, the bridge collapses the first time a traveler steps on it, which can also be taken as a comment on the artist's fate in the modern world.

"The Bridge" shows that Kafka was increasingly skeptical about language itself, as we see in the meditations he began in 1917 after he was diagnosed with tuberculosis. The fifty-seventh of the Zürau aphorisms gives a good sense of Kafka's doubts. According to the aphorism, with the exception of the physical (*sinnliche*) world, language can express nothing except by allusion or indirection, certainly not by approximate comparisons, since in referring to the empirical world language deals only with possession and the relations of possession. Kafka resembles a positivist here, saying that language can either possess the material world or get lost in indirection—what the Viennese positivists after Wittgenstein called metaphysics. These limitations of language imply that metaphor is a trap, which is well illustrated by the experiment in "The Bridge." Its metaphor fails (which is an ironic sign of success for Kafka). For if the text is an allegory or a parable, then it refers to itself to indicate what happens with metaphor in the empirical world, which is catastrophe: it collapses and falls.

Language can seemingly lay its metaphorical hands only on its own failure, which is also comically pointed up in the play of perspectives in "The Bridge": the artist/bridge digs his toes into one side of the chasm and lays his hands on the other side while he bites into the earth to take physical possession of it—the earth to which Nietzsche's Zarathustra exhorts us to remain true. But the artist/bridge has the physical earth only momentarily in his/its possession. The first traveler who uses the bridge leaps solidly onto its middle section, and the bridge falls onto the waiting rocks below, to be solidly impaled upon them. After this description of the bridge, the reader may wonder about the fate of the traveler. We infer that his fate is not to continue his journey, for the way is broken. Or, to borrow from information theory, we can say that the channel has been broken, and no message can get through—though that is perhaps the meta-linguistic message implied by a collapsing bridge.

Messages not only are blocked, they also go astray, and this is the allegorical implication of the fragments Kafka left behind in his musings on the sad fate of "Der Jäger Gracchus" ("The Hunter Gracchus"). Biographers point out that Gracchus sounds like the Italian word for the "jackdaw," a bird that in Czech is *kavka*. However, one hardly needs to seek the *Corvus monedula* wandering in the text to see that one sense of the meta-text is a dramatization of the impossibility of the artist sending his message to its destination. The hunter Gracchus has died in a hunting accident in which he fell on the rocks from a precipice in the Black Forest. His fate is now to be on board a *Todeskahne,* a burial ship or ferry, that has for no apparent reason gone astray and now wanders about, putting in at various ports. The parallel to Charon's ferry suggests that the hunter has entered the world of cultural history and literary legends in which, if he surely has Greek origins, he also has analogies to more recent legends such as that of the wandering Jew, the subject of a popular novel by Eugene Sue, or the flying Dutchman that Wagner brought to the operatic stage. Kafka offers an eclectic mixture of possible symbols and allusions in his comic myth-making, throwing in doves that make annunciations and decorating the ship with pictures of bushmen. Gracchus, though dead, seems well aware of his cultural importance in a second fragment about him. In it Gracchus begins an argument with an ill-informed interlocutor, a practical businessman, who does not know who Gracchus is. By asking for some coherence from Gracchus, the businessman puts Gracchus on the defensive, and in reply Gracchus charges him with intentionally refusing to admit he knows Gracchus. The unfinished comedy stops here. The Gracchus story, with the image of the dead body gone astray forever in search of its destination, is one of the most haunting images of the failure to find a destination in Kafka. Even death is a trip that goes nowhere.

Another unpublished text from 1917, "Eine alltägliche Verwirrung" ("A Common Confusion"), also shows that, as in his tale of the Gracchus, Kafka remained obsessed with travel and distance. The daily confusion is that character A finds that each time he goes to see character B on business, the time required for the trip varies from a second to ten hours. Finally, in his confusion, A rushes by B, who has come to see him, thus making B wait for A to return. Returning home, A starts to rush up the stairs to explain all to B, when he twists some cartilage and falls down in pain, unable to move. B leaves and thus receives no message from A. The elasticity of distances and time seemingly foils all attempts at communication, and, if it does not, the body's own propensity for failure does.

Messages are also central to a longer story from this period, "Beim Bau der Chinesischen Mauer" ("The Great Wall of China" or, recently "Building the Great Wall of China"). As we have seen, Kafka detached from it, for publication in *A Country Doctor,* "A Message from the Emperor," a depiction of the impossibility of traversing the distance that separates you, the message's receiver, from the message's source, the distant emperor in his palace. The longer story opens up other perspectives. We recall that, in 1917, the demise of the Austrian empire was already probable, even without the death of the long-ruling emperor Franz Joseph in 1916. It is certain that the patriarch in Vienna appeared more and more remote as World War I progressed. Another perspective is metaphysical, for it is a perennially absent emperor who rules over the absurd structures that make up the cosmos. From this perspective, the tale is a comic attempt to make sense of the void at the heart of the senseless. The text at once points to the war, the empires involved, and the nomads invading from all sides, whoever they might be, and alludes to an absent patriarch, perhaps the God of Christianity and Judaism, as well as other metaphysical puzzles. Rarely did even Kafka write a text with such a potential for semantic expansion.

The first-person narrator of "The Great Wall of China" begins by presenting a deceptively objective description of the building of the wall. He recognizes that it appears strange that the wall is being built in unconnected sections. Great expanses are left open, to be filled in someday, which, as the narrator admits, allows the northern nomads to go easily around them and even destroy them. Like a theologian explaining the necessity of evil, the narrator wants to explain why the construction could proceed in no other way and why this plan is optimal. Drawing upon the Leibnizian rationality that justifies God's handling of the cosmos, the narrator gives the impression that the construction could be done no other way and that therefore this is the best way. Certainly, as he declares, the project was well thought out: fifty years before it began, architecture and masonry were declared the most important fields of study. Given such elaborate rational preparation, the narrator thinks the piecemeal building must be part of a rational plan. Austro-Hungarians may have had similar thoughts in 1914, though probably not in 1917.

The narrator reached maturity as the building of the wall was about to begin. He explains that he was hired to work on it because of his low level of educational achievement. There is an excess of people with superior educations and the project does not require their redundant architectural skills. The main problem of construction is that armies of workers are needed to work endlessly in distant regions far from their homes. The only way to keep the masses involved is to build sections with a length of five hundred meters that take five years to construct. Then the workers have a leave of absence, return home, see the ongoing preparations for new sections, and experience the joy of those who prepare them. They are renewed by contact with their fellows. The picture of the creation of community, in which the workers sing of their unity and find joy in the work to come, is sharply satirical. Zionists could have felt under attack with this depiction of how a state of believers can be created, as might have nationalists or socialists of various sorts. Kafka's vocabulary seems forebodingly proleptic when the narrator declares that every fellow countryman is a brother for whom one is building a protective wall and who gives thanks, shouting Unity! Unity! The workers' blood now flows not just in their veins but, supposedly, throughout the empire in a joyous community of mass renewal.

The building project has generated many strange ideas, especially among the Chinese scholars, one of whom, for example, has sought to prove that the wall will surpass the Tower of Babel and even serve as the foundation for a new tower. Since the Tower of Babel is the symbol of human disunity, one wonders why one would want to transform the wall into the foundation for a new tower—to create a new perfect state storming the heavens? The narrator does not understand this idea, but his thought suffices to show that no project of this scale will be undertaken without scholars erecting a superstructure of hypotheses about what it means. By contrast, the humble narrator admits that nobody really knows why the wall is being built, though he is at pains to discount the importance of their ignorance. Popular wisdom has evolved a parable about the wall that justifies not thinking about it: you should not think about the wall because if you do, you will be like a river that sometimes overflows its banks. As this parable shows, popular wisdom is hardly more helpful than metaphysical speculation. All speculation can be reduced to this reasoning: since the wall is in fact being built, there must be a reason for its being built. In all probability, somebody in the ruling power wants it built.

To return to Leibniz, I note that this reasoning is not unlike the reasoning used by believers in providence or intelligent design. The problem of knowing what the leadership, like God, has in mind is intractable, and the narrator knows he must try to explain what is as unknown to him as are the northern nomads whom he has never seen even once. Nobody knows what is in the distant emperor's mind. Here, as in all of Kafka's work, the upper reaches of authority, of power, of the law and decision making are remote and obscure, like the judges in *The Trial* or the officialdom in *The Castle*. Leadership must exist, since nothing else explains what happens in the world. It has probably always existed, for what could cause it to begin to exist? Like the beneficent God of rationalist theology, leadership is a necessary postulate to explain and justify things, such as creation, in this case, the creation of the absurd wall.

So the narrator's reflections on the wall take a turn from the created to the creator, namely the emperor, about whom nothing can be known, so great are the distances that separate him and his palace, in space and time, from his remote subjects. It is possible that they who, like the narrator, live in the provinces honor dead emperors and do not know that whole dynasties have gone under. Untold years must past before messages can reach them, if indeed the messages ever cross the vast expanses that lie between them and the leadership. Kafka's satirical presentation of the narrator's doubts offers a reflection on the nature of power: power emanates from an imagined patriarch about whom empirical data are of no consequence, since they can never be really known, and if they could be known, they would matter little to those in the sway of the power that dominates them. Power holds dominance in the abyss of ignorance filled in by imaginative projections about what the patriarch desires or does not desire. That the emperors exist like so many deities that the people confuse with one another is of little import. People live their lives honoring the emperors they believe exist and scoff at imperial officials who occasionally visit them in the name of some emperor who, the people believe, does not in fact exist.

The net result of all this, the narrator says with some regret, is that people live as if they had no emperor at all. That does not stop them from being loyal to their imagined leader, but because life in Peking is more foreign to them than life in the great beyond, they are also free. Freedom exists as a gift granted by the chaos in which nothing is certain. However, it is not certain that the narrator's conclusion is consonant with his picture of the absent emperor's power to enroll armies of workers to perform grinding labor on a pointless project that would be hateful to them if they were not rejuvenated by patriotic rallies. But then, the narrator is not a philosopher, he is merely reporting on what he sees from his distant province in some corner of the empire. He has no desire to criticize what may be seen as a weakness of their world, for, as he emphasizes, to criticize would be to undermine their unity; it would shake their conscience and their legs, which is to say the very foundations of their being. And thus he decides to go no further.

Brod's edition of "The Great Wall of China" ends at this point, appropriately so, for there is a sense of ending with the narrator's silence. However, in the manuscript Kafka added additional text and perhaps even envisaged beginning again, with a narration in which his narrator, now a child of ten, is listening to his father. Apparently Kafka's principle of incompletion made him unhappy with a closure to "The Great Wall of China" that was neither paradoxical nor ironic in itself, simply the affirmation of silence.

From Kafka's short fictions and parables of 1914–1917 three of the most challenging are the short texts that offer new versions of three classic figures of Western literature: Don Quixote, Ulysses, and Prometheus. These are whimsical musings about reading and literature, written apparently for Kafka's own meditation. Each text transforms, with humor, the classic version by offering a variant reading that changes the reader's perspective on the original. These fragments are invaluable for their demonstration of the way Kafka could reinterpret by rewriting three of the best-known of our classical images of literary culture. For example, in a paragraph offering "Die Wahrheit über Sancho Pansa" ("The Truth about Sancho Panza"), Kafka's narrator revises Cervantes by saying that Sancho Panza supplied his personal demon (*Teufel*) with numerous romances about knights and robbers in order to divert the spirit, later named Don Quixote. Then Sancho, perhaps feeling responsible for the demon, followed him about on his adventures, which offered a great deal of useful entertainment until the end. In Kafka's version, the effect of Sancho's reading—keeping him sane—is the opposite of the effect that, according to Cervantes's novel, books had on Don Quixote, which was to drive the knight crazy. Books of chivalry and romances keep Sancho's personal demon at a distance, an effect that might be liked to a kind of catharsis. Through literature, evil demons are kept at bay. Moreover, Sancho can enjoy his demon—at a distance. So the narrator finds the truth about Sancho Panza by taking a different perspective on literature, one revealing its useful function, which is nothing less that the promotion of sanity through the creation of distance. This is not unlike the distance that Kafka himself created in his works through humor and irony. The therapeutic function of literature has perhaps never been so concisely explained while being illustrated.

Another perspective on a famous classic is offered by "Das Schweigen der Sirenen" ("The Silence of the Sirens"), a rewriting of a key event in *The Odyssey,* which reads, I think, as follows. The narrator says that Ulysses wants to outwit the sirens, but not by placing wax in his crew's ears so that they are not drawn to their death on the rocks by the sirens' singing. Rather, he puts wax in his own ears before being tied to his ship's mast. No mention is made of his crew. Kafka's Ulysses then faces the sirens, well knowing that the power of desire generated by siren songs can pierce all things. Yet, he seems protected since he reflects only on his limits, on his bonds, the wax and chains, which make him joyous. However, says the narrator, the sirens can use even more powerful means than song to lure their victims, namely their silence. Perhaps they do not sing, though it is not clear whether the sirens then try to conquer Ulysses by their all-powerful silence or whether the look of happiness on Ulysses's face makes them forget their song. For Ulysses's look conquers the sirens in the end. He may think they are singing, but they really are looking upon him, wanting to hang onto the radiance of his eyes for as long as possible. Had the sirens had consciousness, the narrator suggests, they would have been nearly destroyed by this moment.

This capriciously convoluted text offers a description of the sirens' being seduced by Ulysses as much as the contrary. This is an extraordinary example of aspect viewing. After this image of desire, the text concludes with a pirouette describing the literary text itself as a protective shield. For, with a self-reflective turn in the narration, Kafka adds a coda saying that Ulysses was so clever that he used as a shield the preceding fictive text—the narrated *obrigen Scheinvorgang*—meaning the "preceding apparent happening" or fictional occurrence. Ulysses's shield is in effect the text we have just read about the sirens, preceding the coda's ending lines. The shield is the mirroring text by which the sirens' desire turns against itself when it contemplates itself, as in a mirror, for the sirens are impotent to use their wiles when they face a man who holds up the tale of their own doings to their vision. Thus, a literary text's function is to divert the sirens and, perhaps, the gods. Much as for Sancho Panza, romances keep Ulysses's demon at a distance, and his tale protects him from the wiles of seduction and the looks that destroy. For the reference to the shield recalls the myth of Perseus and the polished shield he used to defend himself against Medusa, whose very look was deadly. The text, like a mirror-shield, reflects the image back at those who look at it, with the result that Ulysses, a teller of tales, is the vanquisher of all who listen to him—for is it not really Ulysses who has told the fictive text about his dealings with the sirens? Mimesis is not only aping, as in "A Report to an Academy"; here it is also the mirror power to overcome the dangers of the real and the imaginary by reflecting their own image back at them. Again, literature is, for Kafka, an act of survival.

The third transformative reading takes up one of the fundamental myths of the tragic tradition, the myth of Prometheus. Aeschylus's *Prometheus Unbound Bound* can serve as a main source, though the myth is found in various sources, especially Hesiod. At the play's beginning, Force and Strength chain Prometheus to rocks in the Scythian desert as punishment for having helped humanity against Zeus. With something like this version of the myth in mind, the narrator of Kafka's "Prometheus" says there are actually four versions of Prometheus's fate. The first is that he is chained to the rocks and an eagle is sent to eat his liver; the second is that the eagle eats so deeply that he and Prometheus become one; the third is that in the course of the millennia everybody forgets Prometheus's crime; and the fourth says that finally the gods get tired of it all, as does the eagle feeding on Prometheus's liver, and that even his ever-renewed wounds are tired of it. The list of versions draws out the humorous truth of a punishment of infinite duration: it allows infinite permutations. But the concluding paragraph of this brief text subverts the preceding readings by offering a rule for hermeneutics. All the preceding versions can be explained as a part of the truth, except for one thing about them: the presence of the rock presupposed by every version. The rock is a brute inexplicable fact of being. So perhaps the real conclusion is that, wherever there are possible truths, one always ends up with the disgruntling presence of the inexplicable. Truth always emerges against a backdrop of the irrational, against something like the gratuitous presence of rocks. This is one of Kafka's most subtle epistemological fables.

Much critical attention in recent years has been given to the short meditations and aphorisms Kafka wrote in 1917 while staying with his sister Ottla in Zuräu. Kafka made a selection and numbered them, making some additions in 1920, perhaps with some thought of publishing them. (Brod published them later under the title *Meditations on Sin, Pain, Hope, and the True Way*.) There are 109 such brief numbered texts, now known as the Zürau aphorisms, though few are aphorisms in the classical sense of offering a concise statement of a sententious general truth (such as those the master of the classical aphorism La Rochefoucauld makes when he gives an aphoristic résumé of the foundation of social life with the proposition "Hypocrisy is an homage that vice pays to virtue"). Kafka's texts are brief meditations, mini-parables, and contain some concise aphorisms, but most are closer to Pascal's ruminations than to La Rochefoucauld's maxims.

With regard to their themes, some critics have argued that in the aphorisms Kafka, for the first and only time, directly uses theological concepts. This idea is misleading. After all, one can find theological concepts indirectly evoked throughout his work. Moreover, Kafka never thought he could directly use theological concepts at all. He used terms like "original sin" and "the Fall" as quasi metaphors, taken from Judeo-Christian theology, with which Kafka positioned himself on a textual playing field where he was, to use his constant metaphor, seeking the way. The way is a metaphor, moreover, that belongs as much to Taoism as to the Western religious tradition that sees Christ as the way. Kafka, like Peter the ape, constantly sought the way out and, sometimes, the way back but, in any case, the way. It is perhaps more accurate to say that for Kafka, as for his Sancho Pansa, these theological metaphors, like romances, offer help in finding the way, minimally the way to retaining sanity in a world in which the truth seems often to be absurd anguish.

For all their variety, the Zürau aphorisms can be divided thematically into three groups. Roughly a third of them deal with the way or with variants thereon, such as themes of movement or the impossibility thereof. A second group of some twenty-five or twenty-six meditations is devoted to ethics, often in terms of Kafka's idiosyncratic views of the Fall, evil, and sin. Kafka wrote about morality in theological terms, using terms he transformed as he sought a way of dealing with the human psyche and its reliance on received language. Notably, he did not use psychoanalysis. Since Kafka declared roundly that one should abolish psychology, we may infer that Kafka preferred traditional language for dealing with the psyche and ethical problems, rather than scientific and pseudo-scientific concepts of his time. Finally, there is a third group of texts that play with perspectival viewing of things, often in the form of paradox, showing different ways of seeing the same thing. Perspectivism is affirmed, in fact, throughout the collection of aphorisms dealing with the way.

Perhaps in a category by themselves are a few texts that refer to the "indestructible." For instance, the fiftieth aphorism says that we all need to have trust in something indestructible (*zu etwas Unzerstörbarem*), though both the indestructible and trust in it may remain hidden. The text says that one expression of this remaining hidden is the belief in a personal God/god. (Both "God" and "god" are capitalized in German.) This is the only reference to God/god in the aphorisms. It is not necessarily metaphorical. It says that belief in a personal deity is a way of dealing with one's needs, perhaps by remaining blind to them. With this interpretation of God as an expression of psychological need, one can argue that, if Kafka's quest for the way is in some sense mystical, it is a kind of lucid atheistic mysticism that shows a willingness to be without illusions—such as the belief in personal deities or the myths fostered by modern psychology.

The first aphorism sets out the difficulty of finding the true way: the true way may appear to be a rope upon which a performing circus artist might walk, but it is set so low that it appears designed to trip one up. Two perspectives on the image of the rope are set out here, and with them the aphorisms begin their marvelously tortuous way, asking how to find the way, accompanied by an equally pressing ethical question concerning the way's goal. The second part of the twenty-sixth aphorism offers little hope of an answer, for if there is a goal, there is no way (*Weg*), since what we call a way is only our wavering (*Zögern*)—or, alternatively, our procrastinating, our bumbling, our failure to make up our mind. And our mind is of little use in any case, for, according to the twenty-ninth aphorism, whatever reservations we may have about evil, we should not think we hold them by our own design: those thoughts are what evil puts in our mind to further its purposes.

Thus our ethical failures are manifold. In speaking of ethics, of evil (*das Böse*) and the devilish, Kafka seemingly found it natural to use the language of the Judeo-Christian tradition, undoubtedly because the Fall is a powerful myth to account for what is occurring at every second of our lives. It is a powerful metaphor to account for our relationship to past ideals. And, as the sixth aphorism puts it, the decisive moment in human evolution is always at hand in the present moment (*immerwährend*). From this Kafka derived the time-abolishing conclusion that nothing in the way of a spiritual revolution has ever occurred: it can only be occurring. The eternal present has the only ontological reality. That perspective on time seems to help elucidate what Kafka meant by evil. In the fifty-fourth aphorism he states that there is nothing other than the spiritual world—*ein geistige Welt.* ("Spiritual" is perhaps misleading, since I think Kafka affirms that there is only the world that can be entertained by the mind.) What we call the physical (*sinnliche*) world is evil (*das Böse*) in this spiritual world. And what we call evil (*böse*) is only the necessity of each second of time in our eternal development. Kafka contrasts a noun, *das Böse,* and an adjective, *böse,* in contrasting two realms, the spiritual or mental world and the physical or sensual world. This is admittedly a metaphysical construction in which physical appearance, erupting into our spiritual life, is deemed the origin of evil while the evil we do, the devilish or diabolical we perform, is an ever-recurrent momentary event. The evil event is our ongoing fall in every successive moment of time, as we rush downhill toward eternity, as the thirty-eighth aphorism puts it. With these metaphysical metaphors, Kafka's view of evil leads to a view of ethics that strongly resembles that of an ascetic puritanism that his own sensual nature constantly put in question—whence the debate with himself and the constant perspectival changes.

In these aphorisms Kafka's humor also reasserts itself in the perspectival games he plays that relativize all assertions. The game is highlighted in the eleventh aphorism, in which Kafka says that our view of an apple depends on whether it is being viewed by the child who must stretch his neck to see it on the table or by the master of the house who looks down and lifts it up to give to a guest. A third of the texts explicitly play in this manner with perspectives and perspectival viewing of this sort, and even more if we include perspectival viewing of the way and of ethics. Perspectival vision is affirmed as the basis of truth in the eightieth aphorism, which states that truth is indivisible and that truth therefore cannot recognize itself. The awkward conclusion is that whoever would recognize/know truth must be (a) Lie. With Nietzschean irony, Kafka affirmed that truth stands out only when falsehood offers the right perspective on it. And, not unlike later Wittgenstein, Kafka entertained the idea that perspectival viewing is a necessity for understanding the way language functions in connecting images to the world in what appear to be constantly contradictory ways. In eliminating these contradictions, we can have belief—belief, which is like a guillotine blade, so light, so heavy, as the eighty-seventh aphorism concisely puts it, from Kafka's ironic perspective, in suggesting that belief abruptly cuts off alternative perspectives. A skeptic's irony underwrites many of these meditations.

In short, many of these texts are ironic and playful demonstrations of the way perspectival seeing determines meaning. Thus Kafka mused that crows maintain that a single crow could destroy heaven. That is doubtlessly true, says the narrator, but that shows nothing against heaven, since "heaven" means precisely the impossibility of crows. The mind reels, wondering whether this aphorism proves the vacuity of the notion of heaven or whether it shows that storming the heavens is a form of hubris that the bulwark of belief will never allow. Or both. One may call this dialectics if one desires, though I think it is truer to the texts' semantic intent to regard Kafka's thinking in images in them as a way of thinking out the alternatives that emerge from the same gestalt. This is explicitly the point, for example, of the ninetieth aphorism. In describing the pursuit of the way, the aphorism says that one has two possibilities with regard to what one can do: to make oneself infinitely small or to be, that is, to be infinitely small. The first possibility is action, which is the beginning or the continuing of an act. The second is being in a finished state, hence complete, in a state of inactivity and thus immobility. The range of interpretative possibilities for what it means to make oneself small or to be small is enormous—I immediately think of Christian humility. Be that as it may, Kafka's double perspective is clear: either one is or one is making; one is doing or one is immobile. However, at any given single point in time the image is the same, for one has become what one is, and one is what one has become in that very second. The image differs only if one changes the perspective, yet it remains the same. Interestingly, this perspective points up the belief that only the eternal present exists, for this conclusion imposes itself if there is no immediate difference between being and becoming, just a perspectival choice.

This brief introduction to the aphorisms can only suggest the dazzling intellectual play to be found in these short, often enigmatic texts that Kafka wrote after the medical diagnosis that, in 1917, was something like a death certificate. These texts ironically bear up under the weight of that judgment as they seek to put in order thoughts about a life perhaps nearly over. However, fortunately, that life was not over, and I conclude here by pointing out one of these aphorisms that seems to be a point of department for seeking the way to *The Castle*, the novel that Kafka was soon to begin. This is the hundred and second meditation. It says that a human being's development follows constant growth, hence constant change, in which the individual body is constantly changed and replaced by the body's new being in stages on life's way. The text affirms we develop ourselves through the suffering of the world, for we are not less bound up with humanity than with ourselves. And it concludes with the thought that there is no place for justice in this context but also no place for fear of suffering, nor is there a place for the interpretation of suffering as a merit. With its affirmation of human solidarity as the grounds for existence, the mediation offers a first perspective on *The Castle,* the novel in which we watch the protagonist, the land surveyor named simply K., struggle to be integrated into a community that refuses to accept him. From this perspective, *The Castle* is the story of a man trying to find the way that will integrate him into the community, with no question of justice or merit but simply as a matter of his being bound to others. Only in this way can he realize himself as an ordinary mortal living with others, the others to whom existence binds us before any questions of justice or the law. Let us now turn to that great unfinished novel.

Chapter 7

The Castle

After a spurt of creativity in 1920, Kafka apparently wrote little in 1921. Most critics and biographers agree that Kafka then undertook to restore his confidence in himself as a writer by working intensely on his final novel, *Das Schloss* (*The Castle*). They support this argument with a diary entry written just before Kafka began to write *The Castle* in the mountain resort Spindlermühle in northern Bohemia, where Kafka went in early 1922 because of his tuberculosis. In the diary entry of 16 January 1922, Kafka speaks of having suffered something like a nervous breakdown. The entry shows he clearly felt himself against a wall. His health problems had not abated, and he now found his solitude to be almost unbearable. He writes, moreover, that a disparity between his inner sense of time and the passage of time marked by clocks shows that his senses of inner and outer reality are split. In tortured language he describes an inner life of chaotic introspection characterized by the pursuit of one idea after another, a pursuit (*Jagen*) springing forth from humanity (*Menschheit*)—which is not an altogether clear idea, though the previously mentioned hundred and second Zürau aphorism implies that Kafka came to view himself as bound up with human existence in mutual solidarity. However, in the diary Kafka seems to think that his meditation on the human condition is pushing him toward madness. He goes on to say that this pursuit of ideas is the product of solitude—it, too, a compulsion—and he wonders where it will lead him. If it does not lead to madness, he says, then perhaps he can stay upright and let himself be carried on by the pursuit.

In the diary Kafka's psychic struggles are expressed by an image that foreshadows the basic spatial configuration of *The Castle,* with its portrayal of the domination of the lower village by the Castle situated on high. When he describes his struggle, he muses that since "pursuit" is just an image (*Bild*), he can just as well use another image and speak of making an attack or assault on the last earthly borders; this will be an attack from below, from where human beings are; and since this, too, is only an image, he can replace it with the image of an assault from above, coming down against him.

The translation of this diary passage uses "metaphor" to translate what Kafka calls a *Bild* or "image" of attacking forces. Given Kafka's suspicion of metaphor, "image" seems more accurate to underscore that in this entry Kafka is thinking directly in images, images of the forces that besiege him, as well as humanity, at this precise moment in his and humanity's history. He is thinking in spatialized images in which forces rain down and forces rear up in a conflict that sets the lower against the upper, as well as the upper against the lower. This spatialization of conflicting forces corresponds closely to the dynamics between the upper and lower realms found in *The Castle* in which the Castle and its bureaucracy, situated above the village, rule over the lower realm of the simple folk where the land surveyor K. begins his struggle with the remote forces above him. In fine, the novel corresponds to a moment in which Kafka, affirming human solidarity in his personal writing, also felt torn by psychic conflict that imposed itself on his perception of it in spatial terms—terms that also correspond to social conflict.

Kafka concluded this January diary entry by saying that all of this kind of writing—he says "*Literatur*"—is an attack on boundaries and that if Zionism had not come along, it might have developed into a new Kabbalah. What Kafka meant by this possible development is not entirely clear—presumably his own work is an exemplar of what he had in mind by the term "literature"—yet nothing in Kafka's writing resembles what he calls, in thinking of the Kabbalah, a *Geheimlehre* or a secret doctrine. In any case, Zionism had come along, and, he says, there will be no new Kabbalah. Apparently social thought has replaced mystical doctrines. This entry shows, moreover, that Kafka was thinking historically as well as personally, for he concludes the diary entry by saying that a genius will be needed who can plant his roots anew in centuries past or one who can create again the centuries gone by without expending himself but only begins to give of himself. This task would be presumably complementary to or even an alternative to Zionism.

Why Zionism? Zionism is probably listed here for its political program, for the idea that a people can think historically in the creation of a new state—one that Kafka undoubtedly hoped might be the antithesis of the state found in *The Castle*. Kafka sympathized with Zionism insofar as he saw in it a program for the creation of a better society. Thus, standing in opposition to the social solidarity Kafka could find in Zionism, the dominating Castle reflects at least two images that tortured Kafka's mind. The Castle seems to offer an image of what political and cultural history have culminated in, that is, political states in which solidarity is minimal. The Castle is also, as we can infer from the diary, an image of those forces that were besieging Kafka's solitary self—an image that concentrates psychological and perhaps metaphysical forces, demons like the one Sancho Panza exorcised by creating Don Quixote. In Kafka's mind, then, it appears that humanity and the individual were mutually implicated, with this image representing in the present moment the history of repression.

After considering Kafka's diary, the reader who turns to the novel relating the land surveyor K.'s misfortunes may at first be baffled by a novel that seems to be composed of a disparate series of texts narrating loosely connected scenes and dialogues. However, the reader should not be put off by a first impression, for it is clear that Kafka was guided by a sense of organization that, for whatever reason, he was not able to bring to closure. The novel is divided into four distinct but interrelated parts, each having its own purpose. The first part consists of the opening chapter, which functions as a prelude to the whole and differs in tone from what follows. In it Kafka sets out the information necessary for negotiating the ways that do not lead to the Castle. After this prelude, the novel unfolds as the narration of what the protagonist K. does in an attempt to secure his position in the village while seeking, through the agency of the mysterious bureaucrat Klamm, to get to the Castle. This narration, which centers on the futile quest to see Klamm, occupies roughly the second through the fifteenth chapters. Then follows a third section, which offers a complementary image to that of K.'s travails in the preceding chapters: Olga tells K. the tale of the disgrace of her family after her sister Amalia refused to obey the summons sent to her by a Castle functionary who wanted to have sex with her. Olga's narration tells a story embedded within the novel's main narration, a story that reveals to K. another aspect of the way social order is maintained. The Castle's order is based on the power of shaming and ostracism. The final section of the novel consists of a series of chapters centered on farces that point up the ineptitude of the bureaucratic order. The scenes include descriptions of K.'s going to a hearing at night, his entering the wrong room and falling asleep, the total disorder that characterizes the distribution of files to the bureaucrats in the inn, and, finally, K.'s apparent readiness to live secretly with servant girls. In describing in these chapters the disorder of the Castle's order, Kafka pulls out the stops on farce and satire.

The novel has no closure, though Brod said Kafka told him that the novel would end with K.'s death. While dying, K. would learn that he had not been granted official permission to live in the village; however, he would be tolerated there. Brod's comments suggest that officially K., with his demands to be heard, could not exist under the reign of the upper powers, though indeed K. does exist. Brod describes a conclusion that would have affirmed what is evident in the novel: that there is permanent separation of two worlds, the private sphere and the public, of desire and official realization, that coexist in the tension that characterizes social reality and, undoubtedly, metaphysical longings. The Castle would thus continue to refuse the solidarity that the one hundred and second Zürau aphorism described as fundamental to humanity. However, Kafka did not write this ending or even attempt to write it, although during his last two years he enjoyed enough health to write some of his greatest fiction.

The first chapter of *The Castle* acts as a prelude that is hauntingly evocative of a remote society outside any precise historical coordinates, situated on the margins of our world and yet central to it in the way that it reflects basic social reality. Almost as in a dream or perhaps as in a fairy tale, the land surveyor K. arrives at a remote village, presumably called by the Castle authorities to work there. These authorities have power over a land covered with snow, in which, because of the fog and the darkness, K., upon his arrival, can barely see where the Castle might be. Nonetheless, this land of darkness is the region that the land surveyor is to survey, or so he thinks, though a challenge to his work is laid down from the beginning in the description of an obscure place where K. can make out only dim outlines of things.

Some critics, like some characters in the novel, do not believe that K. is a land surveyor; some even suggest that he is a swindler. It is true that he seems to forget himself what he is. Identity is at issue in the novel, but not only in the case of K. For instance, his assistants are chameleons, and it is never clear who Klamm is (perhaps even if he is). But there is no reason to think K. is lying, even if he never surveys a single acre. Some, more trusting critics have taken a different tack with K.'s identity. They propose that the word for K.'s profession as surveyor, *Landvermesser,* suggests the Messiah. The idea of a Messiah is plausible only if the surveyor has somehow brought a message of salvation for the villagers. Is K. a messenger in that sense? Perhaps. He brings new ideas to the village in his demand to be treated as a recognized equal of all, which seems indirectly to reflect a Christian viewpoint. However, if we recall Kafka's parody of the Messiah legend in "Jackals and Arabs," we may be a bit dubious about the apparition of the savior in this land that, admittedly, is in need of salvation.

Let us accept that K.'s occupation is the truly Kafkaesque one of measuring land, spaces, and distances and of laying out ways—the *Wege* that structure the development, or lack thereof, of much of Kafka's fiction. A land surveyor would, we hope, be able to cross those infinite distances that keep the country doctor from ever returning home. He must do so if he is to function successfully in measuring out society's spaces as an organized series of ways and byways and precise tracts where people can live. That K. is a failure at negotiating ways that lead anywhere is hardly surprising. But even in failure he is nonetheless a representative of the scientific culture that believes it is possible to use measurement to achieve order and understanding. Perhaps that culture is on trial here, even more than in *The Trial,* for the rational K. is baffled and humiliated at every turn, since the culture of the Castle and village has apparently no need of a rational surveyor of things. Or, as critics from Karen Keller to Ritchie Robertson have rightly argued, the Castle has no need of or desire for the Enlightenment.[1]

In the first chapter, or prelude, K. begins the novel's basic action, that of a quest, as much a quest for lodging as for some meaning about K.'s being in the village. K. arrives in the village, seeks lodging in an inn, is almost thrown out, spends the night there, wanders in the village, enters a house, sleeps, is thrown out, and gets a ride back to the inn, to discover that time is going faster than he thought and that two young men he saw in the road are actually his assistants—though he does not recognize them and they know nothing about surveying. The narration is close to but not quite a dream narrative. As in a dream, logical connections seem missing in K.'s perception of things, though there is a patina of realism to his quite normal desire to get settled and be admitted to the Castle to find out why he has been called and what he is to do.

Translations vary as to the nature of the Castle and what it is perched on. It is a *Schlossberg,* which conveys the image of a medieval castle set on a hill or mountain dominating a plain. However, K. later sees above him an indistinct jumble of rambling houses. The ancient and the modern are melded in these images. However, when he arrives in the dark, K. sees only light and darkness. The description gives the impression that K. has entered a world of eternal snow over which an indistinct power, called simply the Castle, reigns.

In this world immobility reigns. This is conveyed especially well in the first chapter, after K. has spent a first night in the inn and discovers that, though he had been capable of energetically walking to the village from some unknown distant place, he can no longer move along the snowy road. He is stuck in the snow, both before and after he rests in the house in which men are bathing in a vat. The road running through the village is as deceptive as any way or path found in Kafka's work. K. takes the road thinking it will lead him to the Castle, but it only leads him on and on indefinitely. And so the text reads, like an ironic commentary on itself, depicting K.'s hopeless motion: "he was amazed at the extent of the village; it seemed endless, always the same little cottages and frosted window-panes and snow and no sign of life. Finally, he forced himself to leave this street and turned into a narrow lane where the snow lay even deeper; his feet sank into it and it required a great effort to pull them out again. He broke out in a sweat, then suddenly he stopped; he could go no further."[2]

This stasis presents the novel in miniature, something again like a *mise-en-abyme* or inner representation in which a small part or an inner image represents the entirety of the work. K. goes nowhere here or at any other time. By implication, transcendence, either physical or metaphysical, or going anywhere at all is blocked in the village that is endless in its labyrinthine finitude.

K. enters a house where he is not welcome, for, as he learns, hospitality is not a part of the village mores. So his paradoxical situation is that he can go nowhere and remain nowhere. Nonetheless, the entry into the house affords him, and the reader, an introduction to the village culture. People scrupulously obey the Castle's rules, for reasons that become clear later when K. learns that not to obey entails ostracism. After falling asleep and then awakening, K. is expelled from the house with strong-arm encouragement. He finds himself immobile again in the snow and can return to the inn only because a coachman, refusing to take him to the Castle, transports him to the inn on a horse-drawn sled. (Waiting in the snow, K. asks whether a sled might not come by, only to learn that there is no traffic.) At the inn he is astonished to see that the day has gone by, though his inner clock tells him he has not long been absent from the inn. Kafka's diary entry about his own sense of time points up that time is a flexible notion, reflecting psychic instability, both in his life and in his works, for, as the country doctor knows, much can happen in an apparently short period of time and trivial things can seemingly take forever.

The events of *The Castle* occur in a period of a few days, though the novel conveys a subjective sense of duration demanding weeks or perhaps months. The first chapter's unending present moment is contrasted in K.'s mind with an image from his own distant past. This is one of the few moments in the novel in which the reader gets a sense that K. comes from another place and perhaps another time. He recalls his hometown, finding it not inferior to the Castle, though he has not seen the town for a long time. In K.'s mind the church spire of his hometown strikes him as having been built for a higher purpose than the tower or spire he sees above him on the Castle hill: the spire of the past seems to have been built for a noble purpose, whereas the spire before him is simply part of a crazy jumble of buildings, against which the lone spire stands out as if it were a melancholy inhabitant of the place, perhaps resembling a mad person who should have remained locked in the attic rather than be exposed up on the hill. It is noteworthy that later in the novel, when walking with Barnabas, K. recalls his climbing a wall as a childhood victory, but little else seems to remain to K. of his past, just a spire suggesting nobility and a boyhood triumph. The past, in any case, is somehow superior to the present, for it recalls a perhaps imagined moment of something better.

This kind of polarizing of past and present is implicitly present in much of Kafka's work. For example, the law is often a text that was known at some time past but is now only hazily present, perhaps only in old tomes. In *The Castle* the spire of memory is a reminder of a past when society's architecture embodied the noble vision of a culture that, perhaps, once had contact with transcendence, before it lost contact with the Word. But in the present moment, set somewhere in the Castle complex, the spire is a part of the irrational sprawl that stands above K., though perhaps endowed with significance for all that: it is somehow part of the Castle's power.

The first chapter establishes a basic pattern in the world of the Castle: messages are sent back and forth, often contradicting each other, others failing to take other messages into account, but in any case always generating other messages. Sending messages begins with K.'s arrival in the village, when he comes to the inn to seek lodging, is offered a straw mat on the floor, and goes to sleep there, only to be awakened by somebody telling him he needs an authorization from the count to stay in the village. K. says he will go get the permit, to which the young man who has awakened him shouts that he cannot bother the count with a message at midnight and K. must leave immediately. K. then identifies himself as the land surveyor whom the Castle has summoned. The young man, supposedly the son of the Castle's castellan, telephones the Castle, first learns there is no record of a land surveyor, then is called back with the message that there has been an error. K. is recognized. Messages proliferate, though nothing is ever really decided. It is not really made clear whether K. can stay.

Another aspect of dream logic that seems to preside over the narration is that K. does not respond to the recognition accorded him with anything like a realistic response. His first response to the message is that it is unfortunate he has been recognized, since it shows that the Castle had weighed the balance of power and, in some translations, had accepted K.'s "challenge"—though the German text says that the Castle is ready for the *Kampf*—fight or struggle—with K. From the outset, then, K. views his relationship to the Castle as a struggle, not really as a job to be done. And the idea of *Kampf* recurs in the novel at various crucial moments. The transformation of a banal work task into the basis for a fight is not unlike the labile metamorphoses that characterize dream and fairy tale, though here the disjunction between K.'s response and the apparent context is designed to underscore that, in the world of the irrational, responses cannot be logical: the Castle's recognition is a way, he suddenly thinks, of keeping him in a state of terror. He accepts it. He is there to work, and he is there to struggle, and all this in a near dreamscape that may be the nightmare side of a modernity enslaved to its past.

The Castle represents a modernity invested with the vestiges of history. These vestiges are connoted, for example, by the term *Kastellan,* the medieval term "castellan," to designate some of the Castle's officials. Recent translations prefer "warden," though that sounds like a church or prison official to an American ear. The Castle has a castellan, many lesser castellans, and a medieval count Westwest. It also has a telephone whose very modern existence in 1922 is another sign that time is polarized and stretched out, running from a distant past into the era of technological modernity. A castellan and a telephone inscribe history into the text as a dimension in which past and present coexist in irrationally interpenetrating ways.

The peasants in the inn are immediately aware of the perturbation that K. may bring into their static world, for when he is recognized in the inn, they hurry from the room, comically averting their faces as if from a horrible apparition that threatens the stability of their world order. Their reaction is illustrative of the treatment K. receives in the rest of the novel. To varying degrees nearly everybody wants to avoid K., to divert him, and to send him on his way. He is a threat to the order that the village inhabitants honor, for reasons that are not always clear. What is clear is that they fear and obsequiously respect the Castle and its authorities.

From the beginning of *The Castle* it is evident that Kafka is illustrating ways in which power orders culture and culture is a reflection of power. In Kafka's earlier stories power is an irrational emanation from the father's presence. In *The Trial* power flows from a bureaucratic organization that supposedly has access to the law that establishes the order of things. This power is immediate in its effects: it can arrest people and put them on trial before it kills them. The power that orders things in *The Castle* is somewhat different. The bureaucratic order from which power emanates is less hidden, if equally remote. However, it appears beholden to few laws but many procedures. It does not kill but maims the disobedient with the psychological harm inflicted by shame and ostracism. It is a power over daily life that fixes the routines and beliefs of all who are bound by ties that link them together in the same culture.

K. arrives in the village and, asleep, is awakened to be told that one man holds the power to allow him to stay: Count Westwest. But K.'s first belief that he can simply deal with a patriarch or one aristocrat who holds the key to all power is quickly dispelled as K. begins to seek a way to get to the locus of power. Here there are no personal interviews as in days when favors were once granted by the emperor or the king in the more felicitous days of patriarchal empires. All quests and requests in *The Castle* are deflected toward various other sites of power—hence the untold numbers of messages—such that the outline of the hierarchy disappears as the novel unfolds. Various officials are named; they function something like lightning rods toward which energy is directed and that carry it away, and no authority is ever really encountered. In his quest K. fixates on the presumably important functionary Klamm, for the land surveyor must have some goal if his quest is to have a direction. Klamm should be available, for he apparently comes down to the inn called the *Herrenhof;* he sleeps with women there; he has undersecretaries there. I say "apparently" since no positive statement about Klamm, much less the Castle itself, is ever certain. K. may stare through a peephole at a man identified as Klamm, but there really is no proof that the person K. sees is Klamm. His former lover, the servant Frieda, can identify Klamm as a man who sleeps with his eyes open, but that is of little help for K.

After this prelude setting up K.'s quest, the novel unfolds for some fifteen chapters, each with a title given by Kafka, during which K. goes about the village, trying to figure out how to make contact with the elusive bureaucrat Klamm, who, he thinks, might further his interests, not to mention approve of his marriage to the servant girl Frieda. Most readers assume K.'s goal is to gain access to the Castle and hence the locus of power, though this is not exactly the case. Rather, the diffuse power structure has deflected him from that ultimate goal and causes him to concentrate his attention on one often absent functionary, the Klamm who receives nobody.

This strategy of diversion is obvious in the second chapter when first K.'s assistants and then K. himself telephone the Castle to ask whether they might go there the next day. A first request is answered negatively, and a second call, during which K. pretends to be somebody else, results in the answer that he will never be allowed to come there. But hardly has this rebuff occurred than K. receives a seemingly friendly letter, carried to him by the messenger Barnabas. In this message K. is recognized and told that his superior is the village *Vorsteher*—roughly "mayor." K. cannot make out the signature on the letter, though Barnabas tells him that it is Klamm's. The purport of the message remains unclear despite its apparent clarity.

Much has been made of the names Kafka uses for messenger and master, both for their ambiguity and for symbolic resonances. "Westwest" is a play on redundancy and perhaps a parody of Kafka's fascination with the west to which Karl Rossmann was to go. Prosaically "Klamm" literally means "gorge" or "ravine" in German—which can suggest what K. is about to fall into. More interesting is "Barnabas," a biblical name for the inept messenger who serves K. (and the title of the second chapter). The biblical Barnabas is a New Testament apostle mentioned in Acts, a Cypriot Jew to whom was once attributed the Epistle to the Hebrews. Kafka's Barnabas brings epistles, though he is doing his first job as a messenger when he gives the letter to K., a task he bungles when he fails to take K.'s message back to Klamm. The biblical name endows messages from the Castle with an ironic historical analogue to messages coming from on high, such as the Evangelic word sent from heaven to Jewish Christians. However, with his first epistle Barnabas delivers obliquely contradictory messages: the obscurity of the signature suggests that K. has hardly made a successful contact, and the absurd surface message suggests that he is doing well. Behind the name "Barnabas" one reads an ironic use of the meaning of *evangelium*, the good news, that Barnabas supposedly brings.

It is at the *Herrenhof*, the inn for the gentlemen from the Castle, that, in the third chapter, "Frieda," K. meets a servant girl who allows him to look at Klamm through a peephole in a door. In a lugubriously comic scene, presenting something rather like a parody of a confessional in which the confessor has gone to sleep, K. peers at a rather ordinary stout man with a pince-nez who smokes cigars and drinks beer. There is no trace of work here, no papers, and none of the ubiquitous files that inundate the bureaucrats elsewhere. This deflationary scene is, in a sense, K.'s first minimal contact with a representative of the powers above—though nothing proves it.

Frieda becomes K.s lover in a scene in which the two lovers writhe on the floor in filth and beer as they consummate their sudden attraction. The scene is as much a commentary on the power of eros as a demonstration of K.'s willingness to break taboos and challenge authority. In effect he confronts the sleeping Klamm by taking his current mistress from him. Copulating on the floor may seem a devious way of approaching Klamm. This act will be no more successful than any other in bringing K. into contact with the Castle. But the plot takes a new direction. K. leaves the inn with a lover in his charge, a marriage in view, and the possible beginning of a new life of domesticity.

In both the fourth and the sixth chapters, K. has a long conversation with the innkeeper's wife, the wife of the *Wirt* of the inn called the *Bruckenhof* at which K. briefly has lodging. Both conversations turn on how K. might encounter Klamm. In the first the wife tells K. in no uncertain terms that he is nobody, especially in comparison with Klamm. Klamm is from the Castle, which makes him superior to all beings outside the Castle. And the wife lets K. know that he is an unwelcome foreigner, a stranger who causes problems and who, unbelievably, tried to look at Klamm. The wife has what anthropologists once called a primitive mentality. She cannot believe K. would dare to look upon Klamm and hence violate a taboo that forbids looking upon the sacred. Moreover, even if he were to look, she says, he would not be able to see Klamm. K. remains a rationalist, for he thinks that he could very well share the same physical space as Klamm. If it is impossible for him to speak to Klamm, says K. with rational resignation, then so be it: that is simply a matter of fact. What K. does not grasp is that the innkeeper's wife is also warning him about the disgrace that has fallen upon Barnabas's family. K. only slowly comes to understand this tribe's mores.

K. interrupts the first conversation to go to see the mayor, supposedly his immediate superior in the village. In one of the most comic chapters in the novel, the mayor spends his time attempting to prove to K. that his being called to the village can be only the result of a bureaucratic error. In fact, the village has no need of a land surveyor. To make his point, the mayor explains the workings of the Castle's bureaucratic system to demonstrate how an apparently infallible regime can provisionally allow an error to take place. For example, one department may not know what another department is doing, so the control system may not intervene until it is too late. The major assures K. that this can happen only in trivial matters, such as K.'s case. Many years ago an order was probably issued for a land surveyor, and it should have been attended to then. Somehow it may have resurfaced these many years later. Clever peasants may have wanted a land surveyor so that they could ferret out secret land dealings, but the mayor and a bureaucrat named Sordini have worked to thwart the peasants and their leader, Brunswick. With this elaborate and absurd explanation, K. sees possible schisms in the village's social fabric. Finally, the mayor sets his wife to searching through the voluminous files that the mayor used to keep, when he thought it worthwhile to keep everything. The search turns up nothing, though it makes a farcical demonstration of the impossibility of ever having enough information to account for putative facts.

The second conversation with the innkeeper's wife again turns on Klamm, whose lover the wife once was. Roberto Calasso sees in the Castle's use of women a depiction deriving from historical anthropology, for he argues that the women in *The Castle* resemble the sacred prostitutes of religious cults of antiquity.[3] Building on Walter Benjamin's work, Calasso stresses that *The Castle* incorporates traits of antique cultures in its characterization of the village mentality. Illustrative of this ancient mentality is the fact that the only meaningful moments in the wife's life occurred the three times she was called to copulate with Klamm. Then she knew the supreme honor of being allowed to prostitute herself to the equivalent of a high priest and have an encounter with the sacred. These memories of Klamm are now an object of religious veneration. She keeps this memory alive with relics, for example, a photograph she shows K. in which one can supposedly see the messenger who came to tell her that Klamm was calling her. For K., however, the blurred image in an old photo is something less than an annunciation.

The pedestrianly rational K. is worried by the wife's revelation. If the innkeeper's wife has remained so "faithful" to this memory, he wonders what effect Frieda's memory of Klamm may have on their forthcoming marriage. After K. reveals his worry, the wife assures him that Klamm totally forgets women after contact with them; otherwise, women would run back to him. K. retorts critically that Klamm must remember women afterward, since, for instance, he had influence in the innkeeper's decision to marry her—by setting up a situation in which the innkeeper would see her and in which she would be ready to marry him. To return to an anthropological perspective, it appears that the near-priest Klamm sends the consecrated prostitute to the marriage market, where a peasant is glad to have a woman who had been honored by divinity. Or from a different historical perspective, one can compare Klamm's sex with the wife to the medieval rite/right that supposedly allowed a manor lord to use his superior vigor to deflower virgins before their peasant husbands took them—his *droit du seigneur*. Klamm has exercised his *droit du seigneur* with Frieda, too; from the village perspective this implies that K. is in Klamm's debt. From K.'s rationalist perspective, this is not obvious.

The chapter ends with the wife's saying she will transmit a message to Klamm informing him of K.'s request for an interview with him if K. agrees not to undertake anything on his own initiative. K. refuses, arguing that if the request is turned down, he will look as if he were insubordinate in continuing to pursue Klamm, which is what he intends to do. With this refusal K. sets himself squarely at odds with the community's mores. K. begins to resemble the rationalist rebel here. The theme of K.'s defiance is pursued in the seventh chapter, "The School Teacher," which gives a résumé of how K. has offended everyone. The schoolteacher has in fact written up a report denouncing K. for offending the mayor, and Frieda tells him that the innkeeper's wife is so irritated by his plans for meeting Klamm that she wants him to leave the inn. The haughty schoolteacher is then obliged to offer K. the position of school custodian that the mayor has created for him. No school custodian, anymore apparently than a land surveyor, has ever been needed, but little matter. K., Frieda, and the obnoxious helpers move into the two-room schoolhouse to live in a room full of gym equipment. The narrative strategy is ingenious here, for by granting K. a precarious situation as custodian, Kafka keeps K. within the village society while at the same time more or less expelling him. This incongruous situation also increases the increasingly disagreeable contact K. has with his two helpers, those two bouncing balls that may or may not be emissaries from the Castle.

The central chapter tracing out K.'s quest for Klamm is the eighth chapter, in which K. dares to wait for Klamm to come out of the inn. Titled "Das Warten auf Klamm" ("Waiting on Klamm"), the chapter is a poetic text that can be read as K.'s existential manifesto. Here K. shows that he shares none of the fears that characterize the villagers, but he also comes to realize that his resolve is not sufficient, for in his rebellious determination he finds nothing concrete to hold onto. The world seems to dissolve before his eyes; upon going out of the inn, leaving Frieda to take care of preparations for their moving into the school, K. finds himself again contemplating the Castle above him. The lifeless Castle disappears into the darkness that invests this world. K. imagines that the Castle might be an impersonal observer, high above and indifferent to those who look upon it, so that nothing can fasten on to it. The more K. looks, the less clear all becomes. The situation is analogous to his exertions in the village: the more he does, seemingly the less he accomplishes.

K. enters the inn and, going to the door where he may have observed Klamm earlier, finds that the peephole has disappeared or been covered over. It seems that just to see might grant K. some power (which the innkeeper's wife denied him). Upon lighting a match, all he sees, however, is a new serving girl, Pepi. They begin a conversation, the result of which is that K. learns that Klamm is leaving the inn. His sleigh awaits him. K. goes into the courtyard and begins the wait (a wait that might be compared to Beckett's drama of waiting for Godot with its indefinite hints at a meaning to come). He waits; nobody appears; he is invited to drink some cognac by the sleigh driver; a young man appears and asks him to come with him; K. refuses, and then nothing more happens except that the driver is told to put away the sleigh and horses. In a sense K. has imposed himself and shown that he has the power to resist. He perhaps even has the power to have the sleigh called back, though that would mean that K. must leave. K. refuses to leave.

The final lines of this extraordinary scene give a résumé of what K. has accomplished: he thinks that it is now as if all ties were broken off and that he is freer than ever. He feels he could wait there, in a forbidden space, for as long as he wants, for he has won this freedom with a struggle that others had not dared, so that nobody could drive him away. However, from another perspective, he is also convinced that there is nothing more meaningless than this freedom, this waiting, this invulnerability. These fleeting thoughts are perhaps Kafka's most concentrated existential meditation about what K., the modern rationalist, feels as he negotiates the ways of this community in which nobody feels what he feels. He is invulnerable, because he does not take seriously the arbitrary rules that abound here. Yet, no meaning can be found in his floating free without contact with the seemingly seamless web of often harmful relationships that bind the members of the community. It is as if Kafka wanted to show that freedom without community is meaningless.

Going inside the inn, K. demonstrates again his freedom in the face of authority, this time in his confrontation with Momus, Klamm's village secretary. "Momus" is the name of the god of satire and carping criticism. The ironic name perhaps underscores that Momus embodies the kind of bureaucratic thinking upon which the Castle's power is based. The title of the ninth chapter, "Kampf gegen das Verhör" (literally, "fight against the hearing"), with its confrontation between K. and Momus, is significant in this regard, for it highlights again the struggle that K. has seen as his from the outset. The confrontation shows that the "fight" is between two different mentalities. K. makes clear to Momus that he wants to see Klamm only in order to find a way to the Castle, where, he hopes, decisions are really made. His struggle is based on a rational analysis of what he thinks should be the decision-making process. Momus, assisted by the innkeeper's wife, shows that, for the Castle, rituals are all that counts. With a quasi-medieval sense of procedure, Momus insists that it is through the observation of the prescribed ritual that one can placate the powers that be. Therefore, first a protocol must go to Momus. And, as the wife points out, that should be enough to satisfy K. It is of no import whether the document is then given to Klamm, since he will not read it in any case—how would he have time to read all these papers? Kafka's satire of the rites of procedure is Swiftian in its marvelous absurdity, though it also brings out that the real issue here is the maintenance of power. For this purpose it suffices that the supplicants be granted hope and little more. K. categorically refuses to play this game and leaves wondering again who Klamm is. He imagines him like the eagle to which the innkeeper's wife had compared him, an eagle soaring above them all, with a gaze looking down upon them that can never be contradicted. The invulnerability of power seems embodied here in the image of the perpetual gaze or *regard*, as a Sartre or Foucault might have later put it. For K., Klamm has become the emblem of power's omniscient gaze that everybody has interiorized, such that all feel constantly exposed and vulnerable.

In Chapter 10, "On the Street," K. must again try to understand the absurd procedures when Barnabas comes to him with a letter congratulating him on the good work he is doing. The letter demands interpretation. One wonders if it is a bureaucratic accident or part of a calculated strategy to keep K. off balance. Nothing is certain, though the compliment offered by the message for the good work K. is getting from his idiot helpers is certainly calculated by Kafka to underscore the manifest absurdity of the procedures that K. must deal with. The satire of communication continues, moreover, when K. learns that Barnabas has not delivered the message K. gave the messenger. Apparently only the wrong messages get delivered.

In the chapter "At the School," K. once more demonstrates his resolve not to be mistreated by the abuse of power. He refuses to be discharged by the schoolteacher for having broken into the woodshed. This violation of rules was done, justifiably, to keep K. from freezing to death for lack of heat in the night. And in the following chapter, "The Assistants," he decides to discharge his unruly helpers despite their possible relation to Klamm. He is justified, in his own eyes, because of their less than innocent antics with regard to Frieda. It is also true that, like the assistants that the bachelor Blumfeld must deal with, K.'s helpers are idiotically incompetent. I pass over the ambiguities of Frieda's relation to the two young men—who first appear to be young and randy but who age quickly. Of central importance is that they present another test case for K.'s ability to assert his resistance, as well as his honor and sense of self.

Kafka brings in a new character, the boy Hans Brunswick, in order to bring out another side of K.'s character. K. is now close to despair, for each act of resistance brings him no closer to the Castle. K. asks the boy to arrange a meeting between K. and the boy's sick mother in the hope that the woman might help him in his struggle. K. justifies the request by claiming to have medical knowledge that might help her—a new talent about which the reader may have some doubts. In any case, during the mother's earlier brief meeting with K., she had identified herself as a girl from the Castle, which provides motivation enough for K. to want to see her. None of these strands are developed subsequently, so the meeting with the boy Hans stands as an isolated moment in which K. plans one more strategy for getting to Klamm. But the narrative development does turn on Frieda's reaction to the scene with the boy.

Frieda reacts to what she sees as the single-mindedness of K.'s endeavors and berates him for what the innkeeper's wife has told her: K. has taken up with her only in order to use her to get to Klamm. K. recognizes the plausibility of this accusation. K.'s life is, as he recognizes himself, dominated by his attempt to anchor himself in the village, which, he thinks, necessitates his meeting Klamm. The question whether K. has a hidden motivation for marrying Frieda is subject to interpretation. What is clear on the surface is that K. has been physically attracted to Frieda—about whom Pepi will spend much effort later assuring K., and the reader, that his fiancée is not attractive. The question of K.'s motivation remains open, since all is a question of interpretation, for K. as for the reader.

Interpretation is a topic that merits further comment before we turn to the third section of the novel, in which K. himself becomes a surrogate reader when he listens to the narrative describing the fate of Barnabas's family. Throughout the chapters in which K. is seeking Klamm and a way through him to the Castle, he attempts to determine the meaning of various signs and messages offered to him. He must decipher, for example, the meaning of what lies beyond the closed door through which he peers at a beer-drinking cigar smoker. He must ponder letters that are wrong. There is a self-reflexive dimension in this game of hermeneutics, and the reader's position vis-à-vis K. is analogous to K.'s position vis-à-vis signs in the text. With this implicit meta-textual dimension, the novel designates its quest for its own meaning, and what I have said earlier about self-referentiality largely applies to the interpretative strategies demanded by *The Castle*. Most central is the snow in which K. bogs down: it may well resemble the white page on which readers also bog down in their interpretive quest for the novel's meaning—as if trying to read stumps on the snow, as in *Meditation*.

However, *The Castle* differs from Kafka's earlier works in placing a greater emphasis on the physical means of sending messages that elicit interpretation. From the viewpoint of information theory, one can say that the channels of communication are as much in question in the novel as is the meaning of the messages sent through these channels. I refer to the messages encoded and sent by channels as various as telephone, letter, files, rumors, oral legends, and so on. The materiality of the channel by which the message is sent has, to be sure, already been exploited in various ways in Kafka's work. For instance, the tale

"An Old Manuscript" poses the very problem of the transmission of historical meaning if the past exists only as a shredded page. The law is communicated in *The Trial*, it seems, by books full of pornography. And, in "The Great Wall of China," the emperor's messenger can never traverse the infinite communicative space that separates the emperor from his subject. In Kafka the communication channel often resembles an endless *Weg* or way, which is to say that the channel is the impossibly long path that awaits all travelers, all messages and messengers in Kafka. We doubt that the country doctor ever got home.

Perhaps the most striking image of communication, for its emblematic modernity, are the telephones that K. finds installed in the inn and that may be in the Castle. A first telephone call from the inn results in a denial that K. was even summoned by the Castle. This is a perverse meta-communication about the original communication sent to K. A return call from the Castle a few minutes later says there was an error. K. feels thus encouraged to use the telephone to ask for permission to go to the Castle. Deciding to treat his "new" assistants as one person, he orders them to telephone jointly for the permission, which is refused for the following day and forever. At this point the telephone seems as much a barrier as a conduit connecting the village and the Castle. K. then telephones himself, and, because he has disguised his identity, it is as an "old" assistant that he receives anew the message that he will never be allowed to come to the Castle.

More striking than the refusals of communication by telephone is what K. hears when he listens to the receiver: a buzzing sound, resembling the humming sound of countless children's voices, merging into one powerful voice that might seem to overcome hearing. In some way, perhaps wistful, certainly comic, Kafka proposes an image of the message of transcendence coming down from above as a garbled but powerful voice that, as if emerging from an angel choir of putti, ends up in an unintelligible but mighty sound. To which the Castle's refusal of permission adds a negative twist that apparently only underscores what the real information is. It is only apparent, for the village mayor later tells K. that in fact he has had no contact with the authorities, since there is no regular established telephone line with the Castle. Indeed, the only regular message one gets from up there is the humming and buzzing sound that K. heard—constantly negative phatic communication, the information theorist might say.

One may doubt that the mayor knows what he is talking about, but his description of the caprices of the telephone line seems part of the pattern of arbitrary communication found throughout *The Castle*. Castle bureaucrats leave their phones unhooked, the mayor says, and only occasionally, for a joke to relieve tedium, answer a call. Moreover, if one calls the Castle from below, asking for, say, Sordini, how can one know if the person who answers at the other end of the line really is Sordini? The dilemma of telephone communication as posed by the mayor is a comic variant on the theological problem of communication with the divine. Kafka knew well that if an angel comes to communicate revelation to a person, the recipient of the message must ask how one can be certain that the apparition really is an angel and not the devil in disguise. Communication with certainty at a distance is clearly impossible when communication face to face is fraught with the likelihood of deception. And so the modern telephone brings K. back to medieval problems that the Church, not unlike the Castle, used to ensure its power, for only the Church could decide when communication was valid.

The channel of communication is thus as much a problem for receiving and understanding messages as is the proper interpretation of whatever ambiguous message might arrive. This is true of the letters that are sent to K., namely the missives brought by Barnabas to K. In Kafka the "letter" is rarely lacking, as I have said, in self-reflexive resonances, which means that readers of the fictional text find themselves in the same situation as K., the reader in the fictional text interpreting fictional missives: we must all try to interpret an often obscure text. In *The Castle* the first letter sent to K. is of course contradicted by the novel's development, since in the letter Klamm says—if the letter's unintelligible signature is Klamm's—that he is always ready, when possible, to be helpful to K. K.'s quest to find Klamm begins with this problematic missive, which K. takes and hangs on the wall of his room at the time, replacing one of the pictures of saints and soldiers that servant girls had hung there. If one juxtaposes Klamm's letter with these images, creating a visual metaphor as it were, then the letter seems to announce both acceptance and struggle, salvation and *Kampf*, a saint's business and a warrior's fight. The latter theme seems to be K.'s own interpretation of the letter, for the narrator says K. thinks that it spells out that he is an employee, a worker, hence a being in an inferior position, who must face the dangers of a dispiriting environment, the habitual repetition of disappointment, and the power (*Gewalt*) exerted by imperceptible influences at every moment. Against these dangers he must, he thinks, be prepared to dare a struggle (*Kampf*). His interpretation of the letter is hardly the first one that comes to mind, but as the novel unfolds K.'s belief that that a challenge to struggle lies behind the letter grows in plausibility.

Another interpretation of the letter is offered by the mayor. The ailing mayor, with his overflowing boxes of dossiers and files, is another hermeneutic specialist, representing what we might call commonsense village hermeneutics. Countering K.'s charge that the assignment of helpers to him was thoughtless, the mayor enunciates his principle of interpretation by saying that in the village and in the Castle nothing happens without a reason. The mayor offers a homey version of the principle of sufficient reason that, for example, Leibniz made famous as the bedrock of rationalism (and to which I alluded in discussing the justification of the useless wall in "The Great Wall of China"). The principle that nothing happens without a cause (*Bedenkenlos*) once justified belief in the supposedly transparent rationality of the universe. Everything could be explained, which was the first axiom, historically, of the optimistic view that we live in the best of all possible worlds.

Kafka did not need to read Voltaire's satire of optimism in *Candide* to have some doubt about the principle of sufficient reason. Be that as it may, an interpretation of the mayor's principle for interpretation is not without interest, for he may well think there is a reason behind all that happens, but that is not quite the same thing as saying nothing thoughtless happens in the Castle. The mayor's belief is an invitation to interpretation of every event, that is, an invitation to find the putative thought, if not the reason, behind every act. In addition, the mayor adds to his hermeneutic principle another axiom: no statement from the Castle can be taken literally. The second axiom sounds like a parody of the medieval rules for biblical exegesis. One assumes that the literal text always clothes a figurative meaning. Does this principle contradict the mayor's first axiom? One may think so and find in this contradiction an explanatory principle of much of European intellectual history: it is a history of a thirst for rational explanation joined to a hermeneutic principle that allows everything to mean anything else.

Having enunciated his interpretive axioms, the mayor is ready to interpret Klamm's letter to K. in which the mayor is named as his superior. The mayor and his wife first consult and decide that the letter is genuine. However, it is not an official letter recognizing K.'s appointment as a land surveyor. Actually, the mayor argues, there is nothing in the letter that says K. has been appointed. This seems to be the meaning implied by the clause to the effect that K. has been appointed "as you know." The mayor says this means that K. must prove that he has been appointed, for, the mayor argues, the letter shows only that Klamm will take an interest in K. if he ever is appointed.

K. challenges the mayor's interpretation with an ad hominem rhetorical trick by saying that, in his interpretation, the mayor does not respect Klamm, which is an act no villager would own up to. K. declares that the mayor's interpretation reduces the letter to a vacuous page with Klamm's signature merely appended to it. The mayor is not short on his own rhetorical strategies and adroitly replies that, on the contrary, a private letter from Klamm has even more significance than an official letter, simply not the significance or meaning that K. attributes to it. And, in a final twist to dissuade K. from the belief that he had been recognized by the Castle, the mayor then asserts that there are no telephone connections with the Castle and that the only thing reliable about that channel of communication is the humming and buzzing coming from it, which K. did indeed hear earlier. The channel of communication is thus discredited even before a message arrives.

Once the reader grasps the problems of communicative channels—letters and telephones in the present case—it becomes apparent that much of the novel turns on finding the channel that might communicate a message that might be interpreted without problem. In fact, viewed from this perspective, nearly every conversation and exchange between characters can be viewed as an hermeneutic jousting in which K. tries to find a channel through which a reliable message might come and some paradigm through which he might interpret it. K. is not the only interpreter, of course. That everybody is an interpreter is clear, for example, in K.'s conversations with the wife of the innkeeper and with the mayor as well as the schoolteacher. Perhaps the most emotionally charged example of the intricacies of communication occurs in K.'s exchange with Frieda when K. is upbraided by her for his devious intentions. The communicative channel between lovers is not only spoken language but also the poses and gestures of the body itself that send messages according to a semiotic system as old as love and love literature itself.

At the beginning of their relationship, K. interprets Frieda's submission to him as a message of acceptance, though the meaning of her body language is not so obvious later. In the fourteenth chapter, "Frieda's Rebuke," Frieda shows herself a hostile interpreter of K.'s meanings after listening to K.'s conversation with the boy Hans. It reminds her, she says, of the innkeeper's wife and her interpretation of K.'s conduct toward Frieda: it is part of his self-serving effort to contact Klamm. The wife says that K. is using Frieda. Frieda is torn by different interpretations, including her own. She has just witnessed, she thinks, K.'s trying to use the boy Hans so that he can get to the boy's mother, who may then be able to help him to get to the Castle. Frieda puts herself in the boy's place, and from this perspective K.'s acts and words, his very demeanor, now bespeak a different man from the one who claimed to love her. Frieda's hermeneutic endeavors make her very unhappy indeed. In his reply to her, K. recognizes the facts, both deeds and words. They cannot be denied. Then he attempts to show Frieda another interpretation, recalling that she, too, once seized every opportunity in her struggle to rise from the miserable position she had occupied in the village hierarchy. K. argues for an overdetermination of his motivation in which love and struggle are reconciled as coexisting interpretations. As K. leaves, he looks at Frieda and sees that he cannot interpret the signs her body transmits. She opens the window, a helper comes up, and K. cannot decide whether she is enticing the helper or sending K. a plea for help. He cannot tell whether she is rebuffing or greeting the helper; when the window is closed again, K. cannot decide whether Frieda knows that her facial expression is attracting the helper more than it is deterring him. The body is as uncertain a channel for communication as are all others.

A new development in the novel occurs when the narration moves to Olga's house. In effect Kafka places a short novel within the novel. K. becomes a listener who hears a story that reveals the nature of the village society and the way power works in it. In contrast to the narration of K.'s attempt to enter into the society, Olga's tale tells how Amalia is expelled from the same society. In this sense the two narratives complement each other like mirror images as they portray symmetrical motion in opposing directions relative to village society. In some ways this society is primitive, nearly prehistorical, as Walter Benjamin suggested in one of the most influential essays written on Kafka.[4] But aspect viewing also allows one to affirm that the same village society also resembles the mass society of modernity in which all think alike. Kafka's plastic historicity allows the reader to view the social bonds of culture as at once something very ancient and very contemporary. Kafka is not alone in this perspectival viewing. He was preceded in this by the perspectivism of Nietzsche, who pointed out the primitive herd morality that binds, with bonds of stifling mediocrity, the contemporary Christian society Nietzsche rejected. The ostracism inflicted on Amalia and her family is also at once primitive and modern, for there is nothing more modern than those societies in which the fear underlying totalitarian thinking eliminates difference. In fine, the vision of social ties and cultural bonds underlying *The Castle* is at once an archeology and a critique of modernity.

The section of *The Castle* that deals with Amalia's story begins in the fifteenth chapter, "At Amalia's." K. leaves the schoolroom where Frieda has been entrusted with the tedious task of washing the teacher's cat. He goes to Amalia's house in hope of finding Barnabas. It is relevant to add here that Barnabas's name is translated by the standard English version to mean "son of encouragement," but the modern Lutheran translation offers "Barnabas" as "Sohn des Trostes" or the son of consolation. Actually it seems K. is seeking both encouragement and consolation, although he has a messenger who brings neither. Given Barnabas's dismal incompetence, his name ironically underscores the dysfunctional nature of the myths of revelation that promise communication from above. With sharp irony, the name points up the disappointment that awaits K. when he goes to seek a message of hope or encouragement in this house, about which he knows little. Therein lies a revelation, however, namely the revelation of the fall of Barnabas's family.

K. finds only Amalia at home. She knows nothing about Frieda and, offering encouragement of a terrestrial sort, tells K. that Olga seems to be in love with him. Olga does indeed seem interested in K., for, after returning home, she narrates at great length the story of her family so that he may understand not only more about young Barnabas but also why her family is destitute. Olga begins her main narrative in the untitled sixteenth chapter, in which she offers a long interpretation of what happens in the Castle when Barnabas goes there. The interpretation deflates any hopes K. may have for receiving meaningful communication from Klamm or anybody else. Barnabas has no status in the Castle, not even that of an "upper servant"; perhaps he has that of a "lower servant," with limited admittance, though even that, as usual, is not at all clear. Moreover, when Barnabas does get a message to deliver, it is not clear who has given it to him. To K.'s dismay, Olga says Barnabas doubts that it is Klamm. K. also learns that Klamm's appearance seems to change with circumstances—only his black coat with long tails remains the same. Identity is also a hermeneutic problem.

Olga's description of what Barnabas sees in a room occupied by officials sounds as if it were a satire drawing upon the tea party in *Alice in Wonderland*: officials read books, then, rather than exchanging books, exchange places in order to read what others have read by squeezing past clerks who are seated taking dictation. Barnabas waits while this mad movement goes on. He patiently waits for the random letter taken from the files and papers that have also been waiting, for an unknown period of time. He waits for that random moment when he is randomly given a random document. All seems caprice and perhaps even sham, though readers of Lewis Carroll will feel at home with such serious charades. And Barnabas dares say nothing critical for fear of losing his job, although it is not certain that he has a job to lose.

K. is put to the hermeneutic test: he must try to salvage something from Olga's descriptions by making an ingenious interpretation of them. It must be said, not surprisingly, that he is not very successful. Olga's description of the random operations based on unknown principles is devastating for the seeker, and K.'s reply shows his helplessness. Anthea Bell's recent translation gives a good rendering of K.'s attempt to explain away what Olga has just said, when K. surprisingly avers that people are right to be in awe of the authorities, a topic on which he is almost insulting to Olga:

> Awe of the authorities is innate in all of you here, and it is also dinned into you throughout your lives in all manner of different ways and from all sides, and you yourselves add to it as best you can. I'm saying nothing against that in principle; if authorities are good authorities, why shouldn't people go in awe of them? But an uninformed youth like Barnabas, who has never been far outside the village, ought not to be suddenly sent to the castle and then expected to come back with faithful reports, where everything he says is studied like a revelation, with

> everyone's own happiness depending on its interpretation. Nothing can be more misguided. (*The Castle,* Oxford World Classics [2009], p.161)

In this passage K. contrives an interpretation in an attempt to preserve his hopes, hopes badly placed in Barnabas, not to mention the Castle bureaucracy, whose random messages K. wants to believe have significance for him. He is even willing now to quote the village mayor to the effect that personal letters are significant, which seems to offer some solace to Olga. In interpreting Olga's attitude as showing awe that has gone astray, K. betrays his Enlightenment belief in the sovereign self for which awe should be a sentiment subject to the greatest critical distance. But K. is also desperate in this scene, for if Olga is taken at her word, K. has no grounds for belief in the possibility of communication with the Castle.

Throughout this narration K. acts as an interpreter, and his interpretations also throw light on his own story. His defense of Frieda in the face of severe criticism is relevant insofar as it shows that he intends to stay with her, not least of all because she has empowered him with the hope he might stay in the village. Moreover, by inserting K.'s interpretation into Olga's narrative, Kafka creates another configuration of inner duplication: K. is now in the position of a reader listening to Olga's tale, which is to say that K. is a double of the reader of *The Castle* who must also interpret K. interpreting Olga in this hermeneutic hall of mirrors.

Confronting K.'s attempt at hermeneutics, Olga decides she must fully inform K. about why young Barnabas has been thrust into a role for which K. says the lad is unsuited. She then tells "Amalia's Secret," as the title of the seventeenth chapter has it. It is apparently a secret only to K., since it becomes obvious that everyone in the village knows of Amalia's disgrace and participates in ostracizing her and her family. Ostracism by its very nature means that all must know, for it works by unanimous consent, and in this regard the family offers a paradigm case of how power works diffusively in this society situated on the edge of modernity. The plot of Olga's narrative in the next four chapters, which tell of the family's fate, is straightforward, if perplexing. One day, at a festival celebrating the fire brigade, Amalia's beauty so disquieted a normally quiet bureaucrat that, in anger as much as in lust, he sent her a brutal letter telling her to come to him immediately for his quick gratification. Amalia was outraged. Not only did she refuse, but she tore up the letter and insulted the messenger. It was much as if she were spitefully rejecting an annunciating angel.

Afterwards, everyone in the village broke off relations with the family. For some time the family did nothing, but the father became desperate. A shoemaker, he lost all his business. He first tried petitioning and bribing Castle officials to be reinstated in grace—with no result. He then stood by a road to catch their attention and be forgiven—with no result. Olga then had another plan: they would ask the messenger's forgiveness if she could find him. She spent two years, apparently prostituting herself to the Castle servants, trying to find the messenger—with no result. The family was impoverished, the parents' health gone, and finally Olga decided to use what influence she has in the Castle to get Barnabas a job there as a messenger, this as a propitiating gesture, since she hopes that Barnabas could be seen as a surrogate for the insulted messenger, perhaps a ritual victim to make up for the sacrilege. The fact that carrying a letter to K. has been Barnabas's first work is hardly promising.

Even in this brief résumé it should be obvious that Kafka uses Olga's narration as a foil to the story of K.'s attempts to get to the Castle. Amalia's refusal of the outrageous letter is analogous to K.'s refusal to be interrogated, and her insulting the messenger and the letter is comparable to K.'s attitude toward the communication channels that exist with the Castle: he begins to feel a desperate contempt toward them. The family's expulsion from village society is an image of estrangement that mirrors K.'s. In their estrangement both the family and K. desire to be what he calls, when he learns of Amalia's secret, a member of the village, which is to say, of the *Gemeinde*. This term has many connotations. *Gemeinde* is often opposed to the abstract idea of "society" or *Gesellschaft*, for *Gemeinde* is seemingly a more concrete term that can refer to everything from a village or a small unit of local government to a Jewish or Christian congregation. It is roughly the smallest unit of social organization.

In fine, the father's desire to be recognized by the Castle is analogous to K.'s, which is to say that both want to be integrated into the *Gemeinde*. Their situations are different, even if the image they offer is the same. The father wants his guilt recognized as a precondition for being forgiven and restored, whereas K. demands to be accepted as he is, he expects his status as a free subject to be recognized, and he demands the right to be integrated into the community. Olga's search for the insulted Castle messenger in the belief that he might hold the key to the family's fate is also analogous to K.'s seeking Klamm: both of the objects of quest are elusive and perhaps largely illusionary. And, finally, the two tales are joined by a hope common to Olga and to K. that Barnabas's work as messenger might bring about meaningful communication.

It is worth asking what hope means in the world of the Castle. Hope springs from interpreting signs in a favorable way, as, for example, when in telling K. that she has no intention of scorning the letters Barnabas has brought to him, Olga adds that the two letters are the only signs of grace (*Gnadenzeichen*), however doubtful they be, that the family has had in three years. Manifestly she needs to interpret the letters as signs of grace, not for what they say but simply because they exist. Minimally, and perhaps maximally, their existence implies that the Castle has taken cognizance of the family's existence. In K.'s world the communication channel itself acquires meaning, the meaning of hope, even if no meaning comes through it or the message is so scrambled as to be incomprehensible. Or at least so Kafka's desperate characters are compelled to believe, and thus they come to have the most minimal form of hope.

I have used the term "ostracism" to describe the situation that results from Amalia's so-called fault in refusing a bureaucrat and in insulting his messenger. The ensuing quasi-expulsion of the family from the village or *Gemeinde* is not quite "ostracism" if one has in mind the Athenian practice of ostracism, that is, voting to deprive citizens of their rights and expelling them. The Athenian practice was public and visible, which is not the case with the unnamed procedure behind the verdict inflicted on Amalia's family. It is true that in *The Castle* the culture of the *Gemeinde* itself is the diffuse locus for a judgment that imposes guilt and shame. Power imposes itself in this case not through public institutions but through silent communication based on fear. It appears in *The Castle* that the unspoken laws and demands of the Castle are so interiorized that all citizens know what they are and submit to them—or run the risk of feeling guilty and undergoing exclusion. The father's remarkable case illustrates well this procedure. He recognizes his own guilt by association, it seems, and openly subscribes to the unwritten judgment passed upon him. His sentence is in this respect comparable to the conviction of the son in "The Judgment." In *The Castle*, however, the father believes, rightly or wrongly, that guilt can be forgiven if it is recognized by the authorities. For what can be forgiven if he is not guilty? So the father must find them and beg them to recognize his guilt. The mechanism of punishment here is ferociously subtle, for the Castle authorities have only to withhold this recognition and the ostracism will continue. There is no possible court of appeal since, as Olga says, no *Anzeige* or formal complaint has been brought against him or anybody else. What can be appealed?

In résumé, this novella within the novel portrays a father who finds himself forever guilty with no chance of forgiveness. This perversely motivates his hyperbolic desire to prove his guilt to the authorities. It causes Olga to want to find the actual messenger who was insulted as well as her desire to offer up Barnabas as a surrogate for him. The portrayal of this mechanism of punishment is one reason that Kafka has been saluted for foreseeing the tyrannies of the twentieth century, whose victims often begged to be found guilty for usually fictitious antisocial crimes. But, as said, *The Castle* also portrays a kind of mythical world, one that looks back to the origins of Judeo-Christian society, whose doctrine of original sin inflects Kafka's imagination. I would add another ironic perspective on the world of the Castle and its *Gemeinde*. In a sense it is a distorted version of the world before original sin in which the members strictly obey the prohibitions coming from above, for fear of what might happen if they were driven from the world of grace, minimal though it be, created by their social bonds. In this primeval world the villagers want no threatening changes. And, notably, they are not guilty of the impatience that characterizes K. This impatience takes on special meaning if we recall again that in the second and third Zürau meditations Kafka says that impatience is the origin of original sin. In *The Castle* only K. is impatient. Only K. wants struggle—another aspect of sin according to the aphorisms. Obviously sin is not necessarily something negative in Kafka's view.

After Olga's narration is finished, the novel seems to take a new turn. Kafka began a new development, though the fourth part is not finished in any sense, and the novel lacks any sense of closure. The last five chapters, continuing to narrate K.'s strivings, share a dominant tonality and technique. They are dominated by farce, satire, and a comic representation of the world of *The Castle*. Taken individually, some of these chapters are among the most successful moments in Kafka's entire opus for their comedy.

Farce and satire are genres in which exaggerated descriptions, within their specific context, have an aesthetic intent that is comic; in addition, satire aims critically at specific targets. If we imagine a scale of comic narration running from broad farce to subtle humor, we can see that farce and satire often overlap in technique, though they may have different goals. Pure farce is often characterized by comically absurd aggression directed against some established order. The great film farces of the twentieth century, those of the Marx Brothers or René Clair, illustrate well that farce is often in the service of a desire to overthrow restrictive order. If the comic exaggeration has a specific goal as the object of its destruction, then one can usually speak of satire, as say in the eighteenth-century satires of Swift or Voltaire, which are often aimed at intellectual pretention and ludicrous claims to truth (in these cases, respectively, at the followers of Descartes and Leibniz). Satire and farce share common properties but usually differ in terms of precise goals; it is not mere pedantry to stress the difference, for the difference is essential to how we interpret a text. The difference determines how we answer questions such as whether Kafka parodies the desire for meaning in order to celebrate it or satirizes our own thirst for meaning as a sign of our absurdly impossible desires. With perspectival viewing, we may find that he does both.

K.'s stay with Olga comes to an end when his helper Jeremias comes knocking on the door. His arrival opens a near-farcical development that carries over into the untitled twenty-first chapter. Without his partner, Artur, who has gone to complain of K.'s treatment of them, Jeremias now appears aged and withered. Jeremias says that the two assistants were sent to K. by Galater, working in place of Klamm, to keep K. entertained. "Galater" is the German word found in the New Testament to translate what reads in English as "The

Letter of Paul to the Galatians" (Luther's version is "Der Brief des Paulus an die Galater"). Kafka is again throwing out suggestively misleading ways for reading what might be going on—intentional in the sense that he shows a hermeneutic path and then shuts it off after we follow it. A false path is offered by the fact that Paul's letter is notable for stating that until we as minors throw off our tutelage, we are no better than slaves in the English version, no better than a *Knecht* in Luther's version. In the German version Paul anticipates Kant's definition of enlightenment as freeing oneself from tutelage and hence becoming capable of thinking without the imposition of authority. It seems relevant that the assistants,Artur and Jeremias, are in a sense feudal servants—*Knechte*. However, since K. also seems to be close to being a feudal dependent, despite his attempts to assert his autonomy, one is puzzled to think that one can interpret K.'s situation using a biblical letter that upholds the necessity of accepting Christ's word to be free. Kafka was quite aware of the Christian origins of Enlightenment thought, even if this thought was largely directed against Christianity. As an Enlightenment figure, K. may wonder himself where he can go with this ironic name: Paul's letter went to the Galatians, can K. imagine that the Galatians have responded by sending him his idiotic helpers?

The conversation between K. and Jeremias continues in the following chapter, in which K. tells Jeremias that he can speak frankly since they are no longer in a master–servant relation. Is Kafka making here an oblique reference to the master–slave (*Knecht*) relation that Hegel, in his *Phenomenology of the Spirit,* saw as the origins of self-consciousness when each figure in this tandem pair became conscious of himself through his consciousness of the other? It might seem so. If so, that could throw light on the rather wacky attempt K. had made earlier to treat Artur and Jeremias as only one human being? The development of consciousness demands literally one consciousness on each side of the master–slave relation. Paired slaves are not part of the Hegelian equation. All in all, then, the pair of *Knechte* takes on new dimensions in their opposition to K., showing that Kafka uses them to offer allusive meanings even as he retracts them by the absurd narrative context in which they are embedded. Jeremias (Jeremiah?) is last seen as an old man standing in his underwear but somehow capable of seducing Frieda, who now rejects K., mainly because K. has not respected the ostracism laid upon Olga and Amalia.

Barnabas now brings a message not from Klamm but from Erlanger, a secretary whose name suggests the verb *erlangen,* meaning "to obtain" or "to win." It seems like another ironic trap for the reader. The farce begins to develop in this episode when K. goes to the inn to meet this bureaucrat who is desirous of seeing him at night. In the hallway with doors opening on the bureaucrats' quarters, K. notes that the walls do not reach the ceiling so that, upon arriving at Erlanger's door, a servant can climb up on his shoulders to peer into the room and see if Erlanger is there. The incongruity between the supposed seriousness of the meeting and the physical acts shows that the reader has now entered a world of absurd and aggressive farce. In this world functionaries receive at night—if they are awake, and sometimes even if they are asleep. Such is the comic hyperactivity of the world where the bureaucratic procedures never cease operating.

In the following chapter K. leaves the hall to talk to Frieda. They have an argument, which in effect offers a break in the farce. In this scene Kafka draws upon emotional depths, indeed a tenderness rarely seen in his work, to depict two lovers now estranged and unable to come back together. The image of Jeremias at the end of this scene breaks it off with comic pathos generated by the shabby servant's appearance, which is redolent of an invalid in a hospital. The scene with Frieda is an interlude in farcical scenes, a compelling one that may prompt the reader to ask the futile question about what Kafka might have done with Frieda had he written more. Perhaps one reason that Kafka did not continue *The Castle* is that this scene with Frieda seems so final, so irremediably the end of a love affair, that in itself it seems to impose closure on the novel. Kafka himself had had such an experience, we recall, in the recent past, and biographers are undoubtedly right to see that his experience with Milena is a very personal source for the narration of K.'s encounter with Frieda.

This scene notwithstanding, after the emotional interlude K. returns to the hall and to the world of farce, to find he no longer knows which door he should turn to. Like Karl Rossmann and Joseph K. before him, K. has lost his way in a corridor lined with anonymous doors. Trusting to chance for the revelation of what might be behind the random door, K. knocks at a door, opens it, and finds that he has awakened a bureaucrat in bed, namely Bürgel, the *Verbindungssecretar,* a "communication secretary," appropriately enough in a novel about infrequent communication. And communicate the bureaucrat does, at great length, while K. tries fruitlessly to stay awake. Kafka demonstrates his mastery of satirical hyperbole, in this case, hyperbole in the service of motivated absurdity, or the stringing together of causal chains that end up with a demonstration of the absurdity underlying the chain of events and its final result. Here the final result of the functionary's endless discourse is K.'s falling asleep on a big bed—there is no other furniture in the room—while the communication secretary perorates about why there is no furniture in the room, why there are meetings at night, why clients may accidently get what they desire, and so on and so on. Bürgel's friendly speech is designed to justify its own existence, namely why is there a loquacious bureaucrat at night in a bedroom in which a supplicant is accidentally received and why this accident may be as good as any other random crossing of causal events. It can be argued that causation seems always to unfold according to random crossings in Kafka, which is why strict causality can end up with the greatest absurdity. And little in Kafka's work is more absurd that this nocturnal scene in which K. falls asleep while Bürgel rants on to justify the workings of the absurd order of things in which they find themselves operating.

This hyperbole is satire aimed at a bureaucratic order established purposely to avoid favorable decisions for the petitioner. It is an order based on dilatory tactics that Bürgel nonetheless claims may accidently result in a favorable decision. He makes this explanation for the benefit of the hapless K., who cares not a fig for all this blather as he falls asleep. The juxtaposition of the garrulous functionary and the exhausted supplicant gives way to sleep and to K.'s dream in which he is victorious over a bureaucrat resembling a nude Greek god. K. strides forward, and his very motion is a sign of victory. Yet, the oneiric victory contains within it the grounds for defeat. K. steps on the shards of a broken champagne glass and cuts his foot, which awakens him to the sight of Bürgel's less than divine naked chest. The satirical comparison of a god and a functionary underscores the pretentions of the Castle's ruling class, pretentions having their roots in the ancient history of humanity, in Sumer and Egypt, not to mention Kafka's contemporary Europe, where he had himself been a functionary for many years.

The physical farce of the nocturnal scene continues in the following chapter when K. is the privileged observer of the workings of the bureaucratic order and its procedures for handling communications and distributing information, namely handing out dossiers. The farce is of a physical sort that recalls cinematic comedy. Two orders of events unfold here. One is the entropic collapse of the order controlling the distribution of information, that is, the increasingly chaotic way the files are thrown out at five o'clock in the morning. The second is the expulsion of K. from this inner sanctuary whose workings he has accidentally witnessed. He has violated the sacred realm to which only the initiated priests are allowed access, for nobody is allowed to watch the distribution of the *Akten*.

The beginning of the farce is set up when Erlanger summarily tells K. that he must send Frieda back to the inn: one cannot risk Klamm's being upset by the slightest change in the order of things. The order seems superfluous, since Frieda is already in the inn, but it does point up that nobody seems to know what is going on. Then begins the farce of the distribution of files that wreaks havoc with the idea of bureaucratic order. It begins like a well-ordered ballet as files are handed out, builds to a crescendo of disorder with conflict between functionaries and servants, and then falls to the quiet moment when only one sheet of paper remains. The servant holding it contemplates it for a moment and then tears it into shreds, which seems a proper finale to this farcical ballet for orchestrating communicative acts—and the absurdity that K. finds engulfing him. In brief, the scene unfolds with a frenetic tempo comparable to a scene in Charlie Chapin or, especially, Buster Keaton.

Then begins a second farce, with its tempo set by the bells rung by the functionaries, with first one ringing, then others, until they reach another crescendo, and K. is escorted out of this inner sanctuary by the innkeeper and his wife. On K.'s exit, the bells ring as if they were celebrating a victory. He has unknowingly violated the unwritten law that all know: nobody is allowed to witness the distribution of the sacred acts. In suggesting that K. has entered the inner sanctuary of the Castle's order and defiled it, the satire aims at all forms of ritual order that exclude the profane, whether secular or religious, though the religious side seems emphasized when K. learns that the "gentlemen" prefer nocturnal hearings because they cannot stand to look at the unworthy supplicants. The horror of the profane is too much for the priesthood to bear in the light of day. The modern and the ancient are combined once again in the implicit comparison of bureaucracy and the priesthood, a comparison seemingly implying that both secular and clerical institutions are more in the service of disorder than in the realization of higher designs.

K. understands now that he has no position in the Castle's order of things. He has been formally expelled. The novel's final chapter offers a surprising development, seemingly motivated by the preceding chapter's farcical demonstration that K. has nowhere to go, since possibilities for the future then spring up. As a way out of his impasse, K. might end up living with chambermaids, or he might be taken in by the coach driver Gerstäcker, or he might perhaps even become a fashion consultant for the innkeeper's wife. The latter seems an unlikely choice, though it could resemble what happens to Karl Rossmann when he is sequestered by Brunelda, who needs help with her perfume. In any case, when K. is expelled from the inner sanctuary wherein the gentlemen functionaries conduct their absurd nocturnal business, K. reaches a nadir vis-à-vis the Castle. Offered the sudden alternatives K. then has, the reader is disappointed to find that the novel ends in the middle of a sentence.

The lover of hermeneutics will note, however, that Kafka seems to have envisaged a change in the novel's development with a new interpretation of its events, presenting them from the perspective of the barmaid Pepi. Pepi is persuasive with her interpretation that puts in question much of what has been narrated up to this point. Epistemological uncertainty is always part of Kafka's narrative strategy, and Pepi's narration undercuts certainty by effecting the juxtaposition of discordant narrative viewpoints. Using *erlebte Rede* or free indirect discourse, the third-person narrator offers Pepi's overview of everything that has happened in the novel from the moment K. ran away from the inn with Frieda. After the surprising revelation that Pepi loved K. for inadvertently helping her in her advancement at the inn, Pepi then offers a dismal interpretation of things, stressing K.'s lack of importance in what has happened. Frieda, she suggests, was not Klamm's lover, and her latching onto K. was Frieda's idea of what she might do to call attention to herself in order to show how indispensable she is. According to Pepi, Frieda actually wanted to create a scandal. K. has thus no importance for her except for his role in her devious plan. After she left, Klamm did not come down anymore, and the reason for this was that Frieda did not let him. From Pepi's perspective K. has been oblivious to how Frieda has used him, even after she kicked him out and returned to the inn to appear to the innkeeper as a savior. In Pepi's interpretation, it seems the novel's events mainly show what an insignificant fool K. has been.

K. does not accept this version of the events in which, after all, he has been the protagonist. In his counterinterpretation, the narration changes from indirect to direct speech, to dialogue, as K. rather mildly criticizes Pepi's version. His critique has little effect. What is of interest is that Pepi now wants K. to come live with her and two other chambermaids in their small room at least until spring. She proposes that she, K., and two other chambermaids live together in a *ménage à quatre* that would be the antithesis, one thinks, of what it means to be accepted in this society. One wonders whether Kafka was envisaging a fairy tale or a pornographic novel with this surprising idea. The fairy tale side is stressed when K. asks when spring comes, only to learn from Pepi that spring and summer together do not last more than two days in that region, and it may snow on those days. The physical world of *The Castle* remains the realm of a dark fantasy in this development. The image of K. living with three women in a tiny room is another wacky image, but no more bizarre than life with Frieda and two assistants in a classroom amid gym equipment; they are all comic images of marginalization and exclusion.

A third possible development is also suggested. Kafka considered finding K. better lodging by sending Gerstäcker to offer quarters in exchange, it seems, for the help K. might give him in dealing with Erlanger. Despite the fact that the idea is not developed, the arrival of Gerstäcker struck the German writer W. S. Sebald as a significant event pointing up the symbolic structure of the entire novel. Building on Ronald Gray's monograph on *The Castle,* Sebald proposed that Gerstäcker's arrival actually is a form of closure to the novel since the coachman Gerstäcker is a Charon-like figure who offers the means of conveying K. into the realm of the dead. Sebald's interpretation depends on a monolithic allegorical reading of the novel in which everything K. does is part of K.'s quest for death. Sebald makes an allegorical reading in which the Castle represents the region allowing entrance into death. From this perspective it is that realm that Kafka, like his character Gracchus, wants to find but fears he may never be allowed to enter. In Sebald's reading, *The Castle* offers an updated version of the myth of the wandering Jew who, for scoffing at Christ, was not allowed to die.[5] By allegorizing *The Castle* from only one perspective, Sebald thus turns the novel into an example of the creation of modernist myth. The modernist draws upon classical myth to show that the myth continues to live on, embodied in recognizable form in modern life. This type of allegory is not unlike what one might find in Europe in Joyce and Cocteau or, in America, in Faulkner, O'Neill, and Wilder. Sebald's is an ingenuous reading, one that a biographical critic might endorse, recalling that Kafka was sick at the time he was writing *The Castle*. Like all monolithic interpretations of Kafka, Sebald's reading suffers only from its dubious coherence, which allows only one restrictive perspective on the novel and its multifarious images.

Sebald's interpretation of *The Castle* is not unlike the reaction of many German intellectuals who have sought a way of dealing with Kafka's representation of a world situated on the margin of, if not outside, history. They have often felt obliged to interpret it as a kind of myth. Ten years after Kafka's death, for example, the critic Walter Benjamin wrote the influential essay (referred to earlier) in which he characterized Kafka's work as one that exists in a prehistorical space—which, I add, can surely be only the space of myth having a religious significance. In correspondence with Benjamin, Benjamin's friend the scholar Gershom Scholem contested Benjamin's reading and offered his version of Kafka's mythic text, saying that the fictional space was that of revelation, of the "nothingness of revelation," by which Scholem meant "a state in which revelation appears to be without meaning, in which it still asserts itself, in which it has *validity*, but *no significance*."[6] *The Castle* thus becomes then the locus for the reenactment of biblical myths, revealed for their failure to occur but still full of meaning, as I understand this view. These views of *The Castle* by the Marxist mystic Benjamin and the scholar of Judaism Scholem, both in exile from Hitler's Germany, set the tone for the subsequent debates about Kafka and myth that were united mainly in rejecting Max Brod's view that *The Castle* was an allegory about finding grace.

I conclude here by adding that the reading of *The Castle* contained in this chapter owes something to Benjamin and to Scholem, though it undoubtedly owes more to another German intellectual in exile, Hannah Arendt. She asserted in 1944 that K. was based on the Jew seeking integration into society, though the demands of the excluded Jew were represented by Kafka as universal needs. According to Arendt, K. is an ordinary human being who demands the "inalienable rights" of every human being. In a sense he is the only normal healthy human being in a world in which all that is human and normal has been wrested out of men's hands to become a gift granted from without.[7] Arendt certainly had contemporary totalitarian regimes in mind when she penned these ideas, and her interpretation of the excluded Jew as a universal being springs from a catastrophic historical context in which it made great sense.

(It still does, in fact.) It is perhaps not irrelevant finally that Benjamin's friend the neo-Marxist Theodore Adorno, the last of the influential German exiles to interpret Kafka, apparently wanted to reconcile them all. In the early 1950s, he wrote, rather obscurely, that Kafka was an accuser of dialectical theology and that his work preserves the moment when "purified faith" is revealed to be impure. Yet Kafka "remains a rationalist in his attempt to rectify the myth that thus emerges"; he wants to undertake the trial of this myth and reconcile myth through humor.[8] Unlike many of Kafka's critics, Adorno recognized that Kafka had a great sense of humor.

Many readers believe Kafka wrote perhaps his most ambitious and successful work with *The Castle*. In it Kafka perfected his technique by which, to paraphrase what the novelist Martin Walser wrote many years ago, the narrator is absent and the medium itself is the most important character, for all takes place with no refraction pointing beyond the work, all takes place within it, and interpretation is left to us.[9] With this perfecting of his narrative technique, Kafka portrayed the inner world of existential striving that many consider to be the fate of contemporary humanity, one ever subject to many and contradictory interpretations. Kafka did so by creating a world at once historical and before and beyond history on the margin of this world in which we strive to master our sense of the absurd imposed upon us by our metaphysical vacuum and at the same time to survive in a world in which social forces often seem to be beyond our control. The narrative space that Kafka framed for K. in *The Castle* remains a touchstone for understanding what we once considered our modernity, then our postmodernity, and undoubtedly whatever is now, perhaps, replacing both.

Chapter 8

A Hunger Artist and the Last Stories

After the Zürau aphorisms, Kafka wrote short texts in spurts of creativity from 1918 until his death. This writing of short stories, parables, and meditations was marked by fallow periods in 1919 and 1921 and by his work on *The Castle* in 1922. However, 1919 was not entirely fallow if we consider "Letter to His Father" of that year to be part of Kafka's literary opus. It can be argued that this letter is a work of the literary imagination. It is undoubtedly part of Kafka's ongoing attempt to find his identity as a writer, a preoccupation that is reflected, in his last writings, in the frequent portrayal of artists and the nature of their art. Kafka himself probably did not consider the letter he wrote to his father as an artist's manifesto. In fact, before sending "Letter to His Father" to Milena, Kafka warned her, in a letter of 4 July 1920, that it is what he called a lawyer's letter. He viewed it as something like a brief filled with what he called lawyer's artifices. From a literary perspective, this brief resembles a courtroom drama in which Kafka stages a debate to decide who is the guilty party, father or son, with Kafka giving voice to both. In it the man of letters faces his father, the man of practical reality, to charge him with a lack of understanding. Of course, it is the intent of the son, Kafka, the plaintiff, to put the father, who as defendant makes rebuttals and counterclaims, on trial. In the father's rebuttal the son's crimes are put on display, crimes as viewed from the father's perspective. Literary text or not, the letter is a remarkable example of self-therapy. In psychological terms, Kafka confronted his father in his imagination and, perhaps, vindicated himself as a writer.

Much of Kafka's later writing, especially the stories of *A Hunger Artist* but also several of the posthumously published texts, portrays artists and shows Kafka experimenting with ideas about what art might be. (The posthumous texts are found in the second volume of Kafka's unpublished works in Fischer's critical edition, referred to in the following as *KA* 2.) In this writing—sketches, parables, narratives, aphorisms—he sought a kind of reconciliation with the art at which he had failed with such brilliant success. Part of this reconciliation involves questioning the nature of art by experimenting with different views of it. It is of extraordinary interest that Kafka sketched out, experimentally, views of art that have become accepted concepts about the nature of art.

Kafka died with the proofs for *A Hunger Artist* in hand. Then Brod culled stories he considered publishable from the manuscripts he held, edited them, and gave them titles as he set about to establish a Kafka canon. It is mainly these writings, available in translation, that I discuss here. However, one should bear in mind that Kafka filled his notebooks with a remarkable variety of texts, many of which remain untranslated into English. In these texts one finds familiar themes—particularly in the writings of 1920 that deal with the shape of power, the law, and the recurrent search for the way. Kafka experimented with representations of power and of individuals caught up in a web of relations in which they are ruled over by the same bonds with which the patriarch dominates the child. Dominance is a vertical relationship that can also spread out horizontally and permeate the world like a form of social glue. It is the world of conformity, which is to say that it is the world of the Castle.

In a few texts Kafka also undertook thought experiments in which he positioned an observer who sees a world that is slipping away from him. This is the case, for example, in two untitled, untranslated semiautobiographical texts of early 1920 found in the critical edition's second volume of unpublished writings. These meditations highlight Kafka's thinking about literature and the grounds for art before he made the nature of art the center of his concerns. In the first text, probably written early in 1920, Kafka imagines looking through the window on a scene set in a November rain and wonders how he can know anything about the people out there in it. Kafka, or his narrator, concludes, with implicit self-reference, that "one is a human being, too, and thus one knows about people's struggle for adaptation, so that one judges by them, one learns something and knows what one has to expect, that the traffic [*Verkehr*] below does not stand still but remains in motion in street after street with lock-jawed untiring impenetrable conviction" (*KA* 2, p. 218). The observer grimly affirms that he can see the world and its workings and that he, too, is human, even if the world of drizzle is impenetrable, and all that he sees is only this world of unending traffic and numbing movement, the recurrent *Verkehr* in Kafka's vision of the city as an unceasingly mechanical being.

This minimal, bleak affirmation of the writer's power to know can be compared with a slightly later text from February 1920 in which Kafka describes another observer, one who cannot participate in the Sunday excursions that other people have organized. The narrator says everything separates him from these people—ancestry, education, physical training (*körperliche Ausbildung*)—and yet the observer feels that he stands very near to them. They are humans, after all, and nothing "human could be totally foreign to them" (*KA* 2, p. 221). Like the observer looking into the rain, this observer feels he must be able to understand his fellow human beings since he is one, too. This is the basic axiom of humanism—one that the growing ethnic hatreds in 1920 may well have made dubious. It is, moreover, a basic axiom that Kafka adapts for his dog-narrator of "Investigations of a Dog," a believer in universal dogdom. This dog satire suggests that the observer of humans in 1920 may have doubts about the possibility of remaining in the universalist camp of the classical humanists. The observer of 1920 suspects that the same feelings that keep him from participating in human community might also be haunting some dark corner of the others' minds (*KA* 2, p. 221). The forces of separation and alienation, not to mention common dislike and suspicion, are as common to all as are the putative bonds of social solidarity. An ironic belief in humanism grounded in universal dislike seems plausible here.

Kafka then goes on to write in this text of 1920, without apparent irony or paradox, what can be taken as a clear statement about the limits of human understanding. His observer recognizes that strong emotions exist in the world—fear, mourning, misery—but he characterizes them as vague, generalized feelings that touch only superficially on the surface of things. Sharing the distrust of emotions that Kafka expressed in his letter to Felice Bauer, the observer asks, "How could it be otherwise . . . since our feelings can never touch or even catch up with true events [*Ereignisse*]" (*KA* 2, p. 222). What constitutes a true event is a question left unanswered, though one suspects that the answer would lie at the end of the "way" that is the goal of Kafka's texts. The true event, that is, would be the object of literature, resembling perhaps something like the mysterious "permanence" (*Unzerstörbar*) that Kafka evokes in the Zürau aphorisms. The true event appears to be beyond emotion, perhaps beyond attainment, which leaves us with the image of humanity locked in the darkness of its emotive subjectivity so that, as the narrator observes, "We live in the quiet of midnight and experience sunrise and sunset when we turn ourselves toward the east or the west" (*KA* 2, p. 222).

Were this haunting image the conclusion of this dour text, the reader might believe that Kafka sees humanity as lost in total alienation in the dark, with only occasional, chance illuminations. However, Kafka concludes the text with a humorous twist: "A meager life force, a misunderstood education, bachelorhood, these all produce the skeptic—though not necessarily—indeed, to save skepticism, many skeptics get married, at least ideally [*ideell*], and become believers" (*KA* 2, p. 222). With ironic deflation, Kafka's sense of humor returns in this self-directed and witty view of reasons for marriage: a chance to safeguard skepticism. Kafka's skepticism is arguably the saving grace that kept him from floundering in the bleak vision expressed in this text's hopelessness about vision itself, for this skepticism is the grounds for his distance from his own vision and for his boundless sense of humor

It is after this text, with its brief critique of feeling as mere appearance and of emotions as fairy tales and deceptive mirror images (*KA* 2, p. 222), that Kafka began the writings found in the notebook called the *Konvolut* of 1920. He began to work out here the consequences of this critique. The rejection of the Romantic belief in feeling and imagination meant nothing less than finding another basis for aesthetics. Indeed, in saying that feelings and images are meaningless, Kafka implicitly disavowed the view that art is either a mimetic activity or an expressive outpouring of the individual's feelings or both—views recurrent from Plato through Goethe. The texts of 1920 only begin to broach this subject, for many of them continue to deal with Kafka's favored themes of power and the law. It is largely in writing done after 1922 that the nature of art and the artist became Kafka's dominant concern.

With this development in mind, I turn first to the texts Brod took from the *Konvolut* of 1920. These were all written after the two untranslated texts I have just discussed. Brod's titles are used here, though these writings are untitled in the manuscript, with the exception of "Zur Frage der Gesetze," (first translated as "The Problem of Our Laws"). Brod used the following titles for these texts of 1920: "Poseidon," "Fellowship," "At Night," "The City Coat of Arms," "The Helmsman," "The Vulture," "The Top," "The Problem of Our Laws," "The Conscription of Troops," "A Little Fable," and "The Refusal" (the latter not to be confused with the same title, "Die Abweisung," that Kafka used for a text in *Meditation*). Each of these is well worth critical attention.

"Poseidon" is Kafka's humorous version of a Greek god, comparable to his earlier rewriting of myth. It is an exercise in pure wit for which no claims can be made for feeling or imagination in the Romantic sense. Rather, with deflationary humor, the god Poseidon is portrayed as a contemporary functionary working for an administration. The gods today are bureaucrats working for Jupiter. Once familiar as a vengeful god inhabiting the sea, Poseidon now sits at a desk to do his work and calculations. Other positions are offered to him, but he shudders at the thought of leaving the Water Department. Besides, it would be hard for him to find another job in the water works that would befit his stature. So he stays there, though his work allows him scarcely any occasion to see the sea. Only at the moment of the world's extinction (*Untergang*) will he have time, after checking over his last calculations, for a brief trip around his dominions. Kafka's humorous updating of Poseidon resembles superficially other modernists' demonstration of the perennial validity of classical myth by using myth in a modern context. However, Kafka's transformation of myth is a thought experiment reflecting his project for rethinking the grounds of literature in an era lacking ideas about foundations of art. It is much the opposite of the modernist attempt to ground literature in mythic archetypes. Not sharing the modernist belief in the eternity of recurrent myth, Kafka shows comically the end of Nietzschean eternal return—in office boredom.

In the same spirit Kafka also rewrote biblical myths. For a relevant example we turn from the writings of 1920 to consider Kafka's ruminations on Abraham in his correspondence. His versions of Abraham's sacrifice of Isaac involve whimsical transformations of religious myth, in part motivated by his reaction to the Christian philosopher Kierkegaard. The latter proposed that Abraham was a "knight of faith" who made a leap of faith into the absurd when he accepted God's order to sacrifice his son. Kafka was irked by Kierkegaard's ratiocinations to justify his Christian faith, and in a letter of June 1921, to his friend Robert Klopstock, an admirer of Kierkegaard, he offered other versions of the Abraham story.[1] Kafka imagines various Abrahams, all having different characteristics, the most interesting one perhaps being an Abraham who is ready to sacrifice Isaac but who, despite his faith, cannot really believe he has been selected for the absurd task. Kafka's Abraham fears that on the way to the sacrifice he will discover he is Don Quixote and hence a risible object. So much for a leap of faith.

Here Kafka has taken a Judeo-Christian myth and given it universal resonance: Abraham's doubting and fearing ridicule. Underlying Kafka's revision lies the anguish felt at being called, for no evident reason, yet nonetheless called to undertake a mission, like the watch who keeps vigil in "At Night" or, by contrast, the servant who is never called to serve in "The Test." These two texts of 1920 are animated by a comparable concern, indeed, a passionate wonder about the groundless nature of the call made by ethics, which is comparable to Kafka's anguish about the lack of foundations that justify writing. For writing is also a response to a call, an answer to the groundless call that seems to be the basis for ethics.

In the two untranslated texts of 1920 that I discussed earlier, Kafka rejected aesthetics based on the superficiality of emotion. In his reflections on Abraham one sees his doubts about the call to fulfill a vocation, such as art and writing, that should grant access to some divine revelation. In rewriting the myth of Abraham, Kafka foregrounded the fact that there are no criteria for knowing whether one is truly called or not. (This was also Kierkegaard's point about the absurdity of the leap of faith, though it is a situation that could not be communicated to another.) In another version of Abraham, it appears Abraham may come without even being really summoned. Then Abraham would be acting like the worst student in class who, perhaps mistakenly, hears his name called to come forward for a prize; he stands up and then must face the class's derisive laughter at his presumption. Uncertainty about the call seems to be recommended by this parable.

One of Kafka's strangest texts from 1920, "Der Geier" or "The Vulture," can also be read as a revision of myth. The bird in this short tale resembles the eagle of the Greek myth of Prometheus in that it feeds on the first-person narrator, though it eats his feet, not his innards. As in the classical myth, the narrator is destined to be perpetual fodder for the winged beast.[2] But in Kafka's updated version a passer-by obligingly offers to get a gun and shoot the bird. The narrator accepts, the bird apparently understands, and, gathering momentum, it plunges its beak through the narrator's mouth and deep into his body. The narrator takes satisfaction that the bird is now drowning in the blood that flows out, flooding the depths and every shore, as the text puts it. If this is a revision of the Prometheus myth, it is one in which the victim describes his own destruction, caused by his accepting the benevolent intervention of a bystander. The victim can at least take satisfaction in the fact that the vulture is dying. The implications of this bizarre revision are obscure. From one perspective, it appears that answering, like accepting, the call for help does not always have happy consequences—the bystander's offer is deadly. From the narrator's perspective, living a myth apparently entails dying from it. Biographers who argue that the vulture symbolizes tuberculosis, or Kafka's father, or a death wish might also see a certain irony in the writer's self-portrayal as a modern Prometheus, an unnamed one, one simply pinned down by the absurd.

The concern with ethics and art is clear in other texts, for example, the beautiful prose poem mentioned earlier, "Nachts" ("At Night"). An anonymous narrator says he sees people united at night in sleep, though this sight is really a theatrical scene, for they only pretend to be modern sleepers lying on mattresses and under blankets. Actually they are like some nomadic group, flocking together as in biblical times, under a cold sky upon a cold earth. The narrator sees his contemporaries in their sleep as a reincarnation of a tribal scene wherein they lie exposed to the elements. The narrator concludes by directly addressing an interlocutor, asserting that "you keep watch" during this night. One wonders if the narrator addresses himself, or the implied reader, or a guard by the campfire. It matters little, since the import of the apostrophe is to introduce the question as to why you, or anybody, must keep watch. The answer is simple: someone must do so. As the tribe sleeps, there are no metaphysical grounds adduced to justify vigilance; it is a simple necessity. Vigilance demands it, and answering the call is the elementary response that grounds ethics and, by implication, art, for the addressee seems probably to be the writer of this text.

By contrast, in the aforementioned "Die Prüfung" ("The Test") Kafka depicts a loyal servant who is not called. There is something Zen-like about this parable describing a servant who is desirous of duty and the test to which, unawares, he is subjected. The test occurs when he goes to a tavern, is invited by another servant to have a drink, and then is asked a number of questions that he does not answer because he does not understand them. Upon his expressing his regret for his incapacity, he gets up to leave, but his fellow servant tells him to stay, for he has just passed a test in which the mark of success is not to answer. This story is suggestive of the hopelessness of knowing what a calling might be, and one is tempted to compare the text's enigma to the Zen puzzle known as a koan, the understanding of which can be shown only in silence. Can there be an answer to the question of why one is not called? If there is an allegory here, then it seems to mean simply that one may seek a calling but find no service, which is perhaps what Kafka, the writer, felt about his desire for a vocation as writer—vocation means, literally, calling. (This uncertainty is summed up by Kafka's twenty-sixth Zürau aphorism, to the effect that we can know the goal but not the way.) One can also ask whether, if the servant has passed the test by remaining silent, this is commendable or simply the regrettable result of the fact that all meaningful questions are really unintelligible and have no answers. Finally, it appears that "The Test" is itself a self-mirroring test, a generator of questions about itself that cannot be answered except with silent understanding.

Kafka undertook a more extensive revision of biblical myth in "Das Stadtwappen" ("The City Coat of Arms"). In it, Kafka tells of plans for a modern tower of Babel. In the Bible it is told that humanity was once united, speaking one language, before it attempted to build the famous tower reaching to heaven. Kafka's version reflects the Europe of 1920, when diplomats thought they might reshape unity by recognizing a country for nearly every ethnic group in Europe. Kafka's version has a referential dimension spanning from ancient times to his contemporary world, all in a dazzling play of wit. The implications for art implicit in the fact that the tower of Babel has not been built are great, especially for the idea of conceptual art, since nobody thinks it should be built just yet: the very concept of the tower will keep it alive forever, and, as building techniques get better and better, it is better that it be built later. It will naturally be an even better tower than the planners had imagined. For the present one can be content with the concept. The narrator regrets only that the preparation of the project degenerates into quarrels and bloody conflict about quarters for the workers of many different nationalities who gather to work on humanity's tower. The unity of humanity needs no tower to go asunder.

Kafka's tale ends with an epilogue prophesying an apocalypse for the tower's city. The city will be destroyed by the blow of a giant fist, the fist that now decorates the city's coat of arms. The title Brod invented for this tale, "The City Coat of Arms," points up that Kafka's ending alludes to Prague's official city seal, which represents an arm holding an upraised sword. One may surmise that Kafka's final image is not only a jab at Prague's coat of arms but also an expression of pessimism about the European politics that had led to World

War I and that, one suspects, Kafka in 1920 saw as laying no foundation for a future peace. The upraised sword awaits every community that presumes to reach beyond itself, demonstrating the hubris behind the building of the tower that would allow humanity to storm the heavens.

Themes of politics and ethics are central to other texts from 1920. Power is held by the rulers of states that, though not situated on any map, look much like existing states, both past and present. For example, "Die Abweisung" ("The Refusal") is set in a city so far from the country's borders that nobody in the city has ever seen them. As in "The Great Wall of China," distances are so immense and the land's capital so distant that nobody can get there, with the exception perhaps of the officials who claim to have made the journey. In this remote city surrounded by infinite waste, one man has the power to rule. It is not clear to anyone exactly why this is so. Though people call the ruler the *Oberst*—the "colonel"—he is really a patriarch figure with no definite position. Power resides in him, it seems, because power must reside somewhere. It is true that he has soldiers under his command. They speak an incomprehensible language, but, unlike the jabbering barbarians of the "Old Manuscript," they are not especially harmful. The colonel holds power mainly so that people have somebody to address when they wish to make petitions asking for things from the government. In this capacity he rules as patriarch, since he is really the final point in the chain of command; there is no recourse beyond him. His power functions automatically and efficiently: when petitions are presented to him, they are regularly refused. The law can function only if it functions predictably; thus, the colonel's power functions, and all accept this state of affairs. That is, all except some young people who have other ideas. With this conclusion Kafka implies that absolute power may be reliable, but it can always face a desire for change, that is, the possibility of revolution. This is hardly a surprising conclusion. Kafka had just seen three empires disappear before his eyes, with an attendant revolution and several attempts at revolution. The recent war had revealed the unfounded and arbitrary nature of patriarchal authority in ways that not even Kafka had imagined earlier.[3] As *The Castle* shows at length, Kafka now saw power as depending as much on the willingness to be dominated as on the imposition of brute force.

The loss of power recently seen in Europe is dramatized concisely in "Der Steuermann" ("The Helmsman"). The story's narrator is a helmsman who is dispossessed suddenly of his hold on the ship's tiller by a man stronger than he, while the ship's crew passively, indeed, indifferently acquiesces to this coup d'état. If one takes the ship to be something of a traditional trope for the state, then it appears that Kafka is depicting the capricious ease with which the control of state can change hands—in an historical blink of the eye, as the recent war had shown. Equally important is the way the helmsman's lament emphasizes the passivity with which the crew envisages the change of power. It offers no resistance and shows no concern, since one leader is as indifferently good as another.

This facile willingness of the people to accept whatever the authorities—or perhaps fate—decide is described in "Die Truppenaushebung" ("The Conscription of Troops"). Kafka offers a humorous depiction of the practices in some unnamed land where soldiers must be regularly conscripted to fight the incessant border wars waged by the authorities. The borders are distant, and wars are constant there. The narrator acts somewhat like an anthropologist who describes the habits of the inhabitants of a distant land. To raise and maintain its armies on its remote borders, the inhabitants must gather periodically in their homes on a certain day when a nobleman with a whip comes to select new soldiers. A few try to evade military duty. They hide, are found, and then are beaten by the aristocrat, who is, however, so feeble that, when he drops his whip, as he often does, the victim must pick it up and give it back to him. Remarkable in this depiction of the demands of power is the fact that more people show up for recruitment in a given house than are officially listed for it. Men want to be called up, even those who make a pretense of fleeing. There are women who come regularly, hoping to be recruited, only to be regularly driven away by blows on their backs. In short, power can rely on willing acceptance of its demands, and the regular arrival of a debilitated nobleman with the trappings of power resembles a pro forma performance. This is another perspective on the question of ethics and its calling, one with the recent war as its backdrop, for those who answer the call are willing performers who undertake what may appear to be a senseless duty but a duty that keeps the nobleman in power. At this point readers, having in mind the way civilians of all nations had readily answered the call to arms, may also recall Kafka's diary entry in which he wished, at the war's outset, the worst on all sides.

Contemporary European society is also the backdrop for a brief allegory about social ties,"Gemeinschaft," usually translated "Fellowship" but better rendered, with irony, as "Community." It describes the arbitrary community, created when five men come out of a house one day and, because they are together, become friends. The grounds for the founding of their *Gemeinschaft* are arbitrary. It happens because of a fortuitous joining together due to proximity. The five men thus united are then bothered by a sixth man who wants to be a part of their community, but the narrator says that, since they do not know him, they do not want him despite the fact that at one time the five of them did not know one another either and even if it is pointless for the five to hang around together. They will not explain all this to the sixth, since offering an explanation would in effect bring him into their group. So they just push him away, though, curiously, he keeps coming back. The immediate context for this view of the arbitrary nature of social ties is surely the growing nationalism in Europe in which the demands of various ethnic groups constituted an explosive issue. Some groups sought to justify their exclusive solidarity by promoting a belief that some kind of metaphysical ties united their community—say, the strength of their imagined blood ties. Such imaginary metaphysics are the target of Kafka's ironic perspective on nationalism—the five friends are united because they were arbitrarily in the same place one day. And from the perspective of those rejected by such a community, Kafka's story presents an ironic view of, say, the desire of some Jews for assimilation into societies that could not explain why they do not want them. Kafka's irony about community is, to say the least, understated.

Kafka himself gave a title to another text that addresses the question of power, the law, and the foundations of society, namely "Zur Frage der Gesetze" ("The Problem of Our Laws," though literally "On the Question of the Laws"). He describes an imaginary land where an aristocracy reigns supreme. This description is surely a direct reflection on and a critique of Nietzsche's theory of the origins of the law and ethics. Nietzsche was a proponent of the right of superior classes to define morality and to impose their views on lower classes, indeed, of the desirability of such an arrangement. (This can be found, for example, in Nietzsche's *Beyond Good and Evil,* in which in the thirtieth section he observes that whatever nourishes the higher class will almost certainly be a poison for the inferior classes.) Kafka depicts a society in which the Nietzschean ideal that the law is the preserve of the elite is realized. Thus the narrator in "The Problem of Our Laws" describes, from below, a version of the good society as imagined by Nietzsche, one in which life is not easy for the rabble. Indeed, the laws of his land are not even known to the rabble since they remain the secret possession of the small group of noblemen who rule over them. Admitting that this is a painful situation for the people, the narrator then says that actually the very existence of the law is a matter of tradition, since nobody can say for sure that the law exists. Refusing to share their power, the nobles do not reveal the law to the plebeians. In effect, the law appears to be whatever the nobles want—à la Nietzsche.

The situation has created a new class of scholars who scrutinize the records to see what the nobility has done and does. In this way they infer the law for the present day. The results are that one group of these interpreters—resembling lawyers, priests, philosophers—finds that understanding the law is only an intellectual game. And, recognizing that the laws may not even exist, another group has arisen that openly declares that the law is simply whatever the nobles do and decree and that tradition is meaningless. The narrator draws back from accepting this radical viewpoint, preferring to think that only a few more centuries of scholarship are needed before research into tradition can offer a complete picture of the law. But the only certain conclusion, according to another pundit as cited by the narrator, is that the only law that exists is that the aristocracy imposes the law, which is to say, itself. Society's need for security is such that nobody wants to do without this one law that grounds whatever law they happen to have. The society thus lives with the nobility and takes the desires of the powerful as the law. In this way power is grounded by the circular view that the law is law if it has the power to impose itself as the law. This circularity confirms that the grounds for law and morality are what Nietzsche declared them to be: the will to power. Kafka's irony seems to admit what it condemns at the same time. Kafka's brilliant perspectival pirouettes in these reflections on the law and its origins oblige one to ask whether there is a basis for morality and law at all or whether they exist only as the arbitrary will of superior spheres—human, divine, or whatever.

The nature of power is also reflected in "Kleine Fabel" ("A Little Fable"), a few whimsical lines in which a mouse laments that the world becomes narrower each day. Wanting to go forward, the mouse finds its way increasingly constricted as the circumambient walls grow narrower until finally the mouse finds itself going into a room in which a mouse trap awaits it in the corner. A cat that happens to be present commonsensically observes that the mouse need only change its direction, whereupon, however, the cat eats the mouse. The powerful are always waiting to help the weak, it seems, with good advice that is beside the point. Critics have pointed out that this concise parable describes the metaphysics of everyday life, to which I add that it also reads like a description of the unfolding of political fate. It is a description of the way, the wrong way, that is usually taken not just by ordinary mortals but also by policymakers and nations and of the consequences in a world where fate, with destructive power, is lurking to pounce on the weak at the end.

The derisive humor of "A Little Fable" is also at work in the description of a philosopher found in "Der Kreisel" ("The Top"—the name of a spinning cone, once a favored toy). The tale's philosopher thinks that if he were to study one object until he fully understands it, he would have knowledge of all things. Like some natural historian from a tale by Hoffmann, the philosopher wants to reduce the world's variety to something seen from a single viewpoint. Thus Kafka's philosopher is eager to see the universe in a spinning top. In his field work he finds a top to study and is not bothered by children's cries when he interferes with their play. But his progress is rather mouse-like, for his way leads him to the unremarkable discovery that a top is merely a dumb piece of wood. However, the exterior world will have its due, for once the children's cries break in upon his attention, he stumbles away like a top beaten by an inexpert whip—"wie ein Kreisel unter einer ungeschickten Peitsche" (*KA* 2, p. 361). This image alludes to the way children once used a leather strap for striking tops in order to set them in motion (images available online!). This strap in Kafka's tale represents the mute world's power to render derisive the designs of an epistemological seeker. The philosopher himself is reduced to a top turning on itself with a circular motion, yet another way of going nowhere. The spinning philosopher-top is an image of immobility in motion—which offers another concise self-referential allegory about the quest. In brief, it narrates a tale of going nowhere of which it is a prime example itself.

The quest for the way resurfaces in other texts in Kafka's late writings, especially in "Der Aufbruch" ("The Departure"), "Fürsprecher" ("Advocates"), and "Geduldspiel" ("A Chinese Puzzle," found in *Parables and Paradoxes*). These were probably written in 1922, after Kafka had given up on *The Castle*, and can in some sense be considered responses to Kafka's own failure to find a way to the Castle. "The Departure" describes a man's preparation for flight or breaking out, in effect, to find the way. A caveat: this parable in the most available translation is based on a truncated version resulting from Brod's decision to cut the final lines. (I discuss both versions here.) In the first part of the text the first-person narrator orders his horse saddled, but he must take care of the horse himself when his servant does not understand what his master wants. Hearing trumpets sound in the distance, he asks his servant what they mean, but the servant says he has heard nothing. As the master departs, the servant finally asks where he is going, to which the master replies abruptly that he is going "out of here." And to the servant's question about what his goal is, the master cries out that that is it: to get out of here. Brod ended the text at this point. In this truncated version it reads much like Baudelaire's prose poem "Any Where Out of the World" in which the poet, repeatedly asked where he wants to be, angrily expresses his anguished desire to be anywhere, provided it is out of this world.

However, in the final lines of the manuscript text of "The Departure," the practical servant then observes that his master is taking no food, thus bringing up the question of the nourishment he will need along the way. To which the master answers, with a flourish of bravado, that the trip will be so long that if he does not encounter food along the way, no supplies he could take with him would keep him from starving (*Verhungern*). For, he says, it is his good fortune (*zum Glück*) that it will be a very long trip (*KA* 2, p. 375). Why it is a felicitous thing that the way will be so long is not immediately apparent, and one is inclined to contrast this travel with the unending struggle portrayed in *The Castle*. The deleted last lines of "The Departure" show that the trip is envisaged as having no end—since the goal is to move unendingly toward the goal, with hopes that travel itself can nourish the traveler. The idea that the movement itself may offer nourishment is rather new, though it somewhat resembles the Romantic topos that what counts is not discovery but the infinite movement toward discovery. Be that as it may, this image of movement again represents self-reflexively the movement of the literary text itself, but with nuanced hope about what the quest itself may or must offer: a self-sustaining project.

Another description of the way occurs at the end of "Advocates." The story is narrated in the first person by a defendant who is not without analogies to Joseph K. and the businessman Block of *The Trial*. Block notably believes he must have as many lawyers as possible. This also seems to be the case for the narrator of "Advocates." However, the latter narrator is in a greater state of uncertainty than Block or Joseph K., for he is not certain if he is in a courtroom or even if he has lawyers. The unfriendly people around him, he says, do not resemble lawyers, since they look like fat old women who strike their bellies and sway as if benumbed. The expressionist scene is permeated by a noise coming from somewhere, about which the narrator says, with the logic of dream association, that it reminds him of a court. And, with more pedestrian, if absurd, reasoning, he asks why he is looking for a lawyer if he is not in a court. His answer is simple. An advocate is needed everywhere, he says, actually less in court than in the world at large, since the fact that the court supposedly functions according to the dictates of the law lessens the need to have a lawyer there. By contrast, the narrator says, somewhat contradictorily, verdicts are based on the opinions of people in the world, relatives and strangers, friends and enemies, and for this reason one needs a lawyer everywhere; one must collect lawyers, as it were, to deal with the multitudes of slippery plaintiffs that life throws up at every step on the way.

"Advocates" resembles a comic dream in its display of pseudo-reasoning and expressionist juxtapositions. It culminates in the image of the unending way the would-be defendant must take. The narrator declares the necessity of going forward in the quest for the forever-elusive goal—for, he implies, how else can one define justice? He despairs at the hopelessness of the quest but then defiantly says that one cannot turn back, that one must continue forward, through the labyrinthine corridors, up the stairs, in order to make use of the short time allotted to one in life. The narrator uses the rhetoric of ethics, saying it is imperative that the seeker not stop, that the only solution is to continue the way forward so that the stairs under "your climbing feet . . . will go on growing upwards" (*KA* 2, p.380). With this remarkable image, it appears that the quest itself generates the way. "Advocates" is another allegorical description of the writer's quest, which is itself a quest for justice, in its assertion that motion itself creates the way. The writer writes as the quester quests so that the self-scaffolding stairs unfold before him. With this image of forever going upward, one is reminded of *The Castle,* a work for which K.'s steps did not, however, generate stair steps going upward.

The text translated as "A Chinese Puzzle" is not about what is usually called a Chinese puzzle in English. Moreover, the title in German today is *Geduldspiel* (also, *Es war einmal ein Geduldspiel*, literally, "once upon a time there was a game of patience," though the text is untitled in the manuscript). As described in the text, the word refers to something more like a miniature pocket pinball machine. This game of patience involves getting a ball to go into a groove, one of the device's "labyrinthine paths," and then making the ball roll into a hole. That is the goal of the game. The ball used in the game is personified so that it can complain that, when it is not being tortured with the device's narrow paths (*Wege*), it wants to be left alone to stroll on the open fields (*KA* 2, p. 415). The ball objects that it is not really made for a narrow way. About this the text's narrator observes that the ball's viewpoint is partly true—the ball is too wide—and partly false, for if the paths were wider, it would not be a game of patience. The humor concerning the way and the labyrinth resembles in part a self-directed joke about Kafka's own lack of fit to the game's demands, that is, the patience required by the world's demands, as well as by literature, a tortuous game of patience that forces one into a narrow labyrinthine way that leads to an uncertain hole. We have seen that in the Zürau aphorisms Kafka says that impatience was at the origin of original sin. The game of patience may appear, from this perspective, to be an image of the most difficult game of all, the game of necessary patience if one is to play the game, whatever the game, since in impatience lies the fall. In *The Castle* K. is, I argued, an impatient man. The reader is invited to see the humor in Kafka's putting complaints about being patient into the mouth of a rolling ball after his failure to finish the novel.

The final parable dealing with the way and the quest that I discuss here is the text Brod titled "Gibs auf!" ("Give It Up!"). However, in the manuscript of late 1922 the parable appears to be called "Ein Kommentar" ("A Commentary"). My reading of the manuscript is that the parable is probably the conclusion to a letter that Kafka drafted but did not send to Franz Werfel. In the letter Kafka explains his objections to Werfel's play *Schweiger*, in which Werfel presents, among other things, an anti-Freudian psychiatrist with strong right-wing beliefs. Kafka writes that he does not like to be involved with psychoanalysis, but nonetheless it is a part of their generation. Making an implied comparison with psychoanalysis, he says that Judaism has always brought forward "its sufferings and joys almost at the same time as an appropriate Rashi-Commentary" (*KA* 2, pp. 529–530). Commenting in effect on what his generation has done, Kafka accepts psychoanalysis as a fact of Jewish culture, not unlike the Talmud and the well-known medieval commentary on it, Rashi's commentary. Then immediately after this comparison appears "A Commentary," followed by the short parable.

It is a parable in which the first-person narrator finds himself out on the street early in the morning, going to the train station. Looking at his watch and then at a clock tower, he discovers it is much later than he thought. He does not know the city and is not sure of his way, but, seeing a policeman, he runs to ask him about the way (*nach dem Weg*). The policeman smiles and asks if he wants to learn the way from him. To the narrator's affirmative answer, the policeman replies, "Gibs auf, gibs auf," which might be translated "forget about it" as well as "give it up" (*KA* 2, p. 530). This parable has received much commentary. Some see in it another version of the paradox elaborated by Zeno about the impossibility of motion through the infinity of points separating any two points in any given distance. Others view it as a Freudian-like expression of the father's rejection of the straying child (or perhaps the policeman as Freud?). And others read it as an existential parable about the human fate in the cosmos. Heinz Politzer wrote a brilliant introductory chapter to his seminal critical study *Franz Kafka: Parable and Paradox* (1962) to show that this "open parable," like a biblical parable, generates multiple meanings. I add that, in appearing immediately after the unsent letter, the parable can appear to be an oblique "commentary" on the psychoanalysis that Kafka defends in the letter as a part of his generation's expression of its pain. From this perspective, the parable appears to be a commentary on the desire, impossible to realize, to find a way to put an end to pain and disarray, perhaps through analysis. In any case, the train station joins "The Next Village" as one more elusive goal the traveler will never reach.

Before turning to Kafka's concern with the nature of art in his last writings, I turn to two other major texts from the late manuscripts: "Ehepaar" ("The Married Couple," another rare title appended by Kafka), a tale of a businessman's visit to a married couple, and "Heimkehr" ("Homecoming"), a prose poem that imagines a return to the paternal home. Although they differ considerably in tone, one being comic, the other a poetic meditation, both present reflections on the paternal image. "The Married Couple" especially resembles a settling of accounts with the patriarch. Written from the first-person viewpoint of a businessman and containing a portrayal of the ways of the practical business world, it is probably a completed text. The reader learns that business is, as usual, bad, which motivates the narrator to visit his customers. To this end, he goes to see N., an infirm, elderly man who is at home when the narrator arrives. What ensues is a portrayal of the fallen world of family and practical affairs as farce.

The narrator discovers that N.'s son is sick, and, upon entering the son's room, he sees a competitor already sitting there. N. enters wearing a fur coat that N.'s wife has trouble taking off him so that N. can fit into a chair. The narrator begins impulsively to walk about while talking business, while the competitor claps his hat on and off and the bedridden sick son begins shaking his fist. At this convulsive point, the father, N., appears to die—an easy death, the narrator notes. The competitor bides his time while the son sobs. Then the wife says that N. has merely fallen asleep. And the old man wakes up and gets into bed with the son. A good Kafkaesque father, N. begins to read a newspaper and ignores his company, though not without making a few disagreeable remarks about the narrator's business proposals. On his way out, the narrator encounters N.'s wife again and finds that she has confused him with his competitor. The narrator concludes with a disabused remark about paths—the failed ways of business (*misslungene Geschäftswege*)—that come to nothing (*KA* 2, p. 541). Yet the businessman is obliged to go on. Such is the misery of living in the farcical, practical world of the father and the businessman.

"Homecoming" was probably written only a few months before Kafka's death. The title is Brod's, but it is appropriate for this meditation on the possibility of returning to the paternal home. A son has returned home and seemingly speaks to himself in the first person as he surveys the scene of his return. Or, alternatively, he surveys what he would see, were he to return, for the text's hesitant tone suggests that the description may be an imagined scene in which the narrator pictures what would happen were he to go home again. In fact, the narrator knows that "you cannot go home again," as the American novelist Thomas Wolfe said about the artist's longing to return to his origins.[4] Or, from another perspective, in Roy Porter's interpretation in his *Kafka's Narrators,* Kafka rewrites Jesus's parable of the prodigal son to show that the Kafkaesque son cannot return.[5]

The way back would be a way leading to desolation: to an old courtyard with a puddle, a jumble of old tools, and a cat lurking in the background while a torn rag flutters in the wind. This fallen world of detritus is his father's home, and when the narrator asks what he can mean to it, he has no answer. Uncertain, he confronts a kitchen door behind which coffee is being prepared. And the narrator remains distant, listens, hears nothing, and wonders, were someone to open the door, whether he would not act as if he wants to keep a secret —perhaps rather than reveal that he wants to enter his own past. The scene comes to an end when the narrator hears a striking clock; he wonders whether this sound comes from the present scene or emanates from his childhood.

"Homecoming" is comparable to the poet Georg Trakl's meditations in its somber poetic impact. In this encounter with the paternal domain, Kafka shows a narrator permanently estranged from it. The way back to the past is closed to him, and it is not certain that he wants to return to it. The world of the patriarch, of the old farmer imagined here, has secrets that now have no common measure with the narrator's world. In light of "Letter to His Father," it is easy to imagine Kafka staging this scene for himself as an adieu to what he hoped to leave behind in going to Berlin in the fall of 1923. More than simply a biographical text, however, this is a prose poem that makes a critique of the modernist quest for the past, exemplified in works as diverse as those of Joyce, Proust, and Rilke. In Kafka's text there is no epiphanic moment of the past's beauty as in Joyce, no recovery of time lost as in Proust, no vision of the fullness of the child's world as in Rilke. In fine, there is no celebration of childhood in Kafka, only the relentless vision of the present world fallen into time.

After these two final texts dealing comically and wistfully with the domain of the father, I turn to late writings that depict art and the artist. These are often thought experiments that appear to be, in part, Kafka's answer to his own uncertainties about writing. Biographers often comment on a moment of crisis in this regard and point to a manuscript from late 1921 or 1922 in which Kafka wrote that "Writing refuses itself to me. Hence a plan for self-biographical research. Not biography, but research and discovery of the smallest possible components" (*KA* 2, p. 373: "Das Schreiben versagt sich mir. Daher Plan der selbst-biographischen Untersuchungen. Nicht Biographie, sondern Untersuchung und Auffindung möglich kleiner Bestandteile"). Kafka records his decision to make an inward turn and to draw upon his life as a possible way of renewing himself. Undoubtedly he hoped to find grounds for writing in a world in which all appeared groundless. In this respect, he resembles other modernists for whom the writer's self is a sufficient ground to justify writing. To ground writing in the self entails, however, an endorsement of the Romantic belief in something like a metaphysical self. Kafka had much trouble accepting that belief.

In place of belief, Kafka had his sense of humor, and it was from his inimitable ironic perspective that he looked for those smallest components to write a series of brilliantly comic stories about the nature of art, those published in *A Hunger Artist* and also in the manuscripts he did not publish. The portrayal of the artist's plight had been the subject of a few earlier stories, including the depiction of the circus rider in "Up in the Gallery" and the performing ape of "A Report to an Academy." Kafka's delving into the nature of art took a new turn, however, in the previously discussed "The City Coat of Arms," in which he ironically looked at new grounds for art. The idea of building the tower of Babel, a tower that will reach heaven, is conceived by humanity and its architects—but not yet realized. Once the tower is imagined, however impossible its realization, its concept is eternal, for it will never leave humanity's imagination, or so observes the narrator, who says that the essential thing about the whole enterprise is the thought (*Gedanke*). The essential aspect of art is thus a concept. This thought, elevating the role of the concept over actual realization, causes the builders think they should build as slowly as possible, if at all. It is senseless to proceed with the material realization of a concept today when it will be always better realized tomorrow. With no pressures to embody the concept, humanity can fight about housing while enjoying a magnificent idea. There are Romantic antecedents for the idea of conceptual art, though art historians usually attribute the idea to Marcel Duchamp, who, a few years before

Kafka revised the myth of the tower of Babel, put a urinal on display that demanded that one ask what are the grounds for saying something is art. This development of conceptual art culminated some two generations later in the notion that, as the philosopher Nelson Goodman put it, art is when you think it is.[6] And so with the tower of Babel: it is there when you think about it. (Since the same can be said of unicorns, conceptual art is not an idea I immediately accept.)

Kafka undertook no systematic program for rethinking the basis of art. Rather, he experimented with various ideas about the nature of and the grounds for art. He returned to the circus in the first story of *A Hunger Artist,* "Erstes Leid" ("First Sorrow"). Kafka may have interrupted writing *The Castle* to write this story about a manic trapeze artist who is so desperate to perfect his art that he wants never, not for a moment, to stop practicing it. Described in deadpan third-person narration, the artist is depicted in his singular devotion to his art, resolutely defying the demands of the practical world. Offering an image of total devotion, in a constant quest for perfection, the artist quite simply wants never to come down from his trapeze, day or night.

This image of the artist is taken from the world of popular culture. A circus trapeze artist, he is literally a performance artist of the upper spheres. He is thus related to the popular performers about whom Baudelaire was among the first to celebrate their capacity to tear the spectator away from the boredom of existence. In a prose text, "Le vieux saltimbanque," Baudelaire also sees in a miserable "old street acrobat" the image of the modern man of letters who has outlived his time, for the *saltimbanque* is the image of the modern artist as a mendicant entertainer who lasts for as long as the public is amused by him, and in this he anticipates the hunger artist. After Baudelaire, the clown and the acrobat became recurrent images in modern art, often as an ironic or even tragic double for the artist him- or, occasionally, herself. Among painters, artists as various as Toulouse-Lautrec, Picasso, Marie Laurencin, Beckmann, and Kirchner immediately come to mind. The clown became the emblem of the artist in the age of art conceived as a disposable commercial product or as ephemeral performance.

Unlike Baudelaire, Kafka did not interpret his circus artist. He simply showed the difficulties the acrobat encounters as a perfectionist. But Kafka's image of what the artist does also suggests a literalized metaphor: the artist wants to remain forever in the tent's upper spheres, on his trapeze, there where he "transcends" mundane reality. Idealist aesthetics is ironically deflated by this literal image of the artist's contact with the upper spheres. Kafka's humorous irony has rarely been sharper than in this presentation of the opposition between the artist's high demands and the low exigencies of the practical world. For instance, the artist can remain elevated only so long as he does not travel, but, since a circus moves about, he must come down to deal with the messy details of getting from one place to another in a train or an automobile fitted out especially for him. A poor surrogate for the elevation his art demands can be found on a train when he climbs up into a luggage rack. The humor is increased by the narrator's attitude, that of a practical person who tries to justify the trapeze artist's behavior. He points out that the air is better up in the upper regions, though, he concedes, the artist's lifestyle places some limitations on his social life.

By and large, it seems the performer is nearly successful in his quest for perfection, until one day he tells his manager that he must have two trapezes. The compliant manager instantly agrees and tries to reassure the artist that he understands his needs. But the artist's apparent recognition that with only one trapeze he has not been reaching perfection allows doubts to surface, and the seeker for perfection bursts into tears. The manager thinks he sees the first wrinkles appearing on the performer's face. The artist perhaps now realizes the pretense of his groundless ambitions, that of finding transcendence in some kind of achieved perfection, for one can always imagine more of anything, including trapezes or ideal beauty. And perfection, it must be said, has largely ceased to be a category in contemporary discourse about art.

The second story in *A Hunger Artist* is "Eine kleine Frau" ("A Little Woman"). At first glance the story, frequently omitted in anthologies, seems to have little to do with the theme of the artist. Lack of clarity means that there has been critical debate about who is the little woman and who is the text's first-person narrator. Biographers advance the idea, on good evidence, that the woman Kafka is describing resembles his first landlady in Berlin, who apparently disliked him intensely. However, this fact is inadequate to explain the developed narrative and hardly explains why Kafka matched the text with three other stories about artists in *A Hunger Artist,* with its trapeze performer, its mouse singer, and the inimitable artist in starvation.

The biographical fact is not irrelevant, however, for an interpretation of the little woman whose main activity in life seems to be hating the narrator. It seems Kafka's unhappy situation in Berlin was a specific exemplar for his vision of the fate of the artist in contemporary culture. But an adequate interpretation demands that one specify who represents the artist here. The Kafka scholar Malcolm Pasley argued that it is actually the hateful little woman: she represents the literary side of Kafka and embodies the hostile judge whom Kafka holds up to his bourgeois self. Pasley wants her to be in fact the voice of the notebooks in which Kafka was writing at the time.[7] This is a fetching argument, though it can be turned around. If one sees in the woman a hostile judge, as the narrator calls her, who is condemning the writer, she also condemns the narrator who is writing what we read, which in fact she does. She is less the artist figure than the narrator. Hence it seems more convincing to argue that Kafka has placed his narrator-artist and a hostile critic face to face. In a sense they act as facing mirrors; each reflects the other, and in the end it is difficult to tell who is who. This would not be the least subtle of Kafka's ironies about writers and critics.

For example, the narrator says that the little woman is unhappy with him because she always has something to reproach him for; he is the cause of much wrong and irritates her with everything he does. He adds that everything about him goes against the woman's "sense of beauty, her feelings for rightfulness, her habits, her traditions, her hopes" (*Drucke zu Lebzeiten, KA,* p. 322). Given these charges, one then asks whose sense of beauty is offended, that of a modern artist speaking of a hostile critic or that of a hostile critic speaking of a modern artist whose values the critic does not share. The narrative stance works both ways, with irony that allows the reader, moreover, to appreciate the incipient paranoia that animates the narrator's self-defense against the plaintiff, artist or critic. The text ends, however, with a pirouette of rhetorical reversal, for with unjustified self-assertion the writer-narrator says he will keep his hand on this affair, cover it up, and continue to live untroubled by the woman's outbursts of anger. Writer and critic remain unreconciled.

The third story in *A Hunger Artist* allows no doubt about the nature of the protagonist in its portrayal of another circus performer, namely the hunger artist. The story offers an extended development of several amalgamated metaphors that deal with nourishment and art. And with this, it is a pitiless, if ironic, representation of the groundlessness of art. The artist performs by starving in front of the crowds that press forward to view him in his cage. In this display of privation his act certainly foreshadows the "body art" of more recent vintage. However, there is a historical dimension to the hunger artist, since there actually were performers in starvation. The mode began in the seventeenth century and reached its greatest vogue in the late nineteenth century, when, like Baudelaire's *saltimbanque,* hunger artists ceased to be popular. To be sure, the range of reference in Kafka's story goes beyond this past oddity of popular culture. An historical perspective on Kafka's artist should suggest early Jewish prophets, Christ tempted by Satan, not to mention anchorite monks on columns in the desert, certain Hindu and Buddhist ascetics, and all symbolic rituals involving fasting. The denial of the body's needs through negative performance has a long history, and there is hardly a religious tradition that has not used bodily privation to gain access to some superior state. After the trapeze artist's desire for positive transcendence, the hunger artist is a performer in negation who can represent humanity's recurrent aspiration to stop being human. But, unlike later, often pretentious body artists, the hunger artist explains nothing, makes no claims, and proposes nothing positive—except his exceptional capacity for setting records. In fact, he goes hungry because he cannot find the food that he wants.

The story has a plot, elegant in its Kafkaesque simplicity, that mirrors the historical rise and decline of starvation artists. The decline of the art of starvation is described with deadpan irony, underscoring the arbitrary nature of the way in which one world of fashion and culture gives way to another: one day, for no reason, once-celebrated hunger artists no longer have appeal. This loss is no more explainable than the fact that they attracted crowds in the first place. At its zenith, not only did the art of starving gather crowds, but groups formed to verify that the hunger artist was not cheating in his claims. This detail poses an epistemological dilemma, for how can one know that the artist does not cheat? Only the hunger artist can know for certain whether he cheats, a fact that points up the disparity between the objective appearance of art and the subjective world in which it originates. In a sense, of course, the hunger artist knows he cheats since he knows that record-setting starving is all too easy for him.

However, his agent limits his periods of fasting to forty days, apparently with no thought of the biblical allusion: rather, forty days is the longest period of time for which the fickle public can remain interested in the spectacle—which is certainly Kafka's ironic reference to how Jesus felt in Matthew 4:1–11 in holding out for so long against Satan. At the end of each period, the artist is celebrated. Thus he goes from triumph to triumph, misunderstood regarding the reasons he can succeed so easily and easily angered when always congratulated for the wrong reasons but also willing to accept that his manager sells photographs of him nearly dead. Then, just as cinema replaced vaudeville, so starving is replaced in the circus by other attractions, and nobody comes to his cage to view the once-illustrious artist. No longer needing an agent, he hires himself out to a circus willing to stick him in a cage near the animal cages. He is so little popular now that people become angry if, as they rush to the main attraction, they are stopped by somebody lingering in front of the artist's cage—though occasionally a father will explain to his ignorant children what hunger artists were.

Kafka ends the brilliantly ironic exposition of historical change with a logical twist: the circus attendants no longer bother to count the days the artist fasts, so that he now sets record after record, to the indifference of all. Successful beyond all measure, he has almost totally disappeared, having sunk into his cage's straw. One day, before the artist's demise, an overseer wonders why an empty cage stands on display, and the attendants go to find the artist there, still fasting. Wanting to be friendly, the overseer congratulates the artist on his accomplishment, but the artist refuses to be recognized for his feat. He admits that he can do nothing else since he cannot find food (*Speise*) that tastes good to him. Kafka has recourse to the most common language for this revelation that the artist would have stuffed himself if he had found something to his taste. The reader need not be a vegetarian to see that Kafka has taken his own revulsion with *Wurst* and made it a trope for metaphysical longing.

Kafka's hunger artist sets out another ironic image of the modern artist's groundless practice. Moreover, it is arguable that Kafka is making another critical retort to the Nietzsche who saw in asceticism an assertion of the will to power, as exemplified by the Christian ascetics who came to dominate the world of classical Rome. Kafka's critique underlies the hunger artist's confession that his feat has no positive drive behind it: he is hungry, and the earth offers him nothing to eat. The hunger he suffers finds no sublimation in any quest for power whatsoever. However, Kafka does not end his story with this negative demonstration; rather, he offers a complementary image of a creature that does not practice self-denial. The hunger artist is replaced in his cage by a young panther that, as the narrator says, represents to even the dullest spectator, a form of *Erholung*—at once a cure and a reestablishment of health. This beast is the kind of creature that is "true to the earth" to which Zarathustra exhorts the reader to remain true. The beast is fully content with the nourishment it receives, and, says the narrator, from its very jaws emanates the freedom that the cage might seem to deny. Large crowds are now drawn to the cage. They are mesmerized by the sight of this autonomous beast, beautifully complete within itself. Only the image of Gregor's sister, Grete, stretching herself in voluptuous self-delight at the end of "The Metamorphosis" offers a comparable image of delight in the body in Kafka's work. Grete and the panther share the common trait of manifesting themselves as pure flesh, capable of enjoying their material animal existence—though neither seemingly worries about remaining true to the earth.

The next major text Kafka wrote after "A Hunger Artist" was probably "Forschung eines Hundes" ("Investigations of a Dog"). Brod's title focuses on the fact that the first-person narrator, a dog, desires knowledge, though the text could also be called "The Dog as Would-Be Scientist-Artist," since in the dog's attempt to find out where its nourishment comes from, he becomes something of a hunger artist. He begins his quest for knowledge when, as a mere puppy, he sees some dogs conjuring music from the air. This revelation of art lies behind all his pursuits for the rest of his life. For Kafka's dog, in resembling a hunger artist, continues Kafka's experiments in portraying what an artist might be. However, many critics see the story as a parody or a satire of Judaism and Zionism. This interpretation merits a brief commentary before we continue to deal with science and art.

Undoubtedly, the situation of the Jews of the diaspora, with their various schools of law and commentary, gave Kafka one model for a world made up of many types of dogs with their various laws. But Judaism is hardly the only worldview refracted through Kafka's satirical lens in his portrayal of a dog's world, and many targets suggest themselves, ranging from the European world of arts and sciences to the new world order that the American president Woodrow Wilson wanted to create with the League of Nations, a world in which every big and little dog would have its place. Kafka's satirical allegory about dog society and its mores has a multiplicity of possible referents, including, centrally, the Judeo-Christian tradition and the place of the artist in it.

Critics have noted that human beings are absent from the dog's world. They say that it is sufficient to add human beings to explain some of the things that happen in the story, such as singing or soaring dogs, that is, dogs oblivious to the fact that they are being carried by people. Emphasizing the dogs' putative blindness to human beings misses, however, the story's satirical side, which is squarely aimed at human beings, especially those that engage in learning and art. The narrator is not blind to the fact that he overlooks the existence of other species. Though he cannot keep them straight, he knows that dog science recognizes a great many other species, though none have the perfection of the dog. Each species is locked in its own species' worldview—an idea reprised in various nonsatirical ways in writers as diverse as Rilke and Wittgenstein. In other words, dogs may not take much note of inferior species such as human beings, which simply means they speak little of that which lies outside their world. In this, they are notably not unlike human beings.

The dog-narrator, like the rest of us, lives in a self-enclosed world with its own history, tradition, and laws. And like a good humanist—can one say "doggist"? —nothing in "dogdom" is foreign to him, as he says in paraphrasing the line from Terence that has become a foundational thought of humanism. But why dogs and dogdom for a satire of humanism? One reason is that one rarely sees humans without their beloved dogs. A related but contrary reason is that animal metaphors, when used for humans, are often insulting and derogatory. And if a source were needed, one could turn to "Letter to His Father," in which it is obvious that Kafka was accustomed to listening to his father's wide range of animal insults. A friend of Kafka was "vermin," and one of his daughters was both a maid and a worm (he shouted the neologism *Mad* at her, suggesting *Magd* or maid, but also *Made* or worm). With regard to the lowly dog, in German "pig" can be made even more insulting by adding "dog" to it, giving the ultimate insult, *Schweinhund*. Much as in English, such is the contradictory fate of a "dog" in German, a beloved pet by whose name it is insulting to be called—this in contrast, say, to the dog's civilizing image in the fables of Aesop, which Kafka may also have had in mind. Insults and affection set out the comic polarity that underlies this tale of a dog's life, which is apparently not a good life, or so ordinary language often holds, however much Germans love their dogs.

The dog-narrator opens his tale with a panegyric in favor of dogdom—satirically bordering on what today is overt speciesism, to use a term Kafka might well have liked. The aging dog then begins to recall times past in order to evaluate his life, its events, his despair, and his moments of respite, which have eventuated in his present isolation. The dog resembles a modernist writer going in search of time lost, an aging, distracted narrator lost in some indefinite present moment. He sees himself as a dissident, which prompts him to ask himself why he cannot live in silence. Apparently he prides himself on the fact that he cannot easily accept the alacrity with which the other dogs live in the world. A nonconformist, the dog has an image of himself as an artist who is, by his nature, unable to join in the easy conformity with which others accept the received world.

The narrator's memory is fixated upon a moment in his puppy past when he saw dogs that seemingly conjured music from the air and, as he says, could openly face the music without being destroyed by it. If we imagine a connection here between the dogs and men, then these dogs suggest the circus, where dogs often walk on two legs. These dogs did not acknowledge the narrator when he questioned them, which is against a fundamental law of dogdom requiring that dogs reply to greetings from other dogs. Despite their behavior, the music with dancing dogs is a revelation and suggests a mystery that the young dog must explain to himself. The narrator says he has retained his childhood desire to know and implies that his curiosity springs from a disturbance in perception of the sort that lies at the origin of art and science. The curiosity that Aristotle said is innate to the child has lasted into the narrator's old age, providing the continual impetus for both science and art.

His desire to know began with the musical dogs, since this perturbation led to his first investigations. He decided he must learn how dogdom nourishes itself. The connection between music and nourishment is not spelled out. One recalls in this regard that the violin playing of Gregor Samsa's sister inspired thoughts in the vermin about food, notably his astonishment that he could relish garbage. Moreover, for the early twentieth-century reader it was self-evident that music offers the highest form of spiritual nourishment, which is to say that the linking of food and art, especially music, was a received metaphor. Taken literally, however, the dog's investigation into food is a scientific pursuit. Indeed, he hopes to contribute to the vast quantity of knowledge that, from the dawn of time, dogdom has accumulated concerning nourishment. Like the narrator of "The Village Schoolmaster," the narrator finally became aware of the great difficulty involved in contributing to knowledge, and thus at last he is content to simply accept the prosaic wisdom of everyday canine life: dogs urinate, and food grows.

The dog-narrator is then led to consider a different but related question: where does the earth get the food that grows? This question may sound a bit more metaphysical, and it is surely another oblique parody of the aforementioned dictum from Nietzsche's *Thus Spake Zarathustra* that one should remain true to the earth, for then will be born the superman, the superior *Übermensch*. Kafka's satire in this story aims in several directions at once, including himself and the dog writing the text, but Nietzsche is clearly the target when the dog says that the puppy's will to power expresses itself as *Forschungsbegierde*—the lust for research (*KA* 2, p. 332). In his lust, however, he bothers other dogs and soon finds that they are about to drive him from his chosen "way" (*Weg*) (*KA* 2, p. 333).

It is at this point that Kafka parodies classical humanism: the dog proclaims that ultimately his only interest is the Dog, despite dogs' lack of interest in him. After his doggy manifesto, the narrative takes an inward turn, and the dog begins to question himself, recognizing that he has not been able to follow the ways of science. He again asserts that he is really not different from other dogs, despite the great variety of dogs. As an example of difference he offers the *Lufthunde*—"air dogs" or "soaring dogs"—a neologism coined on the model of *Luftmensch*, "air person," meaning a person incapable of practical activity, such as dreamers or artists. The narrator associates this variety of dog with art. *Lufthunde* are weak beings, though they can remain in the air for hours doing nothing, with no relation to life in the community. Yet, one speaks of their "art and artistic activities" (*Kunst und Kunstlerei*) (*KA* 2, p. 337). The narrator is most impressed by the meaninglessness of their existence, for their being is literally without any grounding. These dogs simply hang in the air. In this comic example of Kafka's thinking in images, the artist's lack of grounding is conveyed by the image of soaring, without attachment, so that the dog-artist floats freely (and not being attached to the ground/*Gründ* makes for the same play on words in English as in German). Wistfully, the narrator notes that the dog-artist makes many contributions to science, though, he adds parenthetically, most of them are worthless.

These satirical reflections on the artist lead the dog-narrator to considerations of dog history as a version of the Fall. The dog holds the view that the "progress" of science has been a form of decline as well as movement forward. For those dogs that came before him were, if less scientifically developed, actually better off than the current generation, since these dogs were closer to the true Word. At some point they could have stopped moving forward along the way they had taken, leading away from the Word, and returned to a point where they could keep the Word in sight. But they didn't. The doggy loss of the Word is of course a direct transposition of Judeo-Christian doctrine that the

Fall broke contact with the divine logos that lies at the origin of all things. And the way away, wandering toward progress as it were, has been dogdom's path toward *endloses Irren*—endlessly going astray, leading the hapless dogs to that point today where the Word is absent (*KA* 2, p. 341). Now all are silent in the desert. The dog's meditation on the loss of the Word is a remarkable passage in which there is seemingly no paradox, just the irony, tinged with nostalgia, of a finite dog scientist-artist meditating on the imagined fall of dogs into infinite wandering, like biblical Jews in the desert.

The dog decides to understand how nourishment falls down upon the earth. He reasons that food demands both practical activity such as preparing the soil and, in addition, rituals such as the artistic performance of dance and song. Hence, dogs' faces are ritually turned upward when they beseech the heavens for food. (Can one see the dog-owners' presence in this image, when they throw down food to their pooches, or perhaps one should imagine the now departed gods when they looked down upon supplicants with faces raised in prayer?) After some experimentation the dog hits upon the idea that if he fasts, he can prove that when he retreats from food, it is not the ground that attracts food but his own body. Shunning practical preparations for calling down food, like pissing on the ground, and avoiding artistic incantations and rituals, he decides to fast as long as possible to discover the origins of nourishment. The fasting dog becomes a hunger artist, a voluntary ascetic, or, if one prefers, a hunger scientist for whom fasting is a research tool.

Like every scientist or artist, the dog undertakes fasting in hope of reaping honors for his accomplishments in this field. However, starving has its own momentum, and once it is under way, the dog finds himself too weak to stop and profit from it. He is alone, with nothing under, on, or above the earth to care for him. It simply happens that one day he finds himself facing a strange hunting dog that, manifesting decidedly homosexual tendencies, tells the narrator that he is disturbing him. Subsequently, there arose a song (*Gesang*, or a hymn or song of praise) that floats in the air and moves according to its own laws. Coming from Kafka, who claimed to be unmusical, this second image of music is surprising, for it suggests a power intrinsic to music that defies comprehension. It moves the starving dog. Is this effect a result of the fact that the dog is feeble and hallucinating, or does the music exist in a superior sphere? This is undoubtedly a parody if one views the dog as moved by an invisible hunter's horn, though this is not clear, and, with a change in perspective it may appear that Kafka is offering an homage to music as the most powerful of the arts—or, alternatively, reducing it to a starving dog's hallucination.

Be that as it may, the narrator then begins research into the music of dogs, a field in which much research has already been done, more than into the origins of nourishment. From the narrator's perspective, the two fields are seemingly related, since he wants to study the doctrine according to which nourishment is called down to the earth by music. He is not bothered by his renewed recognition that he is incapable of undertaking serious research or that it is really the silence of the musical dogs that has most impressed him. The narrative comes then to an abrupt and comic end with the dog's discovery that he has an instinct for scientific incapacity. This is not entirely negative, since it is this instinct for incapacity that makes him value freedom. He thinks that this instinct is perhaps in the service of some ultimate science, though what that might be is not named—one that might point the way back to the Word?

"The Investigations of a Dog," like "A Hunger Artist," concludes with a reference to freedom. The panther in the circus carries his freedom in his jaws, which can undoubtedly crunch bones. The freedom that the dog claims to have through his instinct for incapacity is described with a more timorous image, for it is, he says, freedom such as is possible today, which is "ein kummerliches Gewächs"—a "stunted plant" (*KA* 2, p. 354). The dog-artist's freedom is born of his incompetence and valued for that reason. Underlying this view of freedom is the Kafkaesque dichotomy that opposes the artist and the practical man, the latter vaunting himself for his competence and scorning the freedom the artist enjoys by rejecting the dreary conformity imposed by competence. The dog-artist, in his incapacity, knows that his freedom belongs to another sphere, as, in self-directed irony, did Kafka, the celebrator of incompetence in life.

Freedom is also an issue in the posthumously published "Der Bau" ("The Burrow"), a story told by an unnamed animal narrator that laments, in the first person, that he is not free. This is a curious lament from a beast that appears to do pretty much whatever it wants. However, he declares that whenever he finds himself outside his burrow, he is really not in a free and open place and affirms that he is not "destined to a free life" (*dem freien Leben*), because the digging of his burrow takes too much time (*KA* 2, p. 590). The title "The Burrow," a word that Brod took from the story's first sentence, conveys the image of the tunnels the indefatigable burrower digs, and in German it also suggests "building" and construction, the result of architectural planning such as one sees when one looks at a *Baustelle* ("building site"). The narrator is chained to an unending building project, or, as the narrator says, to constructing a labyrinth—with the implied self-reference that the image of the maze has in Kafka's work (*KA* 2, p. 589). The architect-narrator is not free because he cannot escape from the labyrinth that is his own creation. However, in spite of the beast's lamentation about his lack of freedom, it is arguable that he does not really want to be free. This burrower clearly fears the free and open spaces outside his lair. He wants to defend himself against them and what may lurk in the free and open by digging unendingly into the ground. His existence is dedicated to an escape from freedom. To this end he has become an architect and builder.

"The Burrow" can be divided into two parts. In the first the narrator spends his time making multiple hypotheses about the best plan for continuing his maze. In the second he spends his time elaborating hypotheses about what might be the source of a noise he hears, a noise that perhaps comes from without but has no discernible origin. In each part the narrator seeks the way that will lead him to some pacifying knowledge, with a satisfactory hypothesis or plan putting an end to his quest. However, his quest continues, in near paranoia, in manic meditations, since his goal is unrealizable. The end of the quest would be the discovery of the ideal plan or of certain knowledge, which is impossible. This perspective also sheds light on the investigating dog's belief that his recognized incapacity offers the hope of freedom: the incompetent can cheerfully accept that they are unable to reach the end of any quest and, they hope, unchain themselves from its fetters. The burrower, by contrast, remains a captive of his manias.

As a young burrower, the unnamed animal entertained the idea that his labyrinth would confound all his invisible enemies, but today he believes he has done inadequate work and spends his time meditating on his maze's defects, especially the entrance. Occasionally he slips through it, into the open, and lies in wait to see whether any enemies are approaching. Reflecting on the multiple problems an entrance presents, he considers moving elsewhere but decides this decision would be foolish, motivated by "senseless freedom" (*KA* 2, p. 595). His fear of freedom is matched by his need for security, and he contemplates hiring a guard, though he cannot bring himself to believe he could trust one. So his only solace is to dream of the perfect burrow. A would-be Platonist, he tries to imagine the ideal form and how it might be realized on and in the earth. He compensates for his failures in thought by returning to the burrow and gorging himself on his supplies, for he is no hunger artist—just an unhappy conceptual artist in the lineage of those who invented the concept of the unrealizable tower of Babel.

The burrower is in effect another of Kafka's artists. His work is a lifetime of architectural planning devoted to the creation of a maze with, at its center, a *Burgplatz*. This term is translated by the Muirs as "Castle Keep," though the term is really more redolent of a city square with a tower, as found in some German cities. In any case his ideal construct is wackily reminiscent of a labyrinth resembling the city of God (though Augustine might well not have recognized it). The work on the *Burgplatz* in the maze is especially difficult, for he has only his forehead with which to move dirt. To this end he smashes his head into the ground and is happy to know he has done good work when blood runs down his face. This builder is a distant relative of Kafka's supplicant who, in "Description of a Struggle," prays by smashing his head on the ground—the smashed forehead being an image Kafka favored for showing how spiritual needs, as embodied here in the concept, run up against the material world.

The burrower is diverted from his plan for the ideal maze when he hears a hissing, a *Zischen,* coming from somewhere in the material world. Baffled by this intrusion, the animal-artist also shows himself, like the dog investigator before him, to be a would-be scientist, for he has little difficulty framing multiple hypotheses about the source of this ubiquitous vexation. But the explanatory causal sequences he concocts are disproved by investigation. Kafka's burrower is a prototype for the type of scientist that the Viennese philosopher Karl Popper imagined, one whose work consists mainly in disproving hypotheses. The description of the noise, however, seems to draw upon a real scientist-writer whose work Kafka had read with interest, the mathematician Pascal, who wrote in the seventeenth century that nature is an infinite space of which the center is everywhere and the circumference is nowhere (*Pensée* 72 in the classic edition of Pascal by Léon Brunschvicg). Kafka's animal scientist looks for the source of a noise that is everywhere all at once but its origin nowhere, which greatly resembles a transposition of Pascal's image of space. Like Pascal, the burrower is upset by the infinite, though by its noise, not by the silence of infinite space that terrified Pascal with its endless reaches. The burrower's attempts at constructing a causal hypothesis to explain the origin of the noise are fruitless, which allows his mind to indulge itself freely in paranoia about possible dangers while imagining plans to meet unknown contingencies.

At the end, all hypotheses having failed, the would-be knower is tempted by magic and populates the world with an array of imaginary beings. The story ends here, and it is difficult to imagine a closure to this story's demonstration of the infinite narrative possibilities generated by paranoia. Brod did a disservice when he edited the story to make it appear that Kafka had finished it. In fact, "The Burrow" breaks off in mid-sentence—almost as if some beast of the burrower's imagination had attacked him while he was writing. If we return to the incompleteness axiom that I laid down at the beginning of this book, we might say that "The Burrow" is another remarkable success precisely because it is a failure, thus demonstrating self-reflexively by its own existence that the way to the Way has no end. The artist shows that there is no closure to his infinitely proliferating maze that mimes the absurd workings of a mind whose only goal is to create hypotheses—concepts for art, theories for science—which is to say, an infinite labyrinth of possible texts.

The last story Kafka wrote is the fourth story in *A Hunger Artist.* It portrays another, rather special artist, "Josefine, die Sängerin oder das Volk der Mäuse" ("Josephine the Singer, or the Mouse Folk"). With Josephine the singer, Kafka questions the notion that a piece of art is a unique creation. In this regard

Kafka's story of the singing mouse is to be situated somewhere between Duchamp's urinal as artwork (1917) and Walter Benjamin's "The Work of Art in the Age of Mechanical Reproduction," which describes the demise of the "aura" that supposedly once emanated from the uniqueness of the individual work of art (a text first published in French in 1936). The singing Josephine stepped onto the scene in 1924 to offer the artist whose art has no discernible trait differentiating it from nonart: her squeaking is as non-unique as Duchamp's urinal and as reproducible as any of Benjamin's manufactured art objects.

Kafka's title, "Josephine the Singer, or the Mouse Folk," sets out the two sides of the relationship that defines art: Josephine, the individual artist, and her audience, the mouse folk. The term *Volk* has dubious connotations in German—people, ethnic group, nation, and, for some, a mystical soul that unites people, or mice, as the case may be (*Volk* was used by socialists as well as Nazis before 1933); art was often held to be a unique expression of a *Volk*. The story unfolds by first presenting the singer and the nature of her art; then it describes the nature of her relation to her *Volk,* with a depiction of her desires; and finally it comments on her probable fate.

This tale has been interpreted biographically, though I think the identification of the dying Kafka with his singer is misleading. Moreover, interpreting the tale as an allegory about Judaism is also unnecessarily limiting. Undoubtedly, there are critical barbs aiming at the Zionist belief that a Jewish state grounded in the soul of a *Volk* was a feasible goal for political action. Indeed, Kafka may have drawn inspiration from the fact that the verb *mauscheln,* suggesting to speak like a mouse, also means to speak Yiddish. Kafka might also have been bemused by the anti-Semitic musician Richard Wagner's declaration that Jews cannot sing. But these are only some of the components Kafka took from his ongoing historical moment to create a comic allegory. To be sure, this story is to be read in reaction to the ongoing development of art in Europe, a chaotic Europe of multiple states, with multiple peoples, increasingly in thrall to nationalism and totalitarian ideologies that often reduced art to propaganda. This is all part of a historical context that called into question the nature of art itself.

As described by the anonymous first-person narrator, Josephine's art is an incantation that none can resist. But the description of her "aura" is immediately qualified, even contradicted, since the narrator then says that her *Gesang* offers nothing extraordinary. Indeed, one can even wonder whether her singing is music. The sound she makes is only a *Pfeifen,* which various translations offer as "whistling," "piping," and, best of all, "squeaking," since in English, that is what mice do. As the narrator says, it is what all mice do; squeaking is their custom. Yet, Josephine's squeaking is different, even though it resembles the ordinary squeaking of mice's daily speech, so to speak. Squeaking is squeaking, just as language is language, which brings up again a question the young

Kafka had posed early in life: how can ordinary language, the language we use to buy cheese and sell stocks, be used for a work of art? How is fallen language transformed into what the poet Mallarmé called essential language?

The mouse narrator ponders the question and comes up with an answer that sounds very contemporary: he implies that art is what occurs when one says it occurs. The narrator can find no intrinsic difference between a farmer's squeaking and what one hears when Josephine performs. It is simply the case that when she appears before the assembled folk something takes place that they call music. The philosophical mouse-narrator offers a quirky comparison that a contemporary analytical philosopher might endorse: it may be that squeaking in public is not like nut-cracking, though, if it is, then it may be that we have overlooked nut-cracking as an art form. A new artist who performs as a nut-cracker might show us a new art, and this despite the fact that we are actually better nut-crackers than the nut-cracking artist (*Drucke zu Lebzeiten, KA,* p. 353). With this example Kafka is obliging the reader to consider that if there are no metaphysical foundations for artwork, then art itself, groundless and gratuitous, becomes the only thing that grants art its status. This can occur when art says that it is art, when with the magic wand of self-reflexivity art calls itself into being and art occurs.

Josephine is not a contemporary philosopher, and she denies any connection between her singing and ordinary squeaking. Believing in her difference, in her aura, as it were, she gathers the folk around her and entrances them with her squeaking. However, the narrator also says the folk do not take her too seriously, though they willingly protect her in a fatherly way. Indeed, Josephine has an inflated opinion of her worth, for she believes it is she who protects the *Volk* (and there is undoubtedly some savage irony in the fact that the anti-Semitic composer Richard Wagner thought the same thing about himself). The narrator says it is obvious that in fact she neither saves the people nor gives them added strength. True, the people use her, as it were, to gain added unity in times of trouble, though at the same time this recourse is dangerous. The enemy may more easily slaughter the mice if they have assembled to listen to Josephine squeaking. The squeaking may even attract the enemy.

In short, the artist squeaks and does not squeak. Little matter for this practical folk for whom music is a half-remembered tradition, left over from an era when, apparently, art did exist with criteria to define what it was. The narrator offers another variant on Kafka's favored theme of humanity's fall into time and history, such as happened to dogdom when it lost the Word. Leading their workaday lives, the mice *Volk* have reached that nadir at which the mice no longer remember whatever once grounded art. Since they have no time for remembrance, only for work and an occasional concert by Josephine, this forgetting seems of little consequence.

As an artist Josephine makes demands that put her at odds with her society, for she wants to be exempt from all ordinary work—a desire the writer Kafka understood all too well. The people are inflexible in their refusal to accord her special treatment. Nonetheless, in her hubris she wants unambiguous recognition of her exalted status, though no such recognition is forthcoming. Growing old, she begins to practice little forms of blackmail in an attempt to get attention. She even threatens to shorten the moments of coloratura in her songs. The narrator is not sure what coloratura is, so her threat is meaningless and serves only to point up the disparity between the artist's pretentions to difference and the public's reception of her art. She acts as if she were ill, collapses, and even disappears. The narrator says that this behavior will only diminish the power of her art, foreseeing the moment of her last squeak and then lasting silence. With this thought the narrator speculates that it was actually the silence Josephine induced, not her squeaking, that made up her art's appeal. In any case she will soon be lost, as the narrator says at the end, lost in the mass of her people's heroes and hence effectively forgotten. Such is the artist's fate in a practical *Volk* that does not bother with history.

Kafka's last story ends with an oblique homage to silence. This has been a temptation more than once in his work. It is tempting to compare his celebration of silence to the silence offered by the musician John Cage, who wrote a composition in which the performer does not play, presumably to show that silence is full of many circumambient noises that may be called music. However, I do not think this is the silence Kafka evokes, though Josephine's squeaking could be an example of Cage's idea that all sounds are music—if perceived as such. Rather, Wittgenstein's final proposition in the *Tractatus* is probably closer to Kafka's viewpoint, namely that what we cannot speak about, we must remain silent about. Wittgenstein's is an antimetaphysical proposition with metaphysical resonances, which Kafka would have understood. The power of Josephine's song, of her squeaking perceived as music, lies, as the narrator suggests, in bringing about the recognition in her audience of the limits of their world, with a thought for all that lies beyond in silence. For if anything can be perceived as art, art, unlike anything else, is paradoxically sometimes able to hint at something beyond itself. Kafka's work was arguably dedicated from beginning to end to exploring this proposition. Yet, his last works shows in parody and satire that art indeed is when art happens, though this demonstration is not done in celebration in the manner of the celebrators of Pop Art. Kafka's work is an illustration of loss rather than progress, since even a dog recognizes that progress is an illusion.

Epilogue

If Kafka's legacy is a body of work, written with a unique sense of humor, often comic in designating its failure to transcend itself as writing, then perhaps that legacy can be emblematically represented by one of Kafka's best-known parables, "Von den Gleichnissen" ("On Parables"), as Brod titled it. A parable about parables and one of the most teasingly enigmatic texts he wrote, this work is seen by some as a key to understanding Kafka. Without endorsing the idea of a key, I turn to this late parable for a conclusion to this book and present it as a final witty paradox demonstrating that there is no conclusion to seeking a way out of Kafka's textual labyrinths. We can consider a few facts about his writing, however, and they can enrich our understanding of our failure to understand.

The parable on parables appears in a notebook of 1922, a few pages after Kafka wrote "A Commentary" (Brod's "Give It Up!"). Thus it was apparently written shortly after Kafka's unsent strictures to the playwright Franz Werfel in which Kafka recognized psychoanalysis as a fact of Jewish culture, much like a commentary on the Torah. Since the parable could appear to be a continuation of these strictures in the manuscript, it can be considered an outgrowth of the letter to Werfel; furthermore, it is tempting to see in it a commentary on psychoanalysis and the Freudian art of interpretation used therein. For the moment, I refrain from developing that admittedly speculative idea and turn first to what the parable says and then to some interpretive commentary about a parable about parables, or a fable about fables, or a metaphor about metaphors, since all these meanings are included in the word Kafka uses, *Gleichnisse,* in order to designate the advice that the wise offer in their parables and allegories. Then, in conclusion, with Jewish culture in mind, I turn to the only parable in which Kafka mentions something Jewish, "An Animal in the Synagogue." I argue that it shows what it might mean to become a parable, for, in a sense, Franz Kafka showed himself what it means by becoming one himself.

The first sentence of the parable on parables says that many people complain about the uselessness of the words of the wise, for they are simply parables that practical people cannot use. Brod put "complain" in the present tense, and translations have followed him. (See *KA* 2, p. 531, for the past tense.) Kafka writes, however, that people "complained," and the past tense describes a past, historical or mythical, when people were unhappy with the wise men—which also means that there once was a time when there were wise men. The use of the past tense implies that people in olden days were perhaps closer to the truth than we are today, such as was the case when, in "Investigation of a Dog," dogs could still see the Word before their way took them further and further from the truth. The words of the wise thus belong to the past when people complained of them—which suggests that we do not complain today because we have no wise words to complain about.

The text sets up a by now familiar polarity between the world of practical people and that of the impractical other-worldly wise man. A frequent dichotomy in Kafka's work, the opposition is underscored here by the assertion that practical people recognize that they have only this life, no other, in which things must have value now to be of any interest to them. The wise man, seemingly disregarding practical necessities, give people an imperative to "Go over" ("Gehe hinüber!" or "go across" or "cross over"), by which the ironic narrator says that the advice is not to go over to the other side of the street, which people would do if it were worth the effort. No, he says, the sage is talking about some fabulous over-there (*sagenhaftes Drüben*) about which the sage can say nothing very precise or very useful (*KA* 2, p. 532). This disabused description of parables leads the narrator to generalize sardonically that all parables are an attempt to say that the inconceivable is inconceivable, which everybody knew already. The first paragraph ends with the affirmation that practical people have other matters at hand in their daily struggles with existence.

The text then becomes a dialogue when somebody breaks in to ask, "Why do you resist?" and asserts that if you followed a parable, you'd become one and then you'd no longer be caught up in the daily struggle. Another listener then adds, with a popular turn of phrase that is as familiar in English as it is in German, "I bet that that is a parable, too." The first speaker takes the second person's turn of phrase literally and says that the second has won his bet. And the second person retorts that that is only in a parable, too. To which the first speaker makes the enigmatic reply that, no, the second speaker has won in reality but that in parable the second has lost. That one might become a parable is a singular idea, and the idea that, upon betting that that is parable, one wins in reality while losing in a parable is utterly obscure. Before trying to elucidate what these ideas might mean, let me make a few general observations about the parable and possible contexts for understanding it.

Brod invented the title "Von den Gleichnissen" not only because the word appears in the first sentence of the text but probably because this type of concise title, "On Parables," suggests a serious title for a classical work of literature (such as Seneca's *De vita beata* or Montaigne's *Des cannibales*—"On the Happy Life" or "On Cannibals"). Moreover, this type of title recalls the titles Nietzsche, intending the same effect, gave individual parts of his *Zarathustra,* such as "On Overcoming" or "On Poets." Brod was undoubtedly aware, moreover, that Kafka framed the wise man's command, saying that one should undertake a "crossing over," or *Übergehen,* so that it has a decidedly Nietzschean ring. The probable allusion to Nietzsche recalls Kafka's parodying the Nietzsche whose ethics demanded the experience "going under"—the *Untergehen* that Kafka's fat man literally performs in the river in "Description of a Struggle." And every writer who, like Brod and Kafka, had a classical German education was aware that in the section "On Poets" of *Zarathustra,* Nietzsche himself had parodied Goethe and the last lines of the second part of Goethe's *Faust.* In these lines Goethe's chorus sings that everything impermanent (*Alles Vergängliche*) is only a *Gleichnis*—making the claim that the totality of our ephemeral reality is only a parable or a metaphor. The chorus's universal claim for metaphor (or parable or simile) is, to say the least, extensive.[1] If the impermanent is a *Gleichnis* or vice versa, then nearly everything that exists is a *Gleichnis.* Both Goethe and Nietzsche were references for Kafka, and it seems reasonable to infer that Kafka in his use of *Gleichnis,* or parable, was alluding to both Nietzsche and to what Nietzsche parodied in Goethe, the idea that we ephemeral beings live in parable whether we know it or not. If this is the case, then the meaning of "parable" is something like "transient reality." Of course, other sources suggest that reality is a parable and vice versa; Christ's parables are primary examples of wise words, pointing out that the allegorical, though contained in real facts, is superior to the real. In fact, medieval interpretation of the Bible demanded that one see in the literal representation of reality another, allegorical layer so that reality can be seen in fact as a parable.

To return to Kafka's parable, whatever the context one provides for it, one can hardly disagree with the tautology the narrator offers, for it is indeed true by definition that the incomprehensible is incomprehensible. However, there is a bit of narrative sleight-of-hand in the practical narrator's imposing this deduction, reflecting what Kafka probably saw as the trickery used by the practical worldview when it wants to dismiss something troublesome, which is to say, the strategy of often reducing an unwanted idea to a useless tautology. This rhetorical trick is then followed by the question of why a person resists parables when it would suffice to follow one to become one—presumably with the benefit of no longer being involved in the world of toil and trouble. The reader must wonder what it means to become a parable, or an allegory, or, better yet, a metaphor—all possible meanings here. Gregor Samsa arguably becomes a metaphor, but that does not seem an especially desirable state. Certainly the speaker's question is meant, perhaps sardonically, to ask why one does not become something desirable, which would be a metaphor or allegory or a parable oneself. Goethe's chorus suggests that we impermanent beings already are a parable/metaphor. Our literal being in the world can be viewed as an allegory for something else when looked at from the perspective of eternity. So what is the bet about?

One wins in reality if one bets that becoming a parable is a parable, but one loses the bet in the realm of parable. Perhaps that means that becoming a metaphor takes place only in parable, about which one has no choice if all of impermanent reality is parable in the first place. However, the bet takes place in reality, and there one wins if one bets that becoming a parable is a parable. But the bet itself shows that one has lost touch with the parable, and in the realm of parable one loses. Does that mean that the realm of transcendence the parable aims at is not to be attained by a parable? For all parables we have seen in Kafka point out that one cannot transcend the written quest for something else. One is always locked in the parable that designates its own dysfunction. This being the case, then the mundane and the transcendent are two realms hermetically sealed off from each other. Even if one becomes in some sense a parable or a metaphor, one has mere changed positions in a semantic game. One remains in reality, and the bet shows this. One always loses in the parable, for the parable would point to a transcendent realm. But it only points. So one can win in reality—one is stuck in it—but one loses in the parable, for the parable should lift you out of it, though it doesn't. There is a paradox lurking here, to be sure, for the realm the parable points to is unattainable precisely because one is in a parable, a parable designating the failure to realize what the parable promises.

Let me change our perspective and speculate that, in writing "On Parables," Kafka still had Freud in mind after writing the draft of an unsent letter in which he argued, with a tepid defense of psychoanalysis, against what Kafka saw as Werfel's attack on it. Indeed, let us suppose that "On Parables" is part of the unfinished letter, continuing after "The Commentary" and its parable about the impossibility of going anywhere, illustrated by the tale of the man who should give up all hope of ever making it to the train station—so says a policeman. Would psychoanalysis itself then be an example of a parable that urges one to pass over to another realm—in effect, to become a parable? This is arguably the case. In making allegorical readings of the self, with its battle between id and superego, psychoanalysis offers parables about the psyche (a metaphor itself taken from classical sources). The Freudian allegory aims at leading patients out of their neurotic state in their imagined world to another state, closer to the real world. This occurs after one has undergone therapeutic metamorphosis. In simple terms, the Freudian allegory of the self should lead to an understanding that should in turn lead to a "crossing over" from neurosis to health—to use the language of the wise man's command.

To be sure, Kafka kept his distance from the very idea of psychoanalytic therapy, at least to the extent that it purported to cure mental disease. He had spelled this out in a letter to Milena two years earlier (dated November 1920 in earlier editions of the letters and 7 October 1920 in *KA* of *Briefe 1918–1920*, p. 355). In this letter he said that the error of the therapeutic part of psychoanalysis was to characterize as disease those mental states that are actually states of belief (*Glaubenstatsachen*). With this critique he also seemed to reject Freud's interpretation of religion as a form of neurosis. But Kafka clearly saw the analogies between his own fiction and Freud's allegories, especially with regard to the role of the patriarch and the father's law in psychic life. So Kafka might well have thought that accepting a parable and then becoming a parable is something like undergoing psychoanalysis and becoming, so to speak, an example of the allegory in which the father's rule is overthrown by transference to the analyst. Can it then be said that one becomes an allegory? From the Freudian perspective, one seeks to become an integrated self, which is a metaphorical statement in itself. Nonetheless one is constantly thrown back into the practical world of reality—where the father's law continues to reign supreme. Can one then really hope to win in the realm of parable?

To pursue this speculative line, I note that, in the same letter to Milena, Kafka created a schema to explain psychic states. He outlined for her a diagram for the understanding of anguish. The diagram resembles a Venn diagram. (A Venn diagram is one that uses concentric circles contained or not contained in others circles to describe whether or not sets are part of each other.) Kafka proposed three concentric circles, one inside the other, to describe a self encapsulated in anguish. He said that a person's innermost self is the smallest circle, circle A, circumscribed by two larger circles. Circle A explains to the immediately encompassing circle B why A distrusts himself and tortures himself, why he renounces everything and why he can't live. The second circle B does not explain any of this to the outer circle C but just orders the exterior circle C to act. So circle C undertakes acts, more out of anguish than understanding, since he believes that inner circle A has explained everything necessary to B and that B has understood everything correctly and passed it on. The letter breaks off here, but it suggests, with Kafka's inimitable sense of humor, that he wanted to experiment with logical sets to see whether they might work for understanding anguish and self-ignorance, for C acts with no idea about what is going on in A—the inner and outer worlds of the self are in permanent disjuncture. By analogy, one might think that on "becoming" a parable one would want to enter a disjunctive world, though in reality one is still locked inside the self, stuck in reality, without ever having reached the parable's marvelous world at all; alternatively, if one enters the parable, then one may bring the parable into reality, without changing a thing at all. Somehow the parable remains impervious to reality, like parts of the self that Kafka outlined as always separate.

The reader may ask, with understandable perplexity, how one becomes a parable. Kafka seems to have experimented with the idea in one of his strangest animal fables, the unpublished, untitled text that begins with the line "In unserer Synagoge lebt ein Tier" (translated with the title "An Animal in the Synagogue"), the only literary text in which, as I said earlier, Kafka wrote about something explicitly Jewish.[2] On the surface it is not at all apparent what Kafka could have meant by describing an unnamed animal that lives in a synagogue. However, if we have recourse to our interpretive strategy of looking for self-referentiality in Kafka's fables, it appears that a self-referential reading points to a coherent whole that allows the reader to make sense of the details in this allegory, assuming that it is an allegory. I would argue that here, in a quite metaphorical sense, Kafka experimented with becoming a parable by making himself into one.

From this self-referential perspective, the depiction of the animal in the synagogue is Kafka's final text about himself as artist, in this case about himself as an outsider who remains inside the Jewish community. In a sense it is his résumé of his life, written for himself in 1922, shortly after he gave a rather different summation of his life in "A Hunger Artist." For upon reflection I believe that this mysterious beast that cannot be driven from the synagogue can best be interpreted as the Jewish artist himself, tolerated by the practical men there and nervously liked by the women whom he/it frightens and perhaps attracts. The animal is a permanent outsider, living in a community that it seemingly does not want to leave and, perhaps for emotional and social reasons, cannot leave. As a man become a parable, the Kafka artist-animal—slim and with a coat of fur of an unknown color—lives within the *Gemeinde* without being part of it. He is simply a permanent observer who is a witness to the slow, ongoing disappearance of the congregation. Indeed, the narrator thinks that the synagogue may soon be used for storing grain. And in this sense the Kafka biographer Peter-André Alt is right to consider this text also to be a parable about Jewish assimilation.[3] The animal is witness to the ongoing disappearance of the Jewish world in which, by accident, it has found refuge and lived for years.

Legend has it that years ago learned opinions were sought about whether the animal could be tolerated in the synagogue. Opinions appear to have been divided, and, since nobody could catch the animal, it has been allowed to remain untouched. The law probably does not sanction the existence of the animal in the temple—nor of the modern writer who, with skepticism, records the mores of the tribe and the disappearance of the law. It is simply a fact that they, animal and artist, exist, roam about avoiding capture, and observe. Such is the fate of the lonely animal, the Kafka animal-artist, the writer who becomes here a parable about himself for himself. His is an allegorical existence in a world of fruitless wisdom, of hostile powers with obscure laws, characterized by comic incongruity that can be refracted through redeeming humor and incomparable irony. By betting that this text is one in which Kafka became a parable about himself to himself, I trust I have won in reality; in parable it is surely uncertain whether one ever wins.

Notes

Chapter 1. Franz Kafka

1. The Fischer edition is now the definitive critical edition and is referred to as *KA* throughout the present study.

The following biographical sketch is based primarily on three works: Klaus Wagenbach, *Franz Kafka;* Ernst Pawel, *The Nightmare of Reason: A Life of Franz Kafka;* Peter-André Alt, *Franz Kafka: Der ewige Sohn*. Another major source is the three-volume biography by Reinhardt Stach, the first volume of which, *Kafka: Die frühen Jahre,* was published as I was finishing a first draft of this chapter. (Stach's first volume was published last.) See the bibliography for information on these works as well as other biographies. References to these works here are made by reference in parentheses to the author's surname.

2. Wagenbach, Rowolt, 1964, p. 28: There is a picture published here of the invitation, on which one can read "Ich lade Sie höflidist [*sic*] zur Confirmation meinen Sohnes Franz . . . ein . . . " to be held 18 June 1896 in the Zigeuner-Synagoge ("I invite you politely [?] to the confirmation of my son Franz . . . "). My philological searches turned up "höflidist" only in one German Slovenian document. It seems this may be a nineteenth-century Austrianism that has disappeared from the language.

3. The anecdote is found, for example, in the letter to Milena dated 21 June 1920. Stach, Vol. I, reproduces the letter (p. 95).

4. I provide a longer analysis of how Kafka might interpret the meaning of the "law" in the physical sciences in my chapter on Kafka in *Fiction Refracts Science.*

5. Wagenbach says that Kafka's letters to Julie Wohryzek have been lost, though this letter to Julie's sister, dated 24 November 1919, showed up in the 1960s and was presented by him at that time. Thus the letter is missing from early editions of Kafka's correspondence. The letter is noteworthy for the clarity with which Kafka says he views marriage and children as the highest goal on earth—"Ehe und Kinder für das Höchste Erstrebenswerte auf Erden"—but that he could not possibly get married (Wagenbach, Rowolt, 1964, p. 116).

Chapter 2. Kafka's First Experiments in Writing Fiction

1. Writing as a form of prayer is from the *Konvolut* of 1920 in the second volume of Kafka's unpublished texts (*KA* 2, p. 354). It succinctly reads: "Schreiben als Form des Gebetes."

2. Robert Musil, *Gesammelte Werke 9,* ed. Adolf Frisé (Hamburg: Rowohlt, 1978), 1468.

3. Eric Baker, "Para-belle: Jenseits des Schönen in Kafkas *Die Bäume,*" in *Kafkas Betrachtung: Lektüren,* ed. Hans Jürgen Scheuer, Justius von Hartlieb, Christina Salmen, Georg Höfner (Frankfurt: Peter Lang, 2003), 182. For explicit reference to Zeno in Kafka, see the diary entry of 17 December 1910, in which he notes Zeno's answer to the question whether anything remains still: the flying arrow is still.

Chapter 3. *Amerika* or *Der Verschollene* (*The Man Who Disappeared* or *The Missing Person*)

1. Heinz Politzer, *Franz Kafka, der Künstler* (Frankfurt: Fischer, 1965), 195.

2. Wilhelm Emrich, *Franz Kafka* (Bonn: Athenäum, 1958), 223. My translation.

Chapter 4. "The Judgment" and "The Metamorphosis"

1. Elias Canetti has written in *Der andere Process* one of the best books on Kafka, especially with regard to Kafka and power (translated as *Kafka's Other Trial: The Letter to Felice,* trans.Christopher Middleton [New York: Schocken Books, 1974]).

2. There is at least one other candidate for Kafka's allusive irony with the name Gregor. It appears that, while at university, Kafka had read a medieval narrative poem by Hartmann von Aue, *Gregorius or the Good Sinner.* It narrates the tale of Gregorius, born of incest, who marries his mother before becoming pope. Incest is rampant in this morality tale of the good sinner. Kafka's Gregor, unlike the medieval Gregorius, has little chance of becoming pope in his present form, but the quasi allusion to the medieval text points up that Kafka's ironies are multiple.

3. Maurice Blanchot, *De Kafka à Kafka* (Paris: Gallimard, 1981), 73.

4. Einstein asks one to visualize the following image. Two bolts of lightning hit points X and Y behind and in front of a traveler in a train but equidistant from an exterior viewer. To an exterior viewer situated midpoint between X and Y, the bolts appear to hit simultaneously, whereas to the traveler, traveling toward point X, X must appear to occur before the event at point Y—since the light from X would reach him before the light from Y. Hence time is relative to the inertial framework. These images are imaginable images from the phenomenal world but a world now left bereft of absolute temporality. See Albert Einstein, *Relativity: Special and General Theory,* trans. Robert W. Lawson (New York: Bonanza Books, 1961). Those of a speculative bent might pursue how the epistemology of the most influential scientist of Kafka's youth, the Austrian Ernst Mach, might find resonances in Kafka's use of images. One could start with Mach's axiom that only sensations are real.

Chapter 5. *The Trial* and "In the Penal Colony"

1. Walter Sokel, *Franz Kafka—Tragik und Ironie: zur Struktur seiner Kunst* (Munich: Langen Müller, 1983 [1964]), 119.

2. Elias Canetti, *Der andere Proceß: Kafkas Briefe an Felice* (Munich: Hanser, 1969).

3. Wilhelm Emrich, *Franz Kafka* (Frankfurt: Athenäum, 1981 [1961]), 265–266.

4. Albert Camus, *Mythe de Sisyphe* (Paris: Editions de la Pléïade, 1965), 210. My debt to Camus is great: Camus introduced me to Kafka when, as a law student knowing nothing about Kafka except what Camus had written about him, I was led to read *The Trial* in 1962. This then encouraged me in my resolve to drop out of law school.

5. Jean-Paul Sartre, *Réflexions sur la question juive* (Paris: Gallimard Essais, 1985 [1954]), 94.

6. I owe the substance of these comments to James Hawes and his tonically iconoclastic biography of Kafka, *Excavating Kafka* (London: Quercus, 2008), 212–213.

7. The quotation from Benjamin can be found in the very useful anthology of Benjamin's texts on Kafka, *Benjamin über Kafka,* ed. Hermann Schweppenhäuser (Frankfurt: Suhrkamp, 1981), 129: "Mit diesen letzten Worten, die K. erfährt, ist eigentlich ausgesprochen, dass sich das Gericht von jeder beliebigen Situation gar nicht unterscheide. Das gilt von jeder Situation, allerdings unter der einen Voraussetzung, dass man sie nicht durch K. sich entwickelnd sondern als ihm äußerlich und gleichsam auf ihn warten auffasse." It is also quoted by Reiner Stach before the quotation from Stach cited here: Reiner Stach, *Kafka: Die Jahre der Entscheidungen* (Frankfurt: Fischer, 2002), 553.

8. Walter Benjamin, "Franz Kafka: On the Tenth Anniversary of His Death," in *The Metamorphosis,* trans. Stanley Corngold (New York: Modern Library, 2013), 143. This is one of several critical essays on Kafka available in this new edition of Corngold's translation of "The Metamorphosis."

Chapter 6. *A Country Doctor* and Other Stories

1. There are two other short manuscripts from 1914–1915 in the critical edition of unpublished writing, the "Unterstaatsanswalt" manuscript and the "Elberfeld" notebook, the first about lawyers and the second about a student.

2. Bern Neumann, *Franz Kafka und der Grosse Krieg: Eine kulturhistorische Chronik seines Schreibens* (Würzburg: Könighausen und Neumann, 2014), 321. Neumann thinks the play is dealing with a cult of the dead that was the basis for empire.

3. The critic and Bible scholar Robert Alter narrates the tale of this encounter in his highly recommended *Necessary Angels: Tradition and Modernity in Kafka, Benjamin, and Scholem* (Cambridge, Mass.: Harvard University Press, 1991).

4. Helmut Binder, *Vor dem Gesetz: Einführung in Kafkas Welt* (Stuttgart: J. B. Metzler, 1993), 184.

5. Malcolm Pasley, "Drei literarische Mystifikationen Kafkas," *Kafka Symposium,* ed. Jürgen Born (Berlin: Klaus Wagenbach Verlag, 1965), 21–37.

6. For the record, the two other languages Kafka knew beside Czech offer the same identification of *ape* and *imitation.* In the French Kafka read with ease, one uses the verb *singer* to say that one imitates slavishly, like a *singe,* a monkey. Or, in the Italian that Kafka studied now and then and which Joseph K. speaks, the ape or *scimmia* may also be an artist when, with a choice of verbs, it decides to imitate, *schimmieggiare* or *scimmieggiare,* both pejorative. My impression is that Slavic languages do not make this equation, but I have not studied Czech. However, Bulgarian has no such equivalent.

7. Cf. Peter-André Alt, *Franz Kafka: Der ewige Sohn* (Munich: C. H. Beck, 2008 [2005]), 518.

8. Walter Sokel, *The Myth of Power and the Self: Essays on Franz Kafka,* (Detroit: Wayne State University Press, 2002) 130.

9. Reiner Stach, *Kafka: Die Jahre der Erkenntnis* (Frankfurt: Fischer, 2008), 204–205.

10. Translation taken from *Kafka's Selected Stories,* trans. Stanley Corngold (New York: W. W. Norton, 2007), 65. Modified slightly.

Chapter 7. *The Castle*

1. Karin Keller, *Gesellschaft im mythischen Bann: Studien zum Roman "Das Schloss" und anderen Werken Franz Kafkas* (Wiesbaden: Athenaion, 1977). Also, Richie Robertson, "Myth vs. Enlightenment in Kafka's *Das Schloss,*" *Monatshefte* 103, no. 3 (Fall 2011): 385–395.

2. *The Essential Kafka,* trans. John Williams (Ware, UK: Wordsworth Editions, 2014), 183.

3. Robert Calasso, *K.* (Milan: Gli Adelphi, 2005), 99.

4. Walter Benjamin, *Selected Writings,* trans. Rodney Livingston, Vol. 2 (Cambridge, Mass.: Harvard University Press, 1999), 807.

5. W. S. Sebald, "Das unentdeckte Land: Zur Motivstruktur in Kafkas *Schloss,*" in *Beschreibung des Unglücks: Zur österreichischen Literatur von Stifter bis Handke* (Salzburg: Residenz Verlag, 1985), 79–82.

6. Quoted by Robert Alter, *Necessary Angels: Tradition and Modernity in Kafka, Benjamin, and Scholem* (Cambridge, Mass.: Harvard University Press, 1991) 108.

7. Hannah Arendt, "The Jew as Pariah: A Hidden Tradition," *Jewish Social Studies* 5, no. 2 (1944): 99–122; and Arendt, "Franz Kafka: A Revaluation," *Partisan Review* 11, no. 4 (1944): 412–422.

8. Theodor Adorno "Notes on Kafka," in *Prisms,* trans. Shierry Weber Nicholsen and Samuel Weber (Cambridge, Mass.: MIT Press, 1983), 268–270.

9. Martin Walser, *Beschreibung einer Form, Versuch über Kafka* [1952], in *Werke,* ed. Helmuth Kiesel, Vol. 12 (Frankfurt: Suhrkamp, 1997), 42.

Chapter 8. *A Hunger Artist* and the Last Stories

1. These versions of Abraham are partially available in the translations found in the amalgamations of Kafka's texts in *Paradoxes and Parables,* out of print but available online and from Amazon.com.

2. I wonder if Kafka is in fact confusing the eating habits of eagles and vultures, as does Kafka's favored Austrian writer Adelbert Stifter, who, in his novel *Der Hochwald,* thinks vultures attack living mammals.

3. Kafka was also abreast of the course of the Russian Revolution, having read Bertrand Russell's bleak picture of Russia that appeared in a Prague newspaper in August. He mentions it in a letter to Milena dated 1 September 1920.

4. I refer to Wolfe's novel about the artist's return home, *You Can't Go Home Again,* published posthumously in 1940 and considered a defining work of American modernism.

5. Roy Porter, *Kafka's Narrators: A Study of His Stories and Sketches* (Cambridge: Cambridge University Press, 1982) 71.

6. For example, Nelson Goodman developed his argument in the first chapter of *Of Mind and Other Matters* (Cambridge, Mass.: Harvard University Press, 1984). For a complementary view of the idea that art takes place as an interpretive practice, see works by the contemporary American philosopher and champion of Andy Warhol Arthur Danto. I mention them with no intent to endorse either; they are merely symptomatic and widely read.

7. Malcolm Pasley, "Kafka's Semi-Private Games," *Oxford German Studies* 6 (1971): 112–131.

Epilogue

1. On this point I follow Beda Allemann, "Kafka: 'Von den Gleichnissen'" in *Zeit und Geschichte im Werk Kafkas,* ed. Dietheim Kaiser and Nikolaus Lohse (Gottingen: Wallenstein, 1998), 114–125. First published in the 1950s, Allemann's work has been the basis for much of the later interpretation of the parable.

2. This frequently cited text is available in translation under this title in the now out-of-print *Parables and Paradoxes* (also available online). Kafka gave it no title; it is found in *KA* 2, pp. 405–411.

3. Peter-André Alt, *Franz Kafka, der ewige Sohn: Eine Biographie* (Frankfurt: Fischer, 2014), 72–73.

Selected Bibliography

Works by Franz Kafka

Kritische Ausgabe der Werke von Franz Kafka. Ed. Gerhard Neumann, Jost Schillemeit, Sir Malcolm Pasley, et al. Frankfurt: S. Fischer, 1982–2013. (Referred to throughout this study as *KA*.)

Fischer's *Kritische Ausgabe* is the definitive edition of Kafka's writings. It includes in one volume the works published by Kafka in his lifetime; there are also editions of the three novels with a volume of critical apparatus; the diaries; two volumes containing all the currently available manuscripts of works Kafka did not publish, presented in chronological order; his office writings; and four volumes of letters, with one volume more yet to be published at the current date. (This edition is also available, without Kafka's letters, as a Fischer paperback.) The edition includes:

Das Schloss. Ed. Sir Malcolm Pasley. 2 vols. 1982.

Der Verschollene. Ed. Jost Schillemeit. 2. vols. 1983.

Der Proceß. Ed. Sir Malcolm Pasley. 2 vols. 1990.

Tagebücher. Ed. Hans-Gerd Koch, Michael Müller, and Sir Malcolm Pasley. 3 vols. 1990.

Drucke zu Lebzeiten. Ed. Wolf Kittler, Hans-Gerd Koch, and Gerhard Neumann. 2 vols. 1993.

Nachgelassene Schriften und Fragmente I. Ed. Sir Malcolm Pasley. 2 vols. 1993.

Nachgelassene Schriften und Fragmente II. Ed. Jost Schillemeit. 2 vols. 1992.

Briefe. Ed. Hans-Gerd Koch. 4 vols. 1999– .

For the sake of completeness I also note another complete edition of Kafka's works: *Historische-kritische Ausgabe sämtlicher Handschriften, Drucke und Typoskripte*. Ed. Roland Reuss and Peter Stangle. Frankfurth and Basel: Stroemfeld, 1995–. (A largely unreadable edition, reproducing Kafka's handwriting, found in few libraries.)

For Brod's first editions, see the *Chronology*. It should be noted that Brod's edition of the diaries follows chronological order and that the critical edition follows the manuscript order of the entries. Brod's edition of the diaries, first published 1937, also differs significantly in content, having been heavily edited. The English translation has restored some but not all of the text cut from the original German version published by Brod. Brod's versions of the novels also differ from those of the *Kritische Ausgabe*.

The Internet site The Kafka Project has, among other things, all the German critical edition's texts available online with the exception, at the current date, of the correspondence. Caveat: there are errors in transcription.

Selected Translations

The Castle

The Castle. Trans. Willa Muir and Edwin Muir. With an homage by Thomas Mann. New York: Modern Library, 1969 [1930].

The Castle. Trans. Mark Harmon. New York: Schocken Books, 1998.

The Castle. Trans. Anthea Bell. New York: Oxford University Press, 2009.

The Castle in *The Essential Kafka*. Trans. John Williams. London: Wordsworth Editions, 2014.

The Trial

The Trial. Trans. Willa Muir and Edwin Muir. New York: A. A. Knopf, 1937 [1935].

The Trial. Trans. Mike Mitchell. New York: Oxford University Press, 2009.

The Trial in *The Essential Kafka*. Trans. John Williams. London: Wordsworth Editions, 2014.

Amerika (Der Verschollene)

America. Trans. Willa Muir and Edwin Muir. London: G. Routledge, 1938.

Amerika (The Man Who Disappeared). Trans. Michael Hofmann. New York: New Directions, 1996.

Amerika: The Missing Person. Trans. Mark Harmon. New York: Schocken Books, 2008.

The Man Who Disappeared (America). Trans. Ritchie Robertson. New York: Oxford University Press, 2012.

Short Fiction

The Great Wall of China and Other Pieces. Trans. Willa Muir and Edwin Muir. London: Martin Secker, 1933.

Dearest Father: Stories and Other Writings. Trans. Ernst Kaiser and Eithne Wilkins. New York: Schocken Books, 1954.

Description of a Struggle. Trans. Tania Stern and James Stern. New York: Schocken Books, 1958.

Parables and Paradoxes. Ed. Nahum N. Glatzer. New York: Schocken Books, 1961. Various translators.

The Complete Short Stories. Ed. Nahum N. Glatzer. New York: Schocken Books, 1971.

The Metamorphosis and Other Stories. Trans. Malcolm Pasley. London: Penguin, 1992.

Collected Short Stories. Trans. Willa Muir and Edwin Muir. Ed. Gabriel Josipovici. London: Everyman Books, 1993.

Kafka's Selected Short Stories. Trans. Stanley Corngold. New York: W. W. Norton, 2007.

The Metamorphosis and Other Stories. Trans. Michael Hofmann. London: Penguin Books, 2007.

The Metamorphosis and Other Stories. Trans. Joyce Crick. New York: Oxford University Press, 2009.

The Metamorphosis. Trans. Stanley Corngold. New York: Modern Library, 2013.

Diaries and Other Texts

The Diaries of Franz Kafka 1910–1913. Trans. Joseph Kretch. New York: Schocken Books, 1948.

The Diaries of Franz Kafka 1914–1923. Trans. Martin Greenberg. New York: Schocken Books, 1949.

The Zürau Aphorisms of Franz Kafka. Trans. Michael Hofmann. New York: Schocken Books, 2006.

Franz Kafka: The Office Writings. Trans. Eric Patton and Ruth Hein. Ed. Stanley Corngold, Jack Greenberg, and Benno Wagner. Princeton: Princeton University Press, 2009.

Letters

Letters to Felice. Trans. Elisabeth Duckworth and James Stern. New York: Schocken Books, 1973.

Letters to Friends, Family, and Editors. Trans. Clara and Richard Winston. New York: Schocken Books: 1977.

Letters to Ottla and the Family. Trans. Clara and Richard Winston. New York: Schocken Books, 1982.

Letters to Milena. Trans. Philip Boehm. New York: Schocken Books, 1990. (Restores passages cut from translation based on an earlier edition.)

Secondary Sources

Bibliographies and Research and Study Guides

Singularly useful is the Internet site The Kafka Bibliography. It shows where individual stories by Kafka in German are located in English translation.

Beicken, Peter. *Eine kritische Einführung in die Forschung*. Frankfurt: Athenaion, 1974.

Binder, Hartmut. *Kafka-Kommentar zu Sämtlichen Erzählungen*. Munich: Winkler, 1975.

———. *Kafka-Kommentar zu den Romanen, Rezensionen, Aphorismen und zum Brief an den Vater*. Munich: Winkler, 1976.

———. *Kafka-Handbuch*. 2 vol.Stuttgart: Kröner, 1979.

Caputo-Mayr, Maria Luise, and Julius Michael Herz. *Franz Kafka. Internationale Bibliographie der Primär- und Sekundärliteratur: Eine Einführung*. Second ed. 2 vols. Munich: K. G. Saur, 2000.

Dowden, Stephen D. *Kafka's Castle and the Critical Imagination*. Columbia, S.C.: Camden House, 1995.

Engel, Manfred, and Bernd Aurochs. *Kafka-Handbuch*. Stuttgart: J. B. Metzler, 2010.

Flores, Angel. *A Kafka Bibliography 1908–1976*. New York: Gordon Press, 1976.

Gray, Richard. *A Kafka Encyclopedia*. Westport, Conn.: Greenwood Press, 2005.

Jagow, Bettina von, and Oliver Jahrhaus. *Kafka-Handbuch*. Göttingen:Vandenhoech and Ruprecht, 2008.

Järv, Harry. *Die Kafka-Literatur: Eine Bibliographie*. Malmö: Bo Cavefors, 1961.
Kempf, Franz R. *Everyone's Darling: Kafka and the Critics of His Short Fiction*. Columbia, S.C.: Camden House, 1994.

Biographies

Alt, Peter-André. *Franz Kafka: Der ewige Sohn. Eine Biographie*. Rev. ed. Munich: C. H. Beck, 2008.
Brod, Max. *Franz Kafka eine biographie (Erinnerungen und Dokumente)*. Prague: H. Mercy Sohn, 1937.
———. *Franz Kafka*. Trans. Humphrey G. Roberts and Richard Winston. London: Secker and Warburg, 1947.
Canetti, Elias. *Der andere Proceß: Kafkas Briefe an Felice*. Munich: Hanser, 1969.
———. *Kafka's Other Trial: The Letters to Felice*. Trans. Christopher Middleton. London: Calder and Boyars, 1974.
Friedland, Saul. *Franz Kafka: The Poet of Shame and Guilt*. New Haven: Yale University Press, 2013.
Gilman, Sander. *Franz Kafka, the Jewish Patient*. New York: Routledge, 1995.
Hayman, Ronald. *Kafka: A Biography*. New York: Oxford University Press, 1982.
Hawes, James. *Excavating Kafka*. London: Quercus, 2008.
Murray, Nicolas. *Kafka*. New Haven: Yale University Press, 2004.
Pawel, Ernst. *The Nightmare of Reason: The Life of Franz Kafka*. New York: Farrar, Straus and Giroux, 1984.
Stach, Reiner. *Kafka: Die Jahre der Entscheidung*. Frankfurt: S. Fischer, 2002.
———. *Kafka: Die Jahre der Erkenntnis*. Frankfurt: S. Fischer, 2008.
———. *Kafka: The Decisive Years*. Trans. Shelley Frisch. Princeton: Princeton University Press, 2013.
———. *Kafka: Die frühen Jahre*. Frankfurt: S. Fischer, 2014. (Note that the first volume of this biography was published last.)
———. *Kafka: The Years of Insight*. Trans. Shelley Frisch. Princeton: Princeton University Press, 2015.
Wagenbach, Klaus. *Franz Kafka*. Hamburg: Rowohlt, 1964.
———. *Franz Kafka*. Trans. Ewald Osers. Cambridge, Mass.: Harvard University Press, 2003.

Books of Criticism

Alter, Robert. *Necessary Angels: Tradition and Modernity in Kafka, Benjamin, and Scholem*. Cambridge, Mass.: Harvard University Press, 1991.
Beissner, Friedrich. *Der Erzähler Franz Kafka*. Frankfurt: Suhrkamp, 1983 [1952].
Benjamin, Walter. *Benjamin über Kafka*. Ed. Hermann Schweppenhäuser. Frankfurt: Suhrkamp, 1981. (Includes various writings of Benjamin.)
———. *Sur Kafka*. Trans. and ed. Christophe David and Alexandra Richter. Paris: Nous, 2015. (Includes translations of everything Benjamin wrote on Kafka.)
Binder, Hartmut. *Vor dem Gesetz: Einführung in Kafkas Welt*. Stuttgart: J. B. Metzler, 1993.

Blanchot, Maurice. *De Kafka à Kafka*. Paris: Gallimard, 1981.

Bridgwater, Patrick. *Kafka and Nietzsche*. Bonn: Bouvier, 1974.

Calasso, Roberto. *K*. Milan: Adelphi, 2005.

———. *K*. Trans. Geoffrey Brock. New York: A. A. Knopf, 2005.

Corngold, Stanley. *The Commentator's Despair*. Port Washington, N.Y.: Kennikat Press, 1973.

———. *Franz Kafka: The Necessity of Form*. Ithaca, N.Y.: Cornell University Press, 1988.

———. *Lambent Traces*. Princeton: Princeton University Press, 2004.

Corngold, Stanley, and Benno Wagner. *Franz Kafka: The Ghosts in the Machine*. Evanston, Ill.: Northwestern University Press, 2011.

Dentan, Michel. *Humour et création littéraire dans l'oeuvre de Kafka*. Geneva: Droz, 1961.

Duttlinger, Carolin. *The Cambridge Introduction to Franz Kafka*. Cambridge: Cambridge University Press, 2013.

Emrich, Wilhelm. *Franz Kafka*. Bonn: Athenäum, 1965 [1958].

———. *Franz Kafka. A Critical Study*. Trans. Sheema Zeben Buehne. New York: Frederick Ungar, 1968.

Gray, Ronald. *Kafka*. Cambridge: Cambridge University Press, 1973.

Greenberg, Martin. *The Terror of Art: Kafka and Modern Literature*. New York: Basic Books, 1968.

Heidsiek, Arnold. *The Intellectual Contexts of Kafka's Fiction: Philosophy, Law, Religion*. Columbia, S.C.: Camden House, 1994.

Keller, Karin. *Gesellschaft im mythischen Bann: Studien zum Roman "Das Schloss" und anderen Werken Franz Kafkas*. Wiesbaden: Athenaion, 1977.

Koelb, Clayton. *Kafka's Rhetoric: The Passion of Reading*. Ithaca, N.Y.: Cornell University Press, 1989.

———. *Kafka: A Guide for the Perplexed*. New York: Continuum, 2010.

Kuna, Franz. *Franz Kafka: Literature as Corrective Punishment*. Bloomington: Indiana University Press, 1974.

Löwy, Michael. *Franz Kafka rêveur insoumis*. Paris: Stock, 2005.

Neumann, Bern. *Franz Kafka und der Grosse Krieg: Eine kulturhistorische Chronik seines Schreibens*. Würzburg: Könighausen und Neumann, 2014.

Neumann, Gerhard. *Franz Kafka: Experte der Macht*. Munich: Hanser, 2012.

———. *Kafka-Lektüren*. Berlin: De Gruyter, 2013.

Pascal, Roy. *Kafka's Narrators: A Study of His Stories and Sketches*. Cambridge: Cambridge University Press, 1982.

Politzer, Heinz. *Franz Kafka: Parable and Paradox*. Ithaca, N.Y.: Cornell University Press, 1962.

———. *Franz Kafka der Kunstler*. Trans. from English and revision by author. Frankfurt: S. Fischer, 1965.

Preece, Julian, ed. *The Cambridge Companion to Kafka*. Cambridge: Cambridge University Press, 2002.

Robert, Marthe. *Seul, comme Franz Kafka*. Paris: Calman-Lévi, 1979.

———. *Franz Kafka's Loneliness.* Trans. Ralph Manheim. London: Faber and Faber, 1982.

Robertson, Ritchie. *Kafka: Judaism, Politics, and Literature.* New York: Oxford University Press, 1985.

Rolleston, James, ed. *A Companion to the Works of Franz Kafka.* Rochester, N.Y.: Camden House, 2003.

Shepperd, Richard. *On Kafka's Castle: A Study.* London: Croom Helm, 1973.

Sokel, Walter H. *Franz Kafka: Tragik und Ironie.* Munich: A. Langen, 1964.

———. *The Myth of Power and the Self. Essays on Franz Kafka.* Detroit: Wayne State University Press, 2002.

Thiher, Allen. *Franz Kafka: A Study of the Short Fiction.* Boston: Twayne, 1990.

———. *Fiction Refracts Science: Modernist Writers from Proust to Borges.* Columbia: University of Missouri Press, 2005.

Walser, Martin. *Beschreibung einer Form, Versuch über Kafka* [1952]. In *Werke,* vol. 12. Frankfurt: Suhrkamp, 1997.

Zilcosky, John. *Kafka's Travels: Exoticism, Colonialism, and the Traffic of Writing.* New York: Palgrave Macmillan, 2003.

Essays and Articles

Adorno, Theodor. "Notes on Kafka." In *Prisms,* trans. Shierry Weber Nicholsen and Samuel Weber. Cambridge, Mass.: MIT Press, 1983. 268–270.

Allemann, Beda. "Kafka: 'Von den Gleichnissen.'" In *Zeit und Geschichte im Werk Kafkas,* ed. Dietheim Kaiser and Nikolaus Lohse. Gottingen: Wallenstein, 1998. 114–125.

Anderson, Mark M. "Kafka, Homosexuality, and the Aesthetics of Male Culture." In *Gender and Politics in Austrian Fiction,* ed. Ritchie Robertson and Edward Timms. Edinburgh: Edinburgh University Press, 1996. 79–99.

Arendt, Hannah. "The Jew as Pariah: A Hidden Tradition." *Jewish Social Studies* 6, no. 2 (1944): 99–122.

———. "Franz Kafka: A Revaluation." *Partisan Review* 11, no. 4 (1944): 412–422.

Baker, Eric. "Para-belle: Jenseits des Schönen in Kafkas *Die Bäume.*" In *Kafkas Betrachtung: Lektüren,* ed. Hans Jürgen Scheuer, Justus von Hartlieb, Christina Salmen, and Georg Höfner. Frankfurt: Peter Lang, 2003. 184–194.

Banakar, Reza. "In Search of Heimat: A Note on Kafka's Concept of the Law." *Law and Literature* 22, no. 3 (2010): 463–490.

Beck, Evelyn Torton. "Kafka's Traffic in Women: Gender, Power, and Sexuality." *The Literary Review* 26, no. 4 (1983): 565–576.

Butler, Judith. "Who Owns Kafka?" *London Review of Books* 33, no. 5 (2011): 3–8.

Coetzee, J. M. "Time, Tense, and Aspect in Kafka's 'The Burrow.'" *Modern Language Notes* 96, no. 3 (1981): 556–579.

Cohn, Dorrit. "Kafka's Eternal Present: Narrative Tense in 'Ein Landarzt' and Other First Person Stories." *PMLA* 83 (1968): 144–150.

———. "K. Enters *The Castle*: On the Change of Person in Kafka's Manuscript." *Euphorion* 62 (1968): 28–45.

———. "Trends in Literary Criticism: Some Structuralist Approaches to Kafka." *German Quarterly* 51 (1978): 182–188.

Flores, Kate. "The Judgment." *Quarterly Review of Literature* 3, no. 4 (1947): 383–405.

Furst, Lilian. "Kafka and the Romantic Imagination." *Mosaic* 3, no 4 (1970): 81–89.

Gross, Ruth V. "Kafka's Short Fiction." In *A Cambridge Companion to Kafka,* ed. Julian Preece. Cambridge: Cambridge University Press, 2002. 80–94.

Hinderer, Walter. "An Anecdote by Kafka: 'A Fratricide.'" In *Kafka's Selected Stories,* ed. Stanley Corngold. New York: W. W. Norton, 2007. 246–251.

Koelb, Clayton. "Critical Editions II: Will the Real Franz Kafka Please Stand Up." In *A Companion to the Works of Franz Kafka,* ed. James Rolleston. Rochester, N.Y.: Camden House, 2002. 27–32.

Kurz, Gerhard. "Nietzsche, Freud, and Kafka." In *Reading Kafka: Prague, Politics, and the fin de siècle,* ed. Mark Anderson. New York: Schocken Books, 1989. 128–148.

Neumann, Gerhard. "Hungerkünstler und Menschenfresser: Zum Verhältnis von Kunst und Kulturellen Ritual im Werke Franz Kafkas." *Archiv für Kulturgeschichte* 66 (1984): 347–388.

———. "'The Judgment,' 'Letter to His Father,' and the Bourgeois Family." In *Reading Kafka: Prague, Politics, and the fin de siècle,* ed. Mark Anderson. New York: Schocken Books, 1989. 215–228.

Pasley, Malcolm. "Drei literarisch Mystifikationen Kafkas." In *Kafka Symposium,* ed. Jürgens Born. Berlin: Klaus Wagenbach, 1965. 21–37.

———. "Kafka's Semi-Private Games." *Oxford German Studies* 6 (1971): 112–131.

Rolleston, James. "Strategy and Language: Georg Bendemann's Theater of the Self." In *The Problem of the Judgment: Eleven Approaches to Kafka's Story,* ed. Angel Flores. New York: Gordian Press, 1976. 133–145.

Reuß, Roland. "Running Texts Stunning Drafts." In *Kafka for the Twenty-First Century,* ed. Stanley Corngold and Ruth Gross.Rochester, N.Y.: Camden House, 2011. 24–47.

Ritter, Naomi. "Art as Spectacle: Kafka and the Circus." *Österreich in Amerikanischer Sicht* 2 (1981): 65–70.

Robertson, Richie. "Myth vs. Enlightenment in Kafka's *Das Schloss.*" *Monatshefte* 103, no. 3 (Fall 2011): 385–395.

Sattler, Emil E. "Kafka's Artist in a Society of Mice." *Germanic Notes* Vol. 9, No. 4 (1978). 49–53.

Sebald, W. S. "Das unentdeckte Land: Zur Motivstruktur in Kafkas *Schloss.*" In *Beschreibung des Unglücks: Zur österreichischen Literature von Stifter bis Handke.* Salzburg:Residenz Verlag, 1985. 79–82.

Sokel, Walter H. "Kafka's Poetics of the Inner Self." *Modern Austrian Literature* 11, no. 3/4 (1978): 37–58.

Spann, Meno. "Don't Hurt the Jackdaw." *Germanic Review* 37, no. 1 (1962): 68–78.

Steinberg, Erwin R. "The Judgment in Kafka's 'In the Penal Colony.'" *Journal of Modern Literature* 5 (1976): 492–514.

Stockholder, Katherine. "'A Country Doctor': The Narrator as Dreamer." *American Imago* 35 (1978): 331–346.

Thiher, Allen. “The *Nachlass:* Metaphors of *Gehen* and Ways toward Science.” In *Kafka and the Contemporary Critical Performance,* ed. Alan Udoff. Bloomington: University of Indiana Press, 1987. 256–265.

———. “The Legacy of Kafka’s Short Fiction: Knowledge of the Impossibility of Knowledge.” In *The Legacy of Kafka in Contemporary Austrian Fiction,* ed. Frank Pilipp. Riverside, Calif.: Ariadne Press, 1997. 193–222.

Index

Absent-Minded Window-Gazing," ("Zerstreutes Hinausshaun"), 59
"Abweisung, Die," (from *Meditation*) *see* "The Refusal."
"Abweisung, Die," (from notebooks of 1920) *see* "The Refusal."
"Advocates," ("Fürsprecher"), 238
"Aeroplanes in Brescia, The," ("Die Aeroplane in Brescia"), 15
"alltägliche Verwirrung, Eine," *see* "A Common Confusion."
"altes Blatt, Ein," *see* "An Old Manuscript"
Amerika, (Der Verschollene, also translated *The Missing Person* and *The Man Who Disappeared*), 7, 16, 22, 32, 34, 63, 65, 66–97, 98, 107, 116, 123, 137, 147, 163
"Animal in the Synagogue, An," (Untitled text in German beginning "In unserer Synagoge lebt ein Tier..."), 259, 264–65
anti-Semitism, 14, 25, 27–28, 30, 31, 155, 180, 255
Arendt, Hannah, 225–26
art and the artist, the image of, 43, 45, 46, 52, 61–62, 147–48, 175–178, 183–84, 227–228, 233, 243–258, 264
"At Night," ("Nachts"), 230, 231, 232
"Auf der Galerie," *see* "Up in the Gallery."
"Aufbruch, Der," *see* "The Departure."
"Ausflug ins Gebirge," *see* "Excursion in the Mountain."
Austro-Hungarian Empire, the, 1–3, 14, 21, 25, 68, 81, 86, 106, 136, 163, 168–69, 185–86, 234
"Bachelor's Ill Luck," ("Das Unglück des Junggesellen"), 58, 167
Bauer, Felice, 11, 18–24, 37, 38, 68, 98, 102, 128, 129, 132, 153, 167, 229
"Bäume, Die," *see* "The Trees."
"Before the Law," ("Vor dem Gesetz"), 150, 151–53, 159, 169, 172
"Beim Bau der Chinesischen Mauer," *see* "The Great Wall of China."
Benjamin, Walter, 2, 100, 152–53, 156, 172, 205, 214, 225, 256
"Bericht für eine Akademie, Eine," *see* "A Report to an Academy."
Beschreibung eines Kampfes, see "Description of a Struggle."
"Besuch in Bergwerk, Ein," *see* "A Visit to a Mine."
Betrachtung, see *Meditation*
Blanchot, Maurice, 121–22, 123
"Blumfeld, an Elderly Bachelor", ("Blumfeld, ein älterer Junggeselle"), 163, 164, 166–68
"Blumfeld, ein älterer Junggeselle," *see* "Blumfeld, an Elderly Bachelor."
"Bridge, The" ("Die Brücke"), 183–84
Brief an den Vater, see Letter to His Father
Brod, Max, 7, 9, 10, 16, 17, 18, 24, 25, 29, 30, 31, 32–33, 34, 42, 53, 55, 66, 68, 82, 86, 92, 96, 137, 188, 197, 225, 228, 233, 238, 240, 242, 253, 255, 259, 260, 261
"Brücke, Die," *see* "The Bridge."
"Brudermord, Ein, "*see* "A Fratricide."
Buber, Martin, 17, 20, 179
"Bucket Rider, The," ("Der Kübelreiter"), 181

"Burrow, The," ("Der Bau"), 31, 43, 165, 253–55
"Businessman, The," ("Der Kaufmann, Der"), 58–59

Camus, Albert, 82, 134, 138–39, 140, 149, 153
Canetti, Elias, 99, 133, 153
"Cares of a Family Man, The," ("Die Sorge des Hausvaters"), 172–74
Castle, The, (*Das Schloss*), 29, 30, 32, 34, 37, 40, 66, 105, 108, 137, 143, 145, 149, 166, 168, 182, 187, 194, 195–226, 227, 234, 238, 240
"Children on a Country Road," ("Kinder auf der Landstrasse"), 15, 55
"Chinese Puzzle, The," ("Geduldspiel"), 238, 239–40
"City Coat of Arms, The," ("Das Stadtwappen"), 230, 233–34, 243
"Clothes," ("Kleider"), 61
"Common Confusion, A," ("Eine alltägliche Verwirrung"), 185
"Conscription of Troops, The," ("Die Truppenaushebung"), 230, 235
Contemplation, see *Meditation*
"Conversation with the Drunk" ("Gespräch mit dem Betrunkenen"), 15
"Conversation with the Supplicant" ("Gespräch mit dem Beter"), 15
Country Doctor, A, (the collection, *Ein Landartz*), 34, 150, 163, 169
"Country Doctor, A" (the story, "Ein Landartz"), 39, 180–183
"Crossbreed, A," ("Eine Kreuzung"), 174

Darwin, Charles, 9, 176–78
"Departure, The," ("Der Aufbruch"), 238–39
"Description of a Struggle," (*Beschreibung eines Kampfes*), 14,15, 35, 40–53, 55, 57, 61, 72, 101, 109, 114, 126, 128, 141, 254, 261
Diamant, Dora, 31–32
Diary, Kafka's (*Tagebuch*), 17, 28–29, 32, 53–55, 58, 68, 98, 101, 103, 110, 121, 132, 138, 163, 195–97, 235
Dickens, Charles, 76, 80, 97, 115
"Dorfschullehrer, Der," *see* "The Village Schoolmaster."
Dostoyevsky, Fyodor, 9, 110, 136–137, 178
"Dream, A," ("Ein Traum"), 133–134

"Ehepaar," *see* "The Married Couple."
Einstein, Albert, 2, 125, 126, 268n4
"Eleven Sons," ("Elf Söhne"), 174
"Elf Söhne,"*see* "Eleven Sons."
"Enlarvung eines Bauernfängers," *see* "The Unmasking of a Confidence Trickster."
Entropy, 38, 39, 44, 61, 85, 87, 116, 118, 119, 120, 121, 222
"Entschlüsse, " *see* "Resolutions."
"Erstes Leid," *see* "First Sorrow."
"Excursion in the Mountain," ("Ausflug ins Gebirge"), 57–58

"Fahrgast, Der," *see* "On the Tram."
"Fellowship," ("Gemeinschaft"), 230, 235–36
"First Long Train Journey, The," ("Eine kleine Reise durch mitteleuropäische Gegenden"), 15, 53
"First Sorrow," ("Erstes Leid"), 244–45
"Fratricide, A," ("Ein Brudermord"), 170
Freud, Sigmund and themes of psychoanalysis, 2, 6, 7, 12, 49, 59, 73, 100, 103, 104, 115, 117–18, 119, 123, 126, 133, 144, 181–82, 183, 191, 240, 241, 259, 262–63
"Fürsprecher," *see* "Advocates."

"Gassenfenster, Das" see "The Street Window."
"Geduldspiel," *see* "The Chinese Puzzle."
"Geier, Der," *see* "The Vulture."
"Gemeinschaft," *see* "Fellowship."
"Gespräch mit dem Beter," *see* "Conversation with the Supplicant."
"Gespräch mit dem Betrunkenen," *see* "Conversation with the Drunk."
"Gibs auf!" *see* "Give It Up!"
"Give It Up!" ("Gibs auf!), 240, 259
Goethe, Wolfgang, 8, 16, 37–38, 75, 76, 124, 261, 262
"Great Wall of China, The," ("Beim Bau der Chinesischen Mauer"), 171,185–188, 210, 212, 234

"Gruftwächter, Der," *see* "The Warden of the Tomb."

"Heimkehr," *see* "Homecoming."
"Heizer, Der," *see* "The Stoker."
"Helmsman, The," ("Der Steuermann"), 230, 234–235
Hochzeitsvorbereitungen auf dem Lande, see "Wedding Preparations in the Country."
Hoffmann, E. T. A., 110, 177, 237
Holitscher, Arthur, 67, 70–71, 88–89
"Homecoming," ("Heimkehr"), 241, 242–43
Hunger Artist, A, (the collection, *Ein Hungerkünstler*), 30, 32, 34, 227, 244–48, 255–58
"Hunger Artist, A," (the story, "Ein Hungerkünstler"), 31, 106, 119, 246–48, 253, 264
"Hunter Gracchus, The," ("Der Jäger Gracchus"), 184–85

images, thinking in, 35, 71, 76, 95, 123–30, 131, 140, 193, 195–96, 251
Incompletion, the axiom of, 36, 68, 86, 121, 161, 188, 255
"In der Strafkolonie," *see* "In the Penal Colony."
"In the Penal Colony," ("In der Strafkolonie"), 17, 22, 23, 26, 34, 39–40, 131, 132, 142, 144, 149, 153–62, 163, 166
"Investigations of a Dog," ("Forschungen eines Hundes"), 31, 155, 164, 229, 248–52, 260

"Jackals and Arabs," ("Schakale und Araber"), 178–80, 198
"Jäger Gracchus, Der," *see* "The Hunter Gracchus."
Jesenka, Milena, 7, 13, 26–28, 29, 32, 227, 263
Jewish issues, 2, 5, 14, 16, 30, 90, 102, 109, 132, 134, 137, 157, 178, 224, 236, 252, 255, 259, 264
"Josephine the Singer, or the Mouse People," ("Josefine, die Sängerin oder Das Volk der Mäuser"), 31, 255–58
Judaism, 1, 4–6, 16–17, 106, 135, 151, 154, 170, 180, 240, 248–49, 255
Judeo-Christian culture, 1–2, 58, 71, 78, 88, 90–91, 92, 101–102, 110, 118, 120, 122, 135–36, 138, 139, 148–49, 150–51, 153, 154–56, 157–58, 159, 161, 170, 173, 185, 191–92, 200–01, 203, 210–11, 214, 218–19, 219–220, 231, 242, 246–47, 249, 251–52, 257, 261
"Judgment, The," ("Das Urteil"), 22, 34, 34, 50, 53, 68, 70, 78, 97, 98–107, 118, 128,130, 131, 137, 153, 218

Kafka, Franz; attitude toward Jews, 260, 293–297; career as lawyer, 13–14; early writings, 35–36; education, 8–11, 12, 13, 53–54; eroticism, 11–12, 47–49, 73, 78, 82, 143, 144, 204; father, Kafka's, 3–4; letter to Oscar Pollak, 127; mother, Kafka's, 4–5; siblings, Kafka's, 5–6, 19, 24, 26, 29, 30, 31, 190; Kafka's writings: *see* individual titles
Kafka, Hermann, see Kafka's father
Kafka, Julie, see Kafka's mother
"kaiserliche Botschaft, Eine,"*see* "A Message from the Emperor."
Kant, Immanuel, 11, 99–100, 220
"Kaufmann, Der," see "The Businessman."
Kierkegaard, Søren, 24, 28, 30, 136, 231
"Kinder auf der Landstrasse," *see* "Children on a Country Road."
"Kleider,"*see* "Clothes."
"Kleine Fabel," *see* "A Little Fable."
"Kleine Frau, Eine," *see* "A Little Woman."
"kleine Reise durch mitteleuropäische Gegenden, Eine," *see* "The First Long Train Journey"
Klopstock, Robert, 28–29, 231
Konvolut of 1920, 230
"Kreisel, Der," *see* "The Top."
"Kreuzung, Eine," *see* "A Crossbreed."
"Kübelreiter, Der," *see* "The Bucket Rider."

Landartz, Ein, see A Country Doctor [collection]
"Landartz, ein," *see* "A Country Doctor." [story]

language, the deceptions of, 35–36, 43, 122, 125, 173–74, 255
Letter to His Father, (Brief an den Vater), 7, 17, 26, 28,98, 103, 119, 227, 242, 249
"Little Fable, A," ("Kleine Fabel"), 230, 237
"Little Woman, A," ("Eine kleine Frau"), 245–46

Mann, Thomas, 12, 16, 24, 28
"Married Couple, The," ("Ehepaar"), 394–95, 241–42
Meditation, (Betrachtung), 14, 15, 34, 41, 46, 50, 51, 55–65, 86, 92, 98, 107, 209
"Memoirs of the Kalda Railway," 68
"Message from the Emperor, A," ("Eine kaiserliche Botschaft"), 105, 185
"Metamorphosis, The," ("Die Verwandlung"), 17, 22, 34, 37, 44, 68, 70, 74, 103, 106, 107–24, 131, 137, 139, 153, 163, 164, 248, 250, 261
modernism, 2, 42, 43, 44, 47, 55, 126, 127, 226, 227, 230, 242–43, 250
movement and distance, themes of, 36, 38–40, 41, 42, 47, 51, 55–60, 62–63, 63–64, 65, 72, 78, 92–93, 94–95, 101, 107, 140, 156–57, 162, 169–70, 171–72, 175–76, 180–82, 183, 185, 186–87, 191–92, 197, 198–99, 210, 237, 238–239, 241, 255
Musil, Robert, 13, 24, 55, 101

"Nachhauseweg, Der," *see* "The Way Home."
"Nächste Dorf, Das," *see* "The Next Village."
"Nachts," *see* "At Night."
"neue Advocat, Der," *see* "The New Lawyer."
"New Lawyer, The," ("Der neue Advocat"), 169–70
"Next Village, The" ("Das Nächste Dorf"), 171–72, 241
Nietzsche, 9–10, 42, 44, 46–47, 50, 51, 58, 120, 180, 184, 193, 214, 231, 236–237, 248, 251, 261

Odyssey, The, 50–51, 57, 189–90
"Old Manuscript, An," ("Ein altes Blatt"), 170–71, 210, 234
"On Parables," ("Von den Gleichnissen"), 259
"On the Tram," ("Der Fahrgast"), 60, 61

Pascal, Blaise, 255
"Passers-by," ("Die Vorüberlaufenden"), 60
"plötzliche Spaziergang, Der," *see* "A Sudden Walk."
"Poseidon," ("Poseidon"), 230
Prague, 1–2, 3, 17, 27–28, 82, 101, 141
"Problem of Our Laws, The," ("Zur Frage der Gesetze"), 230, 236–37
"Prometheus," ("Prometheus"), 190
"Prufung, Die," *see* "The Test."

"Reflections for Gentlemen-Jockeys," ("Zum Nachdenken für Herrenreiter"), 62
"Refusal, The," (from *Meditation:* "Die Abweisung"), 61, 92, 230
"Refusal, The," (1920 text: "Die Abweisung"), 230, 234
"Report to an Academy, A," ("Ein Bericht für eine Akademie"), 175–78, 243
"Resolutions," ("Entschlüsse"), 57
Richard und Samuel, 53

Sacher-Masoch, Leopold von, 112
Sartre, Jean-Paul, 5, 83, 134, 208
"Schakale und Araber," *see* "Jackals and Arabs."
"Schweigen der Sirenen, Das," *see* "The Silence of the Sirens."
Sebald, W. S., 224–225
self-referentiality, 40, 43, 45, 56, 64, 65, 102, 104–5, 122–23, 140–41, 142, 146–47, 148, 151, 160, 165–66, 169, 170, 171, 173, 174–75, 184, 189, 199–200, 209–14, 216, 239, 253, 255, 257, 262, 264
"Silence of the Sirens, The," ("Das Schweigen der Sirenen"), 189–90
"Sorge des Hausvaters, Die, " *see* "The Cares of a Family Man."
"Stadtische Welt, Die," *see* "The Urban World."
"Stadtwappen, Das," *see* "The City Coat of Arms."
"Steuermann, Der," *see* "The Helmsman."

"Stoker, The," ("Der Heizer"), 16, 66, 68, 70–76
"Street Window, The," ("Das Gassenfenster"), 62, 79
"Sudden Walk, A," ("Der plötzliche Spaziergang"), 56–57

"Test, The," ("Die Prufung"), 231, 232–33
titles of texts from *Konvolut* of 1920, 376
Todorov, Tzvetan, 111–12, 164
"Top, The," ("Der Kreisel"), 230, 237–38
"Trees, The," ("Die Bäume"), 63–64
Trial, The, (*Der Process* or *Der Prozess*), 22, 32, 34, 36, 40, 66, 68, 69, 74, 77, 82, 108, 115, 131–54, 159, 161, 163, 165, 166, 172, 187, 199, 202, 210
"Truppenaushebung, Die," *see* "The Conscription of Troops."
"Truth about Sancho Panza, The," ("Die Wahrheit Über Sancho Pansa"), 188–89

"Unglück des Junggesellen, Das," see "Bachelor's Ill Luck"
"Unglücklichsein," *see* "Unhappiness."
"Unhappiness," ("Unglücklichsein"), 64–65, 91
"Unmasking of a Confidence Trickster," ("Enlarvung eines Bauernfängers"), 56
unpublished manuscript text of 1921 or 1922, 243, 259
unpublished semi-autobiographical texts of 1920, 228–30, 231
"Up in the Gallery," ("Auf der Galerie"), 175–76, 243
"Urban World, The," ("Die stadtische Welt"), 54
"Urteil, Das," *see* "The Judgment."

Verschollene, Der, see Amerika.
"Verwandlung, Die," *see* "The Metamorphosis."
"Village Schoolmaster, The," ("Der Dorfschullehrer"), 105, 163, 164–67, 250
"Visit to a Mine, A," ("Ein Besuch in Bergwerk"), 174–75
"Von den Gleichnissen," *see* "On Parables."
"Vor dem Gesetz," *see* "Before the Law."
"Vorüberlaufenden, Die," see "Passers-by."
"Vulture, The" ("Der Geier"), 51, 230, 232

"Wahrheit über Sancho Pansa, Die," *see* "The Truth about Sancho Panza."
"Warden of the Tomb, The," ("Der Gruftwächter"), 168–69
"Way Home, The," ("Der Nachhauseweg"), 59
"Wedding Preparations in the Country," (*Hochzeitsvorbereitungen auf dem Lande*), 14, 15, 35, 36–40, 49
Weiler, Hedwig, 13
"Wish to Be a Red Indian, The," ("Wunsch, Indianer zu werden"), 63, 92
Wittgenstein, Ludwig, 2, 123, 126, 127, 128–29, 135, 184, 193, 249, 258
Wohryzek, Julie, 25–26
World War I, 21–23, 25, 233–34
"Wunsch, Indianer zu werden," *see* "The Wish to Be a Red Indian."

Yiddish culture, 2, 16–17

"Zerstreutes Hinausshaun," *see* "Absent-Minded Window-Gazing."
Zionism, 9, 17, 18, 24, 25, 30, 179–80, 186, 190–94, 196, 219, 227, 229, 233, 248–49
"Zum Nachdenken für Herrenreiter," *see* "Reflections for Gentlemen-Jockeys."
Zürau Aphorisms, 24, 44, 138, 148–49, 163, 167, 184, 198, 240
"Zur Frage der Gesetz," *see* "The Problem of Our Laws."